The First Latin American Debt Crisis

THE FIRST LATIN AMERICAN DEBT CRISIS

The City of London and the 1822–25 Loan Bubble

Frank Griffith Dawson

Yale University Press
New Haven and London
1990

ENDPAPERS

Front

Bubbles for 1825 – or – Fortunes made by Steam, C. Williams (1824), British Museum. Caricaturists found ready targets for their satire during the lending and investment boom when speculation eclipsed prudence. The over 600 companies organized for a variety of improbable schemes in Latin America and elsewhere were called 'bubbles' because most soon burst, leaving investors with little to show for their improvidence.

Back

The Bubble Burst – or the Ghost of an old Act of Parliament, R. Cruickshank (1825), British Museum. The legality of the Latin American and other companies formed in 1824–5 was called into question when the Court of King's Bench found that the Equitable Loan Society's activities violated a 1720 Act of Parliament passed to prevent a recurrence of the South Sea Bubble scandal. The act was repealed soon afterwards in order to allow the company formation boom to continue. A number of the companies named in the 'bubbles' shown here are discussed in the text.

Map on p. viii is reproduced by kind permission of J Lynch from the Cambridge History of Latin America, vol. III.

Set in Linotron Bembo by Best-set Typesetter Ltd., and
printed in Great Britain
at The Bath Press, Avon

Library of Congress Cataloging-in-Publication Data

Dawson, Frank G. (Frank Griffith), 1934–
The first Latin American debt crisis : the city of London and the
1822–25 loan bubble / Frank Dawson.
p.   cm.
Includes bibliographical references.
ISBN 0-300-04727-4
1. Loans, British—Latin America—History—19th century.
2. Loans, Foreign—Latin America—History—19th century.   I. Title.
HJ8514.5.D39   1990
336.3′435′09809034—dc20
89-78102
CIP

CONTENTS

For the Princess of Poyais

A NOTE ON MONETARY EQUIVALENTS

In the text reference is made to Sterling (£) and US dollars (US$), the currencies in which loans to Latin America have been mostly denominated.

In the 1820s the local currency unit in Mexico and the other Latin American nations was the peso, which is indicated in the text as $. This unit was the equivalent of the Spanish silver dollar or *Peso fuerte*, and, in theory, sometimes equivalent to the US dollar. Although exchange rates fluctuated considerably, the peso's equivalent in Sterling was roughly 4s.

Map of Latin America (Colonial c.1800) This shows the various administrative units into which Spain and Portugal divided their American possessions.

Map of Latin America (Independent 1830) Basically all the major modern states of Latin America were in existence by 1830, with the exception of Panama and the five Central American republics. The border disputes would continue into the 1930s however. Mexico meanwhile would lose a substantial amount of her territory to the United States in 1848.

'History has a way of repeating itself in financial matters because of a kind of sophisticated stupidity'.

John Kenneth Galbraith, *The Sunday Times*, 25 October 1987

PREFACE

LATIN AMERICAN NATIONS today owe their international banking and other creditors over US$416 billion, nearly a half of the total Third World indebtedness. Many observers doubt if this vast amount can ever be repaid. Meanwhile, the cost of debt service impairs economic growth from the Río Grande to Tierra del Fuego, undermining the continent's already fragile political and social structures.

This book analyses a neglected chapter in Anglo-Latin American relations, the disastrous 1822–5 investment boom. During this brief period, over £20,000,000 in Latin American government bonds were floated in the London capital market, together with the shares of companies capitalized at over £36,000,000 to operate Latin American mining, commercial and other ventures. All these investments quickly came to grief. Some of the consequences of that disaster are with us still today.

At the same time, the saga of Latin America's first unhappy experience with a capital-exporting nation is also part of the history of the City of London, that unique, semi-autonomous square mile enclave located within London itself. Those were years of transition, when the City and its institutions first began wholeheartedly to adapt themselves to their roles as the financial arbiters of the world, when Sterling was about to become a universal medium of exchange, and British wealth, talents and commercial expertise began to influence the most remote corners of the globe.

In addition to the usual primary material including correspondence and diaries, my most important sources have been contemporary newspapers, which has meant examining over 6,000 issues. The period chronicled here, however, antedates the era of the popular press. In the 1820s high prices and illiteracy assured a limited if educated audience for what would today be termed quality newspapers. Since few people could afford to pay the equivalent of £2 a day for a four-page newspaper, there was no point in sensationalizing the trivial or in oversimplifying and distorting news items in order to increase circulation. Newspapers therefore provide a dependable but largely neglected record of the lending and investment boom.

I am grateful for the assistance of the staff at the British Library in London and at its newspaper depository in Colindale, the Guildhall Library in the City, the London Library, the Public Record Office in Kew, the National Library of Scotland and the Scottish Record Office in Edinburgh, the University Library in Cambridge, and the Bodleian Library in Oxford. Across the Atlantic, I found the New York Public Library, the Archivos Generales de Centro América in Guatemala City, and the Fundación John Boulton in Caracas, Venezuela especially helpful.

This book was written while I was a Visiting Fellow and Research Associate at the Research Centre for International Law at the University of Cambridge. I am grateful to the Centre's Director, Eli Lauterpacht Q.C., for making the Centre's library and other facilities available to me.

Numerous individuals have encouraged me with their sound advice. Special thanks are due to Professor Harold Blakemore, formerly Secretary of the Institute of Latin American Studies of the University of London, and now affiliated to the Research Unit on European-American Relations of the University of Bradford; to Steven Neff of the Law Faculty at the University of Edinburgh; to Dr Pedro Grases of the Fundación Casa de Bello in Caracas; to Dr Manuel Pérez Vila of the Fundación John Boulton, also of Caracas; and to my banking and stockbroking colleagues in London and in New York, including George M. Gunson, Managing Director of Euro-Latinamerican Bank; Peter Harrold, former Senior International Executive at National Westminster Bank Plc and former Director of Libra Bank Plc; Gerard Legrain, Managing Director of the International Mexican Bank Limited; F. Paul Seabrook, Executive Director of Daiwa Europe Limited; and A. Blake Friscia, Vice President, Economics Group, The Chase Manhattan Bank, N.A., New York. Most of all, I appreciate the patience and support of Richard B. Lillich, Howard W. Smith Professor of Law at the University of Virginia and Director of the Procedural Aspects of International Law Institute, Inc.

Finally, this work is part of a larger study of the impact of Latin America upon the development of public international law, financed by the Dana Fund for International and Comparative Legal Studies. I am deeply grateful for their generous financial assistance.

Frank Griffith Dawson,
University of Cambridge, 1989.

INTRODUCTION

THE CAUSES AND ramifications of the present Latin American debt crisis are complex and interrelated. The suggested remedies, many of which seem novel if not hazardous, are the subject of intensive discussion and scrutiny. Not surprisingly the crisis has spawned a torrent of articles, reviews, books and conference reports which are fast becoming a literary genre of their own. Despite the corpus of information now available, however, probably few of the politicians, economists, bankers and lawyers who today strive to avoid the far-reaching consequences of a massive debt default are aware of the early nineteenth-century antecedents to the situations they now confront.

The current difficulty is not an isolated, unique phenomenon which began in August 1982 when Mexico informed her foreign bankers that she could no longer service her international indebtedness. Instead it is but the latest and largest of the continuing series of financial upheavals which have punctuated Latin America's relations with its creditors since the 1820s, when the first Latin American debt crisis shook the British financial community and caused tempers to fray and angry voices to reverberate throughout parliament, in Downing Street and in the foreign office.

Between 1822 and 1825 seven Latin American nations – even before their independence was secure or recognized by Great Britain – issued over £20,000,000 in bonds in the City of London. The manner in which the loans were launched precipitated brawls in the Stock Exchange, accusations of fraud, and lawsuits. Worse, after discounts and deductions the borrowing nations received approximately only 60 per cent of the face value of the loans they had contracted. This first Latin American lending boom, however, assured high profits at little risk for the selected financiers and merchants who organized the credits. Unlike their post-World War II counterparts, the early loan contractors did not keep any significant portion of the bonds on their own books, and passed the risk of non-payment on to more gullible investors in the form of bearer bonds.

Unfortunately by 1829 nearly £19,000,000 of the bonds issued in 1822–5 were in default. Thousands of investors suffered, and over a generation would pass before most Latin American countries could expect to borrow new funds in London. Meanwhile, bondholder attempts to recover their investments provoked frustrating cycles of renegotiations, reschedulings, litigation and further defaults which lasted throughout much of the nineteenth century. The high expectations, mutual trust and goodwill which had initially characterized relations between the new Latin American states and Great Britain were superseded by disillusion and resentment.

The pattern of dashed hopes and broken promises will seem distressingly familiar to bankers who over the last eight years have watched the Latin American loans which they happily put on their books in the 1970s turn inexorably into non-producing assets. The total borrowed in 1822–5 is of course dwarfed by today's US$416 billion debt overhang. Moreover, the structure of today's international capital market is vastly different from the far simpler financial environment in which the first Latin American credits were launched. Nevertheless, many of the remedies which modern bankers and the creative lawyers have devised to ameliorate, if not resolve, the present debt crisis, were invoked by their financial predecessors one hundred and fifty years ago. Capitalization of interest arrears, extension of repayment periods, interest rate concessions, exchanging equity for debt, providing new money with which to service prior obligations, and accepting goods in lieu of monetary repayments were all suggested or utilized to cope with the first Latin American loan defaults – with but limited success.

The roots of both the first and the later debt crises extend deep into the past. From the earliest days of the discovery and conquest of the New World, Europeans had regarded Latin America as an inexhaustible source of riches, an almost magical land where with modest effort newcomers could become wealthier more quickly than at home. The old Spanish *conquistador* Bernal Díaz del Castillo recalled in his memoirs the sense of wonder which he and his companions in Hernán Cortés's small army had felt as young men in late 1519 as they marched along stone causeways into the heart of the Aztec empire in the Valley of Mexico. They passed innumerable cities and towns adorned with magnificent temples and palaces as they neared their destination, the splendid, glittering Aztec island capital Tenochtitlan, twinkling like a jewel on the bosom of the vast blue Lake Texcoco. Surely these were 'cosas de Amadis', the rough soldiers exclaimed, like the enchanted things and places described in *Amadís de Gaula*, one of the then immensely popular so-called epics of chivalry. This book, and others like it, drove Don Quixote mad and sent him charging down dusty Spanish roads seeking evil giants to slay and lovely, distressed damsels to rescue.

In a sense, Latin America was never thought of *except* in terms of *Amadís* by many Spaniards and Portuguese. They tended to see it as a land of mystery and promise, a cornucopia of wealth to be tapped through a variety of techniques, that is to say, by the overt plunder of the aboriginal empires, by the exploitation of mines with forced native labour, by the imposition of an agricultural serfdom on the conquered races, and, ultimately, by the sale to the highest bidder of positions in the colonial bureaucracies. Even a minor appointment in the Americas promised Spaniards and Portuguese a sure and certain release from poverty at home.

Particularly in those parts of Latin America under Spanish domination, this prevailing attitude left little room for the economic and political aspirations of the *criollos* and *mestizos*. These comprised the social and racial mixtures created by the conquest and the colonial system but who were excluded from effective power. Eventually, however, these new groups, assisted by British money, military supplies and goodwill, would overthrow their Spanish masters, and in the years immediately after independence this new, native, Latin American elite would actively court additional British capital and investment.

The informed British response to these independence movements was enthusiastic. For centuries British merchants and seamen had been attempting with but limited success to challenge Spain's claim to monopolize the trade and wealth of the New World. Once Madrid's hold was broken, the British could replace the Spaniards as *conquistadores*. They would, however, obtain their share of the 'cosas de Amadís' not by swords and cannon, but by providing capital, technology and commercial expertise. It was a new type of conquest which was dilligently pursued throughout the nineteenth century and up to World War I when the United States began increasingly to displace European commercial and financial dominance.

The first loans extended to Latin America as part of this British 'rediscovery' of the New World were launched within a particularly exciting international and domestic political, social and economic milieu. The defeat of Napoleon and the appearance of the infant new American states heralded an era of political change and transition in which the European monopoly of membership in the family of nations was forever broken. Moreover, the emergence onto the world stage of the United States of America and of the Latin American nations affirmed the rights of revolution and self-determination, and undermined forever the principle of monarchical legitimacy. The potentially disturbing impact of this development upon the existing political order was foreseen by British statesmen, and accounts in large measure for the vacillating policy which preceded British diplomatic recognition of some of the Latin American nations in 1825, when commercial realities eventually eclipsed political misgivings.

Socially, the 1820s in Great Britain were years of lavish display and opulence co-existing with the squalor, poverty and crime later described so accurately and poignantly by Charles Dickens. The habits and characteristics of regency England did not vanish over-night when the Prince of Wales was crowned King George IV in July 1821. The decade of 1820–30 was still an era of raffish regency-style bucks, Beau Brummel imitators, brutal bare-knuckle prize fights and extravagant gambling. Draconian penalties – death, whipping and transportation – were imposed for a wide range of minor, petty offenses. Landowners could still install man-traps with impunity to maim and mangle rural labourers who sought to feed their half-starved families by poaching. Gory murders and assaults were re-ported in lavish detail by the press, and public hangings were con-sidered salutary mass entertainment. The embezzling banker and ladies' man Henry Fauntleroy, for example, was hung before an admiring crowd of 100,000 at Newgate prison in 1824.

Despite the callousness which afflicted so many areas of daily life, however, the period after Waterloo was also the age of Jeremy Bentham, Byron, Shelley, Keats, Jane Austen, Constable and Sir Walter Scott. Indeed, London with its population of over 1,600,000, had become the intellectual centre of Europe. Books from all over the world appeared in the shops shortly after publication, and many were even translated into English. Lack of press censorship encour-aged vigorous political debate among daily and weekly newspapers, while quarterly magazines carried in-depth reviews of domestic and foreign publications. Private and public manuscript and book col-lections were accessible to serious scholars at the British Museum and elsewhere. Public lectures and courses on literature, chemistry, science and philosophy at The Royal Society, The Royal Institute and other venues were constantly advertised in the press, while paintings and engravings were exhibited in galleries along the Strand and Bond Street. Architect John Nash was transforming the avenues and buildings of London's West End. Regent Street was completed in 1823, and Cumberland Terrace in Regent's Park four years later. The elegance of Mayfair, however, contrasted sharply with the lawlessness, degradation and squalor prevalent in the criminal 'rook-eries' of St Giles and Whitechapel.

Meanwhile, although the nation was still predominantly rural, the rumblings of profound economic change were becoming increas-ingly loud and more persistent. The industrial age had arrived, accelerated by war, and mills and factories with their regimented workforces were quickly replacing smaller domestic industries. Perhaps the most significant innovation since the steam-engine itself burst upon the national scene in the 1820s – the steam locomotive. The new railways launched in the mid-decade company formation boom were destined to change forever the industrial and commercial landscape of Britain, as well as the entire country's social habits.

By 1822 Britain was poised for an unprecedented expansion in manufacturing and trade and increasingly would look abroad for outlets for its products and energy. The markets opened in Latin America by the collapse of Spanish power would therefore have an almost hypnotic attraction for traders, manufacturers and investors. The loans to the fledgling Latin American nations were a natural outgrowth of this attraction, as well as an early flexing of that awesome financial muscle-power which would assure worldwide British commercial dominance well before the end of the century.

I

NAPOLEON SETS THE STAGE

THE FIRST LATIN American debt crisis was a direct product of the Napoleonic wars. Not only did the years of conflict turn London into the financial capital of Europe, but they also disrupted the links between the Spanish and Portuguese monarchies and their Latin American colonies, thereby encouraging the emergence of seven new sovereign nations in the New World. Between 1822 and 1825 these would turn to London to finance their early years of independence.

In May 1808, Napoleon forced the abdication of his erstwhile allies, Spain's King Charles IV and his son and heir Ferdinand, and placed his brother Joseph Bonaparte on the Spanish throne. The betrayal precipitated anti-French rebellions all over Spain, which were repressed with the eager brutality portrayed so vividly in Franciso Goya's paintings and etchings. Provincial self-governing units or juntas sprang up to organize resistance, and by September a central junta had been formed in Seville to rule in the name of Ferdinand.[1]

Reports of the French usurpation soon reached Spain's Latin American colonies. The Captain Generalcy of Venezuela, the Spanish administrative unit in the northern part of South America nearest to Britain's Caribbean possessions, was the first to learn of the events when in late July copies of *The Times* were received in Caracas via the British colony of Curaçao. To his credit, Spanish Captain General Vicente Emparán then issued public proclamations in Caracas denouncing the French occupation, acknowledging Ferdinand as the legitimate king and later recognizing the authority of the Seville junta. When, however, the junta was replaced in Spain by a more conservative body known as the Regency, Caracas Creole activists deposed Emparán in April 1810 and formed their own junta. This too aimed ostensibly to preserve and protect the rights of Ferdinand VII, as Charles IV's son came to be known.[2] Eventually, however, the more radical members of what had begun as an essentially Creole, upper-class revolt would prevail and provoke the final break with Spain. It was a pattern which, with local variations, would be followed in the neighbouring Viceroyalty of New Granada, the larger, adjacent administrative unit, and, with the exception of Peru, from the Río de la Plata to Mexico.

Napoleon had not confined his attentions only to the Spanish portion of the Iberian Peninsula. In November 1807 the Portuguese royal family had fled Lisbon just ahead of General Junot's invading French troops. Under British naval escort and with a numerous entourage of courtiers and assorted hangers-on, they sailed to Brazil to preserve the monarchy and await better days at home. This conversion of Portugal's largest colony into the administrative centre of the country's vast empire set in motion a train of events which would lead inexorably to Brazilian independence.[3]

Official British reaction to post-1808 events was ambivalent. Until Ferdinand's deposition Spain had been a French satellite. Admiral Nelson had cheerfully sunk the Spanish fleet at Trafalgar three years before, along with the vessels of their French allies. Prior to 1808, British policy-makers therefore had listened to London-based exiles such as the Venezuelan patriot Francisco de Miranda, who had already led one aborted expedition to destroy Spanish power in Venezuela. Miranda and his adherents with some success persuaded Cabinet members that Spain could be weakened and extensive trading advantages obtained for Britain by military intervention in its American colonies.

Indeed, when news of Ferdinand's enforced abdication arrived in London, an expedition was already preparing to sail from Ireland to invade Mexico, where extensive silver deposits could help finance the struggle against the French. After the events of May, however, Lord Castlereagh, Secretary of State for War and the Colonies, perceived that Britain's best interests lay in preserving the Spanish overseas empire so that it could aid the mother country against Napoleon. The expeditionary force was diverted to fight in Portugal, and in January 1809, Britain and the Spanish Central Junta signed a treaty converting Britain's traditional enemy into an ally in the common struggle against France. Plans to undermine Spanish control in the New World were postponed indefinitely.[4]

By mid-1810, however, the Caracas junta had exiled most of the Spanish colonial administration, and felt dangerously exposed to retaliation from the Peninsula. By affirming Ferdinand as Spain's rightful ruler, the junta had alienated France. Moreover, by rejecting the Regency the patriots risked being considered traitors by Spain. The junta therefore dispatched the young militia Lieutenant Colonel Simón Bolívar, together with Andrés Bello, First Officer in the Caracas Department of State, and Luis López Méndez, another

1. *Portrait of Simón Bolívar in Lima*, José Gil de Castro, 1825. Bolívar was the liberator of what are today Venezuela, Panama, Colombia, Ecuador, Bolivia and Peru. By sending his colleague Francisco Antonio Zea to London to negotiate a loan with European bankers, Bolívar was indirectly responsible for starting the first Latin American lending boom.

Venezuelan patriot, to London to seek British protection from this twin danger.

When, however, the Venezuelan delegation reached London in July, it was only received unofficially and with extreme reserve by Marquis Richard Wellesley, Foreign Secretary and brother of Lord Wellington, at Apsley House, his London home. Wellesley realized it would be unwise to undermine the Spanish war effort by encouraging what could develop into breakaway movements in Latin America. Nevertheless, it was evident that British commercial interests had benefited from recent developments in Latin America. The new juntas in Venezuela and elsewhere had declared their ports open to ships of all nations, and even had reduced import duties. These privileges would be terminated if Spain regained control. Wellesley therefore did not reject the mission out of hand, and, despite his professed neutrality, the Venezuelans managed to extract a pledge of protection from French invasion, while British authorities in the Antilles were instructed to allow Venezuelan merchant ships access to their ports. Finally, to avoid further offending Britain's new ally, Wellesley urged the Venezuelans to settle their differences with Spain and offered to act as mediator.[5]

Bolívar then returned home on a British warship in September, leaving Bello and López Méndez behind to represent the Venezuelan junta. Subsequently Bolívar and Miranda, who also had left London to enlist in the patriot cause, helped convert the Caracas junta into a genuine independence movement. The so-called Venezuelan First Republic, however, was crushed by royalist troops in 1812, soon after its birth. Bolívar escaped into exile, and Bello and López Méndez suddenly found themselves unemployed in a strange country.[6] Both would later play central roles in the lending boom which began in ten years time.

British popular reaction to the first faltering Latin American steps towards independence was much less circumspect than that of Wellesley and the Cabinet. Important segments of informed public opinion largely supported the aspirations of the embryo nations, either as a result of basically republican inclinations frustrated by a series of conservative governments at home, or because Latin America offered new markets for British capital and manufactures. Until the end of the eighteenth century, the exclusive Spanish imperial policy had discouraged Latin American trade with other nations. Foreigners were not allowed to travel to Latin America without special permission, and even shipwrecked British sailors were treated as interlopers, if not pirates. Independence promised for the first time to open that vast territory and its fabled mineral and commercial wealth to outside exploitation. Both the intellectual and commercial community therefore had an interest in the success of the patriots.

Indeed, already by 1808 a substantial unofficial trade had developed between Britain and Latin America. The British fleet blockaded Spanish ports, and British exporters supplied the resulting shortages in the colonies either directly through smuggling or via neutral intermediaries. Even Spanish authorities in Buenos Ayres and Havana succumbed to the pressures of local merchants and opened their ports to British shipping. The City and the British merchant community, which since Elizabethan times had resented and challenged the Spanish commercial monopoly of the New World, would view any reimposition of firm Spanish authority with alarm. In 1810 then, in contrast to their unofficial reception at Apsley House, Bolívar, Bello and López Méndez were lionized during their visit. The Duke of Gloucester, the king's nephew, invited them to dine, and their carriage rides in Hyde Park, their attendance at the theatre and the visits of several members of the nobility to their hotel suite did not pass unnoticed in the press.[7]

The new commercial opportunities presented by the disintegrating Spanish American empire stimulated an intense public curiosity about Latin America, its resources and people. In response to the new demand for knowledge, streams of books by scientists, travellers, diplomats, adventurers and visionaries were published in London and Edinburgh, describing in glowing terms Latin America's mineral, agricultural and commercial potential. They were eagerly devoured by the more affluent literate public, who either purchased them in fashionable shops along Bond Street and The Strand, or read reviews of them in prestigious literary magazines such as *The Edinburgh Review*, *The Quarterly Review* and others. The essays published in these journals were not mere summaries of the volumes being reviewed.

Instead, the books simply provided the excuse for extended commentary upon the internal affairs of the new nations and their political and economic relationships with Great Britain. Because they were expensive – six shillings per issue – readership of the reviews was composed of the prosperous middle and upper classes. Nevertheless, the *Edinburgh* and *Quarterly Reviews* each had a circulation of approximately 14,000 copies in the years after Waterloo at a time when *The Times* was barely selling 8,000 copies a day.[8] Consequently these journals to some extent moulded the perceptions of Latin America shared by important and influential groups directing British public policy – specifically the landed gentry, the professions, and the new industrial and commercial bourgeoisie.

The Quarterly Review had been founded with the encouragement of George Canning, a future prime minister, and other Tories to counter the more liberal editorial policy of the Whig's *Edinburgh Review*. Despite their basic differences in general domestic political orientation, as far as Latin America was concerned their anonymous reviewers' comments not surprisingly reflected the ambivalent, shifting state of both educated public opinion and official foreign policy, both of which were torn between an instinctive distrust of republicanism and desires to grasp the new commercial opportunities offered by the disintegrating Spanish empire. As early as 1817 a reviewer from *The Quarterly Review* probably reflected readers' expectations when he observed

> whether the colonies become independent nations, or whether they continue to be governed by Spain, advantage must accrue to British commerce ... South America presents a market for the skill and expertise of our merchants, which we hope and believe will not long be withholden from them.[9]

While some writers for *The Quarterly Review* were supportive of Latin American independence, others were less enthusiastic and ventured that the British volunteers who had sailed to Bolívar's aid were unnecessarily prolonging the bloody conflict for personal ends. *The Edinburgh Review* was, with exceptions, generally cautious in endorsing the independence movements, despite a general inclination towards liberalism and reform.

So great was the desire for information on Latin America that even works originally published abroad in foreign languages were either translated or republished for an English readership. For example, German scientist Baron Alexander von Humboldt's travel experiences between 1799 and 1804 in Latin America – a vast compendium of geographical, botanical, zoological and geological data – were translated from French, published in London and discussed in a series of essays in *The Quarterly Review* between 1815 and 1821. The publishing of Humboldt's now outdated and sanguine assessments of the continent's commercial and mineral wealth would eventually mislead the public into believing they could reap great profits by investing in Latin American loans and mining ventures.[10]

Commercial optimism was further stimulated by newspaper reports sympathetic to Latin America's independence efforts. The exploits of General José de San Martín and Lord Cochrane in Chile, Peru and Brazil were followed closely, and public esteem for Bolívar in particular was reflected in the press. Newspapers all over the country regularly reported the victories and defeats of the patriot armies in which numerous British volunteers had enlisted, while editorial columns extolled the commercial and trading benefits which would surely flow from diplomatic recognition of the former Spanish colonies.

British papers did not, however, have their own correspondents in Latin America, and had to rely for copy upon letters from merchants, who might not be dispassionate observers, and upon local Latin American and Jamaican newspapers. Events were reported weeks after their occurrence. At least six weeks might elapse before a ship arrived from La Guayra, Venezuela's chief port. Worse, there were no regular, scheduled transatlantic mail packets until 1823, so ship departures from the Spanish Main and the River Plate were irregular and unpredictable. Newspaper owners also operated under other great handicaps. As part of a deliberate British government policy to inhibit the growth of a radical, anti-establishment popular press, newspapers were burdened with heavy taxes to prevent them reaching wider, less-affluent audiences. A stamp duty of 4d. per copy was levied on each edition, together with a paper duty of a farthing a page. In addition, a 3s.6d. tax was imposed per advertisement, regardless of size. Printing and distribution expenses raised the sales price per copy to 7d., equivalent to over £2 today. Consequently, in the interests of economy the pages were crowded with small, closely-set type. There was no space for banner headlines, and sharp eyesight was essential lest an item in the tightly-packed columns be overlooked.

Given such impediments, a circulation of 8,000 per day for *The Times* in the 1820s was considered respectable. Nevertheless, actual readership was higher since newsdealers would lend papers for 1d. per hour, and they were also available in clubs, coffee houses and libraries.[11] The influence of *The Times*, *The Morning Chronicle* and their competitors in shaping public perceptions of Latin America in the early nineteenth century therefore was undoubtedly far greater than circulation figures would suggest. Moreover, despite the high taxation and sales price, and the devotion of nearly a third of the usual four pages to advertising, Latin American items frequently occupied over 20 per cent of the total columns devoted to news reports – a proportion with which today's Latin American press coverage compares poorly.

In order to survive at all, however, the newspapers sought financial support from the various political groups. *The Times* received £300 per annum from the government, and the more conservative *Courier* sometimes seemed virtually a foreign office house organ. Perhaps as a result, although *The Times* might print paid advertisements and petitions from merchants urging recognition of the new Latin American states, editorial policy towards independence was initially cautious. Nevertheless, by the end of 1821, *The Times* had become convinced that the commercial and other changes which would flow from the independence of the Spanish colonies would 'be of a nature essentially beneficial to the world'.[12] Once freed of Spanish commercial restrictions, trade and agriculture would be stimulated, the rich mines worked 'with greater skill and activity', and the consumption of European manufactures greatly increased. At the same time, the thinly-populated New World would be a ready and welcome outlet for Britain's surplus population, provided the emigrants concentrated 'on the healthy provinces of the River Plate and of Chile, where a climate congenial to European constitutions, together with a friendly disposition of the natives, are such as to obviate many of the evils experienced by new settlers in distant countries'.

In addition, *The Times* reminded readers that now an opportunity would exist to unite the Atlantic and Pacific by a canal through Central America via Lake Nicaragua and quoted passages from a recently published work on Mexico. 'It is impossible to contemplate without a mixture of awe and exultation ... accomplishment of a work which would unite the billows of two mighty oceans, and by an easy process of human labour and enterprise, change as it were the physical boundaries of the world.' These three themes – commercial opportunity, emigration and inter-oceanic communication – would preoccupy the public's and investors' minds over the next four years, and in 1822–5 embolden thousands of individuals to risk – and lose – their savings in Latin American loans, mining and other ventures.

The Morning Chronicle, founded nine years before *The Times* and its closest rival in circulation and prestige, and with a better financial coverage, demonstrated greater earlier uncritical enthusiasm for Latin American independence. In early October 1818, it published a long article supporting the Latin American liberation movements and extolling the new commercial opportunities it offered. 'From experience and conviction South America hails our commerce, and invites us to augment her comforts and conveniences and to receive in return her various valuable productions.' European arts and technology would inevitably 'dissipate the gloom of abject superstition and intolerance' which had been fostered by Spain 'to bar all intercourse with strangers, who would encourage their industry by teaching them the value of it'.[13] Five years later the paper would even assure readers that 'there is no better way to dispose of surplus money than by investing in South America'.[14]

Some newspapers, such as *The Courier*, which was deeply suspicious of *The Morning Chronicle's* liberal inclinations, joined *The Morning Herald* and the weekly *John Bull* in warning readers of the perils of investing in countries about which little was known. Others, such as *The Sunday Times* and *The New Times* were less consistent. Still, so great was the interest in Latin America that the continent's fortunes were even followed in provincial papers, including *The Scotsman*, *The Manchester Guardian*, *The Edinburgh Advertiser* and *The Edinburgh Evening Courant*. Any journalistic Cassandras went largely unheeded. The prevailing note was one of optimism.

In general, then, the press both chronicled and helped stimulate the early, intense widespread optimism with which the loans were issued and received, and a few short years later similarly reflected and sympathized with the public disillusion and disgust which followed. Newspapers were thus participants in, as well as measures of, the speculative mania which swept the nation after 1822.

The twenty-two years of conflict preceding Waterloo had disrupted established international trading patterns and disorganized traditional continental banking centres. When French troops overran Holland they had assured the displacement of Amsterdam, once Europe's recognized financial centre, by London. Continental merchants and bankers fled with their expertise and capital to Britain, where they could profit from political stability and growing British overseas trade. The City of London thus became Europe's new financial capital to which continental statesmen must resort to repair the ravages of war. By the time peace returned, the European governments were bankrupt. Only Britain, whose fleet had shielded her from the devastation which had afflicted the continent, was solvent despite the great increase in the national debt occasioned by the expenses of war and the subsidies with which she had kept her allies in the field. Moreover, she was at least a generation ahead of Europe and the United States in industrial development. Insulated by the Channel from the destruction of war, British inventors and entrepreneurs had perfected the steam-engine and developed new techniques for iron manufacture, spinning and weaving. They were ideally placed to meet the new, expanded global demand for products and goods which peacetime eventually would generate.[15]

Institutionally, the City also was well equipped to assume its new role. The banking system had been functioning for hundreds of years, dominated by the Bank of England. Although established in 1694 as a private bank, the Bank was increasingly assuming the role of a semi-public institution, responsible for issuing the national currency, providing funds for the government, discounting the paper of other institutions and generally acting as the cornerstone of the nation's financial structure. Over seventy small banks in London, generally partnerships, conducted retail banking business with the public. Only a handful – including Coutts, Drummonds, Samuel Hoare and Glynn Mills – survived into the mid-twentieth century, however. Other houses still influential in the city today were also already in existence by 1822, including N. M. Rothschild & Sons and Baring Brothers. Contemporary commercial directories did not, however, list them as banks but as 'merchants', suggesting that they were not engaged in traditional retail banking business, but in trade finance and related activities.[16]

In 1802 the Stock Exchange had left behind its coffee house origins and moved into its own building in Capel Court. Limited trading among non-members who did not wish to pay for brokers licenses was, however, still carried on in nearby coffee houses, as well as in the Royal Exchange, a long-established commodity trading centre. Although distinctions between brokers, who acted as purchasers' agents, and jobbers or market-makers, who dealt as principals for their own accounts, were now established in practice, members could act in both capacities. Strict separation of the two functions was still some years distant. Stockbroking, however, was becoming increasingly specialized, and members who carried on other businesses were in a dwindling minority. By 1822, the ancestors of some contemporary member firms were operating at Capel Court – including Cazenove, de Zoete and James Capel – and the Stock Exchange had become an essential national fund-raising institution without which the British government would have had immense difficulty financing the war effort.[17]

Foreign bonds generally were not traded at the Stock Exchange, however. Indeed, international sovereign lending in the pre-Napoleonic era had largely been arranged through Amsterdam, to which the new United States of America had turned in its infant years. British-managed or originated bond issues were few and small. The first appeared in 1706, when a personal loan was raised by the Austrian emperor. In the 1730s London merchants lent to the emperor of Prussia against the security of properties in Upper and Lower Silesia, while a small Danish credit was quoted in 1753. By the 1790s, some British firms, especially Baring Brothers, were dealing in United States securities in competition with Dutch houses. The pace of foreign lending did not increase after the French Revolution. With the exception of British government guaranteed credits to Austria and Portugal, and two small treasury credits of £200,000 each to Holland and France in 1813 and 1814, Britain supported its allies with subsidies of arms, uniforms, munitions and goods, rather than with loans.[18]

There were not then, in 1815, many foreign government loans available in which the investing public could participate. British government securities and lotteries provided the bulk of Stock Exchange business, in addition to the shares of the Bank of England,

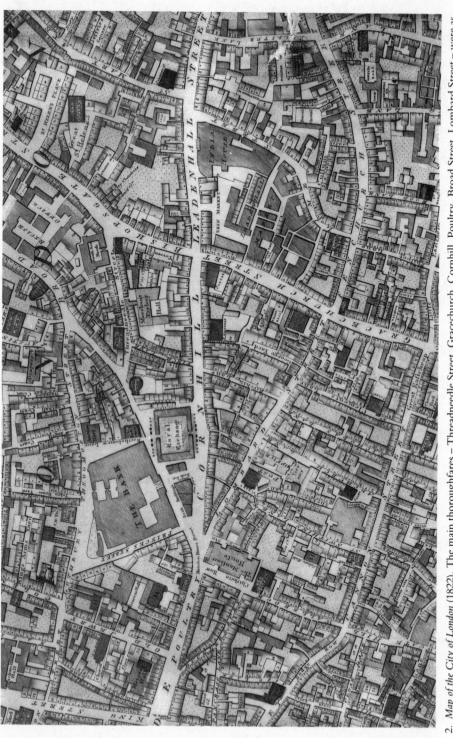

2. *Map of the City of London* (1822). The main thoroughfares – Threadneedle Street, Gracechurch, Cornhill, Poultry, Broad Street, Lombard Street – were as they are now. A modern banker, stockbroker or tourist could use this map today with confidence (The Guildhall Library, London).

East India and South Sea Companies. A handful of canal, road, bridge, insurance and water companies were listed, although generally such groups obtained their financing through family and local bank connections, rather than by relying on the investing public.

Perhaps reflecting the paucity of investor choice, the financial press was virtually non-existent. The bi-weekly *Course of the Exchange* provided price lists of the securities traded, but without comment. *Lloyds List*, founded in 1762, chronicled ship departures, exchange rates and United States stock prices. No specialized financial newspapers or journals providing investors with information vital to decision-making existed. The *Bankers Magazine* would not appear until the 1840s and the *Stock Exchange Yearbook* would first be published in 1875.[19] Nor was the daily press of much assistance until 1822, when regular money-market and City columns first appeared in reaction to the lending boom. They would remain the principal printed source of investor information for years to come.

Despite such differences in Stock Exchange and money-market structures and practice from those prevailing today, physically the City in the early nineteenth century would be easily recognizable by a modern visitor. The principal thoroughfares – Bishopsgate, Cornhill, Leadenhall, Poultry, Throgmorton and Lombard Streets – were all in existence and jammed with traffic – horsedrawn to be sure. St Pauls dominated the skyline which was not yet segmented by towering office blocks. The Mansion House, the Guildhall, the Royal Exchange and the bulky shape of the Bank of England on Threadneedle Street also would be familiar landmarks. The principal external differences from the modern City were not just the height of the buildings and vast number of horsedrawn vehicles which clogged its cobbled thoroughfares: the City in 1815 was still largely residential. Some 130,000 people resided within its densely populated confines, often above the many shops which lined the narrow streets. Drapers, greengrocers, booksellers, ship chandlers and provision merchants of all sorts worked and lived side-by-side with financiers, stockbrokers, insurance and shipping agents. Even bankers sometimes dwelt on their premises, and Charles Dickens as a young man courted a girl living next to her father's bank on Lombard Street.[20]

In 1817, however, the opportunities for foreign investment open to the stock market began to broaden. In that year the new financial power and expertise now concentrated in the City enabled Baring Brothers, in association with the Amsterdam banking house of Hope & Co., to float a loan to finance French war reparations. After Waterloo the victorious allies had imposed a 700,000,000 franc indemnity upon France, payable in five annual instalments. In addition, the French were expected to provide 150,000,000 francs per

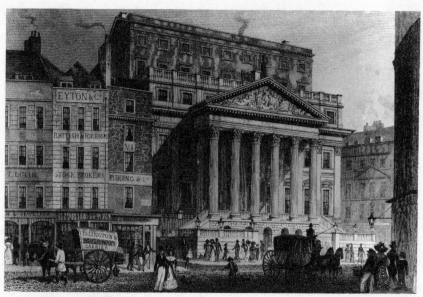

3. *The Mansion House from the Bank*. The official residence of the Lord Mayor of London on Threadneedle Street. It was here that the Poyais survivors complained of their treatment to the Lord Mayor in the Magistrates Court which still functions in the building (The Guildhall Library, London).

4. *The New Stock Exchange*, 1809. The building at Capel Court opened in 1802. This print by Rowlandson and Pugin was published seven years later by Rudolph Ackermann, who designed and printed the 1822 Colombian Bond Certificates (The Guildhall Library, London).

5. *The Stock Exchange Interior*, 1847. The interior of the Stock Exchange at Capel Court, substantially unchanged since 1822 when the Latin American loan boom began. Latin American bonds were still traded on the Exchange, but at substantial discounts and mostly by speculators who would sell them when news of a loan renegotiation would cause prices to rise (The Guildhall Library, London).

annum to support the Duke of Wellington's army of occupation. The French treasury, however, was empty.

Barings, the City's most prestigious merchant banker, and other international financiers believed that France could raise the funds by borrowing abroad. The initial loan, denominated in francs, was issued at a 58 discount, which meant that for 58 francs investors could purchase a bond which at maturity would pay 100 francs. The loan was the first of several similar French borrowings at 5 per cent per annum interest totalling the franc equivalent of £28,000,000, upon which Barings received a 2½ per cent commission. As the loans were issued over the next two years, French credit improved, and so great was the demand by British and continental investors that the discounts on the bonds rose as high as 68. Thanks to Barings' efforts, the victors received their indemnity immediately, and the army of occupation was withdrawn. Meanwhile, France's repayment burden was spread over the maturity of the loans, allegedly provoking the duc de Richelieu's admiring remark that there were six great powers in Europe – Britain, Austria, France, Prussia, Russia and Baring Brothers. At the same time, the episode whetted the British investor's appetite for foreign government bonds.[21]

In 1818, not to be outshone by his major banking rival, N. M. Rothschild, who had been excluded from the indemnity financing, arranged a £5,000,000 thirty-six-year loan for the kingdom of Prussia, represented by bonds paying 5 per cent per annum with an issue price of 72. This was a more significant issue historically than Barings' French loans. Secured by a mortgage on the kingdom's revenues and various royal domains in the Prussian provinces, it was the first postwar foreign loan to be denominated in Sterling. A sinking fund to provide repayment was created by the investment of 5 per cent or £150,000 per annum of the loan in London to be accumulated by trustees at compound interest until maturity. The Prussian credit, followed by loans launched by Rothschild to Austria, Russia and Spain, established enduring precedents of structure, technique and documentation which would be followed in the Latin American loans.[22]

By 1822 not only was the economic structure requisite to servicing an international borrowing boom in place in the City, but the country as a whole had recovered from the economic dislocation which had prevailed during the transition from the years of warfare. The general liquidity produced by prosperity and good harvests was increased when in March 1822, the government, no longer needing to borrow heavily for the war effort, announced plans for consolidating the national debt. Traditionally much of the British public's surplus funds had been invested in government stocks known as consols, which generally paid 5 per cent per annum. Now, however, the interest on government stock was to be reduced to 4 per cent. Stock totalling £214,000,000 was affected, and holders were given the option of converting to the new, lower-yielding issues. Dissenting investors were given twelve days from 12 March to register their dissatisfaction with the new arrangements at the Bank of England and thus qualify to receive back their principal and accrued interest.

Numerous holders, hoping to find more attractive higher-yielding instruments, decided to reject the conversion offer and to take cash instead. Nearly £2,800,000 suddenly became available for new investment just when interest in the future of Latin America and its economic potential was reaching its peak, and when, after years of repeated defeats, Bolívar and the other patriots seemed to be winning their struggle for independence.[23]

II
PATRIOTS AND BOND ISSUES

THE FIRST LATIN American country to seize upon the novel financing opportunities offered in the City after Waterloo was the Republic of Colombia. The new borrower had been created in 1819, when Simón Bolívar, driven by the military and economic imperatives of the continuing vicious struggle against Spain, united, on paper at least, the three former colonial administrative units of the Viceroyalty of New Granada, the Captain Generalcy of Venezuela and the Audiencia of Quito in Ecuador into the single political entity of the Republic of Colombia. His venture into bespoke nation-building would prove optimistic and shortlived.[1]

Colombia was sparsely populated with less than three million inhabitants. Few economic ties linked its three areas, and almost from inception, provincial identities and local loyalties threatened to fragment the republic once the unifying menace of Spain vanished. The bitter fight for independence from Spain begun in 1810 continued. While the worst of the atrocities of the earlier years were no longer repeated, the civilian populace had suffered horribly, prisoners were still shot, most of the commercial classes had been ruined, and the economy was shattered. Moreover, Colombia had yet to be recognized by any European state, and although two of its components – Venezuela and New Granada (modern Colombia) – had declared independence, Ecuador was still under royalist control.[2]

Despite Colombia's poverty and disunity, Bolívar reasoned that if British diplomatic recognition were obtained trade and commerce could recover, while a substantial foreign loan would enable him to rebuild the economy and finance the concluding phases of the war. Accordingly, on 24 December 1819, he granted a power of attorney to Francisco Antonio Zea, his friend and the republic's vice president, authorizing him as envoy extraordinary and minister plenipotentiary to proceed to Europe and to establish political and commercial relations with the Old World. Zea was also given full powers to negotiate and contract a loan of up to £5,000,000 on the terms and conditions he considered best, and to pledge for its repayment and

6. *Francisco Antonio Zea* (1766–1823). The Colombian diplomat who arrived in London in 1820 and reached a satisfactory financial settlement with the English merchants who had supplied arms and munitions for Bolívar's armies. Two years later he signed the 1822 loan agreement on behalf of Colombia, which was the direct inspiration for the Chilean and Peruvian loans launched shortly thereafter. (From A. Walker, *Colombia* (London, 1822), courtesy of Cambridge University Library.)

servicing 'the most productive branches of the public revenue' as well as the 'lands, mines, and other property of the state'.[3]

The choice of Zea was unfortunate. Although highly respected in European liberal and intellectual circles, Zea was also headstrong, vain and without business or financial experience. Born in Medellín, Colombia, in 1766, Zea was a former director of the Madrid Botanical Gardens who had been imprisoned for distributing copies of *The Rights of Man and the Citizen*. In 1816 he had joined Bolívar in Haiti to sail with an ill-fated expedition to oust Spanish forces from the mainland. The following year he became the secretary of government in Bolívar's temporary capital at Angostura, Venezuela, and editor of the *Correo del Orinoco*, the official government newspaper. He was president of the 1819 Constitutional Congress, and for six months served as vice president in overall charge of the government while Bolívar was concluding the last stages of the war against Spain in Colombia.[4] As one of the intellectual founders of the republic, Zea initially enjoyed Bolívar's enthusiastic support. Sadly, within three years the Liberator would call Zea 'Colombia's greatest calamity'.[5]

When Zea arrived in London in late June 1820, he soon realized that the ·conservative British administration would not recognize Colombia's unstable republican government despite increasing pressure from City merchants, who foresaw vast marketing opportunities once the rebellious colonies were freed. The outcome of the independence struggle was still uncertain, and the Cabinet was reluctant to offend Spain, now its ally, by recognizing its former colonies. In addition, many of Britain's ruling class distrusted republicanism. The Cato Street conspirators, who had plotted to assassinate the Cabinet as part of a plan to force fundamental political change had been apprehended only the previous February. New, radical doctrines of suspected French revolutionary origin were not in favour therefore.

Zea also discovered that Colombia's credit rating was non-existent. Prior to their unification, Venezuela and New Granada each had sent representatives to London to obtain diplomatic recognition. Their efforts had been fruitless. Therefore Venezuela's Luis López Méndez, who, as noted, had arrived in London with Bolívar in 1810, and New Granada's José María del Real instead had devoted their time to recruiting discharged and unemployed British servicemen and purchasing military supplies to send to Bolívar. The widespread British enthusiasm for Latin American independence had greatly facilitated their efforts. As one of the volunteers recruited by López Méndez in 1817 to fight under Bolívar's banner recalled later, 'The shouts were now for independence: and success to the enterprize of the South American patriots, and a glorious triumph to their cause, came from the mouth of nearly every Briton! It was not sufficient for me to wish them success ... I determined to lend my personal assistance in promoting it.'[6]

Both López Méndez and Del Real had borrowed heavily from British merchants in the names of their governments to equip these ambitious expeditions, including one led by the persuasive adventurer Sir Gregor MacGregor, a general in Bolívar's army.[7] MacGregor had served in the Peninsular War in the 57th Regiment of Foot, and in 1811, accompanied by his personal piper, had sailed to Venezuela to fight in the struggles for independence. Bolívar promoted him to general and awarded him the young nation's highest decoration for valour, the *Orden de los Libertadores*. In 1817 he returned to Britain to enlist troops with which to help Bolívar destroy the remaining Spanish armies. López Méndez borrowed £1,000 which he advanced to MacGregor for supplies and recruits. The Scotsman, however, dissipated the funds without leaving Britain. López Méndez had already been in debtors' prison several times, but found himself once again behind bars while MacGregor offered his services to New Granada's Del Real. MacGregor, on behalf of Del Real, recruited some 1,700 discharged officers and soldiers in England and Ireland, whom he shipped in chartered vessels to the Spanish Main in 1818–19. Instead of joining Bolívar, however, the doughty general decimated his forces in disastrous assaults on Panama and the

7. *Sir Gregor MacGregor* (1786–1845). Born in Scotland, MacGregor fought in the Peninsular compaign, then became a general in Simón Bolívar's army. Besides his military accomplishments, he occupies a unique place in British financial history as the only man ever to market successfully the bonds of a non-existent country when he launched the Poyais issue in 1822–3.

Colombian coast. Bolívar was furious, while back in London Del Real could not pay the merchants who had provided supplies on credit for MacGregor's expedition and, like López Méndez, he was imprisoned for debt.[8]

Including MacGregor's ventures, Del Real and López Méndez enlisted over 5,000 men and purchased large quantities of munitions, ordnance, uniforms and other military equipment, principally in London. After the British government's 1819 Foreign Enlistment Act effectively forbad recruiting or munitions shipments, the two patriots decided to concentrate on raising money for their joint cause. In November 1819, they combined forces to issue an amateurish prospectus for a £100,000 loan represented by 1,000 'shares' of £100 each. Purchasers were assured that if they paid but 50 per cent of their subscriptions within six months, they would receive full face value of their shares (i.e. double their money) within the following next three months from the sales proceeds of Venezuelan and New Granadan exports.[9] Not surprisingly, even before Zea had left Colombia the nation owed over £500,000 to increasingly angry and impatient British merchants.

Zea therefore quickly convened a creditors' meeting at which he promised that Colombia would honour the commitments contracted by López Méndez and Del Real. Hoping that restored financial credibility would lead to recognition as well as pave the way for a further major loan, on 1 August 1820 Zea signed a refinancing agreement with Messrs Charles Herring, William Graham, and John D. Powles, an association of merchants trading with the Caribbean and who represented Venezuela's and New Granada's one hundred or more creditors. In the agreement Zea promised, after reviewing all outstanding accounts, to deliver to the creditors 10 per cent per annum debentures up to the full amounts of their claims. Zea secured the debentures by pledging the income from the government's tobacco monopoly and one-fifth of Colombia's gold and silver production.[10]

The following month, Herring, Graham and Powles wrote to Zea from their City offices at Freemans Court, Cornhill, reminding him that the British creditors had born patiently Colombia's failure to honour their claims as long as the struggle for independence had continued unabated. With the victory at Boyacá in April 1819, however, the Spanish armies were virtually swept from New Granada. Nevertheless, no payment had been made, the merchants wrote, leading to serious complaints and providing Spanish sympathizers with excuses to indulge 'in the most injurious insinuations against the honour, the good faith and the respectability of the Republic...'.[11]

Herring, Graham and Powles then reminded Zea of the linkage between the nation's credit-standing and diplomatic recognition. It was in Colombia's best interests to see that the new debentures were properly serviced, because 'we can hardly conceive any object more desirable to a Government seeking the recognition of its independence than that its integrity in the discharge of engagements of so just and sacred a character should be vindicated in the eyes of the world.' The letter concluded by hoping that the Colombian government would not regard the arrangement just concluded with Zea as an excuse for any future payment delays.

Two months later the contractors addressed a similar letter to Bolívar. Thanks to Zea's efforts, they wrote, the fears of Colombia's creditors had been temporarily allayed, and the government's credit had begun to recover. Continuation of this happy state of affairs depended, however, on punctual adherence to the agreement Zea had signed, the details of which had already been sent to Colombia. If funds for the first interest payment due 1 May were not received, all the good work would be undone. A default would lend credence to the arguments of Colombia's enemies that the new state was too immature to merit diplomatic recognition. British creditors had supported Colombia in its hour of greatest need, relying upon the solemn engagements of its representatives. 'If obligations such as these are not to be respected, all the bonds of civilized society are at an end.' The contractors then entreated Bolívar, if he had not already done so, to take immediate measures to remit the necessary funds for the May and all subsequent payments.[12]

After spending seven months reviewing creditors' claims, on 9 March 1821 at a meeting in Leicester Square's Hotel Huntley Zea recognized £547,783 in debts owed to British merchants. Unfortunately for his future peace of mind, he imprudently accepted many claims almost without question, asserting that his country's dignity would not allow him to examine them closely. As a contemporary wrote, '[t]oo minute an examination might have accelerated the fall of a credit which stood in need of support on an imperishable basis'.[13] The debentures Zea then issued began circulating at 70 per cent of their face value, rose to 95 and eventually reached 115. The nation's credit was restored – temporarily at least.

Meanwhile, Zea actually increased the amount of indebtedness outstanding by issuing further debentures to support his lavish lifestyle. When criticized for his extravagance, he replied that 'the Republic of Colombia is a skeleton and it was necessary to cover it with a cloak of gold'.[14] For example, he signed £66,666 in 10 per cent debentures to raise £20,000 which he squandered on an absurd and unsuccessful mission to Madrid, where he had hoped to secure

Spanish recognition of Colombian independence. Another issue became necessary when the May 1821 interest payments for the March debentures fell due and no funds had been received from Colombia, despite the contractors' letter to Bolívar. Zea persuaded Herring, Graham and Powles to advance him the required £91,712 in return for £140,000 in additional debentures at a price of 65½. They later presumably sold the debentures at a profit once the interest had been paid and debenture prices risen in consequence.[15]

When news of Zea's March 1821 agreement eventually reached Colombia, an outraged congress bitterly criticized him for accepting dubious claims without supporting documentation, and for agreeing to high interest rates secured by onerous guarantees. Moreover, it was alleged that he had exceeded his authority. The new constitution adopted at the Conference of Cúcuta in July 1821 to replace the former provisional government and formalize the union of Venezuela, New Granada and Ecuador, provided that congress alone could contract loans on behalf of the republic. Indeed, General Francisco de Paula Santander from New Granada had even replaced Zea as vice president. As early as March, however, Bolívar decided he could not approve Zea's August 1820 agreement, and had ordered Secretary of Foreign Affairs Pedro Gual to cancel Zea's power of attorney. Perhaps because he wished to avoid offending the British financiers, or hoped first to consult personally with Bolívar, Gual did not write to Zea until mid-October 1821.[16] Zea always insisted that the revocation was not received in time to prevent him on 13 March 1822, from contracting with Herring, Graham and Powles a larger loan of £2,000,000. Even given the poor communications of the day – six weeks sailing time from Colombia to Britain – Zea's excuses seem forced, unless, of course, the vessel carrying Gual's letter was intercepted by a Spanish warship as the envoy later suggested.

The new £2,000,000 loan, signed in Paris to avoid British usury laws limiting interest to 5 per cent per annum, was to be represented by bearer bonds bearing 6 per cent per annum interest payable semi-annually in London.[17] The handwritten prospectus which survives in the British Library allows subscribers to purchase their shares in three instalments over six months. Parties paying their full subscriptions at once, however, would receive a small further discount from the issue price of 84 for a £100 bond.[18]

One of the purposes of the loan was, of course, to redeem the outstanding 1820 debentures, which now totalled £890,128. Debenture holders were therefore allowed to exchange their 1820 paper for the new bonds at a special rate of £80 in debentures per £100 in bonds. Even though the bond's interest rate was lower, debenture holders who converted to bonds to take advantage of the 80 discount could make a 4 per cent profit by selling out at 84, the price at which the issue was initially offered to the general public. If they decided to retain their new bonds, they would become the beneficiaries of the more ample collateral security offered by the loan.[19] Considering that the 1822 Danish and Russian 5 per cent loans had been issued at 77½ and 81, the Colombian pricing was highly complementary to the public relations efforts of Powles and his colleagues.

Once their subscriptions had been paid, bondholders would receive the elegant bond certificates designed and printed by London's most fashionable engraver and bookseller, Rudolph Ackermann of The Strand. Never before had such artistic talent been lavished upon a bond certificate. Each was surmounted by the Colombian eagle and coat of arms, with scantily-clad male and female allegorical figures representing the Orinoco and Magdalena rivers. Interest coupons, payable every six months to the bearer through final maturity, were attached. The text of the certificate was arranged in parallel columns in English, Spanish and French and promised that the loan would be secured by import and export duties, the entire state income from gold, silver and salt mines, and the income from the government tobacco monopoly.[20]

Potential bond purchasers were assured in the prospectus that the country's resources were 'unbounded and require but a moderate time to organize ... The revenue from the mines is considerable when they are in full work which it is expected they will shortly be'. Investors who might have been worried over Colombia's political future were told that 'the country having now established its independence and having no interests that can bring it in collision with any other nations seems likely to enjoy a long course of uninterrupted tranquility'. The authors of this bald statement ignored the continued presence of a strong Spanish army, and, more understandably, could not foresee the sad future which awaited Bolívar's praiseworthy dream.

Moreover, they alleged Colombia was, despite years of terrible, debilitating warfare, in at least as good a position as the United States of America had been when it had attained independence thirty-five years before. In 1786 these former British colonies had had a foreign debt of £2,488,455 and an internal debt of £9,012,992. By contrast, even including the proposed loan, Colombia's entire indebtedness would not amount to £2,500,000. Investors who might have doubted Colombia's good faith because of its unfortunate past payment record were told that, given its natural resources, the government had no reason not to keep to its bargain.

Rising states are seldom indifferent to their Character in the world and indeed with all governments the importance of sustaining

Public Credit ... is so much felt that, where means are to be found, the will is seldom wanting. As to means perhaps no nation on Earth can be pointed out so rich in resources and so little encumbered with debt as Colombia.[21]

Aided by encouraging books and newspaper articles planted by the contractors, this loan for £2,000,000 was quickly over-subscribed. The 6 per cent interest was more than domestic British government securities could produce. The return was, however, ostensibly even higher. For £84 an investor could acquire a bond which would pay £100 on maturity in twenty years or sooner if redeemed earlier. The so-called 'true' yield to maturity or redemption therefore was over 7 per cent per annum, assuming, of course, that the loan was properly serviced.[22]

Herring, Graham and Powles did not have to wait so long to realize their own profits. They had underwritten the £2,000,000 loan at 80, which meant that the most Colombia could gross from the operation would be £1,600,000. From these proceeds the contractors deducted their 2 per cent commission, based on the face amount of the loan, an additional 2½ per cent to cover the first four interest or dividend payments, plus a further 1 per cent with which to begin the sinking fund out of which the loan would be repaid in equal annual amounts through 1849. The net due Colombia was further reduced by subtracting legal, advertising and promotional expenses incurred by the contractors. An additional 4 per cent of the total face amount also went into the contractor's coffers, representing the difference between the underwriting price of 80 and the issue price of 84. The contractors were moreover entitled to charge an additional 2½ per cent commission on all the interest payments they made on behalf of Colombia, as well as a 1 per cent commission on any bonds redeemed.[23]

The Colombian loan was considered a great success by the British political and financial community. If Zea had heard any murmurs of dissent from Colombia, he kept them firmly to himself. He was in fact extremely popular and respected, and on 10 July 1822 was feted at a public dinner at the City of London Tavern on Bishopsgate. Among the guests were several prominent MPs, including Samuel Wilberforce, the slavery abolitionist, and the solicitor general, all of whom urged early British government recognition of Colombian independence.[24] After toasts to 'The King', 'The Duke of York and the Rest of the Royal Family' and 'The Army and Navy', the Duke of Somerset as host offered a toast to Zea's health, praising Colombia for sweeping away the double tyranny of an oppressive government and an intolerant church. Zea responded in French, expressing gratitude for Britain's support during his country's struggle for independence. 'It was in Great Britain that, at the time of her utmost need, Colombia found firm and faithful friends to come to her support. The injuries of Spain will soon be forgotten; the friendship of Great Britain will be cherished warm in our hearts as long as life shall beat in them.'

Unfortunately the euphoria and good will demonstrated that July evening were not destined to last. Nevertheless, the loan negotiated by Zea had excited the financial community to a degree unknown for many years. Obviously great profits were to be made from such arrangements by the merchants and bankers who, acting as middlemen, passed on the risk of non-payment to the public. At the same time, the theory went, with funds lent by British capitalists the new nations would consolidate their independence and out of gratitude invite Britain to replace Spain as their principal trading partner. In brief, the City could only do well by financing the new republics.

Not surprisingly, therefore, the Colombian loan's success almost immediately triggered a series of new issues by other Latin American borrowers. The structure of the 1822 loan provided a convenient model for future loan promoters. The use of bearer bonds, signing on the continent to avoid inconvenient usury legislation, pledging national revenues and assets, withholding interest and amortization funds in advance, exacting high commissions and issuing a laudatory prospectus before sales to the public via jobbers and brokers on the Stock Exchange, were all techniques which would be employed with but minor refinements in subsequent loans to Chile, Peru, Mexico, Buenos Ayres, Brazil and Central America. Bolívar's correct assumption that Colombia could find in London the finance it so sorely needed had indirectly inspired the first Latin American loan boom.

The next Latin American state to borrow was Chile, which, like Colombia, in 1822 was still unrecognized by Great Britain. During colonial times Spain had not ascribed great importance to this narrow strip of land along the Pacific. The country was a neglected rural backwater, ruled by a governor appointed from Madrid and for many years an economic appendage of the Viceroyalty of Peru, its wealthier neighbour to the north. Much smaller than Mexico, Peru or Colombia, it was a compact country where an aristocratic Creole upper class ruled the large, passive mass of rural labouring poor. Much of it, in fact, was still controlled by fierce, unsubdued indians.

The Chilean independence movement began in 1810, as elsewhere in Latin America, with the formation of juntas initially loyal to King Ferdinand but which soon opted for independence. By 1812 a single patriot leader had emerged – Bernardo O'Higgins, the son of the former Chilean Captain General and Peruvian Viceroy Ambrosio

O'Higgins. When in October 1814, Spanish troops routed the patriots, O'Higgins sought refuge across the Andes in what is now
Argentina, but was then a loose union of independent provinces
under the ostensible leadership of the city and province of Buenos
Ayres. He returned in early 1817 as second-in-command to Buenos
Ayres General José de San Martín. Spanish troops were routed by
the combined Buenos Ayrean and Chilean forces, and Chile's independence was assured. O'Higgins, elected Supreme Director of
the Republic, then energetically set about ridding Chile of the last
Spanish troops and helping San Martín organize an expedition to
carry the independence struggle up the coast to Peru.

The Chilean loan was the inspiration of José Antonio de Irisarri, a
Guatemalan who had emigrated to Chile and been befriended by
O'Higgins. Thanks to the Supreme Director's patronage, in 1819 he
was sent to London as Chilean minister plenipotentiary entrusted
with obtaining British recognition of Chilean independence and
authorized to offer in return commercial concessions and import
duty exemptions. In addition, he was empowered to raise a loan of
2,000,000 pesos. Like Zea, Irisarri was never received officially by
the British government, and diplomatic recognition was consistently
denied despite the proffered concessions and three years of constant
lobbying.

Meanwhile, also like Zea, Irisarri pursued an entravagant life style
to maintain his agreeable façade as representative of a prosperous
new nation. He rented a house on Baker Street, hired servants,
horses and a coach, and, as the funds he had brought dwindled,
wrote frequently and vainly to Chile for more money. During this
period Irisarri met and befriended Andrés Bello, who was still living
in London in exile from Venezuela. Since Irisarri had few official
duties he, like Bello, spent considerable time reading and writing at
the British Museum. He admired the Venezuelan so much that he
offered him a post at the Chilean legation.[25]

Just as his attempts to obtain diplomatic recognition were constantly thwarted, Irisarri's initial efforts to raise a loan also were
frustrated. In August 1819, he signed a financing agreement with
the small London merchant house of Hullet Brothers, but Latin
America's credit rating was so poor due to fears of Spanish reconquest and the antics of López Méndez and Del Real that the transaction was stillborn. Zea's successful refinancing of the Colombian
debt in August 1820, would radically change this situation, however.

On 20 May 1821, Irisarri wrote to various prominent Chilean
leaders describing the favourable reception of the recent French,
Prussian and Spanish loans, and suggesting that Chile attempt a
similar borrowing before Colombia and other borrowers flooded the

market with their paper. The Chilean senate was unconvinced, and Irisarri was ordered to suspend any negotiations and to rescind any loan agreements he might have signed. Once again, however, as in the case of Colombia and Zea, the undependability of transatlantic communication intervened, and a year would elapse before Irisarri received the reply to his letter.

In March 1822, Zea contracted his £2,000,000 Colombian credit, which inspired Irisarri to further efforts. Although no instructions had arrived from Santiago, on 18 May 1822, Irisarri signed another contract with Hullet Brothers to raise £1,000,000. In the wake of the favourable reception of the Colombian issue, the new Chilean credit received ample press coverage, and was to be represented by 10,000 bearer bonds of £100 each, issued at 70, with 6 per cent per annum interest payable semi-annually in London free of all taxes and deductions. The bonds were to be redeemed at par over thirty years from a sinking fund for which £20,000 was deposited in the first year, with further annual allocations of £10,000 plus accumulated interest on redeemed bonds. Additional amounts were withheld to pay the dividends due in September 1822 and March 1823, as well as to defray Hullet's and Irisarri's commissions and expenses. The loan was launched in good company. On the same day it was announced, N. M. Rothschild's new 5 per cent Russian loan of £2,500,000 was issued at 80, and rose quickly to 84.[26]

According to the neatly printed prospectus, the Chilean loan would be secured by all the national lands, mines, and state revenues, as evidenced by a general mortgage bond to be deposited in the Bank of England until the loan was repaid.[27] In addition Irisarri specifically pledged the net revenues from the Mint and from the Land Tax, which he estimated respectively at approximately £60,000 and £50,000 per annum, 'nearly double the amounts of the yearly interest and contributions to the sinking fund'. These revenues were to be collected and kept segregated from other income. No part of them could be applied to other government expenses. Also, bond subscribers could nominate a commissioner to reside in Santiago where he would receive quarterly payments from the treasury to be remitted to London for servicing.

Lest prospective bond purchasers doubt the nation's political stability, the prospectus observed that while Chile was still nominally at war with Spain, in fact the country was 'at peace with the entire world'. Unfortunately it had not reached the level of wealth and progress it would long since have attained 'had not ages of sluggish, perverse, and impolitic administration checked its progress'. After this appeal to investors' anti-Spanish prejudice, the prospectus concluded by stating that the loan was being raised to 'call forth' at last

the productive capacity of the nation's hardy population, long coast-
line and 'diversified territory'. Because Chile's annual revenues were
nearly fourteen times the yearly debt servicing requirements, interest
payments could be made with ease and punctuality.

The loan was welcomed in the City, and with the £20,000 commission he had awarded himself, and £18,000 which he deducted
from the proceeds as back salary, Irisarri resumed his grand life style.
Leaving Andrés Bello in charge in London, he travelled frequently
to Paris, ostensibly to obtain French recognition of Chile's independence. Not surprisingly, Louis XVIII's government refused to consider recognition of a republican regime in open rebellion against
their royal cousin Ferdinand in Madrid. The Guatemalan's mission
was not a total failure, however. Although rebuffed at the French
court, his persuasive charms were more effective elsewhere, and he
acquired one of the most beautiful women in France as his mistress.
Confidently expecting his patron O'Higgins to endorse his actions,
he was soon spending virtually all his time on the continent, where
he purchased a twenty-gun corvette his government had not requested, and speculated in sugar and naval stores with the dwindling
loan proceeds.[28]

For the moment, however, the investing public ignored Irisarri's
unedifying conduct and must have been gratified when the bonds
which had been initially offered at 70 rapidly rose to 72¼ on the first
day of issue. Although the bonds themselves would not be ready
until the end of June, subscribers were given provisional certificates
or scrip, each of which entitled the bearer to receive five bonds of
£100 each upon a 10 per cent downpayment, with the additional
60 per cent payable on or before 31 December. This arrangement,
to be followed in subsequent issues to other countries, enabled
speculators to play the market for relatively small sums and trade in
the scrip in the hope it would increase in value before they were
obliged to make all their further payments by the end of the subscription period.[29]

Chile's venture into the City was quickly followed by Peru. The
motivating force behind this latest loan was not, however, a Latin
American diplomat or entrepreneur, but General James Paroissien,
an Englishman of French Huguenot descent from Barking, Essex,
who had trained as a medical doctor and sailed to the River Plate in
1806 in search of adventure. He eventually joined the Buenos Ayres
rebel forces, and crossed the Andes to Chile as San Martín's chief
medical officer. In 1820 he became an aide-de-camp to San Martín,
whom he accompanied to Peru where he was made a brigadier
general. In 1821 he was sent by San Martín to Europe with Juan
García del Río, former Peruvian minister of foreign affairs, to find

a European prince to rule as emperor in Peru, as well as obtain diplomatic recognition, negotiate treaties of alliance, amity and commerce, and raise a loan of six million Spanish dollars, or approximately £1,500,000.[30]

Paroissien and Del Río arrived in London in September 1822 and opened the Peruvian legation at 21 Grosvenor Street. They could not have come at a more propitious time. Popular sympathy for the Latin American revolutionaries was more widespread than ever before. Bolívar's victory at Carabobo in Venezuela in June the previous year, which shattered Spanish military power in Colombia, and in which British volunteers had played a crucial role, had been widely reported in the press, albeit several months after the event.[31] The general interest in Latin American affairs had continued unabated.

The United States had already announced its intention to recognize the new republics, a decision which provoked great concern among British merchants who feared that the former North American colonies now would obtain special trading privileges to the detriment of British commerce. Consequently a group of merchants, shipowners, manufacturers and financiers, including Baring Brothers, Reid, Irving & Co., and Anthony Gibbs & Sons, petitioned the government to regularize trade with those South American nations which had adopted a policy of only admitting into their own ports the ships of nations which admitted and recognized the flags and merchandise of the South American States. Due to these increasing pressures British diplomatic recognition now seemed inevitable, and lending to the Latin American nations was no longer perceived to be as risky as before.[32]

Also, after the recent lucrative Colombian and Chilean loans, brokers and investors alike were eager to absorb more Latin American paper. During the first week in October *The Courier* was remarking that 'speculation in Chilean and Colombian bonds exceeds all belief; the former is five per cent higher; the latter four per cent since the morning'.[33] By mid-month Colombian bonds had risen to 95, while Chile was quoted at 88¼.[34]

Despite the favourable omens, however, the Peruvian envoys could not persuade the British government to receive them officially, and soon gave up all attempts at obtaining recognition. Nor did they pursue their search for a European princeling for Peru. Instead they approached Messrs Herring, Graham and Powles, who had launched the Colombian loan, and requested their assistance in raising £1,200,000. Armed with a verbal commitment from the Colombian contractors to underwrite the credit, Paroissien and García del Río then persuaded Thomas Kinder, a rival merchant on Basinghall Street, to take the loan on better terms at 75. Powles and his colleagues were furious, and circulated an indignant printed handbill in the City, published in *The New Times* in mid-October: 'When strangers come among us to treat for large and important transactions, they ought to understand enough of the national character to know that English Merchants, acting on their part with openness and good faith, are not to be met by cunning, evasion and artifice'.[35] Nevertheless the City and the public generally did not care about such niceties, and the new issue was eagerly awaited.

The loan agreement with Kinder provided for a £1,200,000 credit bearing 6 per cent interest payable semi-annually and represented by bearer bond certificates of £100, £200 and £500. The loan was to be raised over six months from 25 October 1822 during which the proceeds would be made available to the borrower in six periodic instalments. Subscriptions by potential bondholders were payable in four portions over six months, and the bonds, which would be redeemed periodically at par until final maturity in 1856, were secured by mortgaging all the national revenue, in particular income from the customs and the Mint, as had been done with the Chilean credit. The prospectus did not bother readers with boring economic details, stating simply that 'the extent of the resources of Peru is too well known to require any relation of them'.[36]

Nor did information available to the public reveal that the contractors received a 2 per cent commission on the face amount of the credit. The contractors would, of course, also have the use of funds withheld in advance for interest and sinking fund payments, and were entitled to deduct from the proceeds all their out-of-pocket expenses and to retain the difference between the price at which they had agreed with Paroissien and García del Río to take the loan 'firm', and the price at which they sold it to the public. Even before any deductions, the most that Peru could expect to receive from the loan, due to the heavy discount of 75, was £900,000.[37]

Located in the middle of the west coast of South America, Peru was more geographically isolated from Europe than Colombia, Mexico, Brazil or Buenos Ayres. Its main seaborn link with Spain was via Valparaiso, Chile, and then either directly through the Straits of Magellan or via Buenos Ayres. As a result the new liberal philosophies current in Europe in the early 1800s and even in the rest of Latin America had had little chance to circulate among its populace. The Vice Royalty had thus remained loyal eighteenth-century in its outlook when, beginning in 1810, local juntas established in other parts of the Latin American continent questioned for the first time Spain's exclusive right to determine their future destinies.

So interwoven into the entire fabric of Peruvian society were the social and political structures, traditions and ceremonies of old Spain,

8. *The Royal Exchange, 1822.* This was the scene of the launch of the Peruvian loan in 1822, which caused a near riot. The building burned down in 1838 and was replaced by the present structure (The Guildhall Library, London).

that there was little popular clamour for independence until General José de San Martín arrived in Lima in July 1821 with his victorious troops from Buenos Ayres and Chile to impose freedom from Spain. Bolívar eventually displaced San Martín as leader in Peru, but royalist sentiment and allegiance was so strong that not until 1824 at the battles of Junín and Ayacucho could even the great Liberator defeat the Spanish armies and their Creole adherents. In 1822, therefore, Peruvian independence was far from secure. Royalist armies still controlled large areas, and the nation's economy, based upon sugar, cotton and mining, was in chaos. The treasury was empty, vast expanses of agricultural land laid waste, the best mining areas occupied by Spanish troops, and the Spanish flag flew over the port of Callao, effectively hindering all trade.[38]

Nevertheless, when the Peruvian issue the first offered at the Royal Exchange on the morning of 12 October 1822 – appropriately enough the anniversary of Columbia's discovery of America exactly 330 years before – an unprecedented pandemonium errupted. Instead of inviting written tenders or announcing a price at which he would be willing to sell down loan participations to brokers and jobbers, Kinder took the unusual step of inviting verbal bids from those already assembled in the Exchange and eagerly awaiting the opportunity to buy into what promised to be another profitable Latin

American issue. Recalling the high commissions on the Colombian and Chilean loans, jobbers and brokers frantically shouted their bids, scarcely audible over the din. Kinder and his colleagues pretended not to hear, waiting for the bids to rise. According to *The New Times*, when the bidders were joined by other hopeful subscribers from the Stock Exchange the press of near-hysterical humanity forced the contractor to retreat 'from the Dutch Walk, where the confusion began, to the opposite side of the exchange, where the Swedish merchants assemble'. The mob then pursued the contractor out onto Bartholomew Lane before order was restored and bids of between 88 and 90 accepted.[39]

Deploring the public's overeager haste to purchase Peruvian bonds, *The New Times* declared that 'a more adventurous speculation has scarcely ever been brought into the market'. The editor continued 'if the very respectable Mr Lemuel Gulliver were to appear on stage again, and to issue proposals for a loan to the Republic of *Laputa*, he would run a hazard of being suffocated by the pressure of subscribers to set down their names.' It was difficult to understand why representatives of a country which purportedly had such quantities of gold and silver should need to come to Britain to borrow money. Moreover, 'here is a country on the other side of the globe, of which we absolutely know nothing, but that it is or has lately been the scene of a desperate conflict between two contending parties.' The leader noted that a Bank of England director was among the loan's promoters, and confessed, tongue in cheek, 'we must own that this last piece of information has a little upset the notions we had formed of Bank Directors. We thought they were a prudent, cautious, calculating race of people – the last in the world to plunge into mad speculation of loans to nobody knows whom, secured on nobody knows what.' Initially all went well, however, and a week after the loan subscriptions were opened Kinder paid £120,000 out of the bond proceeds into the Peruvian government account at bankers Everett, Walker, Maltby and Ellis.[40]

The Chilean and Peruvian loans confirmed for subsequent Latin American transactions the patterns of origination, negotiation and sale established by the earlier Colombian credit. Emissaries from borrowing countries armed with powers of attorney would contact a London banking or merchant house, which, as contractor in return for commissions varying from 2 to 5 per cent, would underwrite the loan at an agreed discount price, such as 75 in the Peruvian case. The bonds were then marketed at a steeper discount – 88 in the Peruvian issue. A borrowing country thus would only receive £750,000 in the case of a £1,000,000 loan underwritten at 75, even though actual bond sales might, where a loan was marketed at 88, generate a total of £880,000. The underwriter, however, would be richer by £130,000 and in addition would receive commissions for supervising subsequent interest and redemption payments.

Bond purchasers were content with this arrangement because due to the 88 discount the true yield to maturity on 6 per cent bonds was 6.8% per annum. Sometimes if the issuing house did not wish to incur underwriting risks it might simply act as agent, preparing prospectuses, press releases and securing the services of brokers, all for a flat commission on the face amount of the loan. At the same time, a group of insiders, as was evidently the case in the Peruvian saga, kept prices as high as possible through artificial sales among themselves until the entire issue had been sold to the public.

With few exceptions the contractors or issuing houses were not themselves full service banks, but, like Herring, Graham and Powles, associations of merchants with established connections with Latin America. They might also take deposits, and in some cases had offices in the Caribbean, but they used their own banks for transfers and to receive bond purchasers' instalments. Thus both the bankers and the contractors had the use of the funds left with them as advance interest payments, which they utilized both to intervene in the market to support bond prices through dealings with friendly brokers, and to finance other ventures.

The bond certificates for the loans were generally denominated in £100, £250, £500 and £1,000 par values, and sold to the public by brokers or through jobbers who purchased the instruments on margin for their own accounts from the relevant bank or mercantile house. The bonds themselves had maturity periods of up to thirty-five years, but could be redeemed earlier. According to the loan agreements, a fixed percentage of the face amount of the loan was to be paid off in instalments, after a short grace period, every six or twelve months until final maturity. The contractors would accomplish this by drawing at random the serial numbers of bonds up to the total of the amount to be repaid. The numbers were then printed in the press, and holders who had brought them at a discount would receive their face value without having to wait out the entire maturity period. Money to repay holders, theoretically at least, was to come from the sinking funds which borrowers pledged to replenish annually by depositing with the contractors' bankers small fixed percentages of the loan's nominal value.

As noted, traditionally dealings in foreign funds had been carried on not at the Stock Exchange at Capel Court, but either at the Royal Exchange or in the more informal environments of the coffee houses clustered around Exchange Alley and Birchin Lane. The new lending boom, however, so enlarged the number of non-member brokers and dealers involved with foreign borrowing that Stock Exchange members demanded greater control and supervision of their operations. Consequently in October 1822, the Stock Exchange Committee for General Purposes decided that future loans should be marketed through a Foreign Stock Exchange, to be established in premises connected with the Capel Court Stock Exchange building. The new entity was to be governed by a committee composed of members from the regular Stock Exchange and representatives of the foreign fund brokers. In March 1823 a set of rules for the new market was approved and the first eighty-nine members admitted. Although the original intention had been to keep the two exchanges functionally separate and to prohibit regular Stock Exchange members from dealing in foreign issues, in practice these restrictions were ignored, and membership soon exceeded two hundred.[41]

The public's eagerness to subscribe to the new Latin American loans was not solely attributable to apparently high yields and pledged revenues. The early 1820s were years of extravagant dressing, living, eating and drinking – and of frantic gambling. In elegant clubs along St James fortunes changed hands at the turn of a card. Losers sometimes shot themselves, but more frequently, like Beau Brummel, they fled across the Channel to Boulogne and Calais to avoid their creditors and to end their days in genteel poverty.

The gambling fever infected all classes. In the smoke-filled upper rooms of disreputable London taverns the less affluent even would wager on how many rats a terrier could kill in a few minutes. The rodents were enclosed in a wooden-sided arena and the terrier released among them. In one particularly gruesome encounter one hundred rats were massacred in a record-breaking eight minutes.[42] Nor was the gambling vice confined to towns. In the country, cockfights, race meetings and bare-knuckle prize fights provided additional opportunities to win or lose purses weighted with the newly introduced gold sovereigns. The chance to speculate in Latin American bond issues provided but another outlet for the national gambling instinct.

The lending speculation also had its humorous aspects. In early June 1822, *The Times* announced that 'a new species of security' entitled Chinese Turnpike Bonds had been launched by a City practical joker who wished to trick a rather simple-minded broker acquaintance possessing less wit than money.[43] The broker bought heavily as did colleagues who, however, were in on the hoax. The bonds rose quickly in value until 'the late melancholy news from Canton arrived, that the produce of Chinese turnpikes was not likely to be paid to the subjects of a nation with whom the Chinese prohibited all intercourse'. The bonds plummeted, and the broker disappeared for a few days while his friends feared for his sanity or his life. When he returned the pranksters bought back his stock at the original price, explained the joke, and 'cautioned him to speculate no more' in bonds of the emperor of China or of the Grand Lama. *The Times* used the occasion to reflect that the different kinds of foreign securities offered at the Stock Exchange and at the Royal Exchange had become so numerous, 'as to create not a little perplexity to inexperienced speculators, whose ideas have never wandered beyond three per cent Consols'.

The Poyais swindle, while not nearly so amusing as the Chinese Turnpike escapade and certainly more lethal for its victims, illustrates more than any other incident the absurdities into which gambling investors could be tempted. A few days after the Peruvian loan was launched, General Sir Gregor MacGregor announced an issue of £200,000 in 6 per cent bonds to finance the colonization of his imaginary Central American country of Poyais. After his disastrous expedition to the Spanish Main, MacGregor had been thoroughly discredited in Colombia. Bolívar forbade him to set foot on the mainland and Santander wanted him hung.

Seeking a new outlet for his boundless energy, in 1820 he sailed to that inhospitable, swampy portion of the Caribbean coast of Honduras known as the Mosquito Shore, where during the eighteenth century a small British colony had flourished briefly. At the time of MacGregor's visit the principal inhabitants were the Mosquito Indians, who since the seventeenth century had been staunch British allies in the almost constant warfare against the Spaniards. The Mosquito 'King' was traditionally crowned in Jamaica or Belize, and the alliance cemented by gifts of rum, gaudy uniforms and firearms.

In April 1820, MacGregor met the reigning monarch, George Frederick Augustus, at Cape Gracias a Diós near the present Honduran-Nicaraguan frontier. After many glasses of rum the king granted MacGregor a concession of 8,000,000 acres of his wilderness empire. MacGregor, promising to return with British artisans and settlers to develop the king's territory, then sailed for Britain, where he styled himself Gregor I, Cazique of Poyais, the name he had given his 'country'.[44]

MacGregor then opened a Poyaisian legation and land office on Dowgate Hill, opposite what is now British Rail's Cannon Street Station, to sell chunks of Poyaisian territory to would-be colonists. Ballads were sung in London and Edinburgh streets extolling Poyais' fertile soil and mineral wealth. Handbills described the opulence of its cosmopolitan capital St Joseph, which boasted not only elegant avenues and public buildings, but also an opera house. Books and pamphlets praised this Garden of Eden where with minimal effort poor men could become rich. MacGregor established an order of the Poyaisian nobility, and even created a paper army and navy, selling commissions to ambitious young men with more money than grey matter.

The Poyais loan followed closely the structure of its Colombian, Chilean and Peruvian predecessors, and was to be evidenced by 2,000 thirty-year bearer bonds of £100 each, bearing 6 per cent interest payable semi-annually at the respectable banking house of Messrs Sir John Perring, Shaw, Barber & Co. Repayment of principle and interest was secured by 'all the revenues of the Government', including import duties, and also by the proceeds of all land sales. Although Perring was a former Lord Mayor and an experienced banker, he too was sufficiently mesmerized by MacGregor's persuasiveness to lend his name to this incredible enterprise.

While MacGregor and his cronies were preparing their spectacular fraud, events of much more far-reaching importance for Latin America were developing at Westminster and Whitehall. In August, Foreign Secretary Castlereagh committed suicide by cutting his throat with a razor. His successor was George Canning, who had held the post before but, now out of favour with the king, had been about to sail for India as governor general. After a series of manoeuvres and Cabinet reshuffles, the king was persuaded to accept Canning back into the government, and he was sworn in as foreign secretary on 16 September. It would prove an excellent choice, particularly for the Latin Americans and merchants trading with the New World.[45]

Meanwhile European press reports of the 1822 loan had reached Colombia, provoking another furious congressional outburst when legislators recalled that Foreign Secretary Pedro Gual had informed Zea the prior October that his power of attorney had been revoked. An irate Vice President Santander responded on 1 June with a decree stating that whereas it had come to the attention of the government that

> some individuals residing in Europe call themselves agents of this Republic and ... contract obligations in its name without authority ... it is hereby declared that (1) no Colombian citizen or foreigner is presently authorized to sign agreements, contract obligations or bind in any way the Government of Colombia ... (2) the Honourable Francisco Antonio Zea ... is only authorized to undertake the political assignments with which he has been specially charged by virtue of his instructions.[46]

On 15 September, Gual reminded Zea that his power of attorney had been revoked, writing sarcastically that 'most extraordinary is it, indeed, that you should have ventured to contract fresh engagements in the name of this country, without its knowledge, without its sanction, and in direct opposition to its orders, to the existing laws of the Republic and to what was communicated to you'.[47]

Soon rumours began drifting about the City that Zea's powers had been cancelled. When a copy of Santander's decree was reprinted in the press in late October, a number of investors panicked and began to sell. *The Courier* commented that 'the folly of speculating in foreign loans cannot more clearly be demonstrated than by reference to the Colombian stock; yesterday 95½–96, today 91; and grave doubts are entertained whether there is any authority to negotiate any new loan for the Republic.' Obviously only Bolívar, the sole effective decision-maker in the republic, could resolve the problem, and he was reported to be near Quito, far from Bogotá. Therefore bondholders would have to be patient for at least six months 'till this knotty problem is solved by his Highness'.[48]

Santander's decree was ambiguous, however, and *The New Times* opined that whether the statement that Zea was restricted to political affairs was meant 'to deprive him of the power to negotiate a loan, would be best answered by a publication on the part of the contractors'. Herring, Graham and Powles replied by publishing an English translation of Zea's original power of attorney, together with a letter from Zea explaining that the decree did not apply to him but was directed, as a result of his own urgent requests to his government, to stopping unauthorized individuals – presumably such as his discredited rival Luis López Méndez – from either acting themselves in the government's name and contracting for unwanted material and assistance, or from sub-delegating their authority. Zea insisted he had duly notified his government of the loan contracted in March, and that his power of attorney had never been revoked.[49] Generally the press was not satisfied by Zea's explanation, and a member of Lincoln's Inn in a highly critical, anonymous and widely-read pamphlet insisted that Zea and contractors knew of the revocation of his power of attorney several months before they signed the loan agreement.[50]

On 25 October the Colombian contractors announced that payment of the first half-yearly dividend would be made 1 November as required by the loan agreement. Unimpressed, on the same day *The Courier* solemnly informed readers that since South America had been attracting all the new loans, it was not fair that North America should be neglected by the City. It reported the arrival of twelve agents to negotiate loans for 'the improvement and advantage' of various Indian tribes in the Mississippi Valley. They included a £1,000,000 credit to the Quicapouse tribe, which would be repaid over a period of 700 years by shipping wild geese in their feathers to Britain in ice chests, which would not only 'afford food for the table, but feathers for our beds.' Meanwhile a loan to the Pickawillanees would 'enable them to search for gold where it was never known to be found before'.[51]

Debates on the meaning of the Colombian decree and the validity of the loan continued at public meetings and in the press throughout November. Colombian bondholder unease was contagious. Peruvian and Poyais subscribers now refused to pay allotment instalments as they became due, causing the Poyais loan to die a quiet death. The contractors for the Peruvian issue, who in any case were awaiting news from Lima of the loan's ratification, extended the next allotment subscription date a further six months. Worse still, in early November Paris newspapers stated unequivocally that under the new 1821 Colombian Constitution only congress had the right to contract loans or authorize the executive branch to negotiate their terms. Zea's power of attorney was out of date. So, when Zea contracted for the loan in March 1822, he must have known of the existence of the new constitution, and therefore had no authority to agree to the credit. The French reports were reprinted in London causing further dismay among bondholders.[52] A few weeks later, on 28 November 1822, the debate lapsed temporarily when after a long illness Zea died at Bath of dropsy.

Zea's death immediately drove Colombian bonds down to 70 and *John Bull* warned again of the dangers of speculating in foreign loans:

> Of Mr Zea's respectability and good intentions we have no doubt ... but it is worth the while of those who are afflicted with the passion for foreign stocks, to stop, and inquire of themselves seriously, why they should abandon the certainty of the British funds to dabble in others, the value of which, as it appears, so entirely depends upon the unaccredited *Chargé d'Affaires* of an *unacknowledged Republic*.[53]

The Morning Chronicle, while noting that Zea's death had 'added to the misfortune of the holders of Colombian Bonds', printed a generally sympathetic obituary. Although he might have exceeded instructions, reasoned the editor, nevertheless Zea 'in a short space of time raised the credit of his country to a very high point, and it has been remarked that many years elapsed after the independence of the United States before any Minister of that Government could raise a loan at near the terms that M. Zea raised his.'[54]

In addition to the Zea problem that autumn, news from across the Channel had a profoundly disturbing effect on the Stock Exchange.

Barely seven years after Waterloo, France was once again threatening the peace of Europe. Since the Congress of Vienna in 1815, diplomats representing members of the Quadruple Alliance which had defeated Napoleon – Austria, Britain, Prussia and Russia – had gathered periodically in formal conferences to discuss matters of mutual concern, to settle international disputes and to assure continuation of the hard-earned peace.

The first of these conferences was at Aix-la-Chapelle in 1818, when the allies met to determine their future relationships with France. As a result of their deliberations, a rehabilitated France was invited to join the Alliance to preserve the peace of Europe on an equal diplomatic footing with the victorious powers. The army of occupation was withdrawn, and arrangements made to pay the war reparations. At the conference, Russian Czar Alexander continued unsuccessfully to press the pet policy he had been mooting since Vienna, that is, an affirmative dedication by the great powers to protecting existing monarchical governments against revolution. This proposal, aimed at quelling any liberal threat to despotic government, was treated with great suspicion by Britain's Foreign Secretary Castlereagh, who in May 1820 had maintained that the alliance to defeat Napoleon was never 'intended as a union for the government of the world, or for the superintendence of the Internal Affairs of other States'.[55]

Alexander persevered, and at the Conference of Troppau in December 1820 persuaded Austria and Prussia to join him in what became the Holy Alliance, aimed at destroying any efforts by a people to restrict the rights and powers of their king. At Troppau, and at its continuation at Laibach, it was accordingly agreed that Austria should forceably suppress the new constitutional governments in the Piedmont and Naples. Castlereagh objected strongly the following January. Although the British government, he wrote, recognized a state's right to intervene in another state where its own immediate security was imperilled, this right could only be justified by the strongest necessity. Such exceptions to the proper conduct of states 'never can, without the utmost danger, be so far reduced to rule to be incorporated into the ordinary diplomacy of states, or into the institutes of the law of nations.'[56]

Nevertheless, Britian did no more than protest and the following year in 1822, at the Congress of Verona, Austria, Prussia and Russia urged France to invade Spain to destroy the Liberal consitution of 1820 and restore the stubborn, bigoted Bourbon King Ferdinand VII to absolute power. Canning, Castlereagh's successor, in September 1822, wrote to the Duke of Wellington, the British delegate to the conference, that such interference was useless, dangerous and impracticable. Wellington should therefore if the opportunity arose, tell the allies 'frankly and peremptorily' that Britain would not be a party to such a scheme.[57]

But once again Britain did no more than object verbally. The news of the resolutions taken at Verona, however, enraged the very considerable anti-French, anti-Catholic and liberal sectors of British public opinion. This new development was potentially much more threatening than the earlier Austrian intervention in Naples. France, the old enemy, was rearming and would be on the march again. Moreover, thoughtful merchants as well as politicians now realized that if France and Spain were once more to become allies, they might combine to recover the rebellious Latin American colonies and to close these newly acquired markets to British commerce. Also, it would be extremely unlikely that a restored Spanish government would honour the bonds issued by liberal republican governments either in Spain or in Latin America – hence the concern on the Stock Exchange and in the City generally.

Reflecting the uncertainties generated by worries over the Colombian loan and a threatened French invasion of Spain, from mid-October to the end of November Spanish 1820 bonds dropped from 87 to 65, Spanish 1822 bonds from 73 to 53, Colombia from 97 to 69, and Chile from 90 to 75.[58] Numerous individuals and firms were either ruined or their credit seriously impaired by the brief market collapse. They probably were not amused when the editor of *John Bull* reprinted some lines of anonymous warning doggerel from a Lancashire newspaper:

'What's a loan? Tis a *paper* for sums in advance to
Austria, to Russia, Prussia, France.

'What's a loan? Tis the rage; every day brings a new, to
Hanover, Sweden, Colombia, Peru.

Honest John! Mind your hits, or you'll whimper and groan
When you find a loan paper, is paper alone.'[59]

III
INDIGESTION IN THE CITY

DURING 1823 DOUBTS over the validity of Minister Zea's Colombian loan and the difficulties encountered by the Chilean and Peruvian loan contractors temporarily blunted investor appetite for new issues. After a hectic beginning, the Latin American loan boom suddenly halted.

In early January 1823 Zea's replacement, José Rafael Revenga, finally appeared in London after his first attempt to cross the Atlantic had been frustrated by a shipwreck. Investors' hopes were now raised by rumours that the new envoy had been authorized to ratify Zea's engagements, and Colombian bonds recovered to touch 68.[1] Shortly after his arrival, Revenga met with Herring, Graham and Powles, who, hoping to obtain confirmation that the Colombian government would honour Zea's commitments, reviewed with him the loan documentation and the use made of the loan proceeds. Revenga remained non-committal, awaiting further instructions from Bogotá. Meanwhile, to bolster their case the contractors sought the advice of Dr Stephen Lushington, MP, a respected and leading attorney.[2]

On 10 January, Lushington – who later participated in various of Powles' Latin American enterprises – signed an opinion letter stating that Zea's powers were sufficiently broad to bind Colombia, and, moreover, that since the Colombian government had not made its revocation of Zea's powers known publicly, it would still be bound by his actions. 'Whosoever delegates his own powers to another, is bound by the acts of his agent within the power delegated, until notice of the revocation has been actually received, or the publicity of that revocation so notorious, that the presumption of universal knowledge of the fact must prevail', the doctor wrote.[3] On the same day Solicitor General Copley submitted a separate concurring opinion. Because the revocation of Zea's authority had been communicated to him alone 'and not published to the world, I am of the opinion that it would not affect the validity of the loan as between the contractors and the Colombian Government.'[4]

The legal opinions were circulated by the contractors the follow-ing day at a crowded bondholder meeting at the City of London Tavern, which was attended by the Lord Mayor and two City aldermen.[5] After reviewing again Zea's power of attorney and the circumstances surrounding the alleged revocation, Powles informed the gathering that whatever misconceptions the Colombian govern-ment had regarding the loan were due to the inexplicable non-arrival of the despatches Zea had sent to Bogotá shortly after signing the loan agreement in Paris. In order better to present their viewpoint to the Colombian government, the contractors had sent an agent to Bogotá with a copy of the loan contract and an accounting. Bond-holders could now await the results of the mission 'confident that on no principle of honour, of justice, of good faith, or of interest, can the contract for this loan be questioned'.[6]

Despite these efforts to alleviate bondholders' worries, investors must have shuddered when in late January they read a letter in *The New Times* from a merchant recently arrived from Jamaica who had had 'some interesting intercourse with the people of Colombia'.[7] The anonymous writer warned that Colombians 'are by no means in that state of moral advancement which I find many persons in England erroneously suppose them to be'. British investors should not place too much faith in the opinions of British lawyers on the validity of the loan agreement nor expect observance by Colombia of 'those sacred principles upon which the established Governments of Europe maintain their credit'.

Early in 1823, Luis López Méndez continued to embarrass the Colombian government and its new London representative, Revenga. In 1822 he had contracted for two ships laden with cargoes of overpriced arms, uniforms and munitions which had arrived at Cartagena in mid-November of that year. In mid-March 1823 the London press reported that the Colombian government had found that the terms to which López Méndez had agreed were exorbitant and, moreover, that upon examination only one vessel proved seaworthy – and then only after extensive repairs.[8] One of the suppliers was a James MacKintosh, who was furious when the government had refused to honour the debentures signed by López Méndez on its behalf and delivered to MacKintosh in payment. When Revenga arrived in London, MacKintosh demanded that he acknowledge and confirm the validity of the contract and of the debentures. Revenga refused, pleading lack of authorization and asserting that in any case López Méndez had exceeded his authority.

In March, alleging Revenga was indebted to him for £90,000 in goods sold and delivered, MacKintosh had the envoy arrested. Revenga, stoutly maintaining his innocence and total lack of knowledge of the affair, refused on principle to pay the guaranty deposit which the law demanded of foreign defendants, and was sent to Kings Bench Prison in London pending trial. In May Revenga was released on bail, and a few months later sued MacKintosh for malicious arrest. In December a jury found that MacKintosh had not brought the action in good faith to recover a personal debt, but to compel Revenga to recognize the debentures. Consequently the jury awarded the Colombian damages of £250. The case, affirmed on appeal the following year, must have fueled the frustration and anger of other merchants – as well as bondholders – who had been dealing with the Colombian and other South American governments and who could find no relief in the English legal system when their contracts were dishonoured.[9]

The dispute over the Colombian loan's validity continued into the summer, becoming progressively more bitter. By July even the once-supportive *Morning Chronicle* was describing the loan as a hoax.[10] Meanwhile the contractors' agent, Mr Jones, had arrived in Bogotá and, after consulting with the congressional committee appointed to review the loan, wrote to the contractors that he was certain congress would ratify the transaction. Powles then posted up a summary of the letter in the Stock Exchange. On 25 July, however, the same day Jones' missive was published, *The Morning Herald* printed a discouraging letter from a 'Mercantile Gentleman' at Bogotá, who wrote that Colombia was 'entirely destitute of funds'. Because the 1822 bonds 'were given by persons who had not the power to do so, they are disputed, and unquestionably will be liable to heavy deductions, and, indeed, to an entirely new agreement'.[11]

The same edition reprinted sections of a report by Pedro Gual to Santander for presentation to congress which concluded that Zea's original powers were purely political and 'none of the financial operations in Europe of M. Zea was in the remotest degree supported by the positive instructions given him on his departure' from Colombia. It is difficult to reconcile Gual's conclusions with the actual text of the 1819 power of attorney, which clearly did authorize Zea to raise a loan for Colombia. It is possible, however, that Gual was attempting to avoid responsibility for the loan debacle falling on himself, since he had not obeyed punctually Bolívar's instructions the prior April to revoke Zea's powers. If Gual had acted earlier, perhaps Zea might have been dissuaded from signing the 1822 loan agreement.[12]

Any solace afforded investors by Mr Jones' confident predictions was totally undermined when the press reprinted an extract from *The Jamaica Chronicle*, reporting that the Colombian Congressional Committee had endorsed Gual's report and branded Zea's loan as

unauthorized. The committee also, however, recommended arrangements be made to pay merchants and contractors who had actually
supplied ships, arms, stores and munitions. 'The sensation which
was excited in the minds of some English traders of Bogotá . . . was
inconceivable, as they were previously under the strongest impression that the Government would at once recognize this loan . . .' *The
Edinburgh Evening Advertiser* exclaimed.[13] The leader then commented heatedly that 'what we have long apprehended is now
realized; that the late Mr Zea, in the contract into which he so adroitly
inveigled the monied people in London, had played a deep game,
such a one as will, no doubt, become as memorable . . . as the South
Sea Bubble', and 'many innocent persons may yet have to lament the
precipitancy of those who ought to have deliberated before they
became victims of this passion for Colombian independence'.

Bondholders received yet another shock when a month later *The
Morning Herald* printed without comment a translation of an act
passed on 9 June by the Colombian Chamber of Representatives.
The legislation, which still required senate concurrence, declared Zea
had exceeded his instructions. Consequently the Chamber declared
the loan null and void. Nevertheless, the act, as suggested earlier by
the investigating congressional committee, recognised Colombia's
financial responsibility for any moneys or supplies which were
actually secured, and empowered the executive branch to authorize
new bonds and debentures for their payment.[14] That same day *The
Examiner* noted the great sensation produced in the City by the act.
Zea's 'authority is denied, but the Colombian Government will issue
new bonds and debentures for value received, thus getting rid with
more economy than policy, we fear, of the effects of his very bad
bargain'. The news caused Colombian bonds to fall by 15 percent,
and *The Examiner*'s financial correspondent predicted that 'much
individual loss and ruin is likely to follow'.[15]

At the beginning of October the London papers printed the
Colombian senate's bill repudiating Zea's loan in language similar to
that of the earlier Chamber of Representatives legislation, thereby
causing the bonds to drop another 5 per cent.[16] For some weeks
Powles and his cronies had been inserting advertisements in the press
vainly urging other holders to stand firm and not sell. On 3 September the front page of *The Times* carried the following advertisement:
'COLOMBIAN BONDHOLDERS be firm. DO NOT SELL; if
you do you will repent. – a Friend'.[17] Nevertheless, Colombian
quotations fell to 54, while, by contrast, on 2 October Naples stood
at 77¼, Prussia at 86, Russia at 83¾, Denmark at 90½, and Chile at
70¾.[18]

Meanwhile, the French intervention in Spain, first threatened in late 1822, had become a reality. On 7 April 1823, some 100,000 French troops crossed the frontier to restore Ferdinand to power. The seeds for this intervention had been planted in 1814, when Bourbon absolutist Ferdinand VII, restored to his throne after Napolean's defeat, had sought with some initial success to destroy the Latin American patriots. Despite reversals, however, gradually the Latin American patriots prevailed, and by 1819 it was apparent Spain could never recover its colonies. Nevertheless, late in that year Ferdinand had assembled another expeditionary force for one last attempt. This time, however, the army rebelled under the leadership of liberal junior officers, demanding a return to the Liberal Constitution of 1812 and curtailment of Church power and influence. Civil war swept across Spain, until in 1820 a victorious liberal government forced Ferdinand to accept the revived 1812 Constitution. It was this chain of violent events which led the Holy Alliance at Verona in 1822 to advocate intervention.[19]

The progress of the French army through Spain was carefully reported in the British press, which on the whole deplored the invasion. When Ferdinand finally was 'rescued' from the constitutional government in September 1823, rumours began circulating in the City that he intended to repudiate the loans contracted in London by the liberals, and that his French saviours would finance another attempt to subdue the rebellious Latin American colonies. Consequently not only did Spanish bond prices plummet, but Latin American issues were also adversely affected by fears that a victorious Ferdinand would repudiate the Latin American republican loans.

In October *The Morning Chronicle* opined that unless Great Britain and the United States intervened,

'the Spanish American colonies will be, without much difficulty, reduced to the laws of legitimacy, and restored to the bosom of the true Church, and in that event the English nation will suffer another robbery in the Chilean and Colombian Loans, in addition to the total exclusion of her manufacturers from the markets of this valuable portion of the earth.'[20]

Spain now was rumoured-falsely- to be organizing an expedition of 12,000 men 'fitted out at French expense, and staffed by French artillery and engineer officers, and the necessary number of priests and licensed spies, who may by bribery, fraud and fanaticism, prepare the way for tyranny'.

Gloom pervaded the Foreign Stock Exchange, and Chilean bonds dropped 1 per cent 'as distance even does not render the independence of this Republic perfectly secure'. Few transactions in Colombian bonds were reported, not only due to fears of what Ferdinand might do, but also because of the congressional repudiation of the loan. The contractors' assurances that all the republic's debts and obligations would eventually be acknowledged fell on deaf ears. Even the prices of European bonds suffered. 'What may be the future conduct of the Bourbons baffles all calculations,' commented *The Morning Chronicle*. 'On the Foreign Stock Exchange, the outrageous conduct of Ferdinand makes a more visible impression, for it has had at all events, the merit of creating considerable distrust in the validity or rather the ultimate security of every description of Foreign European National Bonds in the English Market.'[21]

Andrés Bello expressed many people's fears in a letter to the Chilean Minister of State and Foreign Relations. Because Minister Irisarri would be in France on business until the end of the month, Bello explained, he had been instructed to keep the minister informed on the latest developments affecting Latin America. The continental powers were not about to approve of the Latin American revolutions nor recognize the new states' independence, Bello reported. If French intervention in Spain were successful in restoring the Inquisition and absolute monarchy 'the Holy Alliance will itself declare openly against American independence and France will doubtless assist Spain with arms, money and perhaps fleets of ships'.[22]

By the end of October the market had steadied somewhat at news that Canning had determined to dispatch consular representatives to various Latin American cities.[23] Canning was reacting not only to a possible French and Spanish threat to Latin America, but also in response to intense pressure from the mercantile community. As early as July, twenty City merchants, including Anthony Gibbs & Sons, Hullet Brothers, Barclay, Herring, Richardson & Co. and J. & A. Powles & Co., had written to urge him to send consular representatives to Latin America so that local British merchants could be placed upon an equal footing with their rivals from the United States, Portugal and Sweden, which already had consular representatives to the new countries. British firms had over eighty offices in Latin America, but trade was suffering because of the lack of accredited officials to whom the merchants could 'apply for advice or assistance in the various cases of local grievances or necessity which are constantly occurring.'[24] As a result of Canning's decision, Chilean bonds rose two points, and Colombian bonds 'would have probably undergone a proportionate improvement did not the doubts respecting their ultimate acknowledgement retain their former force'.[25] Even the provincial papers took an interest in the dispatch of the consuls, with *The Edinburgh Advertiser* hoping optimistically that the event would be but the prelude to full British recognition of the independence of the new Latin American governments.[26]

Some speculators in Colombian securities maintained a dogged faith that all would come right in the end. Rumours had been persisting for weeks that the Colombian government would eventually ratify Zea's loan if only because it could not otherwise return to the City for further financing. When on 31 October the contractors produced a letter from Bogotá announcing ratification of the loan agreement, bond prices soared eight points, even though the information was incorrect.[27] In early November *The Edinburgh Advertiser* advised its readers – again erroneously – that the Colombian government had finally decided to recognize Zea's loan. By 9 November the bonds had recovered to 61½ – still considerably below their 84 issue price.[28] Nevertheless, fears of a Spanish reconquest aided by France persisted and the market remained sluggish. As *The Sunday Times* observed, 'the attempts at the subjugation of South America, which have been long predicted as the inevitable consequence of the success of the French in Spain, are now no longer disguised, nor the manner in which those attempts would be made – viz. by France, under the name of Spain.'[29]

Colombian bondholders' hopes finally collapsed at the end of December, when the London press printed a translation of the final version of the joint legislation approved on 1 July by both the chamber of representatives and the senate in which Zea's loan was definitely repudiated.[30] The decree, a combination of the earlier chamber and senate bills already published in London, alleged that (a) even if Zea had been authorized to negotiate the loan, he could not have concluded it or received and disposed of the proceeds without Congressional consent; (b) Zea disposed of the proceeds on his own authority, settling prior unapproved and unaudited claims and other unauthorized expenses which he had incurred; and (c) because New Granada and Venezuela had on 12 July 1821 been formally united into one nation, all powers of 'previous Public Agents ceased', including Zea's power of attorney.[31]

Nevertheless, the decree offered to recognize any amounts creditors could prove to have been furnished to the republic, and empowered the executive branch to settle the claims in the manner it deemed most expedient. The executive was also authorized to call in Zea's bonds, and, insofar as they represented approved obligations, issue replacement bonds or bills. Thus Colombia was by no means repudiating its legitimate indebtedness. Indeed, the government recognized it must eventually settle with the bondholders before it could obtain further, much-needed financing. The same issue of the *Gaceta de Colombia* in which the decree was published noted that congress had also authorized the executive to raise a further 30,000,000 pesos. Colombia without war, the *Gaceta* observed, could even support a much larger debt. Readers were assured that the new funds would not be wasted, but used to pay domestic creditors and to promote agriculture and mining from which more than sufficient funds would flow to service the foreign debt. Colombia would do its utmost to settle all its existing obligations 'so that the history of our independence and freedom will never relate in its valuable annals that Colombians made use of resources under conditions to which war and necessity forced them to agree and which they refused to repay'.

Meanwhile, news of Zea's death had at last reached Colombia. Despite widespread hostility to his loan, Zea's memory was not vilified as it had been in Britain. The *Gaceta de Colombia* in May 1823 praised Zea's record and accomplishments as a patriot and a scientist, noting that, 'this is not the place to discuss the question of his politics and economic negotiations, but we dare to say that he deserves the title which he has been given of the [Benjamin] Franklin of Colombia due to his efforts, scientific merits and personal qualities'.[32] A more recent assessment suggests that considering Spanish troops were still in Colombia in 1822, and that when Zea arrived in London the nation's credit rating was in tatters, his achievements were considerable.[33] Compared with the terms and conditions of loans then being extended to European borrowers, Colombia had not done badly. The problem, of course, was that the nation did not, despite the glowing pictures painted by Zea for his European audience, have the political cohesion or the basic human and commercial resources and infrastructures of borrowers such as France or Prussia, and without which the loan could not be serviced properly or repaid.

By now some Colombian bondholders were clearly exasperated at the persistent excuses of Powles and his colleagues, and at the lack of any positive response from the Colombian authorities beyond vague promises to honour at some unspecified future date engagements which could be shown to have led to the actual provision of goods and services. In September two major investors published an open invitation to fellow bondholders to attend a meeting at the City of London Tavern to discuss a new plan of action. A few days before the meeting a mock theatrical handbill appeared at the Stock Exchange which 'occasioned much merriment'. It advertised a forthcoming play entitled 'The South American Jugglers', the leading performers in which included Don Juan de Rowley Powley and Don Carlos de Herring-Guts.[34]

The meeting itself was less amusing. The instigators, Messrs Major and Lousada, demanded that the contractors deposit the sum of £292,892 in cash and £54,500 in bonds in the Bank of England, in the names of trustees whom the meeting would elect. According to accounts published 17 January this sum was still in their custody. Because the bondholders could no longer rely upon the security offered by the Colombian government in the loan agreement, the proposed arrangement was quite reasonable maintained the two disgruntled bondholders, and one to which the contractors could not possibly object 'as it is correct to presume that they have uniformly and carefully invested the Balances remaining from time to time in their hands, in British Government Securities'. Powles, however, was able to defeat the proposal and retain general bondholder confidence.[35]

Meanwhile, the Chilean, Peruvian and Poyais issues were also running into unexpected difficulties. When details of Irisarri's Chilean loan reached Santiago in November 1822, a furious congress appointed a committee of prominent jurists and merchants to review the transaction's legality. The committee then advised Supreme Director O'Higgins that the loan should be disavowed. The total borrowing exceeded Irisarri's initial authorization and would burden Chile with a crippling £20,000 servicing obligation the first year, the committee maintained. O'Higgins, however, replied that repudiation would injure Chile's credit just when British merchants had finally succeeded in persuading their government to allow ships flying Chilean flags to enter British ports. He therefore suggested that congress concern itself instead with deciding how best to utilize the loan proceeds. The legislature eventually agreed, and proposed to use the funds to create a bank 'to develop the public resources'.[36]

In March 1823, Irisarri learned of the congressional reaction and complained bitterly to O'Higgins of the legislators' ingratitude. Fearing that news of the congressional hostility might reach Britain and frighten investors, he hastened to anticipate any adverse press reports by advertising on 12 March redemption from the sinking fund of 172 bonds worth £14,200, which he and Hullett Brothers had cancelled and deposited with the Bank of England.[37] Then he announced that the second half-yearly dividend due on 31 March 1823 would be paid on that date at the Hullett Brothers 'Counting House' at 102 Leadenhall Street. On that day *The New Times* printed a notice that the second half-yearly dividend of the Colombian loan would be paid on 1 May at the offices of Herring, Graham and Powles at 3 Freeman's Court, Cornhill.[38] All these interest payments, as well as redemptions, were of course made from funds withheld in advance by the agents.

Since January 1823 Irisarri had made Paris his principal residence. Meanwhile, Andrés Bello remained in charge of the London legation, and on 13 September announced jointly with Hullett Brothers the cancellation and deposit in the Bank of England of 160 bonds worth £16,000. The serial numbers of the bonds to be redeemed of the sinking fund were then printed in the press. In addition, the third half-yearly dividend would be paid when due at Hullett's counting house.[39] While only the most naive investors could have been long heartened by these manoeuvres, which paid bondholders out of their own money, nevertheless, on 22 September, Chilean bonds were quoted at 73, three points above their issue price, while Colombia hovered around 56.[40]

A letter dated 1 July published soon thereafter from an English merchant in Santiago again dashed bondholder expectations, however. The writer asserted that the loan was neither desired nor wanted. Some Chilean government officials even had urged returning the proceeds to the bond purchasers, he wrote, but the temptation was overwhelming and £40,000 had been embezzled by the outgoing administration. Chile was desperately poor, and it had been absurd to acquire a foreign debt. There was not, nor could there be, the correspondent insisted, the most remote possibility of paying a dollar of interest, much less the principal.[41]

While Irisarri and Bello were struggling to maintain the Chilean loan's credibility, James Paroissien and Juan García del Río, the Peruvian representatives, were also encountering difficulties. They had forwarded a copy of their loan agreement with Thomas Kinder to Peru for ratification, but while they were still awaiting a reply in October 1822 rumours of the revocation of Zea's power of attorney had swept the City, along with reports that Spanish troops had retaken Lima. Peruvian scrip already issued quickly fell in value. Consequently the promoters decided to postpone the 23 November second subscription instalment date, and suspend attempts to sell additional bonds. When no news was forthcoming from Peru, the third instalment was also deferred, although Kinder was persuaded to pay another £50,000 into the government's account.[42]

Meanwhile, Paroissien and García del Río had sent an agent to Lima to facilitate transmission of the proceeds, and the remittance of interest and sinking fund payments. As with the other loans, the actual physical transfer of any significant amount of the cash proceeds to the debtor was not contemplated. Generally borrowers would use amounts raised in London to pay for imported purchases by drawing bills of exchange on the City bankers holding their funds. Or, as in the Peruvian case, the borrowing government would sell bills of exchange for presentation in London to local British merchants resident in South America in exchange for specie. The merchants' London representatives would then present these bills for payment at the loan contractors or at their bankers.

In addition to uncertainties over ratification, Paroissien and Del Río were also plagued with legal problems. The Peruvian loan's unedifying beginning with a near riot at the Royal Exchange was

followed by a flurry of lawsuits. Press reports of these legal en-
counters shook public confidence further. In mid-November in
Hodgson v San Martín a London merchant brought an action in the
Lord Major's Court in the City to attach £3,000 of the Peruvian loan
proceeds deposited with bankers Everett & Co. In his supporting
affidavit, the merchant alleged that a privateer acting for the San
Martín government had unlawfully seized cargo belonging to him
aboard a ship which had attempted unsuccessfully to run a blockade
of a portion of the Peruvian coast still in Spanish hands.[43]

The defendant's counsel asserted that the court lacked jurisdiction
because the cause of action had arisen abroad. Also, if the capture of
the vessel carrying the merchant's goods had been unlawful, counsel
argued, it was the captor who was liable in damages to the plaintiff,
not the government of which he was a subject. The court found for
the defendant. The purpose of a writ of attachment, it decided, was
to facilitate recovery of commercial debts, not to obtain damages for
alleged wrongdoing. The privity of contract which must exist between a plaintiff and a defendant in order for a debt to exist was not
present, and, in any case, the London court was not competent to
pass upon the legality of the capture of a ship in South America.

The legal skirmishing affecting the Peruvian loan continued. In
February 1823 three scripholders, fearing they had been swindled,
obtained an injunction from the Court of Chancery attaching the
loan funds and restraining Everett & Co. from sending any proceeds
out of the country. The plaintiffs' attorney argued successfully that

> individuals have come to this country in great haste and with high-
> sounding names, one of them calling himself the Envoy Pleni-
> potentiary of the Peruvian Empire ... but there is no such empire
> in existence – we know not the Peruvian Government. If, how-
> ever, there be such it must belong to Spain – but it is unknown to
> us; and as a very large sum of money has been paid out into the
> hands of Messrs Everett and Co. for the purpose of supplying that
> loan, we pray on behalf of the petitioners ... that they may be
> restrained from parting with such money.[44]

The Peruvian envoys also had to contend with a communication
system even slower than that between Colombia and Britain. All
letters from Peru had to travel around Cape Horn via Chile, and then
across the Atlantic at its widest. Nevertheless, they must have been
shocked when, in the same month that the scripholders obtained
their injunction, news finally arrived that General San Martín, whose
government had granted their own original powers of attorney, had
resigned as Protector of Peru and had left the country even before
they themselves had launched the Peruvian loan. Vainly the two

envoys worte to Lima asking that their powers be renewed. In June they received instead a brief notice from the Peruvian foreign office notifying them of a November 1822 decree rescinding their powers to negotiate the form of government Peru might adopt. Whether the rescission also applied to their financial transactions was unclear.

Unlike the receptions accorded to Zea and Irisarri in their efforts for Colombia and Chile, the financing obtained in London was welcomed by most Peruvians. Spanish troops still controlled a significant portion of their country, and patriot military operations were conducted either on credit or through forced loans levied on local merchants. The foreign loan was considered necessary for national survival. Therefore, on 1 June, the Peruvian congress, which had approved the loan provisionally in March, quickly and formally ratified the loan contract brought to Lima by the envoys' agent. At the same time, however, congress replaced Paroissien and García del Río with a new commercial and financial agent, an English merchant then living in Peru named John Parish Robertson, who sailed for England in late August with instructions to raise a second loan.[45]

Meanwhile, back in London, in July Peru's bankers had appealed against the Court of Chancery injunction, alleging that the order had unfairly terminated their contract with Peru's agents 'since now the additional subscription instalments on the bonds need not be paid'. If the injunction had not existed, they argued, the parties withholding their instalments would have forfeited their previous deposits and the contractors might have been able to reorganize the loan with other parties. In reply, the scripholders maintained that the loan was against public policy because it was intended for parties in rebellion against a country with which the British government was at peace. Vacating the injunction might affect the relations of amity which existed between Britain and Spain. The judge, however, noted that the petitioning scripholders who had obtained the injunction in the first place were experienced speculators who knew the risks of lending to countries like Peru, and were now asking the court to protect them from the consequences of their misjudgement and bad fortune. Consequently, he decided in favour of Peru's bankers. The injunction was lifted and the loan proceeds, frozen for five months, released.[46]

Nevertheless, the once-eager Peruvian loan subscribers, thoroughly alarmed by the lack of any official confirmation that the loan had been ratified, now refused to pay their instalments. In a desperate attempt to encourage subscribers to resume payments, Thomas Kinder announced in the press that scripholders who had forfeited their deposits by failure to make the payments due on 15 July and 15

September would now be allowed two week's grace in which to pay their arrears and cure their defaults. His offer elicited scant response.[47]

The envoys' troubles were not over. Although the injunction had been dissolved, and eventually news of the loan's ratification arrived, the bankers now refused to release the £144,000 received as the first loan subscription instalment. With reports of yet another change in government in Peru now reaching London, Everett & Co. felt that ownership of the funds was uncertain and the envoys' authority in doubt. Pending clarification from Peru, the bankers quite prudently would not disburse the unfrozen funds lest they open themselves to lawsuits by other interested parties.[48] By this time, however, the Peruvian government, in urgent need of cash, during 1823 had sold local British merchants some £200,000 of bills of exchange drawn on Kinder. When the merchants sent the documents for collection to London, they were dishonoured. Peru's credit now seemed fatally undermined. At the same time paid-up scripholders were demanding their dividends – which could only be forthcoming from the moneys held by Everett & Co. In desperate need of funds to honour the bills and to pay scripholders' claims, Paroissien and Kinder sued the bankers in the Court of Kings Bench to recover any proceeds still in their possession. 'The Peruvian envoys have a good deal to answer for', *The Morning Chronicle* fumed as it reported the case. 'Whatever may have been their intentions, they have done infinite mischief not only to Peru, but to South America in general, by the lasting discredit of this transaction.'[49]

Meanwhile the new Peruvian envoy Robertson had reached London in December 1823 and informed Paroissien and García del Río that a new agent appointed to assume their political functions would arrive in three or four months. Consequently their services were no longer rquired. The envoys' reception of their replacement would contrast sharply with Irisarri's treatment of his successor, perhaps because Paroissien and García del Río were not unhappy to be free of the frustrations and irritations of the previous months, undertaken for an apparently ungrateful government.[50] In fairness, despite their expensive quarters on Grosvenor Street, unlike Irisarri, Paroissien and García del Río had not enriched themselves at the expense of their employers. Their problems had arisen basically from poor communications and the unstable political situation in Peru where the patriots were even more quarrelsome and disunited than in Colombia. Their dismissal stemmed more from the new government's anti-San Martín bias, than from any dishonesty on their parts.

Nor was 1823 a good year for Sir Gregor MacGregor, the Cazique of Poyais. Although in October 1822, the Poyais scrip had been initially quoted at 80 due to cross-trading among the Cazique's broker friends, the actual marketing of the issue had not progressed as far as that of the Chilean and Peruvian loans when Zea's death and news of the Colombian debt repudiation shook general investor confidence. Subscribers had refused to pay their additional instalments, and by mid-December, 1822 Poyais scrip had fallen to 67. MacGregor meanwhile had been attempting to bolster the credibility of Poyais by organizing well-publicized shipments of colonists to his Central American 'nation'.[51] By mid-January 1823, two hundred men, women and children had sailed for Poyais. Some had purchased land from Poyaisian offices in London, Edinburgh and Sterling. Others embarked as indentured servants, pledged to work for the Poyaisian government. All were ill-suited for pioneering in the jungle, and included teachers, clerks, shopkeepers, cabinet makers, jewellers and a 'gentleman's servant'. Mr Gauger, a banker from the City, embarked as manager of the non-existent Bank of Poyais. Many immigrants carried Poyaisian banknotes, having been persuaded to purchase them with Bank of Scotland currency which, they had been assured by MacGregor's agents, was not valid tender in Poyais.

Despite the Cazique's energetic public relations endeavours, bond sales proceeded slowly. Sales were not helped when in June reports trickled into London from Belize that all was not well with the colonists. The Cazique's colleagues did their utmost to support the bond prices by dealing among themselves for future delivery, but by the end of July 1823 Poyais had fallen to 15 at a time when Colombian bonds, despite fears of repudiation, were quoted at 67.[52] By August the fate of the Poyaisian colonists was common knowledge. The immigrants had not found the well-organized nation described in MacGregor's pamphlets. St Joseph, the Poyaisian capital city which purportedly boasted an opera house, broad boulevards, parks, stately public buildings and even a bank, was comprised of four ramshackle huts built atop the ruins of the British Mosquito Shore colony abandoned in 1787. MacGregor's 'loyal' Indian subjects proved distinctly unfriendly, and the Mosquito King rescinded MacGregor's land grant for his unjustified assumption of sovereignty over the monarch's swampy domain. Poyais banknotes were spurned by the natives, who refused to supply the immigrants with food or help them build shelters from the blazing sun.

Surrounded by swamps and jungle, and plagued by heat, insects, snakes, bad water and insufficient food, the newcomers began to succumb to hunger and fever. A few drowned at sea as they tried to escape to Belize. A cobbler from Scotland who had sold his business to take up his appointment as Official Shoemaker to the Princess of

Poyais lay down in his hammock and shot himself. Eventually the survivors were rescued by a ship from Belize, where many more died in hospital. A few, including Mr Gauger the banker, managed to find passage to the United States. Although less than fifty ever saw Britain again, some survivors went to the Mansion House where their complaints to the Lord Mayor received wide publicity.[53]

To offset the adverse press coverage, in October 1823 MacGregor and his cronies issued certificates for a restructured £200,000 loan, also to be issued through Sir John Perring's bank. They were attractive bearer documents printed in several colours and obviously based on Ackermann's design for the 1822 Colombian issue.[54] Issued at 80 in denominations of £100, they bore 5 per cent interest payable semi-annually at the offices of Sir John Perring & Co. The loan was guaranteed by a general mortgage bond given by 'WE, GREGOR THE FIRST, Sovereign Prince of the Independent State of Poyais and its Dependencies', which pledged 'all the revenues of the STATE OF POYAIS' including import duties as security for the loan. A sinking fund for redemption would be created by an initial deposit of £2,000, and supplemented over a thirty-year maturity period by further annual deposits of £1,000, together with the proceeds of one-sixth of all land sales. By November, however, MacGregor's colourful certificates were worthless, and the Cazique with his long-suffering wife and two children, and the remaining proceeds of his fraud, had fled across the Channel to Boulogne. The return of the surviving colonists with harrowing tales of sickness, hunger and death had brought to an untimely end one of the City's more imaginative swindles.

Despite the vicissitudes of the Colombian and other Latin American 1822 issues, stock market promoters were far from discouraged. While no new Latin American loans were marketed during 1823, two successful 5 per cent bond issues totalling £5,000,000 were launched by N. M. Rothschild and Thomas King & Co. for Austria and Portugal at 82 and 87, respectively.[55] Moreover, even though Colombian bonds fluctuated between 51 and 54 in early October, there was no lack of purchasers who, despite all evidence to the contrary, gambled that the government must inevitably recognize the debt.

Indeed, *The Morning Herald* now asserted confidently that the 'rage for new loans was never so great' and 'anything in the shape of a bond will find a purchaser in the foreign market'.[56] Reflecting the still persistent demand both for British and foreign securities, small jobbers who were not Stock Exchange members were now assembling in such large numbers outside the Capel Court entrance and in adjacent Bartholomew Lane to transact their business that the Lord Mayor threatened to enforce a recent act of Parliament imposing fines of up to £5 for causing obstructions in public thoroughfares.[57]

Yet, at the same time, fears that Spain might regain its former colonies with French assistance nevertheless persisted. Commenting on 'the sinister views of France upon South America', *The Times* suggested that 'one security against French officiousness might perhaps be an early recognition of the independence of the South American States by this Government'.[58] Although the United States had already recognized Latin American independence, it seemed unlikely, despite pressure from the mercantile community, that Great Britain would soon follow due to the opposition of the king and a number of his ministers. Foreign Secretary Canning, therefore, had to pursue a cautious policy while trying to persuade his opponents that recognition would at some point become inevitable in order to thwart French ambitions. In September 1823, French refusal to set a date by which it would withdraw from Spain inspired Canning to utilize a diplomatic strategem to force France publicly to relinquish its Latin American aspirations. As he correctly reasoned, if France could be persuaded to renounce any hostile intentions towards the new republics, Russia and the other continental powers would be unwilling to act alone, and a proposed Holy Alliance conference to discuss a joint Latin American policy would be stillborn.

Realizing that French troops would soon take Cádiz and restore Ferdinand, Canning summoned the French Ambassador, the Prince de Polignac, to a conference on 3 October to explain France's intentions toward Latin America. The meetings lasted several days, during which Canning informed Polignac that any attempt to return Latin America to its former submissive state under Spain would be totally hopeless, and that Britain would without delay recognize Latin American independence should any foreign power (i.e. France) interfere in the dispute between Spain and its former colonies. Britain, Canning explained, had no exclusive territorial or commercial ambitions in the area, and only wished to enjoy the same trading privileges as accorded other nations. She would, however, resent any attempt to restrict her growing trade with the ex-colonies.

Canning also declined to enter into any joint deliberations on Latin America with other European powers which were not as concerned on the subject as Britain herself or the United States of America, which should in any case be included in any future conferences. Polignac, surprised at Canning's forthright explanation of British policy, agreed it would be hopeless to reduce the revolted colonies to their former status, and protested that France had no intention of acting against them forceably and even had recalled its warships from American waters.

Canning's decision to seek confrontation with Polignac was motivated less by a straightforward desire to preserve Latin America's independence, than to prevent France from regaining its old continental dominance. At the conclusion of the meetings Canning drafted a memorandum of their discussions, which he persuaded Polignac to sign. The content of the so-called Polignac Memorandum became known unofficially in European chanceries by the third week in October, although it was not circulated privately until November 1823, nor even published oficially until March 1824.[59] Nevertheless, some of the memorandum's tenor was undoubtedly soon known in the City and surely encouraged bondholders.

Perhaps as a result of Canning's actions, King Ferdinand's declaration in mid-October that he had repudiated the bond issues made by the liberal cortes shook the market only briefly.[60] Now that the Spanish constitutional government had been destroyed, Ferdinand sought to convince the world that he had in reality been a captive of the liberal government, and that consequently his authorization of the bond issues had been obtained under duress and therefore was not binding. His strategy was, *The Morning Chronicle* remarked, 'a convenient one, as it wipes off a large amount of public debt, yet possibly it would not have been so readily adopted, if the greater proportion of that debt had been owing either in Paris or St Petersburgh'.[61]

Despite the results of the Canning-Polignac conference, vocal advocates of recognition of the independence of Latin America maintained their pressure upon Canning and the government. Foremost among the newspapers still unconvinced that the Spanish-French threat was blunted, *The Sunday Times* predicted that France, acting in the name of Spain, would destroy Latin American independence.[62] Only by recognizing the new states and placing them under British protection could reconquest be averted and British trading interests secured – not only from Spain and France but also from the upstart former British North American colonies. Another Sunday newspaper, *The Examiner*, asked its readers, 'could anything be more disgraceful in the British Ministers than to let the North Americans, with nothing like our motives, and even some natural feelings to the contrary, get the start of us on establishing a profitable connection with the immense, fertile, and improving States of Southern America?'[63]

Meanwhile, the Stock Exchange was showing extraordinary signs of vigour. Reflecting perhaps a renewed confidence in investor gullibility and inspired by the example of the Cazique of Poyais, in early November a cabal of promoters issued a prospectus for a £640,000 loan to the Order of St John of Jerusalem.[64] The Order, more familiarly known as the Knights of Malta, had been suppressed by Napoleon but was being revived. Now headquartered in Paris, the Order had signed a treaty of alliance with Greek insurgents who in March 1821 had rebelled against their Turkish overlords. In return for raising the loan in its own name on behalf of Greece, the Order was to be granted Rhodes and two other Greek islands once they had been liberated.

The 5 per cent twenty-year loan was to be offered at 61 through Hullett Brothers, architects of the Chilean issue, and secured by mortgages on all the Order's revenues and estates, including land and forests in France valued at 29,000,000 francs, and which yielded an annual income of 3,790,760 francs. Moreover, the Order would soon receive 12,000,000 francs in entrance fees from 4,000 Knights 'now inscribed and waiting to be admitted'.

By 5 November, reported *The Morning Herald* only half-seriously, the loan was already fully subscribed and 'the money raised, it is further rumoured, is to be applied towards assisting the Greeks in securing to them one of . . . Mr [Jeremy] Bentham's Constitutions'. Moreover, 'amongst the subscribers to the loan are the names of most of the principal men on the money market, who . . . mean to sell this loan again the moment they can realize an eighth per cent.'[65] Unfortunately for its promoters, the transaction collapsed when it failed to obtain the support of Parisian financial interests.[66] Although the offering initially might seem a transparent imitation of the Poyais swindle, it was in fact a forerunner of subsequent more successful attempts which, by appealing to pro-Hellene, liberal elements in British life and culture, would raise two disastrous loans for Greece over the next two years.

As for Columbian bondholders, by early December the future must have seemed a trifle brighter when they read in the press that an executive decree in August had revoked both the powers of attorney of the rather ineffective Minister José Rafael Revenga and of the mischievous Luis López Méndez. A notice also was posted at the Stock Exchange by Herring, Graham and Powles containing an extract of a letter from their Mr Jones in Bogotá announcing Manuel José Hurtado's appointment as Minister for Europe and reporting that the Colombian government was now anxious 'to arrange everything on the subject of Mr Zea's Loan in the most satisfactory and amicable manner.'[67]

The same month many friends of Latin American independence also welcomed President James Monroe's forthright address to the United States congress warning that any European attempt to reintroduce their political systems into the Americas would be considered dangerous to the peace and safety of the United States. 'Were

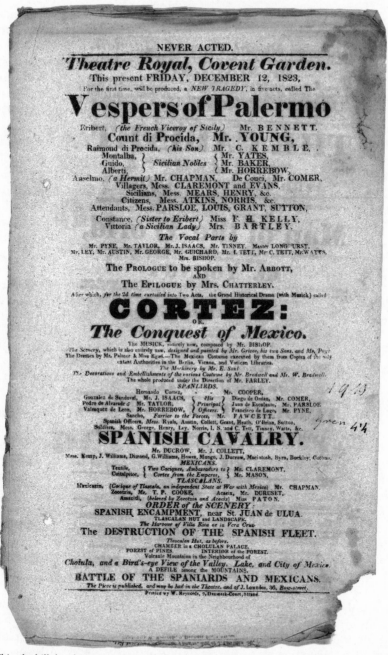

NEVER ACTED.

Theatre Royal, Covent Garden.

This present FRIDAY, DECEMBER 12, 1823,

For the first time, will be produced, a *NEW TRAGEDY*, in five acts, called The

Vespers of Palermo

Eribert, *(the French Viceroy of Sicily)*   Mr. BENNETT.

Count di Procida,   Mr. YOUNG,

Raimond di Procida, *(his Son)* Mr. C. KEMBLE,

Montalba,   ⎫   ⎧ Mr. YATES,

Guido,   ⎬ *Sicilian Nobles* ⎨ Mr. BAKER,

Alberti,   ⎭   ⎩ Mr. HORREBOW,

Anselmo, *(a Hermit)* Mr. CHAPMAN,   De Couci, Mr. COMER,

Villagers, Mess. CLAREMONT and EVANS,

Sicilians, Mess. MEARS, HENRY, &c.

Citizens, Mess. ATKINS, NORRIS, &c.

Attendants, Mess. PARSLOE, LOUIS, GRANT, SUTTON,

Constance, *(Sister to Eribert)* Miss F. H. KELLY,

Vittoria *(a Sicilian Lady)* Mrs. BARTLEY.

The Vocal Parts by

Mr. PYNE, Mr. TAYLOR, Mr. J. ISAACS, Mr. TINNEY, Master LONGHURST,
Mr. LEY, Mr. AUSTIN, Mr. GEORGE, Mr. GUICHARD, Mr. I. TETT, Mr. C. TETT, Mr. WATTS,
Mrs. BISHOP.

The PROLOGUE to be spoken by Mr. ABBOTT,

AND

The EPILOGUE by Mrs. CHATTERLEY.

After which, *for the 2d time curtailed into Two Acts,* the Grand Historical Drama (with Musick) called

CORTEZ:

OR,

The Conquest of Mexico.

The MUSICK, entirely new, composed by Mr. BISHOP.

The Scenery, which is also entirely new, designed and painted by Mr. Grieve, his two Sons, and Mr. Pugh

The Dresses by Mr. Palmer & Miss Egan.—The Mexican Costume executed by them from Copies of the only
extant Authorities in the Berlin, Vienna, and Vatican Libraries.

The Machinery by Mr. E. Saul.

The Decorations and Embellishments of the various Costume by Mr. Bradwell and Mr. W. Bradwell.

The whole produced under the Direction of Mr. FARLEY.

SPANIARDS.

Hernando Cortez,   Mr. COOPER,

Gonzalez de Sandoval,   Mr. J. ISAACS, ⎫ *His* ⎧ Diego de Ordaz, Mr. COMER,

Pedro de Alvarado & Mr. TAYLOR,   ⎬ *Principal* ⎨ Juan de Escalante, Mr. PARSLOE

Velasquez de Leon,   Mr. HORREBOW, ⎭ *Officers.* ⎩ Francisco de Lugo, Mr. PYNE,

Sancho, *Farrier to the Forces,* Mr. FAWCETT.

Spanish Officers, Mess. Ryals, Austin, Collett, Geant, Heath, O'Brian, Sutton,

Soldiers, Mess. George, Henry, Ley, Norris, I. S. and C. Tett, Tinney, Watts, &c.

SPANISH CAVALRY.

Mr. DUCROW, Mr. J. COLLETT,

Mess. Kemp, J. Williams, Dimond, G. Williams, Howes, Mungo, J. Ducrow, Macintosh, Byrn, Buckley, Gibbons,

MEXICANS.

Teutile,   ⎧ *Two Caciques, Ambassadors to* ⎫ Mr. CLAREMONT,

Cuitalpitoc, ⎨ *Cortez from the Emperor,*   ⎬ Mr. MASON,

TLASCALANS.

Mexicazin, *(Cacique of Tlascala, an independent State at War with Mexico)* Mr. CHAPMAN.

Zocotzin, Mr. T. P. COOKE,   Acaxis, Mr. DURUSET,

Amazitli, *(beloved by Zocotzin and Acaxis)* Miss PATON.

ORDER of the SCENERY:

SPANISH ENCAMPMENT, near St. JUAN de ULUA.

TLASCALAN HUT and LANDSCAPE.

The Harbour of Villa Rica or la Vera Cruz.

The DESTRUCTION OF THE SPANISH FLEET.

Tlascalan Hut, as before,

CHAMBER in a CHOLULAN PALACE.

FOREST of PINES.   INTERIOR of the FOREST.

Volcanic Mountains in the Neighbourhood of

Cholula, and a Bird's-eye View of the Valley, Lake, and City of Mexico.

A DEFILE among the MOUNTAINS.

BATTLE OF THE SPANIARDS AND MEXICANS.

The Piece is published, and may be had in the Theatre, and of J. Lowndes, 36, Bow-street.

Printed by W. Reynolds, 9, Denmark-Court, Strand.

9. This playbill dated 12 December 1823 from the Theatre Royal in Covent Garden advertises
a well-received musical extravaganza about the conquest of Mexico which played over
twenty times in November and December 1823. Its popularity reflects the widespread
public interest in Latin America of those days.

anything wanted to strengthen our confidence that South America is happily beyond the Holy Alliance grasp, the Message of the American President to Congress, which has just reached London would supply it', *The Examiner* declared.[68] Other papers were less impressed with what *The Morning Chronicle* considered an overly long and too vague, sweeping declaration. Did the president mean that if Spain invaded Latin America he would help the new nations maintain their independence the leader writer inquired.[69]

By the end of the year it was obvious that a new round of Latin American borrowing would begin in 1824. On 6 November, as if to prepare the public for what was to come, a play *Cortez, or the Conquest of Mexico* opened at Covent Garden. A provincial critic praised its magnificent scenery, wonderful feats of horsemanship, excellent musical compositions, and splendid costumes, all of which were received 'amidst the loudest approbation' of an enthusiastic audience.[70] Later that month the press advised readers that a Mexican loan would soon be offered in the City. Under a congressional decree authorizing the Mexican supreme executive power to borrow $20,000,0000 abroad, a contract had been signed in Mexico City in August with a representative of Barclay, Herring, Richardson & Co. to underwrite a credit at 70. As the loan was rumoured to be the equivalent of approximately £5,000,000, Mexico would receive nearly £4,000,000, 'a sum fully sufficient to enable that rich and populous empire' to defeat any expeditions the French and Spanish might send, one provincial newspaper opined.[71]

In London *The Morning Chronicle* informed the public that the new 5 per cent Mexican bonds would soon be available, but their value would depend on liberating 'this fine country from the Bourbon yoke. For with independence, and the exercise of industry, it produces everything necessary to the comforts and luxuries of man.'[72] Not all the press welcomed the issue so enthusiastically. *The New Times* branded it a monstrous scheme and fumed that 'it seems to be thought there is no end to the *gullibility* of poor John Bull! – A more profligate imposition on his credulity was never attempted'.[73] Readers were urged to reject 'the insane project of sending millions of money to God knows whom at Mexico! Surely poor deluded families enough have been ruined by these wild speculations!'

The Mexican loan announcement was followed quickly by news of an impending Brazilian offering. The £2,500,000 credit was being arranged with a group of City merchants, rather than bankers, and would return 6 per cent interest over thirty-five years. A respectable list of subscribers had been organized, including nearly all the principal houses trading with Brazil and Portugal.[74] One leader writer, however, could not refrain from remarking on the inconsistency of some British investors, who provided money to Colombia to enable it to establish its independence, but were now contemplating a new loan to Ferdinand, who was intent on destroying that freedom and with it the country's debt to Britain. Similarly they had just lent money to Portugal, which might be used to finance an expedition against Brazil, the latest market entrant.[75]

Rumours of still other loans being arranged for the New Year filtered through the City during December, including more credits for Greece and Spain. The public also became aware of the existence of a potential new Latin American borrower when they read in the press of the creation of the United Provinces of Central America, which in July had proclaimed their independence from Mexico, into which they had been briefly incorporated in 1822 following their break with Spain. The birth of this new state was also reported in the provincial journals, demonstrating again that public interest in Latin America was not confined just to London.[76]

The New Year also promised a novel source of income for investors with money to spare and faith in the economic opportunities offered by Latin America. In December the press announced that joint stock associations were being organized to exploit that continent's vast deposits of precious metals.[77] One prospectus circulating in the City promoted in unnamed mining company to extract Mexico's gold and silver 'uniting the scientific and mechanical improvements of the Old World with the already attained practice and experience of the established mines where the operations will be carried on.'[78] Moreover, the prospectus explained, 'there cannot be a better period for accomplishing this object, than when the independence of the new Republic is being consolidated'. Another company, still in formulation, proposed to use British machinery to bring back into operation the rich but flooded silver mines of Guanajuato.[79] Neither entity was identified by name, but from their descriptions they were most likely early versions of the United Mexican Company and the Anglo-Mexican Mining Association which would be officially launched the following January.

Meanwhile, the situation in the Iberian Peninsula was still worrying. Ferdinand began a reign of terror and ruthlessly ordered the execution or exile of all his opponents, both real and imaginary. The British liberal press continued to attack the restored monarch, and on 2 December *The Morning Chronicle* commented that 'The Holy Alliance had brought the refractory Spaniards again within the pale of legitimacy, and has besides punished those credulous and sympathizing Englishmen who were visionary enough to lend them money for the purposes of upholding a representative form of government resembling their own.'[80]

Despite the unpleasant news from Spain, however, no invasion of South America had yet materialized and a cautious optimism replaced the misgivings apparent during preceding months. Although some commentators still feared the worst, the Spanish-French threat to Latin American independence had in fact receded. British consuls were on the high seas en route to Latin America, Colombia had indicated its intention to settle with its creditors, and both the Peruvian and Chilean governments had ratified the loans contracted by their agents. The new mining ventures, as well as projected additional loans, augered a lucrative 1824 for the financial community.

City speculators were not the only one to enjoy a happy Christmas, however. Brighton shopkeepers and property owners were also delighted because, after some hesitation, King George IV had decided to spend the Christmas holidays at the small seaside town. The new Chain Pier, opened in early December, was brightly illuminated to celebrate the royal arrival. A Chinese pagoda was erected at its end, from which a giant fireworks display erupted, while the theatre was thrown open to the public free of charge. In view of the widespread good cheer, it must have seemed a particularly great shame to his family and friends that hard-working George Canning was confined to bed with gout over Christmas.[81] Nevertheless, the foreign secretary could take considerable comfort in the knowledge that his farsighted policies and tireless devotion to the demands of his office had done much to draw the year to a reasonably satisfactory conclusion.

IV
RECOVERY AND
THE INVESTING MANIA

BY 1824 BRITAIN had recovered from the recent agricultural depression, bread prices were low, jobs plentiful, trade and commerce flourishing, and the cotton, wool and iron industries booming. As King George noted in his address when parliament opened in early February, 'at no former period has there prevailed throughout all classes in this island a more cheerful spirit of order, or a more just sense of the advantages which, under the blessing of Providence, they enjoy'.[1] In contrast, the continent was again riven by economic depressions, political crises and wars.

The general euphoria and optimism was reflected in the press, which in mid-January announced the launch of another Mexican loan in addition to the credit reported in November.[2] The Mexican revolt against Spanish authority, waged intermittently since 1808, had triumphed in 1821 when General Agustín de Iturbide's rebel army entered Mexico City after signing a peace treaty with the Spanish viceroy. A provisional assembly then had elected a five man regency to rule the country pending ratification of the treaty by the Spanish cortes and the designation of an emperor for Mexico. When the cortes rejected the treaty, Iturbide seized power, declared independence, and was crowned Emperor Agustín I in May 1822.[3]

Francisco Borja de Migoni, a Mexican merchant several years resident in London, had written to the future emperor in March 1822, offering to raise a loan for the new state. Colombia, he commented, had just negotiated a major financing in London and

> any nation which lends money to another nation acquires an interest in the continuance of the latter's independence. The English Government protects the interests of its people, and if the English people have funds in Mexico ... will not Mexico be given some slight consideration by the Government?

For example, the reconquest of Colombia by Spain would be unwelcome in Britain because of the £2,000,000 British bondholders would lose.[4]

Migoni's offer was well received. Iturbide's government was virtually bankrupt because the traditional colonial fund-raising devices were no longer available. To assure popular support, sales taxes had been reduced drastically, alcohol taxes abolished, the viceregal tobacco monopoly terminated, and annual tribute payments imposed on the Indians since the conquest discontinued. Commerce and mining, once rich revenue sources, had been severely disrupted by the years of violence. Appeals for voluntary contributions to help the country in its difficulties elicited little response, and the government had been compelled to resort to unpopular forced loans. It was a pattern which soon would become all too familiar throughout Latin America.

Accordingly, on 5 June 1822, the Mexican congress authorized the Iturbide government to negotiate a credit abroad of 25–35,000,000 pesos. Fund-raising efforts, however, were halted by the revolution which eventually forced Iturbide's resignation and exile in early 1823. However, the constitutional congress then convened to design a new republican form of government, found an empty treasury, taxes pledged in advance, public credit at a record low, and the paper currency so depreciated that the government was scarcely able to meet current obligations. Consequently on 1 May 1823 congress authorized a further loan of 8,000,000 pesos and revoked all earlier borrowing authorizations given to the imperial government. Two weeks later Migoni was directly empowered to raise the required amount at 5 per cent per annum.[5]

Even before Migoni's instructions had reached London, however, the government was already weighing several additional competing offers, including more from Thomas Kinder & Co. of Peruvian loan fame, and the one from Barclay, Herring, Richardson & Co. The latter group prevailed with an offer of a 6 per cent loan out of which the government would receive £2,500,000. An agreement with Barclay's local representative was ratified by congress in early December, subject to approval by the firm's London head office. This new credit, which had been prematurely announced in late 1823, was designed to supplement, not replace, the amount Migoni had already been authorized to raise.[6] Migoni had formally accepted his appointment as agent to negotiate the loan on 21 August 1824, and had begun discussions with B. A. Goldschmidt & Co. Progress was slow however. Rumours of new revolutions in Mexico, the French intervention in Spain, and the difficulties experienced by Colombian, Chilean and Peruvian bondholders combined to delay final agreement with the contractors.[7] In fact, the contract between Migoni and Goldschmidt was not signed until 7 February, although details of the loan were carried in the press in January. Even though it had been negotiated at an earlier date, the Barclay transaction had yet to be approved by the company's London office and therefore the Migoni-Goldschmidt credit was first on the market. Goldschmidt agreed to place at the disposal of the Mexican government over a fifteen-month period the sum of £1,600,000, the equivalent of the 8,000,000 pesos Migoni was empowered to borrow. This would be raised by selling bearer bonds with a total face value of £3,200,000, and which could be purchased by the public in five instalments up to 21 June.

A general bond pledged 'the whole of the revenues of Mexico' as security, in addition to a special pledge of one-third of the revenues of the customs duties of the Gulf ports. The bond also stipulated that a quarter of the face amount of any future financing raised before complete repayment of the Goldschmidt credit 'shall be applied to the redemption of the present loan'. The thirty-year loan was to be repaid from a sinking fund into which £64,000 would be paid the first year and £32,000 each succeeding year. All redeemed bonds were to be cancelled and deposited at the Bank of England, where, together with the general bond and Migoni's power of attorney, they would remain until the entire loan was redeemed.[8]

Considering the discounted purchase price, the 'real' yield on the 6 per cent bonds to maturity was 8.62 per cent, much higher than the return on British government consols, interest on which was reduced by the chancellor of the exchequer in late February from 4 to 3½ per cent.[9] Mexico's perceived international creditworthiness was now roughly comparable with that of Austria, which had arranged a £2,500,000 5 per cent loan in London at 82 in December 1823. The Mexican scrip issued to subscribers was soon trading at a premium of 3½ per cent.[10]

However, the loan's terms were hardly advantageous to the borrower. Although Mexico issued bonds totalling £3,200,000, Goldschmidt underwrote the issue at 50 so that at most Mexico could have grossed only £1,600,000. From this, £421,360 was deducted for commissions and the first two years of interest and sinking fund payments, leaving a disposable balance of £1,178,640. Since the bonds were sold to the public at 58, Goldschmidt made a profit of approximately £250,000, the eight points difference between the contracting and issuing prices. In addition, Goldschmidt received a management commission of 1 per cent on the first year's interest of £80,000, a 1½ per cent commission for managing the payment of the following three dividends, and a 1 per cent commission for administering the £96,000 retained as a sinking fund. Since out-of-pocket expenses, including stamp duties and newspaper advertisements, also were deducted, Goldschmidt's total profit was handsome indeed.[11]

In contrast to the scepticism expressed by *The New Times* the preceding December, *The Morning Chronicle* had welcomed news of the loan, noting that Mexico 'possesses nearly all the advantages which nature can confer, and it is neighbour of the free Northern Union of America. Much confidence may therefore be placed in its prosperity, when once it begins to feel the blessings of good government, and of a real independence.'[12] The loan prospectus, printed in the press a week later, noted that nearly all the proceeds would be spent on British manufactured goods and 'all the necessary arms and acoutrements for the protection of the populous and rich republic will be speedily as possible forwarded'.[13]

By February 1824 the same newspaper was less sanguine and concerned lest the loan might not have been properly authorized by the Mexican congress: 'The public are already suffering to a large amount by several South American loans; and the grounds on which the Colombian Government refused to ratify that of Mr Zea, render it peculiarly incumbent on the contractors to proceed with the utmost caution.'[14] In March the even more disenchanted *John Bull* leader complained that 'we are sick to death of these impolitic (to say the least of them) foreign loans, and with the highest respect for the persons who in the spirit of speculation engaged in them, cannot but hope capitalists will pause before they embark in such visionary undertakings.'[15] This was, of course, a minority opinion.

In January 1824 other promoters proposed a small loan for another country which had not yet attained independence from its tyrannical overlord – Greece. Like the early Latin American issues, the Greek loan was welcomed in the City. There was a difference, however. The favourable reception of Latin American financing overtures was largely founded on commercial considerations; sympathy for the Greek cause was rooted in cultural ones. Since 1821 the needless barbarity with which the Turks had sought to suppress the latest Greek revolt had appalled classically-educated British Whigs and liberals. Eventually they formed the London Philhellenic Committee which through public meetings and subscriptions provided supplies and money to assist the gallant descendants of Homer and Pericles in their battle for liberty. A few more adventurous spirits, including Lord Byron, even sailed to Greece to offer their lives in the unequal struggle.

Taking advantage of the widespread pro-Greek sentiment, Herman Hendriks, an ex-colleague of Gregor MacGregor, announced he had been appointed agent for the rebel Greek government and was preparing to launch an £800,000 5 per cent loan.[16] Initially the press doubted the project's legitimacy due to the involvement of Hendriks, a City fringe character who at the time was also attempting to broker an improbable loan for Cyprus. Not surprisingly *The*

Morning Chronicle characterized his proposal for Greece as premature and advised investors to wait until duly accredited envoys had arrived from Greece.[17]

Such was the popularity of the Greek cause, however, that by the time an £800,000 loan was officially launched in February at a banquet at the Guildhall presided over by the Lord Mayor, the issue was already heavily oversubscribed at 59.[18] Nevertheless, even though the loan was secured by 'the whole of the national property of Greece', *The Morning Herald*, noting Hendriks' involvement, remained sceptical: 'All that we have to say to John Bull is, remember the Cazique of Poyais.'[19]

While the Mexican and Greek loans were being absorbed by investors in Britain, Colombian Vice President Santander had been implementing plans for raising additional funds. After the Zea fiasco, Colombia's financial crisis had deepened due to Bolívar's expensive campaigns to liberate Ecuador and Peru. In Colombia itself the economy was in total disarray, with mining and agriculture virtually ruined. Santander foresaw that no new financing would be possible unless an arrangement was reached with the creditors Zea had sought to placate in 1820 and 1822. Congress obligingly approved a foreign loan up to £6,000,000, and the new Colombian minister in London, Manuel José Hurtado, was authorized to condition the market for the new, larger credit by settling with Herring, Graham & Powles, the creditors' representatives. Two special envoys and friends of Santander, Francisco Montoya and Miguel Antonio Arrubla, would then negotiate the new loan separately with a more prestigious firm.[20]

All proceeded as planned. On 1 April 1824, Hurtado agreed to recognize the validity of the 1822 loan and Zea's other transactions. In addition he signed £54,550 in debentures to replace the notes Zea had issued. Herring, Graham and Powles in return agreed to surrender £175,000 in undistributed loan proceeds.[21] Colombian bond quotations immediately jumped over 16 points to 85, to the great annoyance of former Colombian bondholders who had already liquidated their positions.[22] On 2 April one 'Ex-holder of Colombian Bonds' wrote to Hurtado demanding to know why upon his arrival in England the minister had not announced his intention of affirming Zea's loan. Earlier Colombia had notified the world that it had repudiated Zea's loan, causing many bondholders to sell. Now Hurtado proclaimed that Zea's bonds could be exchanged for new debentures.

What, Sir, can you say to those unfortunate individuals, whose only fault was to rely on the veracity of your government, and who taking it at its word, preferred realizing 40 or 50 per cent rather than endure further sacrifice? Sir, I will fearlessly tell you, that they have been most wantonly wronged by you...[23]

Nevertheless, *The Morning Chronicle* noted with relief that the dispute between Colombia and its bondholders had at last been honourably concluded, and the new debentures signed by Hurtado sanctioned by congressional decree.[24] The market confidence generated by the settlement would not only benefit the new Colombian loan then being negotiated, but 'will also powerfully operate in favour of the Brazil Loan, about to be contracted'.[25] The ever-sceptical *John Bull*, however, compared the lending boom to events preceding the South Sea Bubble crisis, and commented smugly that 'although the mania for stockjobbing has not yet possessed the minds of our females and established itself in our drawing rooms, it is a duty to prevent by every possible means an evil much to be feared, and which is not to be cured.'[26]

With Colombia's credit restored, Montoya and Arrubla successfully negotiated an agreement in which B. A. Goldschmidt & Co. agreed to underwrite £4,750,000. Meanwhile, the 1822 bonds, now selling at 95, were expected soon to reach par.[27] The new 6 per cent issue was heavily oversubscribed by £25,000,000, and was represented by 23,150 bearer certificates signed in Calais to avoid British usury laws.[28] Unlike the 1822 certificates, they were printed only in English, and, since Mr Rudolph Ackermann's engraving talents had not been employed, were far less elegant. Principal and interest were secured by a pledge of all state revenues and particularly those from tobacco, which the minister of finance was bound to segregate from other income and remit to London semi-annually. The bonds would be redeemed at par over thirty years from a sinking fund into which £47,500 would be paid annually.

The 1824 Colombian negotiators obtained better terms than Zea, with Goldschmidt taking the loan firm at 85 and issuing it to the public at 88½, assuring themselves of only a 3½ point profit. Colombia's credit rating thus, for the moment, was almost equal to that of France and other European borrowers. The nation's political future, moreover, now appeared brighter than it had two years before. Bolívar had won a series of impressive victories, and Canning had sent a commission to Bogotá to assess the nation's stability, presumably as a prelude to recognition.[29]

Bonds dipped a full point, nevertheless, on news that ex-Emperor Iturbide had left Europe for Mexico, presumably to reclaim his throne. As one newspaper commented, however, Colombia had nothing in common with the fate of Mexico and therefore apprehensions were groundless.[30] Whatever the misgivings over the future, on 19 May the delighted Powles and his colleagues hosted a dinner in honour of Hurtado at the City of London Tavern, where the unfortunate Zea had been feted two years before. Parliamentarians, prominent merchants and bankers again attended. Toasts were drunk to all members of the royal family, to Bolívar, and to the speedy recognition of Colombia by Great Britain.[31]

Although most British investors may have liked the loan, the Colombian congress ratified it only over spirited opposition. Santander's political opponents particularly criticized the commissions totalling over £73,000 paid to Hurtado, Montoya and Arrubla. Also, after deducting the discount, retention of two years interest in advance, sinking fund provisions, commissions and other costs, Colombia received only about half of the total face value of the bonds it had issued. A substantial portion of this amount went to defray military purchases abroad, and was probably misspent. Approximately £750,000 was paid by the Santander government in settling miscellaneous internal debts, thus greatly benefiting speculators who had purchased government domestic promissory notes from their original holders at substantial discounts. In the end, little was left to invest in agriculture or in the other productive activities for which the loan ostensibly had been destined.[32]

Meanwhile, the wrangle over the Peruvian loan continued throughout February, with Everett & Co. still refusing to release loan proceeds despite the court action against them. Until the dispute was resolved the remainder of the credit could not be marketed nor certificates issued to replace scrip. Eventually a scripholders meeting in late February persuaded the bankers, Kinder, and Robertson to submit the matter to arbitration. Following a decision against Everett, Robertson crossed to Paris to prepare and sign the bonds to be exchanged for the scrip. Bond quotations then rose to 78, but still ten points below issue price.[33]

The moment now seemed propitious to market the £750,000 remainder of the 1822 Peruvian loan. The issue was well received at 82 and the bonds were confidently expected to rise in value as soon as the remainder of the Spanish troops still in Peru were expelled.[34] The dishonoured bills of exchange could now be paid, and so certain was the prospect of the expulsion of the royalist forces that on 13 April a second Peruvian loan was tentatively announced by City bankers Fry and Chapman of Mildred's Court, Poultry.[35] Unfortunately for Peru, it received, like Columbia, but a fraction of the face amount of £1,200,000 in bonds it had issued. The discount at which Kinder had underwritten the loan reduced gross proceeds to £900,000, from which £20,000 was deducted for the expenses of the Paroissien-García del Río mission, while £72,000 was withheld to pay the first year's interest. Another £20,000 for commissions and expenses, together with other deductions, further reduced the amount Robertson could draw on for the government to £744,293. Nor could Peru benefit from the seven point spread between the underwriting and issue prices, all of which went to Kinder.[36]

Throughout the first quarter of 1824 trading in Latin American issues continued to dominate Foreign Stock Exchange activities 'because they yield more interest than those of Europe, and because the new Republican States are daily becoming more firmly established'.[37] General public interest in Latin America persisted unabated, and newspapers devoted ample, costly space to the conflict in Peru, political intrigues in Brazil and Central America, and even to the bizarre dictatorship of Dr José Gaspar Rodríguez de Francia in remote, isolated Paraguay. Fascination with Latin American public figures continued, Short biographical articles on Bolívar and other patriot leaders were frequent. When in June General San Martín arrived in London en route to his French exile, the press duly reported that he was feted at a dinner at London's Grillons Hotel hosted by García del Río, Manuel José Hurtado and Luis López Méndez.[38]

Recognition of Latin American independence by Great Britain now seemed tantalizingly close. In years past, British policy had been to encourage a rapprochement between Spain and its colonies. As the chances of reconciliation appeared increasingly remote, British policy shifted to one of assuring that no other country intervened in the conflict to obtain special political or commercial concessions, either with the new states or a victorious Spain. Canning in the 1823 Polignac Memorandum had indicated yet another policy change. As he had made clear, ultimate recognition was inevitable and depended only upon time and circumstances.[39] This latest shift was revealed publicly in February 1824, by the king's address to parliament, which almost paralleled the wording of the Polignac Memorandum. His Majesty's and his ministers' conduct, the address maintained, had been open and consistent. Consuls had been appointed to protect the trade of British subjects, and 'as to any further measures, his Majesty has reserved to himself an unfettered discretion to be exercised, as the circumstances of those countries, and the interests of his own people, may appear to his Majesty to require.'[40]

Not all MPs were satisfied with the government's Latin American position as expounded in the address. Some, like Lord Lansdown, while declining to opine whether government should have gone further, hoped it would be disposed to do so at the proper time. Britain should have taken the steps which it had now just done at an earlier date, he thought, because the trading advantages to be derived from an independent Latin America were impressive.[41] In the lower House, Henry Brougham condemned the government's failure to oppose the Holy Alliance and lamented Britain's declining influence abroad. 'Once we could boast of a proud pre-eminence in governing the destinies of states, but no man could point out its existence now.' He hoped Britain would follow the United States in recognizing Latin American independence 'in order to place bounds on that impious alliance, which, if it ever succeeded in bringing down the old world to its own degrading level, would not hesitate to attempt to master the new world too.'[42] Canning replied that while he agreed that no foreign nation had the right to intervene in Spain's dispute with its colonies, nevertheless, Spain had a right to recover her possessions and should be allowed a decent interval in which to do so before recognition of independence was accorded.[43]

During the debates, Lord Liverpool and Canning managed to steer a course between the die-hard opponents of recognition, and the advocates of more radical action. Both Houses eventually approved the address, which now became a public, formal declaration to the world that Britain no longer felt bound to consult with Spain or with its former allies against Napoleon, but would follow a policy which inevitably must result in recognition at the moment of Britain's choosing. Ferdinand had rejected numerous opportunities to reconcile himself to the loss of Spain's New World empire. Canning was now free to prevent a resurgent, triumphant France from profiting from the collapse of Spain's internal and overseas authority.

Responding both to the improved political climate and to the lure of rich profits, the two most respected and conservative banking houses in London, N. M. Rothschilds and Baring Brothers, now for the first time entered the Latin American lending market with credits for the Province of Buenos Ayres and for Brazil. These two prominent firms already had divided the cream of European borrowing between them, with Rothschilds earning the sobriquet 'Bankers to the Holy Alliance'. They now sought to extend their rivalry to the major Latin American states, leaving the more marginal nations to lesser financial and commercial groups. Although in 1824 neither Buenos Ayres nor Brazil seemed to offer the glittering prospects of Colombia, Mexico or Peru – which had been prosperous Spanish viceroyalties – they nevertheless eventually would prove to be better credit risks and would yield more consistent returns to investors. The relationships established in 1824 between these two merchant banks and the two largest countries in South America would endure throughout the century.

In 1824, however, the vast expanse of territory that was to become Argentina was merely a loose union of semi-independent provinces, each jealous of its own autonomy. The strongest and richest province was Buenos Ayres which, with its capital of the same name and located at the mouth of the Río de la Plata, dominated the area's international commerce and aspired to the area's political leadership. Since the first efforts in 1810 to achieve independence from Spain, Buenos Ayres had sought to unite the rest of the area into a cohesive political unit, but with limited success. Santa Fé, Entre Ríos, and Corrientes remained aloof and did not send delegates to the 1816 conference at Tucumán which declared the independence of the 'United Provinces of South America'. Even this union, perceived to be dominated by Buenos Ayres, collapsed in violence three years later to be replaced by a loose federation in which the provinces would maintain their independence. Not until late 1825, would the warfare between the unitarists, who wanted a strong central government based around Buenos Ayres, and the federalists who wanted a looser union, abate sufficiently to enable the formation of the short-lived United Provinces of the Rió de la Plata.[44] Consequently, in 1824 only Buenos Ayres, which was empowered to conduct diplomatic relations on behalf of the other provinces, had sufficient international credibility to attract foreign capital. Therefore the country's first loan was made to Buenos Ayres rather than to the fragile, embryonic provincial union as a whole.

In October 1823, Canning had appointed British Consul General Woodbine Parish to the government of Buenos Ayres. After a twelve weeks voyage he reached his new post in March 1824, by which time the city of Buenos Ayres had 3,500 British residents, including 150 merchants who dominated all foreign, and to a great extent internal, commercial activity.[45] Parish's impressions of the province's political stability and economic prospects were highly favourable. In 1820 the Buenos Ayres leaders had decided to suspend their unification ambitions and to concentrate their efforts on forming an efficient provincial administration. 'From a state of anarchy and confusion the people of Buenos Ayres are now raised to a prosperity hitherto unknown to them', Parish wrote, 'and are at present in the enjoyment of the blessings of a good, well organized, and stable government.'[46] The conclusions of his report to Canning, compiled with the assistance of local British merchants, undoubtedly soon circulated in London financial as well as political circles.

Britain was already by far the areas largest trading partner, exchanging principally cloth, manufactures, pots, pans and cutlery for hides and tallow. Annual imports from Britain were valued at $5,730,952, as against $1,368,277 from the United States and $820,109 from France.[47] While the country would still have to undergo nearly 40 years of more dictatorship and violence before it attained a lasting stability and union, for the moment the economic leadership of Buenos Ayres promised security and profit to foreign merchants.

Even before Parish's appointment, however, the Buenos Ayres provincial legislature, encouraged by the merchant community, on 19 August 1822 authorized the executive branch to raise 3–4,000,000 pesos locally or abroad. Proceeds were to be used to build adequate port facilities for Buenos Ayres, to provide the city with running water, and to establish towns along the southern frontier to discourage Indian attack.[48] The government of Bernardino Rivadavia did not act upon the authorization for over a year, ostensibly, as he later explained to congress, because he did not wish Buenos Ayres' credit standing 'to become enveloped in the shame which the other American loans have suffered in the great cities of Europe'. He advised waiting until the true economic and political state of Buenos Ayres were better known abroad.[49]

In early December 1823, however, five prominent merchants and directors of the Bank of Buenos Ayres, which had been founded largely by British merchants, formed a consortium which offered to negotiate the loan in London on behalf of the government. One consortium member was William Parish Robertson, younger brother of John Parish Robertson, the London Peruvian envoy who was also a member of the Buenos Ayres consortium *in absentia*. John had arrived in Buenos Ayres in 1808, and William in 1813. They engaged in a wide range of activities – importing and exporting merchandise, speculating in land and in money-lending. Their efforts prospered, and they opened a branch in Lima, where John was based at the time he was appointed to replace Paroissien and García de Río in London.[50]

Rivadavia approved the consortium's proposition with but few modifications, and on 16 January 1824 the government granted a power of attorney to the merchants to raise £700,000 through a loan of £1,000,000 to be issued at 70. Don Félix Castro, a prominent merchant and patriot, was authorized with John Parrish Robertson to negotiate the specific terms and conditions, including the interest rate, the form and timing of interest payments, the final maturity date and the commissions payable to the London bankers.

In London, meanwhile, John Robertson had already begun preliminary discussions with Baring Brothers. Two months before Woodbine Parish arrived in Buenos Ayres, Castro sailed for Liverpool aboard the British merchant ship *Lindsay* with the power of attorney in his luggage. He arrived in London on 12 June, and with Robertson began the final loan negotiations. The credit, underwritten at 70 but intended to be sold at 85, would yield £850,000, leaving a handsome profit of £150,000 of which £120,000 was destined for the pockets of the consortium members. Barings would receive £30,000, in addition to a commission and reimbursement of any printing or other costs, as well as 1 per cent on dividend and amortization payments. After all deductions – including two years interest and amortization in advance – the borrower would have but £570,000, which was to prove inadequate to the nation's needs.[51]

On 6 July the loan was officially announced in the press, although Barings had been receiving subscription applications since March.[52] The 6 per cent credit was to be represented by 2,000 bonds of £500 and secured by all the nation's properties and income. Interest was payable semi-annually against presentation of the appropriate coupons at Baring's 8 Bishopsgate office. In addition to the £30,000 in interest payments to be transmitted to London every semester, the government was to transfer £5,000 each year for the sinking fund until final maturity in 1870.[53]

The loan's single unit price of £500 indicates that, even when the discount reduced the purchase price to £350, Barings was targeting a more affluent market sector than prior issues, which had sought to attract investors who could afford an outlay of £75 to £88 per £100 bond. The Buenos Ayres issue was directed at the upper income brackets, perhaps at those fortunate individuals with at least £1,000 a year who should, according to the anonymous 1825 publication *A New System of Practical Domestic Economy*, be able to afford a wife, three children, a cook, a housemaid, a nurserymaid, a coachman, a footman, a four-wheeled carriage and a pair of horses. The bonds' pricing, however, must have seemed justified to its promoters in the light of the general enthusiasm for loans and other Latin American-related ventures rekindled by Canning's policy towards the new states.

The timing of the loan's launch was impeccable. On 6 July, *The Times* had reprinted Canning's letter to President Rivadavia notifying him of Parish's appointment as consul general empowered to take effective measures to protect British commerce and to obtain accurate information on the state of affairs in Buenos Ayres 'for the purpose of adopting such measures as may eventually lead to the establishment of friendly relations'.[54] The next day *The Courier* reprinted the minutes of a meeting Parrish had held with British residents of Buenos Ayres on 26 April. A seven-member committee had been appointed to draft a letter to thank Canning for sending consuls to the various Latin American states and also for arranging 'the important and much-desired advantage, a line of packets direct between England and Buenos Ayres, a measure from which the very best results must accrue to British interests already extensive, and daily increasing, in this part of the world'. As the editor remarked, 'at the present moment, and in reference to the important question of South American recognition, these documents are of considerable interest.'[55]

Barings had also cleverly deferred the launch until the dividend payment date for British government stock. Consol holders would then be liquid and might be tempted by the new, higher-yielding investment opportunities. Barings then made an immediate partial distribution of scrip which it sought to force up to a premium by cross-selling and buying between friendly brokers. At one point the artificially boosted scrip was offered at a premium. The purpose of the exercise, 'the uniform practice attendant upon the introduction of every new loan' lamented the press, was to induce potential investors to believe they would be buying into a successful, rising issue from which they could reap a substantial return provided they placed their orders quickly.[56] The strategem in this case was unsuccessful, and by the end of July the scrip was back at par. Nevertheless, the loan ultimately was heavily oversubscribed.[57]

In contrast to the glad tidings from Latin America, during July the newspapers recounted in great and sad detail the last days of Lord Byron, news of whose death in Greece, had reached Britain in April. Now the press reported attentively the arrival of his remains in England, the lying in state at a friend's house on George Street – 'The coffin is of a most beautiful description, and there are four vases which are to contain the heart, etc' –, and, a few days later the funeral procession attended by the empty carriages of numerous nobility including the Marquis of Lansdown, the Duke of Sussex, the Earl of Carlisle and the Duke of Bedford.[58] Not only had Byron been a participant in the Greek struggle for freedom, but he also had been an early supporter of the Latin American independence movements, and had named his yacht The Bolivar. Years previously, Byron, then living in Italy and perhaps anxious to escape his current possessive mistress, had even seriously considered moving to Venezuela to take up the supposedly idyllic life of a planter.[59] Subsequently he became a symbol both in his poetry and in his life of the romantic struggle against tyranny everywhere, and therefore his death was particularly mourned both by Philhellenes and Latin American enthusiasts. When the ship which had brought Byron back to England arrived, MP John Cam Hobhouse, one of his executors, immediately ordered the 180 gallons of spirits in which his body had been pickled to be thrown overboard rather than risk it being sold to the poet's fervent admirers offering half a sovereign for a few drops of the liquid.[60]

The press in the meantime continued its ample and generally encouraging coverage of Latin American events. In mid-July the cutter *Lion* arrived, forty-one days out of Vera Cruz, with welcome confirmation that the Mexican loan had been approved unhesitatingly by the executive branch. Bond quotations quickly rose to 54½.[61] In that same month the first instalment of the loan proceeds arrived in Mexico. A letter dated 22 May and reprinted in *The Courier* confided that the money was used to pay government and military salary arrears, thus establishing the unfortunate precedent of utilizing what were intended as long-term investment funds to defray current expenses. The same issue of *The Courier* also observed it was now the avowed intention of Liverpool and Canning to recognize the Latin American states as soon as they could demonstrate they possessed regular and permanent governments.[62]

Not even news that in the previous February mutinous Buenos Ayres troops in Peru had invited Spanish forces to retake Lima could dampen the prevailing confident atmosphere. It was assumed Bolívar was now in Peru dealing with the problem. Nor was the City unduly disturbed when in mid-July the assignees of a Captain Edwards, a Colombian creditor, attempted to attach £300,000 of the Colombian loan proceeds still lodged with B. A. Goldschmidt. The attachment was vacated when the lord chancellor decided that the Colombian government could not be a party in English courts since it still was unrecognized by Great Britain.[63] The price of the scrip for the new Mexican loan was unaffected, and on 22 July Goldschmidt announced the first half-yearly redemption of £27,900, represented by 279 bonds.[64]

In August the first Brazilian loan was offered firm at the Foreign Stock Exchange. It was not, however, the 6 per cent £2,500,000 credit reported in the press the previous December. This had apparently been withdrawn due to rumours of a joint Portuguese-French attempt to reduce the new nation once more to European authority. The face amount was now £1,000,000, bore interest of 5, not 6, per cent, and was secured by customs revenues. The managers of this new issue were Baylett, Farquhar & Co., Alexander & Co., and Wilson, Shaw & Co., well-known City bill brokers and merchants who had agreed to share their 4 per cent commission with the Brazilian government emmissaries who had come to London to negotiate the loan.[65]

The issue price was 75, with the bonds payable in ten instalments up to 17 May 1825. The contractors apparently did not attempt the extreme scrip manipulation which had characterized the Buenos Ayres issue. Although Rothschilds were not directly involved, their later leading role in Brazilian financing suggests they may have discretely backed the smaller contractors in order to test the market's appetite for the new paper. The financial correspondent of *The*

Morning Chronicle did not doubt the loan's future success: 'Considering the immense resources of the Brazilian Empire, and the small amount of the loan, the price appears to be moderate and ... no doubt can be entertained that justice will be done to the subscribers in its management.'[66]

The favourable reception accorded the Brazilian loan was not attributable solely to the nation's vast resources of precious minerals, woods and other valuable tropical products. The country was better known to the investing public than any of the other Latin American borrowers, and, given the close political and economic ties which had existed between Britain and Portugal for centuries, it is not surprising the loan was well received. Although in 1824 Portugal had not yet recognized Brazil's independence, the former colony had escaped the bloodshed and devastation that had ravaged former Spanish colonies as the mother country futilely attempted their reconquest. The new Brazilian emperor was the son of Portuguese King João VI, who when still heir to the throne and prince regent in 1807 had escaped with his court to Brazil on British naval vessels, leaving his mother, the insane Queen María I, behind as sovereign.

In return for the British rescue, Prince João had opened Brazilian ports to British trade by the 1810 Treaty of Commerce and Navigation, thus giving British merchants their first legitimate foothold on the South American mainland. Subjects of the two nations were accorded reciprocal rights to trade and reside in each other's ports and towns, to enjoy most favoured nation status as to taxes and levies, the reciprocal right to establish and maintain consuls, and assurance of religious toleration. Duties on British imports were set at 15 per cent, 9 per cent lower than those charged other nations, and 1 per cent below those levied on Portuguese imports. The treaty was technically between Britain and Portugal, not between Britain and Brazil, still linked to Portugal by the monarchy. Nevertheless, it came to be considered as a compact between Britain and the South American nation, as, in a historically unique role-reversal, the mother country now became the subordinate state while Brazil, the colony, became the centre from which the far-flung Portuguese Asian and African empire was ruled.[67]

When French troops were eventually ousted from Portugal in 1812, Prince João refused to return home, much preferring life in beautiful Rio de Janeiro. After Queen María died in 1815 and João assumed the crown, he issued a decree elevating Brazil 'to the dignity, prominence and denomination of a Kingdom', equal with Portugal.[68] The new king continued to live in Brazil, while Portugal was administered by a council of regency headed by British Minister Sir Charles Stuart. Finally, in 1821, after much vacillation and with strong British encouragement, the king returned home to resume his throne lest control of the country pass to a popular liberal faction which demanded a constitution and an end to the regency. The liberals also wished, however, to revive Brazil's colonial status, and therefore rejected King João's proposal of a dual monarchy.

Hoping at least to save Brazil for his family, before he sailed João appointed his son Pedro as regent, and even suggested he seize the Brazilian crown for himself. The younger man followed his father's advice in September 1822, and three months later was crowned Emperor Dom Pedro. After a brilliant Brazilian naval campaign led by Admiral Lord Cochrane, formerly of the British and Chilean navies, by January 1824, all loyal Portuguese forces had been expelled.[69] British recognition seemed inevitable, and on 21 August the first loan subscription instalment was paid in full.

Reports from the other Latin American nations, however, were not always so encouraging, and serious doubts were now raised in the press concerning the validity of the Chilean loan. In June Minister Irisarri had received word from friends in Chile that he was being replaced as Special Envoy and Minister Plenipotentiary by former Minister of Foreign Relations Mariano Egaña, who had also been charged with investigating Irisarri's use of the loan proceeds. Therefore, when Egaña's ship docked at Gravesend in late August, a secret letter from Irisarri awaited his henchman Agustín Gutiérrez, who had travelled from Chile with Egaña. Gutiérrez was told to explain to Egaña that Irisarri was still in Paris and therefore could not be on hand to meet them. Since Egaña spoke no English, Gutiérrez offered to guide the new minister through customs, and sent his luggage ahead by fast coach to Irisarri's London house. By the time Gutiérrez and Egaña were lurching along rutted roads heading for London, Irisarri had had time to search the new envoy's cases and discover the letter authorizing Egaña to obtain an accounting and to remit the remainder of the proceeds to Chile. Amongst the papers was a letter to Irisarri from the Chilean foreign ministry date 13 April 1824, officially notifying him of Egaña's appointment and ordering him 'to give the most punctual compliance' to Egaña's orders.

Realising his financial peculations would soon be exposed, Irisarri resolved to leave the Chilean service at once rather than suffer a humiliating dismissal. When Egaña eventually reached London after his slow coach-ride, he handed the foreign ministry's letter to Irisarri, who read it with feigned surprise before announcing his immediate departure for France. The trip was necessary, he explained, to complete purchasing negotiations for the corvette for the Chilean navy. In any event, Irisarri told the new minister, he considered his own power of attorney to have expired with O'Higgins resignation and Egaña's appointment. Egaña, who had no friends or contacts in London, was dismayed and begged the Guatemalan to stay. Irisarri adamantly refused. He then hastily crossed the Channel, taking the ministry files and seal. Egaña wrote requesting their return. Irisarri replied huffily from Paris that he would send them later, along with his full accounting.[70]

Irisarri's abrupt departure did not go unnoticed and precipitated over the next fortnight a three-way debate in the columns of *The Morning Chronicle* among correspondents who signed themselves 'Plain Dealing', 'A Holder of Chilean Bonds' and 'X' on whether or not the Chilean government had recognized the loan agreement formally and would be bound by it.[71] Finally, in mid-November Gutiérrez, on Irisarri's instructions, delivered the ministry files and seal to Egaña, together with Irisarri's accounting. Of the loan proceeds, £62,518 had been invested by Irisarri in various projects, £18,000 had been deducted as his salary over six years, and £20,000 had been subtracted as his 2 per cent commission. Moreover, he claimed £11,630 for outstanding expenses. Egaña objected vehemently, implying that Irisarri had been deceitful if not dishonest, which remarks Gutiérrez dutifully conveyed to Irisarri.

As Egaña gradually realized he could expect little clarification from Irisarri, he grew increasingly irritated. Andrés Bello was an early casualty of the envoy's frustration, for although he had not been involved in Irisarri's schemes, Egaña nevertheless forced Bello's resignation. Fortunately for the impoverished scholar and his large, hungry family, he eventually found more congenial employment at the Colombian legation.[72]

While Irissarri was attempting to outwit Egaña, some newspaper commentators had come to speculate that recent events in Mexico and Colombia might cause recognition of independence to be postponed. Mexico's political future now seemed uncertain due to reports of widespread support for Iturbide. While at present a republic, in a few months Mexico might again be an empire, *The Courier* remarked. 'Would it be consistent with the just dignity of this country, or with its just interest, to establish relations on so uncertain a basis?'[73] Also, Colombia had recently sent an expeditionary force under Bolívar to drive the Spaniards from Peru. Although 'the great talents of Bolívar are sufficient to inspire confidence', defeat still was possible, and it might therefore be best to delay recognition until the final outcome of the struggle.

In other quarters objections to recognition was more solidly entrenched. The king and a number of his advisers, including the lord chancellor, opposed recognition of republican governments on principle. Other critics based their opposition on more practical considerations. *The Morning Herald* urged the Cabinet to ignore petitions urging recognition. The British empire was extremely vulnerable. If Britain were to interfere with Spain's colonies in the New World, she might provoke retaliatory action in Hanover or elsewhere. War with the Holy Alliance might even result.[74] While journalistic reservations could be ignored by Canning, the opposition of the king and some cabinet colleagues was more serious.

By the third week in August Mexican bonds were down to 48, while Colombian bonds were boosted slightly by news that the government, thanks to the intervention of the British counsul-general, had agreed to pay the full amount of the debentures issued by López Méndez to James MacKintosh.[75] In early September a letter from a British visitor to Venezuela was published describing Caracas and its port of La Guayra in glowing terms, which may have heartened some investors. A considerable number of British merchants were already established in the two towns, with more arriving all the time. Among the business leaders was the 'respectable house of Jones, Powles and Murray, who have distinguished themselves by their active and cordial support of the Republic'.[76] The Mexican bonds' depression was not alleviated, however, even by Goldschmidt's announcement that the fourth quarterly interest payment would be made on 1 October at their Great St Helen's counting house.[77]

It should be remembered, however, that fluctuations in bond prices were sometimes artificially induced. Taking advantage of the lack of rapid, reliable trans-Atlantic communications, speculators would circulate rumours of a patriot defeat in South America, and quotations would fall. Then market manipulators would purchase the bonds at the depressed price for resale when better tidings provoked a rise. Due to the great distance between London and the Latin American battlefields, weeks or even months might pass before the accuracy of a report or rumour could be ascertained. Conversely, good news could upset speculator's plans, as when unexpected confirmation of Iturbide's execution on 17 September, two days after news of the death of France's King Louis XVIII, lifted Mexican and all other Latin American bond prices. Even Peruvian bonds rose 7 per cent at the news, causing *The Morning Chronicle* to ruminate optimistically that 'the blessings of peace, the expulsion of European influence, and the introduction of liberty into these wealthy and immense regions, are now alone necessary to promote the general prosperity of mankind'.[78]

In early November all Latin American bond quotations were boosted by favourable commercial reports from Mexico, Peru and

Colombia. The Brazilian loan had been quickly absorbed, and the scrip now commanded a 2 per cent premium. Mexican bonds, however, fell slightly when the press reminded readers that Barclay, Herring, Richardson the year before had contracted a 6 per cent Mexican loan of £3,200,000, which would soon be brought to market.[79] When the new issue was announced, *The Times* assured readers that a perusal of newspapers recently arrived from Mexico demonstrated that the country was calm, that laws were enforced with regularity and energy, and that the government had been consolidated rather than shaken by Spanish threats and the Iturbide experience.[80] Nevertheless, not all bondholders were pleased with the prospect of the Barclay's credit, which they feared might overstrain Mexico's capacity to service its earlier loan. *The Morning Chronicle* leader bravely argued that the new issue would actually improve the nation's credit since proceeds would be utilized to repay £1,000,000 of the Goldschmidt loan and to finance a navy to protect Mexican coasts from Spanish attack.[81]

December was a generally comforting month for bondholders, with bond quotations rising above their issue prices. Letters received from Jamaica confirmed Bolívar's victory over the Spanish forces in Peru, which now retreated southwards. Lima was evacuated and at the request of local merchants marines from British warships at Callao were landed to prevent looting.[82] Mid-month Goldschmidt announced that the fifth quarterly Mexican interest payment would be made on 1 January. A few days later Goldschmidt advertised that the second half-yearly dividend payment on the 1824 Colombian loan could be collected by bondholders on 15 January, also at his Great St Helen's counting house.[83]

Chilean bondholders finally were heartened when the press published letters from Santiago revealing that the government had taken concrete steps to assure the efficient collection of revenues with which to service and repay the loan. A ten-year contract had been signed with a consortium of local merchants who, in return for yearly government advances of £500,000, would collect the taxes on tobacco, foreign wines, spirits, playing cards and tea, and remit the proceeds semi-annually to Britain for interest and sinking fund payments. If the government itself had undertaken the collection, the theory ran, smuggling would have diverted the proceeds. Confidence in the efficiency and honesty of this consortium, or *estanco* as it came to be called, would prove entirely misplaced. For the moment, however, investors were satisfied and Chilean bonds traded at 80¼.[84]

Coinciding with these reports of more favourable turns of affairs in Latin America, was the announcement that nearly £6,000,000 would be paid at the Bank of England to holders of British government stock who had decided not to exchange their 4 per cent consols, already reduced from 5 per cent two years before, for the new 3½ per cent issue. At the same time, the government was reported to be determined to reduce outstanding exchequer bills by £4,000,000 by the end of the year. These decisions, combined with the payment of government stock dividends in October, *The Times* predicted, meant that 'an influx of capital into the market for investment must take place to an extent seldom known at one period'.[85] Much of this new market liquidity would be reinvested not only in existing and forthcoming Latin American and European loans, but also in the company formation craze then beginning to sweep the country.

Although most British overseas financial commitments had been in government loans, investments in Latin American mining company shares, begun in late 1823, had accelerated at a surprising rate. In early 1824 more information on the mining companies, which had been announced in various newspapers during the last months of the previous year, was again published in the press, and the public invited to purchase shares. The Mexican Mining Association was one of the first offered for public subscription. Capitalized at £240,000 represented by 6,000 shares of £40 each, it had twelve British directors, while Don Lucas Alamán, Mexican secretary of state, was president of the board of management.[85] *John Bull* greeted the announcement with the same scorn and disbelief it directed towards foreign loans. How, the leader inquired, could a capital of £240,000, which would not be adequate for a large brewery, be expected to support a trans-Atlantic speculation of such magnitude and difficulty?[86] Shortly after the debut of the Mexican Mining Association more details became available on the rival Anglo-Mexican Mining Association, formed to work the famed silver lodes at Guanaxuato with a capital of £1,000,000. Charles Herring and John D. Powles were directors, along with other prominent City merchants. The next entrant was the Real del Monte Mining Association, with a capital of £2,000,000 divided into 500 shares.[87] Not all the mining promoters were intent on extracting gold and silver. The Bolivar Mining Association, capitalized at £500,000, was organized to exploit the rich copper deposits of the Aroa mines in Venezuela, owned by the family of Simón Bolívar since 1663. The Liberator himself signed the lease by which the association agreed to pay an annual rental of $10,000.[88]

In colonial times, Spanish legislation had prohibited foreigners from working mines in the Americas. Upon independence, the new states repealed these restrictive laws. British entrepreneurs now were able to lease specific, once-productive mines from their proprietors, often offering share participations as inducements. The owners and their governments, lacking capital to restore productivity after years of neglect and destruction during the wars of independence, were delighted, while the British were convinced that after injections of British money and new machinery to replace antiquated Spanish technology the mines could once again be made to yield the golden and silver streams which had financed the imperial dreams of Charles V, Philip II and their successors. The prospectus of the Anglo-Mexican Mining Association, for example, confidently articulated this theme which soon would be repeated in the solications of future companies: 'It is believed that by the introduction of English capital, skill, experience and machinery, the expenses of working these mines may be greatly reduced and their produce much augmented.'[89]

In itself the successful launch of mining ventures for Latin American operations was not surprising, considering the long-frustrated ambitions of British entrepreneurs to obtain access to the almost legendary sources of Spanish imperial wealth. What was unforeseeable, however, was the sudden surge in share prices in the winter of 1824, when the mines were far from operational. By the end of November, for example, Real del Monte shares on which £70 had been paid were selling at £700, while Anglo-Mexican and United Mexican commanded premiums of £30 a share. *The Times* forsaw nothing but trouble ahead for the mining speculation, and warned readers that the spectacular rise of Real de Monte and other shares would before long 'have a proportionate fall'.[90] The competition to acquire mining company shares which caused their prices to soar was not, however, due to any increase in asset value or productivity, but to a widespread spirit of speculation fueled by low interest rates and a plentiful money supply and which by mid-1824 had developed into a mania for company formation and investment unseen since the days of the South Sea Bubble.[91]

The Latin American mining associations represented but a puny handful of the companies which were now being formed at an increasingly mad momentum. By the time the boom peaked in 1825, over 600 companies would have been organized or projected to operate in Britain and abroad. Their many diverse objectives included agricultural developments in Canada and Australia, sugar refining in Bengal, ice manufacturer, insurance, canal constructions and steam navigation. In such a heady, exciting environment, it seemed the shares of any company, however exotic its objectives, could be sold. Responsible, serious promoters of Latin American ventures inevitably would be joined by more flamboyant colleagues whose projects were more original than sound.

In October 1824 the Colombian Pearl Fishery Association, the first non-mining Latin American venture to be formed, announced its debut with a capital of £625,000. Subscribers were offered £25 shares for a £2 downpayment in order to raise £50,000 quickly for working capital. The remaining £23 per share need not be paid until called by the directors, who included two earls, an MP and a Royal Navy captain. The prospectus noted that the once highly profitable Colombian pearl fishing industry had been discontinued because of 'the presence of certain destructive fish' – presumably sharks and barracuda – around the oyster beds. It was now proposed to revive the industry by the use of diving bells, in which divers could descend 70 to 80ft in safety and remain underwater up to eight hours.[92]

In November the press reported that the share offering made by the Colombian Mining Association has been heavily oversubscribed. A successful outcome to the venture, the prospectus predicted confidently, would result 'from the application of British skill, machinery and experience to mines hitherto but partly worked'. The 'highly respectable' directors included Messrs. Herring, Graham and Powles, as well as four MPs. The president was Manuel José Hurtado, Colombian minister in London.[93]

On 7 December yet another mining company invited public subscription. The Rio Plata Mining Association, capitalized at £1,000,000, had been organized pursuant to a Buenos Ayres decree to exploit gold and silver mines in the provinces of Mendoza, Córdoba, San Juan and Tucumán.[94] The Brazilian Imperial Mining Association appeared on the Foreign Stock Exchange on the same day. With a capital of £1,000,000, the directors intended to work gold and silver mines in the state of Minas Gerais. The area's name itself almost guaranteed success, the prospectus intimated, since it was 'derived from the abundance and rich variety of its Minerals, every district of it containing the precious metals, as will be seen by a reference to the best Authors on the Subject of the Brazils'.[95] Even allowing for the speculative nature of mining, *The Times* concluded, the new Brazilian venture presented 'as fair an opening for the extension for British capital and industry as any of the same kind that has been offered to the public'.[96] Reports next appeared in the press that a new Mexican company was being formed for working mines at Tlapuxahua, some 'thirty leagues' from the capital, and that a further association would soon be exploiting deposits at Pasco, in Peru.[97]

Although the December weather was so damp and dreary that King George IV would scarcely venture outside the Royal Lodge at Windsor, spirits were high in the City. By New Year's Eve heavy trading had driven bond and company share quotations to new highs. Brazilian bonds were at 76, Buenos Ayres 89, Colombians (1824) at 89, Chileans 82½, Mexicans 74¾ and Peruvians at 78¾. By contrast, Austrian bonds were at 95½, Greeks 59, Portuguese 88½, Prussian 102, Russian 96 and Spanish at 22½. Anglo-Mexican Mining Association shares traded at 42 premium, Imperial Brazilian at 15½, Colombian 21½, Rio Plata 12, and United Mexican at 48 premium, reflecting, as did the rise in bond prices, the market's reaction to recognition rumours, the good news of improved Mexican political stability and the retreat of the royalists in Peru.[98]

When a Madrid newspaper produced statistics to show a decline in Mexican agriculture, manufacturing and general prosperity since the revolution, *The Times* refuted the allegations scornfully.[99] Nor could *The Courier* resist sneering at the luckless Spaniards, whose king still had not located a banker who would arrange another loan without first insisting on royal recognition of the cortes bonds. Commenting upon a report in *Le Moniteur* in Paris that a 'general confidence' prevailed in Madrid that Spain would soon repossess its Latin American colonies, the London paper's leader tartly observed that 'the Spaniards are devout Catholics, and we may suppose their minds are well trained to the exercise of implicit faith'.[100]

The self-confident patriotic superiority, if not contempt, with which the British press and its readers viewed the often unruly and inept fashion in which political and military affairs were conducted across the Channel was also reflected in popular entertainment in London over the holidays. The Royal Coburg Theatre offered a new and sanguinary melodrama entitled 'The Reign of Terror, or the Horrors of the French Revolution'. Special painted scenery complemented the drama with illustrations of the trial and execution of the king.[101] Less affluent members of the public were invited to attend the Peristrephic Panorama at which for sixpence visitors could enjoy twelve splendidly painted views which opened with Nelson trouncing the villainous French at Trafalgar nineteen years before, and concluded with the death of the Corsican tyrant on St Helena.[102]

The older year thus ended as happily as it had begun. No one foresaw troubles ahead, and George Canning, recovering from another painful gout attack, put into execution his plan to call the New World into existence in order to redress the balance of the Old which had been upset again by France.

V

RECOGNITION AT LAST

As THE NEW Year 1825 began, Latin American bonds and mining share prices were still rising steadily. When on a wet, windy 1 January Baring Brothers announced payment of the first half-yearly dividend of the Buenos Ayres loan in twelve days at their Bishopsgate offices, heavy buying drove Mexican bonds to 78, Colombia (1824) to 96, and Brazil to 78, while Real del Monte shares purchased for a £70 deposit now traded at 800 guineas.[1]

Meanwhile, still unbeknowst to the press and general public, Foreign Secretary Canning and Prime Minister Lord Liverpool had at last overcome the opposition of the king and Cabinet colleagues to Latin American diplomatic recognition. Persistent French reluctance to fix a firm date to withdraw from Spain, combined with Canning's threat to resign, had extracted the grudging acquiescence of his opponents. So, on New Year's Eve Canning had instructed the British chargé in Madrid to inform the Spanish government of Britain's intention to negotiate commercial treaties with Mexico, Colombia and Buenos Ayres. 'The effect of such treaties, when severally ratified by His Majesty, will be a Diplomatick Recognition of the "De Facto" Governments of those three countries', the foreign minister wrote.[2] Spain had no hope of reestablishing its control over the former colonies, and their continued non-recognition by European governments would be greatly injurious to 'the General Commercial Interests of the World'.[3] England would simply be acknowledging independence as a *fait accompli*, and could not be accused of having brought it about. Also, linking recognition to commercial treaties would assure acceptance by the new states of trading relationships on British terms.

The British financial community was jubilant. When the press reported the news Latin American bond prices jumped again. Feeding on speculation that they might also soon be recognized, Chile rose to 86¼ and Peru reached 81. 'It is a triumph gained by civilization over ignorance', crowed *The Morning Chronicle*, 'a perfect admission of the soundness of the opinions [we] expressed ... when the other daily prints even attempted to convert into ridicule the idea that the former possessions of Spain in America could ever become independent'.[4] Latin American mining-companies' shares also soared, and buying orders poured into the Foreign Stock Exchange from all over the United Kingdom, as well as from Europe.

Continental reaction was predictable. A furious King Ferdinand prohibited imports of British cotton and salted fish. *The Times* thought his retaliation ludicrous, 'for the statues of the Virgin Mary can hardly have proper petticoats without our heretical manufactures, neither can Lent be kept without fish of our importing'.[5] French reactions varied according to individual political inclinations. Liberal newspapers insinuated that France should do the same as Britain for commercial reasons, while supporters of the Holy Alliance hinted at dire consequences to follow.[6]

Loan promoters were quick to take advantage of the renewed optimism generated by Latin American recognition, which had erased from many people's minds – at least temporarily – the worries and scandals of the previous two years. The first new loan was for Brazil, announced on 12 January, the same day B. A. Goldschmidt advertised that the second half-yearly dividend on the latest Colombian loan would be paid at his counting house on 15 January. Although a £1,000,000 Brazilian bond issue had been placed in 1824, the total authorization had been £3,000,000. Brazilian loan commissioners in London had thought that Brazil's credit and resources merited better terms, so had borrowed only enough for the nation's immediate needs. The surge in Brazilian bond prices after January vindicated their caution, and the earlier bonds were now 12 per cent over their original issue price.[7]

When the press announced Rothschild had secured the contract on the remaining £2,000,000, the bonds rose again. Rothschild's remarkable success in improving the credit standing of his continental government clients would, *The Times* was certain, be repeated across the Atlantic. Under his auspices Brazilian government securities soon would bear quotations as high as those of the better European governments. While Rothschild had abstained from raising money for the Spanish American republics in order to avoid offending his Holy Alliance clients, Brazil, a monarchy, was a different matter.[8]

This second Brazilian loan, issued at 85, bore interest of 5 per cent per annum. The scrip quickly attracted a 3 per cent premium, while the earlier bonds issued at 75 held firm at 88½.[9] Participations were payable in twelve instalments over a year, which meant scrip for speculation could be obtained at a modest capital outlay. Rothschild's profit was immediate and considerable, however, and entailed no risk. In addition to a 2 per cent commission of £40,000, the bank received £59,000 representing six months interest, because the loan contract had been signed in January 1825, with interest backdated to the previous October. When the bonds were issued, however, they offered purchasers interest running only from April 1.[10]

The loan proceeds, it was reported, would be paid to Portugal for acknowledgement of Brazilian independence and to compensate former King Dom João VI for property he had left behind when he returned home in April 1821, leaving his son – now Emperor Pedro I – as regent. Dom João had taken with him, however, most of the cash in the Bank of Brazil, and jewels and plate collected from museums and the treasury. Even before his departure the extravagance of his court and the thousands of hangers-on he had brought from Portugal had nearly bankrupted Brazil. Gold and silver had been driven from circulation, and the country overrun with paper money and copper coins. Foreign loans were therefore vital to national survival. Since the projected recognition and peace treaty with Portugal was not as yet signed, however, when the loan proceeds were remitted to Brazil they were not credited to Portugal, but were dissipated in diplomatic missions to Europe and, when war errupted with Buenos Ayres the following January, in purchasing ships and military stores.[11]

A week later Barclay, Herring, Richardson announced that they were putting their £3,200,000 Mexican credit out to public tender. When, however, Mr Barclay entered the City of London Tavern to receive offers, he found but two bidders, B. A. Goldschmidt and a Mr Stokes. Goldschmidt's high bid of £18.15s. per share won him the contract. Other bidders arrived, but they were too late.[12] The new credit was represented by 16,000 bonds of £150 and 8,000 bonds of £100, issued in February at 86¾, a substantial improvement over the 1824 issue price. Reflecting the nation's improved credit rating, the interest rate was now 6 instead of 5 per cent, and £32,000 was to be appropriated each year to fund redemptions of principal over the thirty year maturity period. The loan was secured by mortgaging one-third of the maritime cutoms revenues, while redemption and interest payments, once amounts withheld in London were exhausted, would be remitted from Mexico six and three months ahead of their respective due dates.[13]

The credit was welcomed enthusiastically and oversubscribed by £44,000,000.[14] From the £2,776,000 actually raised, Barclay deducted their 6 per cent commission, interest and sinking fund payments for eighteen months, comissions for administering the interest and sinking fund payments and repayment of an advance to the Mexican government of £200,000 plus £4,142 in interest. The proceeds were further reduced by using £694,000 to redeem bonds of the 1824 loan, as required by a provision in Goldschmidt's earlier contract that a quarter of the proceeds of any new loan be utilized to reduce the amount of 1824 bonds outstanding. Mexico's disposable balance was thus only £1,370,497, from which were deducted repayment of advances made by British merchants in Mexico to the government and interest on the 1824 loan. The net receipts of the proceeds of the 1824 and 1825 loans totalled but £2,549,137, in exchange for which Mexico had assumed a total foreign indebtedness of £6,400,000.[15]

The lending enthusiasm evidenced by the Mexican loan's reception was not limited to Latin America. In February the press announced a 5 per cent £2,000,000 Greek loan to be issued at 56½ by Ricardo & Co., the proceeds of which would be used to retire £250,000 of the bonds of the prior issue.[16] In early March it was announced that a new 3 per cent £3,500,000 Danish loan at 75 would be launched by Thomas Wilson & Co., merchants of Wormford Court, off Throgmorton Street. Part of the loan would redeem the 1823 5 per cent issue, leading one commentator to express surprise that Denmark had preceded France 'in actually concluding a contract for reducing the interest of their public debt'.[17]

Latin American bond prices were boosted further in early March when news arrived via a cutter from Jamaica confirming Bolívar's destruction of the last royalist army in Peru.[18] The Times was delighted: 'The conquests of Cortés and Pizarro – the empires of Moctezuma and the Incas – are now as free from the despotic influence of Old Spain as they were about three hundred years ago, before a Spanish adventurer approached their shores.' The leader enthused that twenty million free people now occupied 'a vast Continent containing unexplored and incalculable resources', having replaced three centuries of bondage and prejudice with political institutions destined to promote commercial prosperity and civil freedom. Indeed, they had quickly reached a stage of political development which older states had attained only after slow, painful struggle.[19]

By mid-March Latin American bond issues were trading at their peak price, and the first Brazilian loan's contractors announced payment of the second half-yearly dividend due in April at Thomas Wison & Co.'s Wormford Court counting house. Chilean Minister Egaña and Hullet Brothers then announced the redemption from the sinking fund of 89 Chilean bonds worth £8,900. Colombia was now selling at 92½, Buenos Ayres at 91¾, Brazil at 85 and Peru at 87¾.[20]

If sometimes bored by the financial reports during the first quarter of 1825, readers even of respectable newspapers could find more risqué amusement in other press items. For example, in mid-January the celebrated Shakespearean actor Edmund Kean was sued by Alderman John Albion Cox for damages arising out of Keans 'criminal conversation' or adultery with Mrs Cox.[21] This type of action, discontinued by the mid-century, was not uncommon and generally, if the outcome were favourable to the aggrieved plaintiff, was a prelude to a divorce petition. The two-day trial was reported at length in the press. Cox had befriended Kean when the young actor was beginning his career, and helpted him obtain his first part at the Drury Lane Theatre. Kean repaid his benefactor by seducing his wife. Their affair continued for four years before Cox discovered Mrs Cox's infidelity and sued Kean for £2,000 damages.

Over thirty letters by Kean to Mrs Cox were introduced in evidence, some of which were reprinted in the daily papers. Others, to the public's undoubted dismay, were not reproduced because they were as *The Courier* explained to disappointed readers 'of so filthy a description that we cannot insert them'. The jury returned a verdict for Mr Cox, but only awarded him £800 in damages, perhaps because it had been influenced by the defence's contention that Mr Cox had been negligent by allowing his wife to stay alone in their house with a notorious womanizer.

On the evening of the day the verdict was given, Kean appeared on stage in Richard III, where the uproar from the audience, which showered him with rotten vegetables and epithets, halted the performance. After such a long absence from the stage, wrote *The Times*' editor, his reappearance on that particular date was in the worst possible taste,

> when any person who can read knows that his offence is aggravated by the most shocking circumstances of indecency, brutality, obscenity, perfidy and hypocrisy ... Let him hide himself for a reasonable time: his immediate appearance is as great an outrage to decency as if he were to walk naked through the streets at mid-day.[22]

The general passion for gambling also still persisted, and afforded no little amusement even to those who only read of it. In early April the press reported an encounter between a five-year-old male African lion named Nero and 'six mastiffs of the True English Breed' for a purse of 5,000 sovereigns. Initially betting among the blood-thirsty spectators at Warwick Race Course was five to four on the dogs. The odds quickly changed when Nero – who stood 4½ ft high and was over 13 ft in length – demolished the first of his opponents with a crunch of his mighty jaws. Four more mastiffs were quickly slain before the wounded lone survivior was rescued by its distraught owner. In subsequent bouts, however, the number of dogs was increased, and Nero badly mauled. The press then carried frequent vigorous protests against such cruel treatment to the king of the jungle and to animals in general.[23] Humans did not fare so well, however. Public hanging and mass transportation to the hell of Botany Bay continued to flourish. Over three thousand men and women rotted in the stinking, floating prison hulks, while victims of stock and bond frauds could find scant relief in the courts. King *Caveat Emptor* still ruled the City and his reign would continue unrestrained for some years to come.

City optimism meanwhile persisted. In early April B. A. Goldschmidt had announced the third half-yearly redemption of the 1824 Mexican loan, cancelling certificates valued at £26,400.[24] It was followed that same month by a further redemption from the 1825 Mexican loan proceeds of 418 more 1824 bonds, while on 17 March, Minister Egaña authorized redemption of Chilean bonds worth £62,700.[25] In May, B. A. Goldschmidt advertised the redemption of an additional £65,100 in Colombian 1824 bonds in *The Times*, 'with funds set apart from the proceeds of the last loan'.[26] Buenos Ayres bondholders breathed easier when news arrived that a commercial treaty with Great Britain had been ratified, and provided for reciprocal freedom of trade on a most favoured-nation basis, with import duties to be no higher than those paid on similar articles from other, non-party countries. The new nation's future prosperity – and that of British merchants – seemed assured.[27]

In mid-May Brazilian bonds recived a gentle boost when confirmation was received that, thanks to the mediation of British Ambassador Sir Charles Stuart, a treaty at last had been agreed with Portugal recognizing Brazil's independence.[28] On 21 May, another 6 per cent Peruvian loan was announced by banker Thomas Kinder for £616,000 at 78. The loan contract had been signed by Peruvian agent John Parrish Robertson and Thomas Kinder in January 1825, but they had postponed the issue until reliable news of a royalist defeat had reached London. Meanwhile Kinder had advanced £166,320 to Robertson, expecting to recoup the outlay as well as out-of-pocket expenses of over £11,000 when the credit was officially launched. After deducting £46,200 in advance to cover the the first fifteen months interest and Robertson's own 2 per cent commission, nearly half the proceeds would be retained to service interest payments on the first loan.[29]

The 25th of that same month was the birthday of the future Queen Victoria, an event reported in full by more enthusiastic royal-watchers among the press. That morning 'the infant Princess Victoria', and her mother the Duchess of Kent, left Kensington Palace to visit Prince Leopold at Marlborough House. The Duke of York, the Duke of Sussex, the Duke of Gloucester and various princesses and duchesses then arrived to present their congratulations, and were entertained by Prince Leopold 'with a most elegant *déjeune'*.[30] Unlike the future queen's birthday party, the new Peruvian loan was no great success. The market, still digesting the recent Brazilian and Mexican issues, was unreceptive and by the end of the first week in June, Peruvian scrip was selling at a 6½ per cent discount.[31] Mexico's credit, however, was maintained by an announcement that 509 shares of the 1824 loan valued at £66,100 would be redeemed on 1 July. Both the first quarterly dividend on the second loan and the seventh quarterly dividend on the 1824 issue would be paid in July at the New Broad Street offices of Barclay, Herring, Richardson upon presentation of the corresponding coupons one day in advance for vertification.[32]

Meanwhile, the company formation craze accelerated as new ventures were announced daily.[33] The Metropolitan Fish Company capitalized at £300,000 would supply fish at low cost to London's poor. 'It is well known' the prospectus recited, 'that, with the exception of sprats and herrings, Fish is almost excluded from the meals of the poor and reserved for the luxury of the rich.' The London Pawnbroking Company expressed a similar desire to alleviate the lot of the poor by proposing to undercut pawnbrokers while at the same time 'to employ Capital profitably, without the slightest Risk of Loss'.[34]

The Metropolitan Bath Company and one other concern were organized to establish swimming bath supplied by seawater piped from the coast, thus making available the salutary benefits of saltwater bathing to people who could not afford a seaside holiday. At the same time, their prospectuses noted, by providing safe swimming places the alarming number of drownings in the Thames and the Serpentine would be reduced. When leaving the baths, one could step into clothes cleaned by the Patent Steam Washing Company, which at its establishment in Merton, Surrey, would, by avoiding the use of soap with its impurities, 'contribute to the comfort, and what is of still more importance, to the health of the inhabitants of the metropolis.'

Even prominent aristocratic figures became involved with the companies, one of which, with Lords Lansdown and Liverpool as president and vice president, sought to revive the silk industry by promoting the cultivation of mulberry trees and silkworms in England and Ireland. Nor were improved modes of transportation neglected. A Patent Steam Carriage Company was projected and sent a prototype puffing and chugging briefly around Regent's Park. Not surprisingly, one newpaper noted, 'The jobbers at the Stock Exchange are bewildered with the variety of new schemes brought forward.'[35]

Meanwhile, parents concerned over their childrens' health were assured that the newly-established Metropolitan Dairy Company would guarantee delivery of pure undiluted milk by utilizing special containers to prevent middlemen from adding water to the cans.[35] Not only parents, however, were concerned about another prevalent problem – the plundering of graves for bodies to sell for medical dissection. Now Londoners who wished to place their mortal remains beyond the reach of body-snatchers or 'resurrection men', and at the same time make a profit, could invest in the £25 shares of The London Cemetery Association for the Security of the Dead. The association would establish a cemetery laid out and planted in the style of the Père la Chaise Cemetery in Paris, and assure 'perfect security for the repose of the Dead, effectively remedying various other evils long complained of, and yielding a very handsome return for the investment'. The profits to be derived from burial fees and the erection and sale of vaults 'considering the number of deaths, will almost exceed the powers of calculation'.[36]

Some people might be able to delay their last trip to the Cemetery Association's establishment thanks to the London Drug Company, which with its capital of £500,000 would supply 'the United Kingdom, the East and West Indies, and all parts of the world, with Unadulterated Genuine Drugs'.[37] Others might avoid catching cold in the first place thanks to the ingenuity of the promoters of The London Umbrella Company, who sought to free the public from 'the inconvenience of carrying an umbrella when the weather is fine, and of being without one when it is wet'. The company planned to establish 'stations' in the West End and in the City where umbrellas could be rented against a deposit. Pedestrians would be able to obtain an umbrella at one location, and, when the sun appeared later in the day, return it at another.[38]

Unfortunately, investing in shares was not confined to experienced speculators and merchants. Instead, retired professional people living on their savings, ladies who derived all their income from government funds and families who normally lent their money only against mortgages now saw the enormous profits to be made by speculation and became ambitious. It was easy for promoters and swindlers to tempt such people to switch out of their safe investments into more exciting wares.[39]

There were those contemporary observers who viewed the mania with dismay. For instance, *The Morning Chronicle*, in contrast to its enthusiasm for Latin American mining associations, was sceptical of most of the new companies, branding them 'bubbles' and 'schemes'.[40] *John Bull* noted soberly that the high price of iron had even induced several bankers and merchants to form The Resurrection Metal Company. According to a mock prospectus printed in the paper, the company proposed to raise tons of iron cannon balls which lay on the seabed, particularly near Trafalgar and other scenes of great British naval victories. A rich harvest was anticipated, 'since it is not the property of iron to float upon the surface of the water'. The government could have no claim on the balls, various admiralty lawyers had opined, because 'by the cannon law, the act of firing guns under proper authority was an authorized surrender of all property in the balls on the part of the Crown'. Share applications were to be directed to the company secretary, William Brassey of Ironmonger Lane in the City.[41] *The Times*, commenting more soberly upon the mania for speculating in Mexican mining companies, predicted that the extravagant hopes would end in disappointment, and readers were urged, therefore, 'not to become dupes of their own imaginations'.[42]

As with the bond issues the public was encouraged to invest by exaggerated accounts in the press and in the flood of published travellers' reports of the unexploited mineral potential of the new states. Although most investor attention focussed upon the mining companies, at least twenty other associations for Latin American operations were also enthusiastically promoted. Their romantic-sounding and impressive names, such as the South American and Hibernian Manufacturing and Trading Association, the South American and Colonial Gas Company, the Haytian Trading Company, the London, Colombian and Mexican Steam Packet Company, and the Honduras Indigo Company, captured the popular imagination and offered modest, stay-at-home investors the opportunity to become vicariously involved with exotic and faraway lands. Thus, for only a £5 deposit widows and bankers alike could become shareholders in the Anglo-Mexican Mint Company, which had been capitalized at £250,000 to coin (at great profit) the legendary, limitless silver and gold of the land of Moctezuma. Both the Duke of York and the Duke of Wellington were patrons of the American Colonial Steam Navigation Company, which with its capital of £600,000 proposed 'to establish lines of steam vessels to communicate from the United Kingdom to North America, the West Indies and the new States of South America'. Although the shares had a nominal value of £100, they could be obtained for a £10 deposit.[43]

Also for a deposit of but £10, armchair travellers could reserve a £100 share in the Atlantic and Pacific Junction and Central American Mining and Trading Association, which planned to open a canal through Nicaragua to link the Atlantic and Pacific by using the navigable San Juan River and Lake Nicaragua as part of the route.

Although the Spanish government had commissioned several surveys, no action had been taken. Now declared the prospectus,

> British capital, combined with British energy, will complete this important work; and it will be reserved for Englishmen, under the reign of George the Fourth, to carry into effect an enterprise, the advantages of which every commercial nation has perceived, and most writers of Latin America have pointed out.[44]

Even the normally sceptical *John Bull* wished this company success, stating that 'Among the many projects of the present day for the employment of British capital, we know of none so pregnant with important benefits to commerce in general, and to that of England in particular.'[45]

Not all the companies had purely commercial objectives. Many Britons had long assumed that an independent Latin America would also provide outlets for the nation's unemployed, who posed a political threat as well as a burden on Poor Law resources. Now, reversing the Spanish colonial policy, the new nations encouraged foreigners to come and settle in their underpopulated expanses. For example, in June 1823 a Colombian Congressional Decree authorized the executive branch to organize 'the emigration of European and North American foreigners into this Republic', and allocated approximately 200,000 acres of land for colonization.[46] Similar legislation was enacted in Guatemala and other states. Thus encouraged, British merchants, politicans and socially conscious individuals formed companies which would promote emigration and also return handsome profits to their shareholders.

In March 1825, sensitive as ever to the public mood, Messrs Powles, Herring and Graham expanded their Latin American lending and mining interests by organizing the Colombian Agricultural Association to take advantage of the benefits offered by Colombian legislation. Capitalized at £1,300,000, the company proposed to convey emigrants to Colombia and settle them upon large grants Powles had obtained near Lake Maracaibo, Medellín and Caracas. The association president was Colombian Minister Manuel José Hurtado, and, in addition to the ever present Herring, Graham and Powles, the officers and directors included five MPs. Whatever the company's merits as an investment, one commentator wrote, the venture 'if judiciously conducted, will greatly benefit Colombia and accelerate its rising prosperity' – thereby presumably enabling it to service and repay its foreign debt.[47] The prospectus presented a glowing picture of Colombian agriculatural potential: 'With a soil capable of yielding almost every species of agricultural production, it possesses a variety of climate adapted ... to the cultivation of the fruits both of tropical and European countries, and to the general varieties of the human constitution'. The association would advance passage money to potential settlers, convey them to this earthly paradise only six weeks sail from Britain, and supply them with housing, tools, provisions and credit until they could produce their first crops. Once the crops were sold the colonists would be expected to repay the advances at 5 per cent interest, as well as rental of 4*d*. per acre per annum for their lands – which they had the option to purchase at 4*s*. per acre.

Further south, the Buenos Ayres government in January 1825, also issued a decree encouraging foreign immigration. In response, various Stock Exchange operators and the Buenos Ayres London representatives formed the Rio de la Plata Agricultural Association, capitalized at £500,000. The twelve directors included four baronets, an MP and an admiral. The company was assigned a tract of fertile land in the province of Entre Ríos upon which to grow wheat and mill flour, and in addition the Buenos Ayres Government promised the settlers exemption from military service, taxes, and import and export duties.[48] The association's basic objective, claimed the prospectus, copies of which were available from its offices in the Royal Exchange, was 'to remove part of the unemployed agricultural labourers of Great Britain and Ireland to the settlements of the Association in South America and to establish them there as independent farmers.' As if to allay any fears potential immigrants might entertain for their own personal safety, investors and settlers alike were assured that the first settlements in Entre Ríos would be enclosed by the Uruguay and Paraná Rivers 'which effectively protect the province from the incursions of the Indians'.[49]

Meanwhile, share prices of the mining associations formed during 1824 jumped to new heights.[50] Anglo-Mexican, Brazilian Imperial, Colombian and United Mexican Mining Association shares, upon each of which £10 had been paid, were trading at £158, £66, £82 and £155 respectively. Real del Monte shares, upon which £70 had been paid, were now quoted at £1,350, while Colombian Pearl Fishery shares for which £2 had been paid were trading at £25. Inspired by this market receptivity, a fresh group of entrepreneurs began promoting further mining companies. Unlike the companies formed during 1824, however, most of the newcomers had no specific mines under contract before they sought subscriptions from the public. Instead, after leafing through Baron von Humboldt's works for suitable districts in which to begin operations, the directors used the first shareholder downpayment to dispatch agents to negotiate leases with local mine owners. Investors were not, however, discouraged by such slipshod practices.[51]

Among the first of these to appear on the Stock Exchange in the New Year was the Chilean Mining Association, capitalized at £1,000,000 to work silver, gold, lead, tin and iron deposits. Minister Mariano Egaña was president of the board of directors. The prospectus reported that Chile was peaceful, had long been independent, and enjoyed a healthy climate, abundant water and wood, and a goodly supply of cheap labour.[52] It was soon followed by the Anglo-Chilean Mining Association, again under Egaña's patronage, and capitalized at £1,500,000. Chilean mines were so extensive, the prospectus observed, that considerable capital in addition to that of the companies already announced would be required to exploit them properly.[53] By the end of January two additional Mexican groupings were soliciting subscriptions from the public, the Tlapuxahua and the Bolaños. Their shares were enthusiastically received, and were soon selling at £200 to £300 premiums.[54]

Mining associations were being formed so quickly as to cause *The Times* to remark that 'a new day seldom passes without the arriving at maturity of some great project, requiring a large amount of capital, independently of numerous minor undertakings which escape notice in the crowd'.[55] For example, the Peruvian Mining & Trading Association organised in March 1825, with an authorized capital of £1,000,000, was probably typical of the associations now being hastily formed by speculators who hoped to make a quick profit on share sales without actually beginning operations. The one-and-a-half page prospectus revealed that of the ten directors, one was an MP, another a lord, and a third a Royal Naval admiral. 'The objects of the Company are to carry on a regular trading intercourse with Peru and to work such mines in that country as, upon careful investigation, shall be found worthy of attention.'[56]

Another example, the General South American Mining Association was capitalized at £2,000,000, twice the usual amount for mining companies. Its intended area of operations was vague. The prospectus merely noted that South America was known 'to abound in valuable minerals and contains inexhaustible Resources in Gold, Silver, Quicksilver, Copper and other metals'.[57] The next mining venture to appear was the Pasco Peruvian Mining Company, capitalized at £1,000,000. A deposit of £15 on the £100 shares would enable investors to participate vicariously in the extraction of the silver and gold which had underpinned the Inca, and later the Spanish, empires.[58] If the Spaniards had succeeded in operating the mines at a profit, wrote a satisfied Pasco Peruvian shareholder to *John Bull*, 'will not the probability be, that these things may be much better

PERUVIAN MINING COMPANY.

This is to Certify, that *Daniel Barclay Chapman Esq*
of *23 Lombard Street* — is the Proprietor
of one Share numbered *4583* in the Capital of the PERUVIAN MINING
COMPANY, as established by an Indenture of Regulations, bearing date the
24th day of March, 1825, subject nevertheless to the observance and performance of the Covenants, Agreements, and Provisions contained in the same
Indenture.

London, 28th March, 1825.

} Directors.

N.B. This Certificate is not transferable, and must be returned upon
a transfer of Shares being made. All transfers of Shares must be made
in such manner as may be prescribed by the Directors.

No Transfer can be made within ten days of the first Thursday in
March in any year, during which period the Books will be shut.

10. Peruvian Mining Company Certificate. The Peruvian Mining Company was organized in
1825 during the company formation boom. The Company soon collapsed and its share
holders recovered but little on its liquidation.

performed by Englishmen, who so well understand the use of machinery, than by Spaniards, who are comparatively ignorant of its application?'[59]

The mining-company prospectuses directed at the buying public contained scant hard economic data. They relied heavily on the general observations of Baron von Humboldt, whose comments were now so hopelessly outdated and unreliable that prospectuses based upon them were at best inadequate, if not deliberately misleading. Potential shareholders in the Potosí, La Paz and Peruvian Mining Association were simply assured that '[t]he mineral wealth of Peru, and particularly of Potosí, is too well-known to require any comment.'[60] Further south, the Anglo-Chilean Mining Association's prospectus avoided distracting investors with boring economic details and asserted succinctly that '[t]he territories of Chili are known to abound in gold, silver, copper, tin and other minerals.'[61]

Not only mining-company prospectuses combined scanty economic data with commercial naivety. Prospective investors in the Brazilian Agricultural and Jewel Company were told that the new entity would 'barter' British manufacturers for the 'Diamonds, Emeralds, Amethysts and the various precious stones and gems which abound in the interior of Brazil'.[62] Although for only a £3 deposit, investors could obtain a £100 share, few purchasers came forward. Perhaps they feared competition from the South American Gem Company, organized with offices on Bishopsgate a few months earlier to procure from Brazil and other parts of South America precious stones of every description for sale in Britain and the continent.

'When we reflect upon the enormous demand for Precious Stones of all sorts ... it is presumed that the Speculating World will immediately see the certain and immense profits which will accrue to a company undertaking, with a sufficient capital to supply the still increasing demand for these objects of luxury and elegance', the prospectus explained.[63]

As with bond promoters, mining venture promoters were not averse to commissioning, printing and circulating pamphlets extolling the virtues and profitability of their enterprise. Among the authors enlisted to boost shares was the young solicitors' clerk Benjamin Disraeli, himself a speculator in mining shares, who wrote three 'anonymous' pamphlets defending the Latin American mining companies against their detractors, who insisted upon comparing the wave of speculation to the South Sea Bubble. Disraeli's faith was misplaced, and he lost over £2,500 he could ill-afford. His correspondence suggests that his principle paymaster was none other than the ubiquitous and not over-scrupulous John D. Powles.[64]

By late January the mania to acquire mining and other shares had reached such proportions that the United States minister in London, Richard Rush, could write to Secretary of State John Quincy Adams in Washington D.C., that

> nothing was ever like it before, not even the days of the South Sea scheme ... Shares in some of the ... companies have advanced to seventeen hundred per cent within a few months, and are bought with avidity at this price. I hear it said that noblemen of great estates, and directors of the Bank of England, participate; also that princes of the blood press forward to obtain shares.[65]

By March, however, concern over the hectic speculation was increasing in parliament. From the beginning of the company share boom, promoters hoped parliamentary approval might immunize their companies from the possible impact of the so-called Bubble Act, passed in 1720 in the wake of the South Sea Bubble scandal. The act forbad individuals from acting or presuming to act as a corporate body, and the raising of a transferable stock or the assigning of such stock without authorization by an act of parliament or royal charter. While the intention was to prevent a repetition of the frauds of 1718–19, the act placed severe hindrances on corporate formation for legitimate purposes.[66] Because of its severe penalties, it had remained a virtual dead letter for many years. The resurgence of the company formation mania in the 1820s, however, caused legislators to consider its revival. Although the applicability of the act was uncertain, and it would eventually be repealed in 1825, to avoid its possible impact most mining companies sought to attract MPs to their boards of directors, who in return for free shares would facilitate passage of the necessary legislation authorizing their activities.

Doubts over the wisdom of endorsing the new companies were expressed with particular vehemence during the heated parliamentary debate over the Pasco Peruvian Mining Association Bill. John Cam Hobhouse, MP for Westminster, called the company a bubble with no substance, the shares of which were selling at a premium artificially engineered by its promoters. The mines, he noted, were located 13,000 ft above sea level and all prior attempts to work them had failed. The effect the mining schemes had upon the public was 'monstrous', and he knew of 'many instances where the hard earnings of many years had been disposed of in those plans which, he had no doubt, would, in the end, come to nothing'.[67]

While *The Courier* mockingly suggested Hobhouse rely more on concrete facts than upon 'loose talk', some parliamentary colleagues were more sympathetic.[68] Alexander Baring, MP, whose bank had studiously avoided association with the mining companies, stated forthrightly that he saw little difference between the noblemen gambling 'in the hells of St James's Street', and the merchant in the Royal Exchange. The mining companies, he believed, would 'turn out to delusions and that many innocent persons who had embarked their little capital in them would be awakened one day unpleasantly from their dreams of grandeur, by the intelligence that their all was lost.'[69] This scathing prediction by the City's most respected merchant banker and a leading MP provoked vigorous protests from John Powles. It was certainly not a 'delusion', he answered in a letter published in the press, appropriately enough on April Fool's Day, that until 1810 the Mexican mines had been the source of 'considerable remittances' to Spain, even after defraying the expenses of the viceroyalty. Sounding a familiar refrain, Powles asked whether it was unreasonable to believe that superior British capital, skill and machinery could render the mines again productive.[70] Over the next two months it appeared as if Powles had successfully neutralized the impact of Baring's remarks. New companies multiplied 'with a rapidity which ought to make prudent men look about them ... before they leap and to reflect how impossible it is that all the current undertakings should succeed', cautioned *The Times*. By mid-June, however, bond and share investors alike were becoming nervous, and training was thin.[71]

Investors must have been both curious and disturbed when in late July *The Morning Chronicle* imprudently, under the clumsy guise of a letter to the editor, alleged the misapplication of the proceeds of a loan to an unnamed country, but which readers could easily identify as Chile. Similarly, they must have recognized ex-Minister José Antonio de Irisarri as the 'Creole Spaniard' whom the newspaper accused of taking 'two hundred thousand pounds Sterling of John Bull's money to Paris, where he now out-tops princes in his style of living'.[72] The Guatemalan promptly filed suit for libel and thus began a litigation which would entertain the public until a decision was rendered in late December.

The summer of 1825 was the hottest in many years. Horses along the post roads collapsed and died in their hundreds. The temperature soared into the high 80s, even reaching 89° in the shade at Bath.[73] The heat was so enervating that brokers sweltering at the Stock Exchange probably scarcely had the energy to wonder or care if the gentle slide in Latin American bond prices which had begun unperceptibly in late April would ever be reversed. On 16 April, Chile had been steady at 85¼, Brazil at 85½, Colombia at 91, Mexico at 78½ and Peru at 85¾. European bonds were only at slightly higher levels, with Austria at 98¾, Denmark at 101 and Russia at 95, while one finanical writer had commented that 'the rage for speculation does not appear to have abated much'.[74] On 15 June, while 'amusing himself . . . with one of his children on his lawn', Nathan Rothschild slipped and dislocated a shoulder. After prompt medical attention he was back the next day at his desk at St Swithin's Lane in the City 'in a fair way of doing well' and preparing to announce a partial redemption of his Prussian loan and payment of the half-yearly dividend on the Neopolitan loan.[75] Latin American bond prices were not destined to demonstrate the same recuperative powers as that redoubtable financier. By the end of July Brazil had dropped to 81¼, Chile to 81, Colombia to 85¾, Mexico to 75 and Peru to 74.[76]

The market did not improve appreciably even when in August Portugal signed the treaty recognizing Brazilian independence, perhaps because of the indemnity extracted from Brazil. Although the improverished former Spanish colonies had steadfastly rejected any suggestions that they might 'purchase' independence and recognition from Spain, Brazilian Emperor Pedro I was less scrupulous. He undertook in return for recognition to guarantee service and payment of the remaining £1,400,000 of the £1,500,000 5 per cent loan Portugal had issued in London in 1823, as well as to pay his royal father £600,000 for the properties he had left in Brazil.[77]

In late August investor unease surely increased when news arrived that Brazilian troops were beseiging Montevideo as part of an attempt to incorporate into Brazil the so-called Banda Oriental, a vast expanse of territory on the eastern bank of the Río de la Plata. Patriot troops were resisting and looking to Buenos Ayres for support. War between the two nations now seemed likely, and, the press opined, in such a conflict Brazil would suffer most. Indeed, the monarchy itself might collapse it the other republican states decided to join Buenos Ayres in freeing the continent 'from the only remnant of monarchial institutions which has been suffered to remain'.[78]

Despite investor misgivings about the future solidity of their Latin American bonds and shares, curiosity about Latin America continued unabated. The proliferation of new travel accounts and histories led one book reviewer to complain that 'the press at the moment is pouring forth such an abundance of volumes on South America, and the danger seems to be that of perplexity as to those that are genuine and really useful'.[79] Public entertainments of varying cerebral pretensions also evidenced this continued fascination with the New World. For only a shilling one could visit Mr Bulloch's Mexican exhibition at the Egyptian Hall on Picadilly and view 'ancient idols and antiquities' together with models of fruits and flowers and 'an invaluable collection of minerals'. A native of Mexico in the costume of his country was on hand to explain the exhibits 'as far as his knowledge of the English language permits'.[80] Elsewhere interest was expressed in more sophisticated forms.

In mid-June the Duchess of Rutland 'and many fashionables of distinction' gathered at the Argyll Room for a musical evening.[81] After several vocalists had done their turns, the celebrated Italian 'Improvisatore' Signor Pestrucci, accompanied by a colleague on the pianoforte, extemporaneously composed sonnets based on themes provided by the audience. When someone proposed 'Bolívar', without hesitation Pestrucci produced a florid improvisation which was enthusiastically applauded:

> Oh! Thou who languished not in love
> But are a true prodigy of glory!
> Thou shalt prove thyself the destroyer of every vice,
> In triumphing more rapid than the wind!
> Bolívar! Though hadst no teacher
> In the art of tormenting traitors...
> Oh! That a Tasso were living to sing thy praises
> Or that I were at least a Terrence for thy sake!

Five year later, after the death of the Liberator, this event, if remembered at all by its participants, would seem sad and even more absurd.

Given the deterioration of financial confidence, it was not surprising that when in late August the last Latin American loan was announced – to the United Provinces of Central America – the response was lukewarm. By the end of 1824 several offers by London financiers had been presented directly to the central government in Guatemala City, including a proposition by Barclay, Herring, Richardson's local representative, John Bailey. Eventually on 6 December 1824, the national assembly authorized the government to contract a 6 per cent loan with Bailey for 7,142,857 pesos (£1,428,571), secured by income from the government tobacco monopoly and the maritime sales tax. In return, Bailey issued a letter of credit to the government for 20,000 pesos to finance a London legation, which could negotiate both recognition and a commercial treaty with Great Britain, as well as control disposition of the loan proceeds.[82]

On 22 August 1825, Barclay put the loan out to tender. Only one offer was made and the following day Barclay planted an article in the press extolling the mineral wealth and political stability of the new borrower, now recognized by the United States, Colombia and Mexico, and to which a British consul-general had been appointed last May. Moreover, 'the character of the people is described as mild and peaceable, and the government is stated to be free from any internal debt.'[83] Nevertheless, when the new loan was offered to the market at 73, it found few takers. Only £163,000 of the bonds were placed, and the scrip was soon selling at a steep discount as a major financial crisis unrolled through Great Britain.[84]

A number of interrelated factors caused the so-called 'panic' of 1825 which, before it peaked in December, threatened to empty the reserves of the Bank of England and leave the country 'within twenty-four hours of barter'. Cotton prices and other commodities had been rising steadily since late 1824, encouraging a heavy speculation in commodities to accompany the already booming market in foreign bonds and company shares. Overtrading streadily drove prices up even more, and helped create an import boom. By 1825 wool imports had grown from 20 to 38,000,000 lb. over the 1822–4 average, cotton from 161 to 222,000,000, indigo from 5 to 7,500,000, silk from 404 to 800,000 lb.[85]

Inevitably, the eventual over-supply triggered a dramatic fall in commodity prices in the last quarter of 1825 and the collapse of several large trading firms in the north of England, which in turn unleashed a general panic. Bank of England directors, already concerned by the speculation which they had facilitated either directly by issuing paper money and credit, or indirectly by discounting bills drawn on other banks, now saw their own gold reserves shrink from £13,500,000 in January 1824, to £6,650,000 by April 1825. The Bank then decided to restrict credit to protect its reserves, and thus further contributed to the collapse of the entire fragile speculative edifice.[86]

Government consols, at 97 a few months before, fell to 89 while money to meet calls on shares as well as to pay instalments on foreign bonds was now virtually unobtainable. *The Morning Chronicle* accused the Bank of England directors of contributing to the crisis 'by having issued paper money heretofore so freely as to make "accommodation" of all sorts easy, and induce extensive speculations in merchandise, in foreign funds and in shares, and by now having limited . . . their issues in a sudden manner'.[87] Not everyone blamed the Bank. As *The Courier* reminded readers, it was not the Bank's function to regulate the economy by issuing or withholding notes. The Bank should play a passive role, answering to market forces but not creating them, and, 'like an Aeolian harp', respond 'with a rich and ready acquiescence to the ever-varying undulations of the atmosphere.'[88] The panic in the City increased daily. Colombian bonds dropped to 73 and Chile to 77, while Brazilian scrip, formerly offered at a premium, by 1 September was trading at a 10 per cent discount.[89]

The loan contractors sought vainly to halt the slide by emphasizing the solvency of their borrowers. On 15 September, Minister

Egaña announced redemption of 82 Chilean bonds totalling £8,200.[90] A week later both Goldschmidt and Barclay, Herring, Richardson widely advertised the 1 October dividend payments on their respective Mexican loans, while Rothschild announced the payment of the half-yearly dividend on the £2,000,000 Brazilian issue.[91] The following month Herring, Graham and Powles declared that the half-yearly dividend due 1 November for the 1822 Colombian loan would be paid at their counting house off Cornhill. On the same day Rothschilds announced redemption of 78 Brazilian bonds representing £29,400.[92] None of these measures had any appreciable effect on bond prices.

On 17 October *The Morning Chronicle*, perhaps hoping to arrest the decline, announced that Peruvian scrip was now fully paid up and turned into stock, and that only some small payments were still due on the Brazilian and Mexican scrip before it too would become stock represented by bonds. 'There will then only remain the Guatemalan scrip, all the others being completely paid up.'[93] The news was certainly misleading as regarded Peru, since it implied that the entire issue of £616,000 had been placed when at least £250,000 in bonds had been retained by Robertson and the promoters and not offered to the public. The bonds later would be gradually sold between December 1825 and May 1826 at discounts far greater than that at which the bonds had first been offered.[94]

The Morning Chronicle's comments concerning Brazil and Mexican scrip were also highly suspect. By the end of the year the scrip was still on offer because funds to complete bond purchases were almost unobtainable. Latin American bondholders had hitherto been able to secure credit to honour their subscriptions or make additional purchases by borrowing against the bonds as security. Since September, however, bankers concerned over the rapid decline of the bonds on the Stock Exchange had been refusing to advance money on them as formerly.[95] The bankers' reluctance to accept bonds as security of course depressed them still further. The increasing gloom at the Stock Exchange was not lightened by news in early October that runs on banks in the west country had caused two failures.[96]

Coinciding with and augmenting the general economic downturn was the realization by investors in Latin American mining and other ventures that some companies were probably swindles and never intended to function, such as the Haytian Mining Association, organized by Gregor MacGregor's former colleague Herman Hendriks.[97] But even where a company's motives were honourable, lack of proper market research could still bring disaster. In 1824 a company had been formed to manufacture butter from the milk of the many cattle reputed to throng the Argentine pampas. Subsequently the directors sent Scottish milkmaids to Buenos Ayres where they were soon churning immense quantities of butter. The product proved unsaleable since not only did it not keep, but the local populace preferred to cook with oil instead![98] Even investors in the more reputable mining associations became disheartened as reports from their engineers on the true state of affairs in Latin America circulated through the Stock Exchange and City coffee houses. By July it had become evident that the obstacles of an unfamiliar climate, a hostile geography, and the lack of adequate ports and roads, combined with the effect on the mines themselves of fifteen years of civil war, had been vastly underrated. Considering the problems they confronted, all the mining ventures were underfinanced. Only two had nominal capitals of £2,000,000, and while the total authorized capital of all the mining companies amounted to £24,190,000, only £3,508,500 was ever paid in.

Moreover, the expertise and technology developed in British coal and tin mines was not readily transferable to the Latin American environment. Experienced Spaniards who might have shared their knowledge had long since fled, or been killed. In any event, local labour was scarce and expensive, and the companies had to bring all their skilled workers, including blacksmiths, carpenters, superintendents and engineers from Britain at great cost. But even such extreme measures were not always successful. Cornish miners sent out by the Colombian Mining Association could not adapt to the climate and soon became addicted to inexpensive local rum. The association's young chief engineer was Robert Stephenson, later to achieve fame with his steam locomotive 'The Rocket'. After arriving in La Guayra in June 1824 he soon discovered to his chagrin with the well-designed machinery cast at his father's plant near Newcastle was too bulky to transport on mules over Colombia's primitive roads and mountain paths. Worse still, during his three years in Colombia Stephenson could never get from any man more than half a day's work, and he always had nearly a third of his hundred and sixty subordinates 'disabled by drink'.[99]

Clearly even the most viable ventures could only return the promised dividends after additional massive capital injections. For example, in 1825, the fabled Real del Monte mines were not yet operational because the men were employed constructing roads to convey the ore to the smelters, and the mine shafts were still flooded after years of disuse. The most sanguine observers now perceived that instead of sending silver and gold up their shafts, the mines simply swallowed the money subscribed and then demanded more. Nor was the outlook any more favourable for colonization ventures. In early August 1825, the Mexican Agricultural and Colonization

Company announced to share applicants that upon 'mature deliberation' it had decided to postpone any share distribution until further notice.[100]

It also now become apparent that the expected Latin American markets for British manufacturers had failed to materialize. As with the loans and the mining and commercial companies, expectations had outrun reality. The achievement of independence did not automatically bring with it the expected expansion into new, profitable overseas markets. After years of war, large sections of the interiors of the new nations were left devastated and depopulated. The expulsion or flight of Spanish merchants produced such a capital shortage that only a thin layer of the more affluent populace in the capital and coastal cities could afford British textiles and other goods which had flooded into their ports. The great majority of people relied instead for their clothing, cutlery, furniture and other items on cheaper, local manufacture.[101] The products of Sheffield and Birmingham were either left to rust and rot on the wharfs at Rio de Janeiro, Valparaiso and Callao, or were sold locally at prices far below their retail value at home.

A writer in The Quarterly Review, commenting in 1824 on two books written by British travellers, noted that while the authors remarked on the large number of British and North American vessels which flocked to South America, they did

> not notice what sales have been made of those cargoes . . . nor the ruinous losses which attended their adventures. The same system of deception which has duped British capitalists, under the name of loans, has tempted traders to send goods to Chile, far beyond the amount for which the commodities of the country can ever pay.[102]

Back in London, company shareholders were ignoring calls to complete their share purchase instalments and had begun to sell, driving prices down further. Other investors who had not signed deeds of association within the prescribed time limits ignored the extended grace periods offered by the directors of the Anglo-Chilean and Chilean Mining Associations, even though they risked forfeiture of money already advanced. By the end of October, Real del Monte shares which once had sold at £1,550 were trading for £200.[103] The non-mining companies were also collapsing, and City coffee houses and traverns were jammed with shareholder meetings voting their dissolution. Shareholders received but fractions of their investments after deducting expenses. The experience of the London and Manchester Equitable Loan Company investors was typical. Of the £6,000 subscribed, £4,000 had disappeared in directors fees and other expenses, leaving but £2,000 to be divided among shareholders.[104] Not all those involved with the companies suffered, however.

Lawyer's fees were calculated at 2s.6d. per share of a liquidated company, causing one commentator to write that '[w]e early anticipated that the Lawyers would have a rich harvest of these associations.'[105] The general panic continued well into November. The alarm at the Foreign Stock Exchange was particularly 'frightful' and Latin American bonds were 'in a deplorable state'.[106] Colombia touched 64½, Mexico 62, Peru 50, Chile 55, and Guatemala scrip was now offered at a seven per cent discount. Trading at the Foreign Stock Exchange virtually had halted by the end of the month.

Widespread fears that Brazil could not remit funds required for debt servicing were not allayed by publication in November of what was intended to be a reassuring communiqué from the Brazilian government. The Emperor of Brazil had ordered that customs revenues collected at Rio de Janeiro be deposited each year 'in a chest' at the Imperial Treasury until they totalled £60,000, which would be remitted twice-yearly to London to meet interest and sinking fund requirements. Of this, £25,000 would be distributed via the contractors for the first loan and $35,000 via N. M. Rothschild as contractor for the second loan. Customs authorities at Bahia, Pernambuco and Maranhão were ordered to provide annual quotas of £60,000 each, thus raising £240,000 for transfer to London.[107]

Latin American loan promoters during November made several other attempts to restore sagging investor confidence by placing favourable letters and advertisements in the press. *The Courier* in particular launched an ambitious attempt to influence public opinion with what was announced to be a series of four articles on Latin American finances. The anonymous author, 'Mercator', was reputedly the best qualified person in the country to discuss this topic 'due to his general knowledge of the actual conditions of the South American Republics, and his access to official documents. In an analysis of Mexican finances, Mercator showed that during the past year receipts had exceeded expenditures by over $2,000,000. Moreover, he wrote, the proceeds of the second loan had not been touched, leaving a fund for contingencies. Mexican finances were therefore presumably quite healthy and there was no cause for investor concern.[108]

Not all observers were convinced, and on 30 November the public was reminded in the press that the sums retained by contractors to pay the interest instalments and redemptions on the Latin American loans would be exhausted in six months. 'And the probability is that not a single remittance has yet been received to pay the dividends;

and it is probably a long time before the South American Governments will be able to remit money...'[109] Even *The Morning Chronicle* now reluctantly confessed that

> the great difficulty with respect to the South American States ... is that there are few public men sufficiently upright in them to whom the disposal of loans can be safely entrusted ... The history of the appropriation of the Chili Loans, for instance, which will soon be laid before the public, will exhibit an extent of profligacy almost beyond example.[110]

Despite the contractors' efforts, on 2 December bond prices had dropped even further – Peru to 46, Buenos Ayres to 76 and Colombia (1824) to 63. Mexican 1824 bonds collapsed to 64, even though two weeks before £78,000 in bonds had been redeemed from proceeds of the second loan.[111]

Meanwhile, during November British government securities and consols also had continued to fall, although money could still be raised on them at 3 to 3½ per cent per annum. Nonetheless, unsecured, well-known merchants' bills were increasingly difficult to negotiate, and people became even more reluctant to take paper money. They insisted on gold, and there was none to be had. By the end of the month the panic became almost uncontrollable when news reached the City that the highly respected Plymouth Bank had suspended payments. Another west country bank failure was made public on 3 December.[112]

The rickety national financial structure had been determined by the Banking Act of 1709, which enabled the Bank of England to dominate banking throughout the nation. Legislation forbade the organization of rival banks as joint stock companies, and limited the number of partners of a bank to six 'so that any small provincial tradesman, a fruiterer, a grocer or a butcher, might open a bank' and issue its own notes, 'whilst the right of issue was refused to genuine companies, well deserving of confidence'.[113] The system would function only so long as the over 500 provincial or so-called country banks in England and Wales with paper money issuing licenses retained customer confidence, and the Bank of England and other London banks were willing to accept their paper. These country banks were particularly vulnerable. In case of a run London banks could convert good security into cash on short notice. Provincial bankers, however, had to rely on their own reserves in a crisis since London was too far away for a supply of money to arrive in time to cope with extraordinary, unforeseen demands.

In addition many banks were undercapitalized and lacked reserves adequate to cope with a sudden crisis, such as that with which they were confronted when the Bank of England, alarmed at the uncontrolled speculation, at first stopped discounting altogether and then raised the rate to 5 per cent.[114] The decline in Latin American bond and share prices contributed to the chaos. Banks which had made advances to customers found that upon liquidation the heavily depreciated securities which they had accepted as collateral would not yield sufficient funds either to satisfy their obligations to other institutions, or to pay depositors when general lack of confidence produced a nationwide banking run.

Incredibly, despite weakening bond prices, the loan contractors with admirable determination continued to deny the obvious. In early December 'Mercator' again appeared in print, this time to reassure Colombian bondholders.[115] Although financial data on Colombia was not as plentiful as for Mexico, Mercator felt justified in making 'reasonable estimates' based on available information. He calculated total government revenue at approximately $7,000,000, half of which derived from customs duties. These could be expected to increase, like they had in Brazil, as trade with Europe expanded. The foreign debt was £6,750,000, of which £82,500 had already been redeemed. Government expenditures totalled but £3,000,000 per annum, which would fall as military expenditure decreased following the successful Peruvian campaign. Mercator concluded by asserting 'that no State in the civilized world which, in proportion to its capabilities, is *less burthened with debt* or more capable to the discharge of its engagements than the Republic of Colombia'.

In early December the City was alive with rumours of more pending bank failures. Then, in mid-month the reputable London bank of Sir Peter Pole, Thornton & Co. suspended payments, sinking with it all but the strongest of its forty-four correspondent country banks. Pole's failure sparked a run on London banks, causing at least three more failures. 'The dense fog which prevailed throughout the day was scarcely more gloomy than the countenances of those affected by the present alarming state of the money market'.[115] Provincial papers echoed the concern of the London dailies, and *The Aberdeen Chronicle* reported that '[t]he alarm in the London money market continues; so numerous are the causes, real and imaginary, that it almost seems impossible to fix a limit to the fall'.[117]

Notes from the country bank survivors poured into the City by the morning mails, forcing London banks to hire extra clerks to examine and pay the unusual amount of claims. Generally, however, tradesmen were reluctant to accept anything but Bank of England notes or gold. But not even Bank of England notes could fill the gap created by the public's refusal to take local bank paper. For some time the Bank had stopped issuing one pound notes, and at one point even ran out of £5 and £10 notes before a fresh supply arrived from the printers the next day in time to stave off total disaster.[118] Pressure to take remedial action mounted, while the Mint worked day and night to produce gold sovereigns. This in turn worsened the drain on reserves without alleviating the coin scarcity. The shortage 'became a veritable famine' after the prestigious London Bank failed, dragging under still more financial houses.[119]

Fortunately by mid-December the panic began to abate following the arrival of 150,000 gold sovereigns from France, paid into the Bank of England by N. M. Rothschild.[120] Then £600,000 to £700,000 in one pound notes were discovered in a box in the cellars of the Bank of England. These had been put aside unissued in 1822 when one pound notes were withdrawn from circulation, and apparently forgotten. The Bank then hired extra clerks to fill in the numbers, dates and signatures so that, along with gold, they could be issued as quickly as possible to the country banks. One commentator a few years later asserted that the crisis had already begun to ease by the time the notes were put into circulation due to the contraction caused by the destruction of nearly all the country paper, the virtual halt in business transactions, and the retention by bankers of funds to increase reserves. Nevertheless, pressure on Bank of England clerks was still so great that they worked through the Sunday before Christmas. Rather than going home some slept instead at the Bank.[121] Although by the end of December money was daily becoming more abundant, failures would continue, albeit at a slightly slower pace.[122]

The year thus ended on a sour note, with bankers and investors wearily surveying the wreckage of over seventy financial institutions which had collapsed in the last three hectic weeks. Even the City rumour mill seemed momentarily exhausted, and the press warned readers against spreading unfounded tales concerning the solvency of commercial houses and banks: 'Credit, like the honour of a female, is of too delicate a nature to be treated with levity – the slightest hint may inflict an infamy which no subsequent effort can repair.'[123]

The New Year promised scant relief. Although some institutions which had suspended payments would recover, reports of the liquidation of the Mexican Mining Association were widely circulated by the press as a foretaste of the future. Letters from Mexico confirmed earlier information that although the Anglo-Mexican, United Mexican and the Real del Monte Mining Associations had expended over £1,000,000 on local labour, their mines were still half-flooded. Once the darlings of the Stock Exchange, their continued viability seemed doubtful. Alexander Baring's prediction in parliament in March that the mining companies would turn out to be delusions was now proven correct, while Powles' vigorous contradiction was exposed as wishful thinking.

The future of the Latin American bond issues was similarly beclouded, although redemptions and interest payments had been made when due throughout the crisis. On 17 December, *The Morning Chronicle*, even though its new editor was already being sued by Irisarri for libel as a result of its reference to him in July, launched a more direct personal attack upon the former Chilean envoy. It had earlier called the Chilean loan a 'notorious transaction, that will occupy a monumental place in the Annals of stock-jobbing fraud'. Irisarri, the newspaper now maintained, had also deliberately and falsely stated in the prospectus, 'on the faith of which Englishmen were induced to advance their money', that Chilean government revenues amounted to $4,000,000 per annum when they were really much less. 'There are but too many South American agents here, who, when befriended by respectable British merchants, can pledge revenues that never existed, and sell mines without a title', the editor sputtered.[124] Unfortunately for the newspaper, two days later Irisarri's attorney convinced the jury in *Irisarri v Clement* that the ex-minister had received personally but £62,000, of which £32,500 had been spent on a warship for the Chilean navy, and the rest for legitimate governmental purposes. After a half-hour deliberation, the jury awarded Irisarri damages of £400.[125]

But no number of court decisions could restore public faith in Latin American bonds. Although some recovered slightly from their tumble at the height of the panic, on 31 December, Colombia was quoted at 59⅞ (1822) and 61¾ (1824), Chile at 55, Mexico at 60 (1824) and 65 (1825), and Peru at 41. Brazilian scrip was selling at 15½ discount and Guatemalan scrip lingered at 18 discount, reflecting investor reluctance to increase their exposure in Latin American issues.[126] Not since the war had the City and the country at large anticipated a New Year with less joy or more despondency.

VI
THE BROKEN BUBBLE

WHILE BOND QUOTATIONS had stabilized momentarily by the end of 1825, Latin American mining shares continued to descend, helping eventually to undermine bond prices. Shareholders were now increasingly asked to honour agreements to contribute additional capital when called upon by their directors, or risk forfeiting amounts already paid. On 6 January 1826, for example, Peruvian Mining Company directors requested in vain for a further £5 per share from shareholders,[1] while on the 27th the Famatina Mining Association, formed by Thomas Kinder to compete directly in the River Plate area with the Rio Plata Mining Association, called up an additional £25 per share.[2] At the beginning of February, Colombian Mining Association directors at a meeting at the City of London Tavern reported they had received but £50,000 in deposits, and so resolved to demand another 2½ per cent per share.[3]

By mid-February the once highly priced Real del Monte shares were selling at par, while Anglo-Mexican traded at a £15 per share discount. Public confidence in the companies was fast ebbing, causing the Money Market columnist in *The Morning Chronicle* to exclaim: 'As for shares, no person thinks of mentioning their names, and thousands wish they had never had a name to mention.'[4] More companies faced the very real possibility of dissolution as shareholders refused to meet the calls and objected strenuously to forfeiture of the payments they had already made.[5] The financial crisis had of course peaked the prior December. Nevertheless, there was still, as Charles Greville, Clerk to the Privy Council, noted in his diary in mid-February, 'the greatest alarm, and every prospect of great distress, and long continuation of it'.[6]

Confidence was further shaken by the publication in late March 1826 of a letter dated the previous November from an Englishman resident in Chile which revealed that the locals were selling their worst mines to the British while retaining the better pits themselves. 'What the deuce are you in England about? Here are ships coming in with miners and machines . . . and none of them will be allowed to work a mine worth having. How the natives laugh at them!'[7]

Perhaps it was no coincidence that five days later a discouraged shareholders meeting at the City of London Tavern voted to dissolve the United Chilean Mining Association and to return a portion of the share deposits to its investors.[8] Another letter, dated the previous September, arrived at *The Morning Chronicle* from Peru. 'Not one of these [mining] companies can do any good – it is physically impossible', the correspondent wrote. British mining companies' agents were everywhere and 'have turned the brains of the Spaniards, who had long given up mining in despair. Potosí ... is all in an uproar, with the competition of Englishmen for pits full of water'.[9]

The letter may have been referring to the activities of the Potosí, La Paz and Peruvian Mining Association. Within a month of its formation in April 1825, an advance agent had left for Potosí to take possession of the mines, followed by a ship containing machinery, stores, miners, carpenters, masons, blacksmiths, a doctor and even a gardener.[10] Unfortunately the company was soon in grave difficulties. Initial deposits of £5 had been paid on less than half the 10,000 shares representing its £1,000,000 capital. Nothing had been paid on the 6,000 or more shares reserved for directors. Consequently, available capital at the end of 1825 approximated only £54,000. In view of the large initial outlays for men and equipment, the company was probably insolvent by the time its miners and other personnel had left England.[11]

Urgent shareholder meetings to raise more capital were summoned in June for the Imperial Brazilian and the Anglo-Chilean Mining Associations.[12] That same month there were angry meetings at Batson's Coffee House on Cornhill of the shareholders of the Honduras Company, which had been formed to grow and export indigo. The shareholders rejected the directors' proposal that only £2 out of each £5 share deposit be returned, insisting upon receiving the entire amount of their instalments.[13] In August the Chilean and Peruvian Mining Association shareholders also voted for dissolution,[14] while the following month the Tlapuxahua Mining Association staged an elaborate public relations exercise to restore confidence in its Mexican operations. A group of supposedly German miners, clad in blue smocks and carrying long pipes in their hands, walked through the Royal Exchange 'where much curiosity was excited as to the cause of their visit to the City. We understand that these persons, with several others, amounting to 40, are about to take their departure from South America, to work the Tlapuxahua Mine.'[15]

The display had a type of mad logic. Unlike in Britain, there were significant silver deposits in Saxony, where German engineers and miners had evolved highly efficient extraction processes. The event's organizers presumably believed therefore that investor confidence would be boosted if it now appeared that British capital was being reinforced by German silver mining techniques. Nevertheless, the Tlapuxahua company too was eventually dissolved, as was the Pasco Peruvian Mining Association.[16]

The latter company's problems had been exposed to public scrutiny in February by the release of figures showing that only £82,315 had been received in shareholder deposits. Expenses had totalled £74,696, the great bulk of which had been spent on driving new drainage shafts, local wages and on the salaries, freight and passage money for the fifty-two miners, sawyers, carpenters, masons, blacksmiths, and rope and brick-makers sent out to Peru. Not an ounce of precious metal had been recovered, however.[17] Meanwhile, *The Times* had noted the demise of the Chilean Mining Association of which Powles and his colleagues had been directors. The financial correspondent commented wryly that at a shareholders meeting at the City of London Tavern the association had 'committed suicide and agreed to bury itself in the mines wherein its property had already been swallowed up'.[18]

The dismay of mining company investors and Latin American bondholders must have deepened when in October 1826 the press printed excerpts from the recently published *Journeys Across the Pampas and Among the Andes* by Francis Bond Head, chief engineer of the Rio Plata Mining Association.[19] The company had been formed in 1824 by investors elated by prospectus claims that in the zone covered by the company's concession grains of gold 'appear in sight when the rain washes away the dust which covers the surface. After a very heavy rain a woman stepping forth from her hut, a few yards from the door, found *a piece of gold weighing twenty ounces* . . . These instances happen so frequently in the rainy season that it would require much time to detail them . . .'[20]

Head, a Captain in the Royal Engineers, had been retained to proceed to Buenos Ayres in charge of a group of Cornish miners and begin operations. When he and his companions arrived, however, they discovered that their concession had been revoked and given to another British company. Before returning home Head rode across the vast pampas of what is today Argentina four times, covering 6,000 miles, to inspect the mines purportedly assigned to his employers. He concluded they were far less rich than those of Mexico or Peru, and too far removed from supplies, transport, water and ports. All tools, machinery and food would have to be imported and conveyed at enormous expense across the pampas. The climate was hot, dry and inhospitable. Moreover, local authorities were corrupt, unreliable, and shameless in demanding bribes. Both the local upper and poorer classes were 'perfectly destitute of the idea of a contract, of punctuality, or of the value of time'.[21]

The demise of the Latin American companies was paralleled by the continued widely-publicized collapses of 'schemes' formed for domestic ventures. *John Bull* chronicled their decline with ill-concealed glee, noting in May 'we are happy to announce the utter demolition of that humbug the *Equitable Loan Company*'. A shareholders meeting concluded that of the £30,000 raised from share deposits, only £14,000 had been applied to company purposes. The solicitors bill exceeded £8,000. Once assets were sold and debts paid, shareholders could expect to receive, with luck, twelve shillings in the pound.[22] It was then revealed that the directors of the bankrupt Cornwall and Devon Mining Company had hatched 'a vile scheme of deception', and had misappropriated the company's money, manipulated its stock, paid excess amounts to friends and cronies for worthless property and services, and grossly overcharged for their attendance at meetings.[23] The Alderney Dairy Company was dissolved soon after in another flurry of scandal, while the Imperial Distillery Company disappeared amidst familiar accusations of improper use of shareholders' funds.[24]

Despite adverse news items detailing the internal problems of the mining and other companies, a contrary current was still apparent. For example, in late October some Mexican mining shares advanced significantly for the first time in several weeks, although they had long passed their peaks. Bolaños rose from £135 to £295 in a week, while Real del Monte now commanded a £150 premium per share.[25] The rally was short-lived and did not include the South American companies. On 1 November Chilean and Peruvian Mining Association shareholders met at Batson's Coffee House and, due to the impossibility of raising more capital, voted for dissolution.[26] More mining companies would expire during the next few months until by 1832 only eight (five Mexican, two Brazilian and one Colombian) would have survived out of the original twenty-six.[27]

Just as by January 1826 only the most incurably optimistic investors in company shares would fail to admit that their initial expectations of quick, easy returns had been wildly unrealistic, so too none but wilfully blind bondholders could now be unaware that most, if not all, Latin American borrowers were insolvent. So sensitive and nervous had the market become, that adverse news concerning any Latin American country to some extent depressed the bonds of all the others. The Latin American economies, moreover, were still too disorganized and shattered after the wars of independence to generate funds for remittances. Central governments were often too weak to collect taxes from outlying districts, much less to set them aside to service the foreign debt as required by loan agreements. The so-called 'security' which had collateralized the loans was therefore either not available or non-collectable. The only solution Latin American govenments could propose was additional borrowings with which to repay and service prior obligations.

The year began badly for Peruvian bondholders when *The Morning Chronicle* published a letter from a reader signing himself 'Pizarro'. The writer complained that he had purchased Peruvian bonds at their highest quotation, but now they had crashed to 45, and he saw no prospect of further dividends because the proceeds retained for that purpose had been exhausted. [U]nless some remittances come from Peru before next April, nothing can be looked for.'[28] Andrés Bello at the Colombian legation would have agreed. After the Colombian treasury minister instructed him to test the market for a new loan, Bello, holding out little hope for another credit, replied that the 'unexampled calamity which presently afflicts commercial credit in England' had undermined the value of all securities, even those of the British government. 'But none have undergone such a considerable fall as those of Colombia, which are now at 53 per cent'[29] – that is, a £100 Colombian bond could now be purchased for £53.

Nor did the future look bright for Buenos Ayres and Brazil when news arrived in early February that the two young nations had declared war on New Year's Day. The bonds of both countries fell, and by mid-February Brazil was trading at 52. The news depressed Latin American bonds generally, so that Guatemala was quoted at 45, Chile at 45, Colombia (1824) at 52½, Peru at 38, and Mexico (1825) at 60. A money market correspondent noted that Latin American stocks on average had fallen 40 per cent from their issue prices, and in a masterly understatement mused 'what revolutions of property this enormous depreciation must have occasioned'.[30]

Worse followed. During the second week in February the City learned that B. A. Goldschmidt & Co. had suspended payments. Even before the Stock Exchange opened it was crowded with concerned brokers and investors, for as well as being a prominent mercantile house, Goldschmidts were one of the City's most active loan contractors, having arranged Danish, Portuguese, Colombian and Mexican issues. Both Colombian and Mexican bond quotations immediately fell to 41 and 50 from fears that funds retained to pay dividends would be lost in the crash.[31] On 16 February *The Morning Chronicle* assured readers that the Colombian dividends had been deposited by Goldschmidt with the Bank of England and that 'with regard to the others, the most satisfactory arrangements will be made for their being met at the proper time'.[32] Nevertheless, when the firm sank it took with it over £350,000 in Colombian loan proceeds which Hurtado had inexplicably left with them instead of depositing in a bank. One commentator has since suggested that the deposit had been used by Goldschmidt and Hurtado to make a market in the shares of the Colombian Mining Association of which Goldschmidt was a director and Hurtado president.[33] Colombia's eventual default was now assured. The next week Goldschmidt died suddenly at his father-in-law's house on Park Crescent, allegedly of apoplexy.[34]

The City was soon shaken by another banking failure when John Perring, Shaw, Barber & Co., the firm headed by the former Lord Mayor whom Gregor MacGregor had persuaded to act as agent for the Poyais issue, suspended payments. Despite its involvement with MacGregor, the firm had enjoyed a good reputation and was agent for eighteen country banks. The failure gave rise to considerable agitation in the City and added to the general depression which still affected all bonds and shares.[35] The bond market improved slightly, however, when Hullet Brothers announced that the 31 March Chilean dividend would be paid at their offices. Chile rose from 49 to 51 and Colombia from 65 to 67½. Peru and Brazil remained steady at 31 and 55.[36] While Hullet's announcement may have boosted bond prices slightly, any favourable impression of the state of Chilean finances must have been offset by publication during March of the difficulties experienced by the mining companies, since the health of the Latin American mining industry was closely linked with governments' capacities to service their borrowings. The collapse of the companies thus affected seriously public perceptions of general Latin American financial credibility.

In addition, the well-publicized candid reports by intelligent travellers such as Captain Head contradicted earlier euphoric press accounts and made clear to the investing public the instability, inefficiency and corruption of many of the infant governments. The Latin American search for political utopia had foundered upon the harsh, divisive realities of geography, poverty and military ambition. The economic circumstances of the new regimes offered bondholders little hope of repayment. Investors therefore were probably sceptical when they read the Mexican finance minister's report showing that after a deficit in 1825 of £5,207,024, a surplus of £992,478 after debt service was projected for the next year.[37] Three days following publication of the report, *The New Times*, which did not generally carry considerable financial news, remarked that some South American bonds 'have declined considerably', and quoted Colombia (1824) at 50½, Mexico at 66, Peru at 29 and Brazil at 57.[38]

The Buenos Ayres bonds were by now seldom quoted. Brazil's fleet blockaded the Río de la Plata and European trade with Buenos Ayres was at a standstill. Proceeds of the 1825 Buenos Ayres loan were spent on war materials rather than the port improvements and other public works as intended, while the government issued large quantities of paper money to finance its current operations. An attempt to raise additional funds in London in early 1826 was still-born, but due to the blockade the government could not have remitted specie to pay its creditors even if it had been financially solvent.[39]

Mexican bonds should have improved on the announcement in mid-April that Barclay, Herring, Richardson had redeemed 206 certificates of the 1824 issue amounting to £25,950 with proceeds from the 1825 loan. Nevertheless all Latin American stocks fell because that same day Thomas Kinder announced that Peruvian dividends due 15 April would not be paid. It was the first Latin American default and caused 'considerable panic' in the City. Kinder somewhat ingenuously blamed the inability to pay on the refusal of the scripholders of the second Peruvian loan 'to fulfil their engagements'.[40]

Kinder insisted that governments finances were in a much more favourable state than could have been expected considering the short interval since December 1824 when the nation's independence was assured by the battle of Ayacucho. Government coffers, he claimed, in fact contained a considerable surplus. Kinder further assured the public that he had impressed upon the government the urgency of remitting future dividends, and that he would 'continue to exert himself to accelerate the payment of those deferred ... even at the expense of his personal responsibility, having no doubt of the re-sources or good faith of the Government of Peru.'[41] At the time of default the total bonds in circulation had a face value of £1,816,000, although many had been sold at extremely low discounts.[42]

The general slide in bond prices continued, but surprisingly Peru still held firm at 29½ due, *The New Times* opined, to 'hopes being entertained that some light will be thrown on the affair of the divi-dends ... by the Peruvian Minister in this country, who is very desirous to afford every information upon the subject'.[43] The market steadied slightly when on 1 May the 1822 Colombian loan dividends were paid, although there were still fears that the July dividend on the 1824 loan would not be met. On 13 May bondholders may have been slightly encouraged by the announcement that 583 shares of the 1824 Mexican loan worth £31,250 had been purchased for re-demption by Barclay, Herring, Richardson with proceeds of the 1825 loan.[44]

Doubts over the July Colombian interest payment persisted, and not even the arrival of a ship from Mexico with £40,000 in specie for interest payments had any appreciable effect on the general gloom, since the shipment was less than expected.[45] Colombian bonds fell six points in July when rumours of a revolution arrived in London. Peru slid to 23½, while Chile dropped from 37 to 32. Even though dividends were paid on the 1825 Mexican bonds the 1824 bonds declined over four points to 35. Both Colombian and Mexican bonds were now selling at one-third of their quotations at the same time the previous year, causing *The Morning Chronicle* to comment that 'the public are, no doubt, the greatest sufferers; not so much the dealers, whose favourite operation is that of selling – followed up with great alacrity ever since the failure of the house of B. A. Goldschmidt and Co.'.[46]

Colombian credit was further undermined when the public learned it planned to pay dividends with funds owed it by Peru for expenses incurred in liberating it from Spanish rule. Peru, equally insolvent and now in default, had intended to raise the money by floating another loan in London. As feared, the 1824 Colombian loan dividends were not paid on 15 July. Although the Mexican minister had lent Hurtado £73,000 from his government's funds in London, it could not cover the full amount due.[47] Hurtado could offer no explanation for the default, and the bondholders were furious. After several private gatherings, they determined to call a public meeting 'where it is probable that the interference of Mr Canning will be sought for, and that a declaration will be put forth, expressing the sense of the meeting relative to the silence of Mr Hurtado'.[48]

The angry Colombian bondholder reaction contrasted with the less acrimonious behaviour of the Peruvian bondholders, who at first consulted privately with the Peruvian government commissioners in London. A bondholders' resolution agreed that, considering the great distance from Peru, the uncertainty over the means adopted by the Peruvian government to provide payment, and the confidence which they had in the government's rectitude, they would for the moment refrain from officially complaining to their own government of the default.[49] The Colombian issue, however, was much larger than the Peruvian and more widely held. Moreover, such high hopes had been entertained for Colombia – in banking, mining, and immigration – that the default's emotional impact was also greater.

On 21 July *The Morning Chronicle* printed a table comparing the respective issue prices of the Latin American loans with their current quotations, and calculating the investors' loss on the value of their holdings. The differences between the issue price and the quoted bond prices were shocking. Brazilian bonds had shed 30 points since their issue date, Buenos Ayres 36, Chile 37, Colombian 1822 bonds 58, Colombian 1824 bonds 60½, Mexico 1824 bonds 50, and Mexican 1825 bonds 45. Peruvian 1822 bonds had lost a staggering 65 points, and the 1825 issue had fallen by 60. The total face value of the bonds issued was £19,775,000, while their present market value was but £7,260,000, provided, of course, buyers could be found. Investors probably derived scant consolation from knowledge that Spanish and Greek bonds had performed even more poorly. Spanish 1822 bonds issued at 56 were now quoted at 7, while Spanish 1823 bonds had dropped from their issue price of 30 to 4. The 1824 and 1825 Greek bonds, issued at 59 and 61½, had collapsed to 10 and 11 respectively.[50]

News reports of the Buenos Ayres-Brazilian war also haunted the Foreign Stock Exchange. A correspondent named 'Pacificus' wrote to *The Morning Chronicle* that the ships of the two contending navies had been purchased from the proceeds of loans raised in London, and that British subjects were serving on both sides. 'Now these same navies are employed in shutting up the River Plate against British commerce. Our Capital is thus turned against ... our industry.'[51] Redirection of loan proceeds from the productive purposes outlined in prospectuses into armaments was not unique to Buenos Ayres and Brazil. At least £40,700 of Peruvian loan proceeds was spent on muskets, while in Colombia the greater part of the 1824 loan was used to purchase military equipment in Great Britain and in the United States. While it was undoubtedly argued that purchases of British arms and munitions aided domestic industry and employment, they did nothing to help borrowing states rebuild their economic bases in order to generate the funds needed for debt servicing.[52]

During August, Mexican and Colombian bonds fluctuated wildly. Barclay, Herring, Richardson suspended payments, adding to the uncertainty since they had been agents for the Central American and 1825 Mexican loans. Even though earlier reports of specie shipments from both Mexico and Colombia proved false, Mexico held at 47 and 46¾, while Colombia's two issues struggled up to 40 and 32½. Brazil was still the investor/speculator's favourite at 61, while Buenos Ayres stayed around 52.[53] These nominal quotations merely indicated the prices at which bonds were offered, not necessarily those at which they were sold. By now there were not as many investor participants as before, so only a few shares needed to be bought or sold against future delivery for perceptible price fluctuations to occur. Early September saw more reports circulate concerning specie shipments from Vera Cruz which, unfortunately, due to a late sailing date would not reach Britain in time for the dividend payment day. The market generally was sluggish, so with the start of the shooting season many brokers and jobbers left the City and went to the country.[54]

In mid-September, however, Mexican bonds recovered sharply when Mexican Chargé d'Affairs Vicente Rocafuerte announced that Baring Brothers had assumed the agency for the Mexican government from Barclay, Herring, Richardson, which had just been dissolved. Dividend coupons for the 1 October payment should be presented, therefore, at Baring's Bishopsgate offices. From 55¾ on 14 September, the 1825 bonds closed at 64¾ four days later.[55] While it was rumoured that a new agent also would be appointed for the Colombian loan, *The Morning Chronicle* opined that since the last dividend had not been paid it was unlikely that a house equally as respectable as Barings would assume the responsibility.[56]

All other bond issues were temporarily bouyed by Baring's designation as agent for the Mexican loan. Even Peru rose from 27 to 29½, and buying orders for Mexican stock were received by post from the 'Hansa towns' where the appointment had 'created a strong impression'.[57] Seeking to take advantage of the new euphoria, agents began to test the market for a £15,000,000 Mexican loan. *The Times* commented sadly that even the unsettled conditions in South America and the ill-repute in which their bonds were held were 'insufficient to alter the restless spirit of speculation for new enterprises'. Nevertheless, there had been so many financial disasters of late that 'the wilfully blind will deserve the ruin they incur'.[58] Although by 28 September no bullion had arrived from Mexico, *The Morning Chronicle* announced that Barings itself would advance the money for the dividends due the next week, in return for which favour 'peculiar privileges are to be granted by the Mexican Government'.[59]

In contrast, Chilean investors must have despaired when on 28 September Minister Egaña informed bondholders with deep regret that no funds to pay interest dividends had arrived from Chile. Nevertheless, 'I confidently expect that the necessary remittances will shortly be received'.[60] Not surprisingly *The Times* was not as sanguine, and revealed that Egaña had urged Hullet Brothers, the agents, either to advance money to pay the dividends or relinquish the agency. They had refused to do either. Moreover, the money market correspondent wrote, 'those who reflect on the Chilean character', and who know that 'not one dollar has been appropriated from the revenue of the mint and land taxes to service the loan as promised', could not be very hopeful that any future payments would be made.[61]

On 30 September Hullet Brothers gave notice that since funds from Chile still had not arrived, they would not receive dividend coupons until further notice. Meanwhile a brawl had erupted on the floor of the Stock Exchange when a broker (also a MP) was accused by a colleague of having sold a large block of Chilean bonds during the past weeks when he must have known from his connections with Hullet Brothers that default was imminent. The charge of insider dealing was denied 'in language the most direct and the least ceremonious'. Cards were exchanged and a duel narrowly averted.[62] On the same day a Stock Exchange report noted that even though it was now certain that Brazilian and Mexican bond dividends due 1 October would be paid, the Chilean failure had tended to increase 'the prejudice against those of all other South American Republics'.[63]

Whilst the larger loans were drifting into default, Central American Minister Marcial Zebadúa was having difficulties with his nation's much smaller issue. On 21 June 1825, the Central American Federal Congress had resolved to appoint a minister plenipotentiary to the governments of Europe in order to obtain recognition of their independence, and to establish a legation in London.[64] Foreign Minister Zebadúa agreed to serve and arrived in London in April 1826, where he opened the legation at 68 Baker Street. On 20 August 1826, Zebadúa wrote to the new foreign minister in Guatemala that Barclay, Herring, Richardson had informed him that the loan proceeds could not even cover the legation's expenses for the forthcoming year. Six days later he wrote again to report that the loan was going badly. Because his own authorization was limited only to remitting funds, he could not interfere with the loan's marketing nor take any action to protect the government 'from the evils which it is to be feared will result from the present state of this affair, and the less-than-favourable public comments about the credit of the lending house'. Guatemalan bonds, he reported, were now at 25.[65]

After persistent inquiries, Zebadúa finally obtained an accounting from Barclays, which revealed that due to the depressed state of the market only £163,300 in bonds had been issued at 63, producing £75,684. Had the loan been offered six months earlier, it might have been more fully subscribed. Even the small amount realized, Barclays claimed, should be offset by £94,384, representing negotiation, legal and other expenses, commissions, withheld dividends, and payments made to suppliers for the government's account. In fact, the government owed its contractors £18,700. Zebadúa disputed the calculations, but before the differences could be resolved, Barclays collapsed. On 5 October Zebadúa wrote to Guatemala saying that he wished to appoint the firm of Reid, Irving & Co. to take over administration of the loan.[66]

The new firm promised Zebadúa they could place a £1,000,000 bond issue during 1827, and meanwhile advanced him £1,000 for legation expenses and paid £2,000 interest on outstanding bonds.[67] News of the appointment caused the bonds to rise to 58, and a few more were sold. Only a small number of bonds were in circulation, however, since most of the scrip had been forfeited for failure to pay instalments as they came due. *The Times* noted that discussions were under way between the new agent and the scripholders to rescind the forfeitures – presumably on payment of a reduced amount – but 'we have not heard of the result'.[68]

Colombian bonds fell into increased disrepute when it became public knowledge that Minister Hurtado had lent his name to a seamy attempt to boost their value just prior to the inevitable default. Although in early October news reached London that General Páez had ceased his rebellion against the central government, the bonds still remained sluggish around 34.[69] Suddenly on 10 October bond prices jumped to 40½ on news that the Colombian government was shipping £160,000 in bullion to pay the dividends, and had ordered Hurtado to insure the shipment at Lloyds. A letter from Hurtado at his office on Portland Place to a broker placing the insurance was exhibited at the Stock Exchange, leading *The Morning Chronicle* to conclude hastily that 'it is certain that a large sum has been under-written this afternoon ... and we believe that little doubt now prevails on the subject'.[70] Speculators thus were led to assume that because an insurance policy had been written, the long-expected bullion shipment must indeed be in transit. *The Times* was more sceptical. Observing that the amount insured was small, 'we would recommend great caution with respect to these bonds till some further *certain* intelligence arrives'.[71]

Doubts gradually turned into hostility. Any dispatches from Colombia ordering Hurtado to effect the insurance must have arrived by the last ship from Colombia which had docked the prior Saturday, reasoned press commentators. Why then did he wait until the following Wednesday before ordering the insurance? Why also, given the supposed urgency of the matter, did he use a broker when he could have gone to Lloyds himself?[72] Moreover, the broker concerned was the unsavoury Herman Hendriks. Hurtado must have known that news of the insurance would send quotations soaring, critics commented, because even if the shipment had not arrived by 1 October, the due date, the fact that it was on the high seas would still boost bond values. Meanwhile, the cost of the policy would be more than offset by the speculating gains made by selling before the true state of affairs became known.

Hurtado protested his innocence. At a meeting with Herring, Graham and Powles he maintained he had not received any letters from Bogotá which they had not already seen, and that he had not met Hendriks, whom he implied suggested the insurance, until two days previously. His despatches from Bogotá had mentioned no specific sum the arrival of which was to be insured at Lloyds, and 'he had been misled on the subject'.[73] *The Times* found Hurtado's explanation unsatisfactory: 'Mr Hurtado's conduct is inexplicable, except on grounds which imply an extraordinary defect in judgement, or an indifference to that delicate sense of propriety which ought to characterize a public functionary to whom the reputation and interests of his country have been committed.'[74]

Amazingly, however, *The Times* was still convinced that the Colombian dividends would be paid. The newspapers' faith seems particularly incredible since on the same day it castigated Hurtado's conduct, it reported that a Dr Foley had left Bogotá with $240,000 to be remitted to London as dividend payments. On arrival at Cartagena, Foley was ordered to pay $40,000 to the garrison and leave the rest with local authorities to defray their current expenses. He therefore arrived in London with his pockets empty except for an authorization to raise a £4,000,000 loan![75] He approached Baring Brothers, who declined the opportunity when he admitted that the Bogotá Mint contained but $300,000 in its coffers. 'How then', *The Morning Chronicle* inquired not unreasonably, 'could Mr Hurtado order insurance upon *One Million of Dollars?*'[76]

In late October Mexican bondholder unease was increased by an ill-timed revelation that the Mexican government wished to consolidate its two issues by increasing the interest rate on the first loan from 5 to 6 per cent, to match that of the second credit. Holders of 1824 bonds would then pay the difference between the quoted prices of the 1824 and 1825 issues to Barings for the government's account. Since 1824 bonds were selling at 53 and the 1825 issue at 64, in theory the gain would have been significant. The Mexican suggestion, however, confirmed suspicions that the country was without resources to make the next interest payment, notwithstanding recent specie shipments. Consequently, the 1825 bonds fell to 62, and on Barings' advice the proposal was withdrawn.[77] Confidence, however, had at last been forever undermined, causing *The Times* to observe that 'the mania for foreign loans is so far cured as to create an obstinate resistance to further advances, until the countries asking them have at least proved themselves in possession of internal resources sufficient to meet the payment of the interest.'[78]

Expectations that the Chilean default might soon be cured were in turn dispelled when a letter from Santiago written the previous June confirmed that the government had not intended to pay the September dividends, which, of course, had already fallen due. Gradually it became clear that the Chilean government no longer regarded itself as the primary obligor on the loan. Instead, bondholders were expected to rely on the *estanco*, the group of Chilean merchants who had undertaken to service the issue. Since the exchange rate was now so unfavourable, however, the merchants, in what could hardly be termed an excess of patriotism, refused to remit any funds unless they could negotiate better terms for themselves with the government.[79]

Meanwhile, Peruvian agents in Paris were still seeking to raise a £1,000,000 loan, a portion of the proceeds of which would be applied to paying the Colombian dividends. French bankers offered to arrange the financing at a ridiculous 40 per cent discount, but the Peruvians refused.[80] *The Times* was sceptical, and could see no reason for seeking the financing in Paris rather than London. If the proposal were as sound and profitable as alleged 'there are abundant means here to entertain it, and even the houses in Paris who listen to it are said to send to London for assistance'.[81]

In late October the Greek Bondholder Committee's final report on the disposition of the loan proceeds was made public. Although the general outlines of the disaster had been known earlier, the specific relevations of mismanagement and corruption were shocking. Of the £800,000 first bond issue sold at 59, the net proceeds raised for Greece were only £350,000 after deductions of £96,000 for two years of interest and sinking provisions, and for £26,000 in commissions. After subtracting other expenses, the remaining proceeds reached Greece as stores or specie, which Lord Byron had helped allocate on behalf of the Philhellenic Committee. The proceeds of the 1824 loan of £2,000,000, issued at 55, were but £1,100,000. From this bankers subtracted £200,000 for two years interest, £20,000 for the sinking fund, and £64,000 in commissions. Of the remainder, £200,000 was lost in open market dealings to maintain bond prices, while generous additional fees were paid to provisional Greek government representatives who had arrived in London to approve the loan. Out of the second loan Greece received but £182,000 in cash, £60,000 in stores, and £33,000 in accepted bills of exchange in return for the obligation to pay £100,000 interest per annum.[82] Reviewing the committee's report, *The Times* exclaimed sadly 'Poor Greece! Little cause had she to expect such treatment from England.'[83]

Meanwhile, by 30 October it was evident that any news of specie shipments from Colombia had been invented by speculators. Although Santos Michelena, Hurtado's replacement, was en route to London with authority to raise a new credit, *The Morning Chronicle* considered 'very questionable whether the contract will be made even at the present price of Greek or Spanish Bonds, unless specie be shipped before any negotiations with the monied interest are attempted'.[84] On 1 November any remaining hopes disappeared when the 1822 Colombian dividends were not paid, and Zea's loan,

the first floated in the City by a Latin American nation, collapsed
into default at last. Letters from merchants in Colombia also painted
a very gloomy picture of the nation's prospects. A series of earth-
quakes over a six week period had wreaked damage estimated
at £2,000,000, and 'a great want of power or energy, even in the
capital, seems to characterize the Colombian Government'.[85]

While Hurtado was attempting to mollify and cajole the Stock
Exchange, Andrés Bello was educating the finance minister in
Bogotá in the realities of the economic situation in Europe. On 16
July the minister again wrote to Bello that congress had resolved that
the interest payments up to June 1827 should be paid with the over
£400,000 deposited at B. A. Goldschmidt and with the 1,000,000
pesos due Colombia from the projected Peruvian loan. On 15
November Bello and Michelena responded that given Goldschmidt's
bankruptcy and the lawsuit brought against the firm by Hurtado,
in no way could Colombia expect to receive even part of the
£400,000.[86]

Hardly less forlorn, they wrote, were hopes of drawing upon
proceeds of a future Peruvian loan since Peru's credit was even more
depressed than Colombia's. In any case, although Hurtado had had
several meetings with the Peruvians, they had not yet agreed definitely to the proposal. But even if they should decide to raise a loan
at great sacrifice 'it is unlikely they would find anyone prepared
to advance money to their government'. Nor were Bello and
Michelena hopeful of raising another loan to Colombia, even at a
steep discount. 'The general opinion is that, without a considerable
remittance of funds from the Colombian Treasury, it will not be
possible to erase the bad impression made on the public by the state
of payment of our dividends, which unfortunately have coincided
with the Peruvian and Chilean [defaults]' and bad news of a revolutionary movement in Venezuela.[87]

The dissentions within the Colombian government over Hurtado's dealings with Goldschmidt became public knowledge in mid-
November. *The Times* obtained and printed a letter from the Colombian finance minister requesting Hurtado to explain why he had left
such a large sum on deposit with Goldschmidt when all the loan
agreement had required was the deposit of two years of interest, and
the funding of the 1 per cent amortization fund.[88] If, *The Times* coyly
suggested, Hurtado would favour it with a copy of his reply to the
minister, their readers would not have 'to wait for the requisite
information until his letter has travelled to Bogotá and back'.[89]

Hurtado promptly wrote to *The Times* rejecting the suggestion as
'without precedent in diplomatic conduct'. The newspaper tartly
replied that Hurtado's involvement in the loan scandal was also with-

out parallel, and that if he could provide a satisfactory explanation of his conduct he should do so at once.[90] As if this unedifying exchange of letters was not sufficient, long-suffering Colombian bondholders were further incensed when they learned that a 'considerable amount of specie' had been received in the United States to pay for warships ordered by the Colombian government.[91] Not only had loan proceeds again been diverted for military ends, but in this instance they went to Britain's principal trading rival in Latin America.

By the end of November Hurtado had brought suit against the surviving Goldschmidt partners as well as the firm's trustees in bankruptcy, who included N. M. Rothschild. Hurtado demanded a full accounting of the monies received by Goldschmidt from bond sales proceeds 'so that if a balance appeared in favour of the plaintiffs, it might be paid over to them'. The defendants countered by alleging that the loan contract was null and void because the Colombian congress had unilaterally modified some of its provisions.[92] Moreover, because Colombia had not been recognized by Great Britain at the time of the loan, the contract could not be enforced in British courts.

Also, the contract was usurious, defendants argued. Considering the discount at which the bonds were offered, the real interest rate was 8 instead of the 5 per cent permitted by law. Although the documentation was signed abroad to evade English usury laws, the agreement was executed with British subjects for money to be raised by bonds to be sold in Britain, the dividends on which were payable in London. The arrangement from the beginning was essentially British, and therefore English usury law applied.[93]

Despite the specious nature of the defense, the vice chancellor, focussing instead on the technicality that the petition had not described who constituted the Colombian government, nor whom the court might require to pay damages in the event of a decision against the plaintiff, rejected Hurtado's petition. After the decision, *The Times* observed that every new disclosure 'makes it more evident that had the independence of Latin America rested on the fidelity, foresight and knowledge of business on the part of the agents ... and contractors in this country, it would have been placed in equal jeopardy with that of the unfortunate Greeks'.[94]

Bello and Michelena on 7 December again wrote to the finance minister, commenting with a realism surely unwelcome in Bogotá that,

Even if the house of Goldschmidt paid the amount it owes or the Ministers of Peru pay the letters of credit drawn on their Government in favour of Mr Hurtado, and consequently one or two dividends are paid, our credit standing would improve little or nothing, and it is not possible to inspire confidence in the public without remitting funds from Colombia.[95]

Because of the litigation, Hurtado had admitted to Bello and Michelena, there was for the moment no hope of obtaining the funds held by Goldschmidt. Moreover, the Peruvian envoys had now conceded it was impossible to raise a loan out of which Colombian dividends could be paid.[96] Meanwhile Colombian bonds fell to 40 upon receipt of reports that the Cartagena garrison was unpaid, and that the government was apparently powerless even to collect and make remittances of monies received as customs duties.

During December adverse news from Colombia and elsewhere drove Stock Exchange speculators to increasingly desperate means to protect their positions or turn a fast profit before Latin American bonds became totally worthless. Early in the month a letter purportedly signed by Hurtado was left at Lloyds requesting one of the underwriters who had insured the specie shipment to call upon him immediately. Hurtado's signature had been forged, however, and the real authors used the letter to fuel a rumour that the insurance had been cancelled. This 'trick of an extremely reprehensible nature', which was a swindle based upon another swindle, caused Colombian bonds to tumble two further points and speculators 'were enabled to realize a handsome profit'.[97] The Committee of the Stock Exchange for once was stung into action and began an inquiry to trace the real authors of the letter.[98] They were, however, soon called upon to deal with another fraud.

Other speculators in early December spread a rumour that Hullet Brothers had received the necessary funds from Chile to pay the overdue 30 September dividends. Bond prices jumped ten points to 48 but fell back when the agents flatly denied the report. 'A more disgraceful, and we are sorry to add, a more successful piece of swindling has rarely been practiced', moaned The Times. While 'responsible men' agreed that something must be done to deter such practices, no one could agree on the remedies. The Stock Exchange Committee should at least publish the names of the offenders as 'a sort of moral pillory', The Times suggested, since the entire Exchange 'suffers in character from such transactions, and, if allowed to pass without notice, will be fixed in the public mind with the opprobrium of having connived at them, for it will not be conceived that it was utterly impossible in any way to punish the offenders.'[99] Such calls for reform went unheeded.

Although 1826 closed with perhaps slightly less depair in the City than in 1825, holders of Latin American bonds and shares could not have enjoyed a carefree holiday season. While the Mexican, Brazilian and Buenos Ayres dividends had been paid, doubts over those nations' future political stability and solvency persisted. The internal Mexican political situation was highly volatile and necessitated maintaining a large military establishment, while war persistently drained Brazilian and Buenos Ayrean resources. Rumours of new loans with which to repay prior obligations continued to worry investors. Even though on 20 December Baring Brothers advertised in the press that the 1 January Mexican dividends would be paid at its offices at 8 Bishopsgate, the 1825 bonds only rose half a point to 64½.[100] News of the ratification of the commercial treaty with Great Britain a few days later pushed the bonds up briefly to 65 but they soon receded.

Nor could Chilean and Peruvian bondholders receive much solace from news that due to straightened economic circumstances the two nations were imposing forced loans on their subjects. On 12 December *The New Times* prefaced its translation of the August Chilean Decree obliging inhabitants to contribute to a 6 per cent per annum $300,000 loan, by commenting that 'the following decree looks as if the Chilean Government was not sanguine in its expectations of being able to raise another loan ... in England at the present moment'.[101] Two weeks later the press reported that in order to consolidate its foreign debt Peru was levying a $50 per head assessment on all male inhabitants between eighteen and fifty-five.[102]

Although by now the unbridled speculative mania had abated, the press continued to expose the human tragedies it had left in its passage. Four days before Christmas the City was shocked to learn that a promiment broker had committed suicide. A Foreign Stock Exchange investigation revealed he had defrauded 'two ladies of property, residing in the neighbourhood of Grosvenor Square', who had given him £30,000 in securities and foreign stock to manage. He had lost the entire amount, as well as a sum entrusted to him by a clergyman. Commenting upon the sad case, *The Times* lamented that the stock-jobbing mania had spread throughout many different levels of society 'and we mention these facts as a useful caution to all those who may feel disposed to listen to similar representations of extravagant profit, and to place their property out of their own control'.[103]

To be sure, in May Parliament had passed legislation to prevent a recurrence of the recent crisis by reorganizing the country credit system and authorizing the establishment of banks of issue 65 miles or more from London with any number of partners. At the same time bank notes of less than £5 were abolished on the theory that smaller notes were 'of no use except to raise prices and encourage speculation'. Not until 1833, however, were banks specifically authorized to be formed as joint stock companies rather than as more vulnerable partnerships.[104] These few reforms probably could not have stemmed the speculation which brought about the recent crash, and certainly were enacted far too late to save thousands of investors and tradesmen from disaster. By the end of the year over 2,200 private bankruptcies had been reported in the press, well over twice the figure for 1825.

By 30 December Latin American bonds had recovered slightly from their mid-year lows, but were still considerably below issue prices: Colombia (1822) stood at 30, Colombia (1824) at 34½, Mexico (1824) at 53¼, Mexico (1825) at 65¾, Chile at 37¾, Peru at 33, and Brazil at 59. By contrast, however, European bonds (except for Spain and Greece) were much higher. Russians were at 84½, Danish at 58¼, Austrians at 88½, Portuguese at 70½, and Prussians at 95.[105] As investors, brokers, merchants, jobbers and other financiers gloomily raised glasses of champagne and tankards of mulled wine on New Year's Eve, they must have looked back sadly on 1826. The three Latin American borrowers which had tapped the London market in 1822 had defaulted. Moreover, there was little realistic hope that the defaults could be cured in the near future, because all the Latin American nations now were involved in serious domestic and external political and economic difficulties.

Latin American political disunity had been highlighted in the summer by the failure of Bolívar's Panama conference to achieve any meaningful results. The gathering had had various laudable objectives, including the creation of a permanent network of treaties of confederation, alliance and commerce, an arbitration mechanism, the codification of international law, and the formation of a defensive alliance against Spain. Although all Latin American nations had been invited, only Colombia, Mexico, Peru and the United Provinces of Central America had attended. Of the several conventions signed, only the Treaty of Union, League and Perpetual Confederation was ratified – and only by Colombia.[106]

The lack of cohesion demonstrated by the conference's participants did not inspire confidence among British investors, and fueled the cynicism which by now was replacing the sympathy and high expectations once entertained for the Latin American political experiment. Thus, *The Annual Register*, commenting upon the 'pompous and futile' gathering, remarked scornfully that the Latin American statesmen who had attended the conference

> speak and write like boys who have just left school, as if their minds had been stationary since they attained the age of puberty: they exhibit scarcely a single trace of a reason accustomed to

observe human affairs, to analyse their combinations, or follow their consequences. For this defective turn of mind they are hardly responsible; the system of education, and the frame of society, which existed in the Spanish colonies, were such as scarcely to permit statesman-like habits of thought to grow up.[107]

Jovial celebrants in the City – and they must have been few – required no crystal ball to predict that 1827 would bring additional disappointments and defaults. Even the most sanguine investor could foresee that instead of bullion shipments very little but empty promises to pay would in future travel eastward across the Atlantic to Britain.

VII
DAMAGE CONTROL
AND GOOD OFFICES

NEW YEAR'S DAY 1827 dawned grey and rainy, and if the skies were overcast so were spirits in the City. As if the recurring press reports during the previous months of the problems encountered by the Latin American loans, mining and other companies were not sufficient, investors were surely appalled when early in the year Stock Exchange broker Henry English published *A Complete View of the Joint Stock Companies formed During the Years 1824 and 1825.*

Although investors certainly had been aware of the collapse of most companies launched during the share market craze, English's work must nevertheless have been shocking. In that pre-radio and television era, the educated public's impressions and awareness of the boom and its collapse had been acquired in piecemeal fashion by word of mouth, through isolated press reports, or by the bitter personal experience of seeing one's own holdings in a particular loan or stock become worthless. English's work for the first time reliably revealed to investors and non-investors alike the overall magnitude and extent of the speculative mania, and the dimensions of the financial destruction left in its wake.

By English's calculations only 156 companies with a total capital of £47,936,650 were in existence when the company formation boom began. With the exception of twenty-five insurance companies, these concerns provided a variety of infrastructural facilities and services – roads, canals, docks, waterworks, bridges – which in a later era would be supplied by local or national governmental authorities. The social and economic value of these activities, English asserted, demonstrated the basically sound and beneficial character of the joint stock company as an instrument for improving national life. It was therefore unfair 'as was the fashion of late' to denounce joint stock companies in general.[1]

In 1824 and 1825, however, a staggering 624 companies – four times as many as those then already existing – were formed or projected, most without the redeeming objectives of the pre-1824 organizations. They included 74 mining companies (26 for Latin American operations), as well as gas, railroads, insurance, trading and other organizations capitalized at a nominal total of £372,173,000, and on which £17,605,625 had actually been advanced.

By 1827, after a brief life, 118 of the companies with a total capital of £50,606,500 had been abandoned by their promoters. Among them were the Anglo-Peruvian, Guanaxuato and United Chilean mining associations, as well as the once highly-esteemed Atlantic and Pacific Junction Company, the Peruvian Trading & Mining Association, the Havana Company and the Brazilian Agricultural & Jewel Company. Shareholders in all these enterprises lost over £2,419,000 in paid-in capital.

A further 236 companies capitalized at £143,000,000 had been projected 'but of the actual formation of which, by the issue of their shares, no precise information can be obtained'.[2] Presumably they functioned only for even briefer periods. They included a Brazilian mining company, the South American & Colonial Gas Company, the Haytian Trading Company, the Island of Cuba Company, the South American and Hibernian Manufacturing and Trading Association, the Havana & Hayti Steamship Company and the Isthmus of Darien Association. English could provide no details on how much capital had been paid in for this group of companies. He could furnish even less data for another category of 143 projected and abandoned companies but which his best information indicated had a total nominal capital of £69,175,000. Among them were the Central American Mining Association, the Isthmus of Panama Canal Company, and the Mexican Agricultural and Colonization Company.

Only 127 of the companies organized in the heady days of 1824 and 1825 were still in existence by 31 December 1826, English's cut-off date. They included 44 mining ventures (including most of the Latin American associations) 20 gas companies and 14 insurance concerns, as well as 49 miscellaneous trading, railroad, agricultural and manufacturing concerns, 6 of which had been formed for Latin American operations.[3] Their aggregate capital totalled £102,781,600, on which £15,185,950 had been paid. A further £87,595,650 was still subject to call. Since most of the shares were selling below par, and the total shareholding investment was now worth but £9,303,950, it seemed unlikely that future calls would be met, given the public's reluctance to throw good money after bad.

For example, Famatina Mining Association shares with £50 paid in were selling for £2. United Mexican shares had £25 paid, but could be obtained at a 13 per cent discount. General South American Mining shares on which £5 had been paid could be obtained for £1.5s. Although the Anglo-Mexican Mint had maintained its £5 paid-in price, shares of the Colombian Pearl Fishing Association on which £2 had been paid were trading at 9½ per cent discount. While these companies had not gone into formal liquidation, most were already bankrupt and their days numbered. It was surely obvious that eventually virtually all their paid-in capital also would be lost.

English's calculations of company failures were in fact out of date by the time of publication. 'The dissolution of joint stock humbugs continues to proceed with undiminished vigour', commented *John Bull* in February. 'Several of these affairs have been brought before the public during the past week, and in some of the proceedings had thereupon, names and persons pretty notorious in the world have been treated with less ceremony than might have been expected.' In January a former MP was summarily ejected from his chairmanship of the board of directors of the Welsh Iron and Coal Company when a shareholders meeting accused him and his fellow directors of overcharging for attendance fees at meetings, and of speculating in company shares alloted to them and on which they had never paid any instalments.[4]

Although he might have been 'a swan among crows', even Lord Palmerston had been criticized the year before for his directorship of the Cornwall and Devon Mining Company, which had collapsed amidst allegations of malfeasance and corruption.[5] The eagerness with which public figures had lent their names to these and other enterprises was now deeply regretted. Attempts to distance themselves from the scandals by pleading ignorance of the activities of fellow directors were rejected scornfully. Of course the counterargument was either that they should have known, or, if in truth they did not, then they were derelict in their duties.

English had also noted that in 1824 and 1825 a total of £32,069,571 in bonds of the Latin American states, Austria, Portugal, Greece, Naples and Denmark had been placed in London, on which £25,308,468 had actually been advanced. When added to the amounts paid in on the companies formed during the same period, he estimated that the total actually invested by the British public in highly speculative ventures was a staggering £42,914,093.[6]

Investors in Latin American loans as well as mining company shareholders must have been further disheartened by press reports of the further misadventures of the Rio Plata Mining Association. The directors, who by now had spent £60,000 of their shareholders' funds, had been furious at Captain Head's conclusion that their doomed enterprise had been formed to mine gold and silver in a country which produced 'only horses, beef and thistles'. When they withheld his salary, he published what had been a private internal document as *Reports Relating to the Failure of the Rio Plata Mining*

Association, which continued the sorry tale of bribery and corruption begun the previous year in *Rough Notes*.[7]

Although Head's comments related principally to mines in what is now Argentina and Chile, only the most obtuse investor would fail to see parallels with the difficulties mining enterprises were encountering elsewhere in Latin America. Head reminded readers that over £2,000,000 had been invested in Latin American mines without a shilling of profit to the shareholders. The implications of his *Reports*, he wrote, transcended the Association's mining operations, and 'the commercial man may consider whether in this and in the other countries of South America, it is prudent to embark his capital in any permanent establishment or speculation, or to furnish these countries with the Loans which some of them are still requiring'.[8]

As far as bonds were concerned, however, the New Year had begun slightly more favourably. Widespread certainty that Barings would pay Mexico's next dividends caused a flurry of buying which pushed 1825 bonds up to 66.[9] Shortly thereafter Colombian bondholders were slightly heartened by news that Bolívar had returned to Colombia instead of remaining in Peru as had been feared, and were led to hope that he would be able to dispel the political discord which had been paralysing both commerce and government.[10] Trading in Latin American bonds other than those of Colombia and Mexico nevertheless was generally sluggish, in contrast to activity in some Mexican mining shares which still commanded premiums.

The Brazilian-Buenos Ayres conflict continued to dampen the market. As far as *The Morning Chronicle* was concerned, Buenos Ayres was mad to continue such an unequal and disastrous war 'with resources borrowed from British capitalists'.[11] In early February, however, news of Bolívar's intention to reform Colombia's financial system caused Colombian bonds to rise to 36½. Brokers now confidently spoke of Colombia curing its default by mid-summer.[12] Mexican bonds were then boosted to 68⅝ in mid-month by news that bullion shipments were on route from Vera Cruz. Peruvian bonds lingered at 34½, while Brazilians, depressed by the protracted war, stayed at 65.[13] By the end of February, City financiers were certain that due to the war's drain on resources Brazil would soon require another loan. The bonds reached 66¼, presumably on expectations that any new loan could be used to pay dividends on the earlier credits.[14] Although Brazil had not defaulted, investors were nevertheless nervous. Indeed, so little business was being transacted in foreign bonds that *The Morning Chronicle* wondered 'whether the Foreign Stock Exchange will not soon be appropriated to some other purpose than originally intended'.[15]

Meanwhile, reports reached the City that after lengthy negotiations the Spanish government had agreed to compensate British owners of property damaged in the recent civil wars and in the subsequent French invasion. No such arrangement was contemplated for holders of cortes bonds. Because part of the compensation would be paid in debentures, a special meeting of the Committee of the Foreign Stock Exchange was convened to consider whether they should be given a Stock Exchange quotation among other authorized securities. Not only did the committee decide against a listing, which would have allowed the bonds to be sold on the Exchange, but used the occasion to resolve by a large majority that 'for the better protection of the interests of the members of the Stock Exchange, and the public in general' the committee would not sanction or recognize any sale or purchase of bonds issued by foreign governments in default on former loans raised in Britain until that government reached 'some satisfactory arrangement' with its creditors.

In an editorial comment *The Times* pontificated that 'it is high time that all Foreign Governments should be informed that they are not to be permitted to commit wholesale plunder in this country without the recoil of injurious consequences upon themselves'.[16] Given, however, that after commissions and other deductions Latin American borrowers had received on average but 60 per cent of the face value of the bonds issued, an impartial observer might wonder who was plundering whom. Nevertheless, the policy established by this resolution would be continued through the century and proved a more effective sanction against defaulting borrowers than court actions.

The Foreign Stock Exchange's policy was later supplemented by the Committee of the Stock Exchange itself, which was troubled by the low esteem in which it was currently held by many members of public thanks to well-publicized scandals involving some of its members. As the date approached for the annual membership re-election in March, the committee announced that 'a stricter degree of inquiry' than usual would be made into members' past conduct. Subsequently a considerable number of members of both the domestic and foreign stock exchanges were refused readmission in the hope that their example would 'go far towards removing the general odium which the public have felt disposed to affix on the majority of the transactions entered into at the Stock Exchange'.[17]

In early March letters from Colombia reported the reconciliation of Bolívar with his fractious colleague General Páez, thus leaving the Liberator free to consider means of satisfying the bondholders. Meanwhile Mexican bonds climbed to 69¼ on the strength of another rumoured specie shipment and publication of the Mexican president's address to congress which provided 'a very flattering view of the prospects of the country'.[18] Brazilian bondholders were surely relieved when the contractors for the first Brazilian loan announced that the eighth half-yearly interest payment would be made on 1 April when due.[19] Future payments, however, would be assured not by remittances of bills, due to the high rate of exchange, but by shipments of coffee, sugar and other produce. Nevertheless, official purchases of these commodities would drive up local prices and prove even more costly to the government, it was feared.[20]

By the end of March the amounts withheld from Mexican bond proceeds for dividends were exhausted, yet Baring Brothers announced that the interest due on 1 April would still be paid. No such glad tidings were conveyed to Colombian bondholders via the Jamaica mail. There was no specie cargo waiting to be loaded at Cartagena, and it was obvious that 'the expectations of the bondholders which have been very sanguine of late, are not in the way of being speedily fulfilled'. Nor was confidence in Colombia's reliability heightened when *The Times* printed an extract from a Bogotá newspaper criticizing the London press attacks on Minister Hurtado's insurance policy stratagem of the prior year. The Bogotá paper did admit, however, that the government had not ordered the insurance to be written, that it had only advised Hurtado of the possibility of funds being remitted, and that he was being recalled.[21]

More depressing news followed in April when a letter from La Guayra reported Bolívar was planning an expedition against Puerto Rico. According to the correspondent, Bolívar considered Colombia's independence insecure as long as Spain retained Cuba and Puerto Rico. Colombian creditors would indeed have cause for concern, *The Times* noted, if instead of restoring the nation's credit Bolívar wasted resources in expensive enterprises 'of very doubtful result'.[22] Misgivings over the projected expedition were soon eclipsed by rumours of Bolívar's resignation as president. Colombian bonds tumbled two points to 36 as fears grew that Colombia would now be without effective leadership. Nearly all other Latin American bonds were also depressed 'by the sympathy that seems to exist between countries which have acquired from the nature of their struggle for independence, a sort of political identity'.[23]

Colombian bonds then slipped to 34½ as more holders abandoned hope and tried to sell.[24] By the end of April the press observed that Colombian bonds, now at 33, were falling to their true value, that of a deferred stock 'the payment of interest on which is extremely remote and altogether indefinite in point of time'.[25] Letters from Bogotá confirmed the gloom, noting that the government administration was in a state of total confusion, with not a thought given to the plight of the nation's creditors.[26] On 1 May Consul General

Michelena destroyed any lingering bondholder expectations by announcing in the press that he had no official information from his government which would 'warrant him in making any specific communication to the bond-holders respecting the unpaid dividends already due, and the one becoming due this day'.[27]

Meanwhile, some months before bondholders had sent an urgent memorial to their agent in Caracas, who had in turn presented it to Bolívar. He promised to reply officially but a letter from La Guayra held out scant hope of any positive action: 'It is quite useless to make representations to Bolívar about money matters, as he does not, or will not, understand them.'[28] By mid-June Colombian 1822 and 1824 bonds, issued with such confidence and high expectations, were quoted at 25 and 29.[29] Although stories that Bolívar had ordered all Church plate to be seized for loan service failed to impress the market, Colombian 1825 bonds rose to 31½ when news arrived in London of Bolívar's favourable reaction to the bondholders' memorial. His reply, when finally made public by Powles, was not all that encouraging, however. Sent over the signature of José Raphael Revenga, former minister in London and now secretary of state for the interior, it merely stated that funds had already been allocated for payment of the foreign debt by a law passed in May of last year. Although 'deviations' from the law had occurred during 'the late dissentions ... with the presence of the Liberator, the laws have again resumed their authority'.[30] Colombian bonds remained steady at a discouraging 28½ and 32.[31]

Neither did Powles and his colleagues find much sympathy at the foreign office. In February 1827 Powles had sent Canning a copy of resolutions passed at the last Colombian bondholder meeting, which had requested that the British foreign office be informed of their plight. Under-Secretary Joseph Planta merely had thanked Powles on behalf of Canning for the communication, without further comment.[32] As Powles must have been aware, the British government did not consider itself obliged to espouse claims arising out of defaulted bonds purchased as speculations on the open market, and in the issuing or guarantee of which the government had not been involved. This had been clearly stated by Canning in parliament, and in reply to a request for intervention from Spanish bondholders. The government had no duty 'to interfere in any way to procure the repayment of loans made by British subjects to Foreign Powers, States or individuals'.[33] Nevertheless, the contractor kept lobbying in order to pacify his irate bondholder clients.

While Colombian bondholders were clutching at straws, Chilean investors were experiencing similar disappointments. On 31 March Minister Egaña announced with deep regret that still no funds had arrived to pay the individends. He attributed the delay to the sudden collapse of the *estanco* charged with servicing the debt. Since then, the government had not had sufficient time to collect the necessary funds elsewhere, he explained. Egaña, however, expected shortly to have 'some gratifying information, which he will lose no time in laying before the Bondholders'.[34] A week later *The Times* printed an indignant letter from a substantial Chilean bondholder who angrily deplored the 'extraordinary supineness' of the holders of defaulted bonds who sat quietly and made no effort to better their situation. The writer, who signed himself 'Amicus Justitial', proposed instead that bondholders, as in private bankruptcy procedures, meet regularly and appoint trustees to take any steps necessary to protect their rights and to call attention to their claims.[35]

The letter produced its desired results, and on 19 April Chilean bondholders assembled at the City of London Tavern. They were addressed by the letter's author, a Mr Hartly, who said he had been told by merchants with experience in Chile that as long as British bondholders remained quiet and uncomplaining, the Chilean's native indolence – together with their conviction that the British were careless with their money – would combine to prevent payment of the dividends. Hartly therefore proposed various resolutions condemning the Chilean government for its breach of good faith and requesting the secretary of state to withhold recognition of Chilean independence until it had satisfied its creditors. Although the meeting did not adopt Hartly's suggestions, it did, however, resolve to invite the loan contractors and Egaña to meet with the bondholders to discuss their claims.

The following day *The Times* remarked that the meeting had set a useful example to other Latin American bondholders. Although it might be difficult to devise means of obtaining immediate relief, the bondholders were right 'to let the Government which owes the money perceive that they are not ... disposed to submit to a heavy loss without causing their complaints to be heard'. The annual interest due on the loan was less than £50,000, for which Chile's revenue if properly administered should be adequate.[36] On 24 April *The Times* followed its earlier comments on the Chilean meeting by referring to a letter just received from Chile via Buenos Ayres dated 16 January and reporting that the government had made no preparations for remitting funds for the April dividend. Consequently 'the situation of the creditors ... is as forlorn as can be imagined'.[37]

Nor was the Chilean creditors meeting on 24 April productive. Neither Egaña nor the contractor attended; but merely sent letters reiterating their prior positions. Chile's 'scandalous breach of faith' and contempt for its engagements deserved the severest reprobation fumed *The Times*, noting that all the country's revenue had been pledged for liquidating the debt. Incensed by Egaña's absence, the bondholders now passed several resolutions condemning Chile's conduct, copies of which were to be sent to the Chilean envoy, the British consul at Santiago and the foreign office.[38] The bondholders then elected a committee to meet on a regular basis, correspond with the foreign office and the Chileans, and generally protect their interests.

Upon reflection *The Times* found nothing surprising in the Chilean government's silence regarding dividends. 'It is a well-known trait in the Spanish character when nothing satisfactory can be communicated, to remain silent, in order to avoid all personal responsibility...'[39] The foreign office was, however, still unwilling to become officially involved, and answered bondholder pleas by stating that because 'the transactions to which these resolutions relate are entirely of a private nature, his Majesty's Government cannot exercise any interference respecting them'.[40]

While bondholders were holding meetings in London, war and insurrection were spreading throughout much of Latin America. Rumours of a pending peace treaty between Brazil and Buenos Ayres would spring up quickly and were as quickly contradicted by a new set of unauthenticated reports. Mail from Buenos Ayres indicated the Brazilian blockade was largely ineffectual and that Buenos Ayres privateers were successfully preying upon Brazilian and other shipping. On land, Buenos Ayres also appeared to be winning, inflicting a massive defeat on Brazilian troops in February. Incredibly, relative to most other Latin American bonds, Brazil and Buenos Ayres issues enjoyed high quotations with the former at 57½ and Buenos Ayres at 59 by the end of May.[41] Unrest was also reported in Peru and Chile, while further north the unity of the United Provinces of Central America was still threatened by a civil war begun by El Salvador. Central America had not as yet defaulted, however, and the February dividend had been paid. Nevertheless, the bonds, quoted at 53 in January, were unsaleable by mid-year and seldom mentioned in the press.

Although the March Mexican dividend had been paid courtesy of Baring Brothers, the availability of funds for the July dividends was doubtful unless Mexico could in the interim remit sufficient silver to Britain. Beginning in late March, rumours circulated that HMS *Tweed* was due to leave Vera Cruz for London with a cargo of bullion and cochineal worth over £1,000,000. An insurance policy on the shipment had been written at Lloyds at a high premium, other rumours revealed. Further reports then stated that ship's departure had been delayed, probably by bad weather.[42]

By the time the *Tweed* arrived at Portsmouth in late April, rumours had escalated the cargo's value to £1,500,000, of which approximately £700,000 was for the Mexican government's account. Mexican bond quotations promptly rose half a point. The ship unfortunately was placed in quarantine and consequently no confirming letters could be brought ashore. Word soon reached London, however, that the cargo was worth far less than anticipated – only £300,000, of which most was for private merchants' accounts. Less than £50,000 had been remitted for debt service.

One disappointed anonymous Mexican bondholder in a letter to *The Times* remarked that during the last year the second Mexican loan contractors had not, as in the past, published any notice confirming the deposit of monies in the sinking fund as required by the loan agreement. He therefore wished to know from 'competent authority' if this obligation between the Mexican government and the bondholders had been suspended, and, if so, 'from what cause, it being an essential condition of the contract, in the regular fulfilment of which we are all interested.'[43] No answer was forthcoming.

Additional apprehension was caused in early May by letters from Mexico reporting on the country's finances, and illustrating the importance of the mining enterprises in servicing the foreign debt. Figures released by the ministry of finance showed Mexico would in future be largely dependent for revenue upon the success of the British mining operations. Given the generally poor performance of the British companies, the minister's 'continued ability to satisfy the English creditors cannot, with anything like certainty, be calculated upon,' *The Times* warned.[44] The 1824 Mexica 5 per cent bonds now were quoted at a lower rate than the 1825 6 per cents, because the obligation in the 1824 loan contract to redeem one quarter of that loan out of the proceeds of any subsequent credit had never been completely honoured. In vain holders of 1824 bonds demanded an explanation.[45]

So great were doubts concerning Mexico's political and financial future that the market was unaffected by Baring Brothers' announcement that the dividends due on Sunday 1 July for the 1825 bonds would be paid at their Bishopsgate office on Monday 2 July. In fact, of the £221,697 interest payment, £131,154 was advanced by Barings, which did not inspire public confidence in the basic soundness of the securities.[46] By 2 July, nevertheless, Mexican 1825 bonds were quoted at 71, higher than even Brazil (59½) or Buenos Ayres (60¼). Colombian bonds trailed at 27¾ (1822) and at 31 (1824), while Peru remained at 24½. Neither Chilean nor Guatemalan bonds were mentioned, and Mexican bonds would shortly slip to 68¾ as the public's misgivings returned.[47] By the end of July, Brazil and

Buenos Ayres quotations had each risen two points on reports that the Buenos Ayres peace envoy had been warmly received at the Brazilian court and that 'every matter in dispute . . . will be amicably settled without delay'.[48] Although in fact the war would shortly resume, demand for Brazilian and Buenos Ayres bonds pushed prices to 67 and 65 by early August. The Mexican 1825 bonds meanwhile dropped over a point when news – later disproved – that Barings was intending to transfer its Mexican agency to Reid, Irving precipitated a heavy selling wave.[49]

The market received a much more severe shock when on 6 August the press announced 'the alarming illness' of George Canning, who had become Prime Minister in April. He had been confined to bed at his Chiswick home for over three weeks with 'a very severe attack of inflammation', and despite four doctors at his bedside and being bled several times, his life was now in serious danger. Medical bulletins reporting his sinking condition were issued periodically over the next three days, while a constant stream of distinguished callers, including the Brazilian envoy extraordinary, arrived at Chiswick House to pay their respects. On Thursday 9 August the newspapers sadly announced his death.[50] All were fulsome in their praise, and the king commanded he be buried between Charles James Fox and William Pitt in Westminister Abbey. The funeral took place the following week. It was a simple service, without music as the family had requested, and attended by approximately 250 mourners, including the attorney general, the solicitor general, the lord chancellor, MPs, the Dukes of Clarence and Portland, and the diplomatic corps. The monarchist statesman, who had done more than any other European to assure the freedom of the new Latin American republics, was then laid to rest in the Abbey's north transept only nine inches from the foot of William Pitt's tomb.[51]

By the time of Canning's death the government practice of remaining aloof from disputes between foreign states and their British bondholder creditors had undergone a subtle transformation. It was now obvious that the total losses incurred by investors in Latin American loans could be quite serious. Under increasing pressure from City merchants and bankers, the foreign office policy softened to allow diplomatic and consular representatives abroad to use their 'good offices' and encourage defaulting states by persuasion rather than force either to honour their obligations, or to negotiate rescheduling arrangements with bondholders. On 8 August 1827 Lord Dunglas wrote on behalf of the foreign secretary, the Earl of Aberdeen, to Colombian bondholders that the chargé'd'affairs at Bogotá had been instructed 'to afford the aid of his countenance and good offices' to bondholders' efforts 'to effect an arrangement' with the

Colombian government. Nevertheless, 'you are not to understand from this ... that His Majesty's Government have thought it expedient to comply with the request of the bondholders, considered as a claim of right.'[52]

This policy shift was not confined to Colombia. By September 1827 Consul General Nugent in Santiago was instructed to utilize his good offices and to meet with the Chilean president to deliver a memorial from Chilean bondholders. On 23 October Chilean Minister Franciso de Zegers replied on behalf of the president, who expressed regret that the bondholders 'should unjustly insinuate that the Government had been dilatory or inattentive in the fulfilment of its contracts'.[53] Great efforts had been made to pay the bondholders, Zegers wrote, but these had been rendered ineffectual by unforeseen circumstances, political intrigues and the government's obligation to submit to the decisions of an obstructive congress. Indeed, he maintained, Chile had sacrificed a large part of the loan in order to pay the first dividends in 1823 and 1824. Then the government had established the *estanco*, to which it had advanced $500,000 from the loan. The monopoly's managers were unfortunately inexperienced, and, moreover, the country had to cope with threats, civil war and maintain a large military establishment. The president now promised new legislation which 'will fix unalterably the payment of the interest and aid liquidation of the debt in conformity with the ... contract'.

At this point Mexican bondholders panicked when on 15 August mail just arrived from Vera Cruz reported the government's failure to raise a loan locally with which to pay the 1 October dividends. The remaining resident Spaniards – still Mexico's wealthiest merchants and entrepreneurs – had refused to participate unless recent anti-Spanish legislation was repealed. The government refused and so an October default and an agency change now seemed more likely than ever. Any decline in Mexican bonds was, however, more than off-set the following day by a counter-rumour that the sloop-of-war HMS *Britomark* was about to load $40,000 in specie at Vera Cruz, thereby causing a one and half point rise in the 1825 issue to 68¾.[54]

Three days later an attempt appears to have been made to bolster public confidence in Mexico through insertion in *The Morning Chronicle* of a report presented to congress by the Mexican finance minister on 1 January 1827. The report described in detail how the proceeds of the 1824 and 1825 loans had been disbursed, leaving a balance of £464,467 still not utilized at the end of the year. Presumably bondholders were expected to infer that the funds had not been wasted, and that enough still remained to pay dividends. Actually, if anything the report demonstrated that the Mexicans had been thoroughly fleeced by its London bankers and contractors, since although the nation had incurred a total indebtedness of £6,400,000, it had actually received less than £2,550,000 in stores, credits and cash.[55] More thoughtful readers also might have reflected that because Mexico had obviously benefited so little from the loans, it might not be over-eager to repay them.

Not all Londoners were concerned by the constant flow of bad news from Latin America. Indeed, most people demonstrated remarkable recuperative powers after the 1825–6 panic. Many of the firms which had stopped payments reopened their doors, while the social season with its constant round of dinners, soirées, concerts and balls occupied the time and attention of society's upper echelons. Between four and six in the afternoon Hyde Park was crowded with well-groomed gentlemen on shining horses paying court to fashionable, beribboned ladies whose open, elegant carriages flowed in unceasing streams along Rotten Row. In the evening the theatres were crowded, with the best boxes at Covent Garden occupied by the most successful courtesans of the day, who used them as show windows in which to display their expensive wares. The gambling craze received a new outlet when William Crockford, a former fish-monger, opened his famous gaming club in 1827. Admission was exceedingly difficult to obtain, and although games of chance were nominally illegal the membership list was filled with prominent names, including the Duke of Wellington. Nor did Crockford neglect the inner man: the club chef was, as a German visitor to London observed in admiration, 'the celebrated Ude, theoretically and practically the best in Europe'.[56]

While the fashionables were recovering from the festivities of the night before, the City swarmed with activity: coffee was sold from barrows to early arrivals, and the streets were soon jammed with horse-drawn vehicles of every description. Countless advertisements for products, medications and services were posted on the walls of buildings and on the sides of large, box-like wagons pulled through the thoroughfares by men and horses. Early versions of the sandwich-board man were everywhere evident: 'One man has a pasteboard hat, three times as high as other hats, on which is written in great letters "Boots at twelve shillings a pair – warranted." Another carries a sort of banner on which is represented a washerwoman and the inscription "Only three-pence a shirt".'[57] For such humble tradesmen, as also for the fashionable Mayfair set, news of Latin American political and economic instability had little relevance. Middle-class investors were, however, gravely concerned.

During July, the anxiety of Mexican bondholders was overshadowed by the despair of Colombian investors as each ship brought news of spreading unrest within Gran Colombia. In mid-August bondholders learned of a separatist movement in Ecuador and increasing opposition to Bolívar in congress, as men who once claimed his friendship now became enemies. On 27 August 'An Anglocolombian' wrote to *The Times* in an attempt to explain the bitterness of Bolívar's opponents. Many legislators were still hobbled by their colonial past, he suggested, in which favouritism, absolutism and corruption had prevented the acquisition of any experience in disinterested self-government. The uncompromising principles of Bolívar were anathema to such men.[58] Many office holders, the Anglocolombian wrote, were primarily interested in enriching themselves by granting concessions and contracts to foreign entrepreneurs in return for large commissions, or by using government funds to liquidate domestic government bills which their agents had purchased at steep discounts. Colombia indeed had the wealth to pay its creditors if its resources were properly applied by honest public servants, 'but, unfortunately, the spirit of public spoliation, so prevalent among the viceroys and governors in the time of the Spaniards, has not ceased to operate on the acts of their successors'.

During the first two weeks in September rumours persisted that Barings would soon surrender the Mexican agency due to the Mexican government's refusal or inability to repay Barings' cash advances. Rumours that a new loan agreement had been signed stemmed the panic briefly, leading to speculation that the October dividends would in fact be paid. Then Minister Rocafuerte dispelled all doubts when he placed an advertisement in the 15 September morning papers stating he found himself 'in the painful necessity' of informing the public that due to a delay 'from accidental circumstances' he could not announce, as was usual two weeks before a due date, that the October dividends would be paid. He assured Mexico's creditors they could expect the payment to be made very shortly and that the Mexican government would faithfully discharge all its engagements.[59] When the Stock Exchange opened that morning 'to a scene of great confusion', excited jobbers and brokers rushed across the floor shouting selling orders. The 1825 bonds dipped to 44 before closing at 47¼, and their fall depressed all other Latin American securities as well.[60]

According to *The Times*, the shock of the Mexican default was one of the most terrible that it could recall because it caught unawares even some of the most cautious Stock Exchange members. Apparently – although it seems incredible given the frequent storm warnings – many investors had still believed either that funds to pay the dividends were already in the hands of Barings or that additional assets had been retained and were forthcoming from the former agents. Nor was it realistic to share Rocafuerte's hope that payment would be made shortly. His tone had resembled too much that used by Colombian Minister Hurtado on a similar occasion to inspire much confidence. It was, *The Times* observed with hindsight, especially regrettable that Barings had lent its name to the proceedings. Although all the firm's partners had repeatedly stated they had no formal connection with the Mexican government and had agreed to pay out dividends as they would any other commercial agency, the general public had received a different impression. Many bondholders would never have retained their positions in the loan 'but for the character which Messrs Barings gave it by undertaking the agency'.[61]

It was to be hoped, the arch-conservative *Courier* commented, that the delay in paying the dividends was, as Rocafuerte had said, attributable only to 'accidental causes' and not to lack of means. Whatever the reasons, the non-payment was 'one of the most unfortunate events that could well have befallen South American interests'. While other South American governments had defaulted, it had been thought that Mexico's resources were so abundant and her government so aware of the importance of maintaining her public credit that nothing similar would be allowed to happen. This confidence had been buttressed by the recent statement of the president to congress that provisions had been made to meet all public engagements for the current year. Mexico's default was therefore 'a severe blow at South American credit, generally'. Rocafuerte, the newspaper continued, was reportedly one of the most able and intelligent Latin American ministers who had ever come to Britain. He had worked unceasingly to establish Mexico's credit in Europe, 'and now he has the mortification to find, in a single day, the fruit of his exertions thrown away. Let us not add to this disappointment which he does not deserve.'[62]

Presumably by now many of the original purchasers of Latin American bonds had already sold them to speculators at less than they had paid, and so were no longer exposed to further loss. Nevertheless they and the present bondholders must have become even more upset – if possible – as during the year they read press advertisements announcing dividend payments and redemptions of the Prussian, Danish, Russian and Neapolitan loans on their due dates. Perhaps, however, some unfortunate Latin American investors found slight comfort in the even worse plight of the Spanish and Greek bondholders – assuming of course, that the Latin American bond purchasers had not been persuaded to spread their risks by diversifying into these other disasters.

Despite Rocafuerte's last minute efforts to obtain bridging finance, 1 October came and went without payment. *The Times* continued to praise the minister's diligence in seeking solutions and intimated that the Mexican government had been served poorly by its former agents – presumably Goldschmidt. 'It is the universal feeling that the general treatment the Mexican government has met with in this country is an affair in which the national honour is concerned. The subject must in future press very much on our attention.'[63] The bonds shed another three points when ten days later HMS *Britomark* arrived with a large shipment of specie – but none for the Mexican government's account. The market's incredible volatility was amply illustrated when on the following day news flashed around the City that an insurance policy for £109,000 had been written at Lloyds and the Alliance Company on instructions relayed to Rocafuerte by swift packet. Bonds jumped to 52, while large wagers were placed that all the dividends in arrears would be paid before April.[64]

Surprisingly, although no specie had arrived by mid-November Mexican bonds in the interim had remained fairly steady. On the morning of 24 November prices rose to 55½ at another set of rumours that $2,000,000 had been shipped from Vera Cruz. In the afternoon, however, newly-received letters told a different story. No specie had arrived in Vera Cruz in time for the sailing of the latest warship, although a large amount had been sent by mule trains from Mexico City in late October. On 17 December a fortnight before the maturity date, the customary advertisement announcing dividend payments failed to appear in the press. A week later bad news arrived from Mexico that while specie worth $1,000,000 had indeed been sent to Vera Cruz from Mexico City and placed aboard HMS *Tyrian*, none was earmarked for the October or January dividends.[65]

When the *Tyrian* actually arrived at Falmouth on the day after Christmas, it brought even more depressing news concerning the nation's miserable financial and political situation. Bonds fell two to three points in the morning, but, incredibly, recovered when a report circulated that Rocafuerte would advertise payment of the dividends the next day. The minister's announcement was disappointing, however. He merely told the public that he had received a further triplicate copy of the earlier 16 October despatch informing him that $500,000 would be sent by the first available warship. *The Times* was not impressed, noting that the copy had been sent two months after the original dispatch and had not provided any additional information.[66] Rocafuerte, however, had achieved his purpose and revived, without actually lying, hopes that the dividends might yet be paid. So eager were distraught investors to find the faintest of silver linings in the darkest of thunder clouds that, despite months of destroyed expectations, the 1825 bonds rose one point to end the year at 46.[67]

As Mexico slid inevitably into default, the cautious optimism which had prevailed among Brazilians and Buenos Ayres bondholders since receiving news in August that peace was imminent had proved shortlived. By the end of September word had reached London that Buenos Ayres had refused to ratify the proposed treaty, and that consequently Brazil had resolved to continue the war. Even though Brazilian bonds were quoted higher than any other Latin American security, they declined quickly to 60½. Buenos Ayres bonds slumped two points to 53 as selling orders were quickly placed. *The Times* dismissed scornfully any expectation that a new Brazilian loan would succeed. Internal paper money issues were trading at 50 per cent of their face value and a debased copper coinage had replaced gold and silver, which had soared in value. It was an inopportune time to borrow, but without funds it would be difficult to continue the war.[68] Unlike *The Times*, which seemed more sympathetic to Buenos Ayres, *The Morning Chronicle*'s assessment of the conflict was more even-handed. Nevertheless, it too opined that attempts to find a further loan for Brazil would be futile and any sums raised would, like the proceeds of the earlier loan, be spent on the armed forces.[69] Despite the lack of foreign funds, however, the war dragged on, financed by paper money, internal loans at usurious rates, and, in the case of Buenos Ayres, by piracy thinly disguised as privateering.[70]

On 21 November the desperation of certain Peruvian bondholders, and their obstinate refusal to believe or admit the obvious, became manifest when a large buying wave drove Peruvian bonds up to 41 before they closed at 38½. The rise had been sparked by news that a £350,000 loan had been raised in Paris from which the three overdue London dividends would be paid. Even Colombian bonds rose on the belief that if Peru could raise money in Paris, Colombia, a stronger, larger country, could do likewise. The story had undoubtedly been concocted by speculators, and within two days Peruvian bonds fell back to 35½, and Colombia declined to where it had been when the report was first mooted.[71] Peruvian bonds then slipped to 30 when letters from France confirmed that 'the moneyed interest at Paris would as soon think of lending to the inhabitants of the moon as to any of the South American States which have not kept their faith with the bondholders.' By 6 December, Peruvian bonds had reached 24, over 16 per cent below the price paid before the hoax had been exposed.[72]

The year thus once again ended unhappily for most Latin American bondholders. They must have been feeling as battered as those scarred professional bareknuckle prizefighters Jack Tisdale and Dick Curley, whose recent gory encounter the press had reported in an argot all its own:

> Tisdale hit him, but Dick was too quick and, among other operations, planted a *muzzler*, which drew *first blood* from Tisdale's *ivories* ... Tisdale came up spitting *claret*, but steady. Dick threw in a right-hander on his left *peeper* but Tisdale was with him, and countered heavily with his right on the ear, drawing some blood, which came from the interior, and to speak figuratively, 'melted the wax'.[73]

After the Mexican default, market confidence in Latin American issues would never be restored, even though rumours of specie shipments would continue to stimulate slight fluctuations. Mexico, moreover, was about to experience a new wave of internal political turmoil, and by December had great difficulty even borrowing domestically. Mexican merchants who could earn 2 or 3 per cent a month on well-secured loans to the local private sector were not interested in lower-yielding government paper.[74]

To the south, the Central American federation was still riven by war, while Colombia, Peru and Chile seemed unlikely to be able to cure their defaults in the foreseeable future. Across the Andes the dreadful state of Buenos Ayres' finances stimulated fears that the January dividends would not be paid, causing bonds to close the year at 44, two points below Mexico. Only Brazil, whose bonds were quoted at 60, maintained a fragile market credibility – and even that soon would be shaken.[75]

VIII
THE LAST DEFAULTS

ON NEW YEAR'S Day 1828, the press reported Latin American bond prices were holding steady, there having been little trading since Christmas. The calm was deceptive and temporary, for on 9 January the press announced the Buenos Ayres dividend due in three days would not be paid.

The market apparently had discounted the bad news in advance, since quotations which were already at 45 dropped initially only to 43, slightly below the Mexican 1825 issue.[1] In any case, the blockade of the Río de la Plata had long prevented any specie shipments for remittances. Moreover, the exchange was so unfavourable if that the government had sought to effect the remittances they 'would have had to raise four dollars for every one paid to the English creditor'. The war had been unnecessarily prolonged for the sake of enriching a few individuals by privateering, while the country's resources were wasted, *The Times* stated. The only solution could be another loan, which Buenos Ayres could never obtain while the war continued.[2]

Soon after the Buenos Ayres default the public was treated to another exposé of Latin American perfidy by the review in the press of James A. Beaumont's *Travels in Buenos Ayres and the Adjacent Provinces of Rio de la Plata*. In 1824, the author's father, James T. B. Beaumont, had organized a group of British emigrants bound for Buenos Ayres, and subsequently had helped form the Rio de la Plata Agricultural Association in order to send settlers to the Province of Entre Ríos.[3] Young Beaumont sailed on one of the later emigrant ships in March 1826. The prospective colonists were sober and well behaved during the voyage from Plymouth, causing Beaumont to comment 'if there ever were a body of agricultural emigrants from this country who were likely to succeed, and deserved to do so, they were these men'.[4] Arriving at the Río de la Plata estuary after a nine week voyage, the ship was prevented by the blockading Brazilian fleet from proceeding upriver. One hundred and fifty of the new arrivals then returned to England, while the remainder settled across the river at Montevideo. Beaumont, however, resolved to proceed to Entre Ríos to discover how the earlier emigrants were faring. He quickly learned that far from receiving the warm welcome and assistance they had been led to expect, the colonists' cattle, tools and stores had been confiscated by local Entre Ríos *caudillos* who refused to recognize the authority of the Buenos Ayres government to settle foreigners on their lands.

In any event, the Brazilian blockade and the generalized violence would have prevented resupply of the colony, and impeded the settlers' products from reaching Buenos Ayres in any great quantity. Even without the war the colony's future would also have been clouded by the jealousy of local economic interests who feared the immigrants' superior agricultural and technical skills. Native farmers, millers and bakers, as well as Buenos Ayres merchants who made their living importing corn and flour from abroad, felt threatened.

In Buenos Ayres, Beaumont reminded the central government that the association had advanced nearly £300,000 for passage, supplies and maintenance for 620 emigrants. He soon discovered that the authorities had no intention either of reimbursing the passage money as had been promised by their London representatives, or of paying the agreed £100 to £200 bounty to each family on arrival. In addition, monies entrusted to Buenos Ayres representatives in London to assist the colonists had vanished without an accounting or explanation. Despite its promises, the government now claimed it was too impoverished by war to render any assistance. Beaumont, totally disgusted, disbanded the colony and returned home.

Although Beaumont ascribed the main reason for the colonization failure to the Brazilian war, he was scathing in his observations on the general standards of political and social morality in Buenos Ayres. Independence had left the vices of the Spanish heritage intact. Although they had 'dismissed their monks and friars there remains with them the hypocrisy of both orders. They have broken their own chains of slavery, but the vices of slaves, dissimulation and treachery, continue rooted in their habits.'[5] Nor could the legal system afford relief against corruption and refusal to honour government contracts. 'What the law really is at Buenos Ayres, I could find no-one to tell me during ten months residence there. It seems a very flexible and varying commodity; and although it yields no protection to a capitalist in Europe, it appears to answer every such purpose for a knave in South America.'[6]

While Beaumont's withering denunciations were directed at Buenos Ayres and its sister provinces, *The Times* when reviewing his book implied that the association's misadventures were typical of what might be expected by any company venturing into Latin America. Narratives like Beaumont's did the public a service by pointing out 'the vanity of any expectation that English capital is likely to be applied in South America, to any other purpose than that of putting money into the pockets of the adventurers who practice upon our gullibity.' The association's subscribers had lost all their investment and gained nothing 'but the valuable knowledge that the South American diplomats are no more to be trusted than any other Stock Exchange intriguer'.[7]

After the Buenos Ayres loan debacle only Brazil and Central America were not in default. While the dividends on the latter – commonly called the Guatemalan loan – were paid on 1 February, a week later the bonds which had been issued at 68 were quoted at 30–1.[8] News that the Central American civil war still continued, and that to finance a further military campaign the government had exacted a $50,000 forced loan from Guatemala City merchants, did not inspire confidence in London. The loan then received particularly unwelcome notoriety when details of a bondholder's suit in the Court of Chancery for fraud against Barclay, Herring, Richardson, the original agents, were fully reported in the daily press.[9]

Consequently, in an attempt to refurbish his country's image, Minister Zebadúa announced on 6 March that while his government had 'suffered great inconvenience and injury' through its agents failure to place the entire loan of £1,421,000, the bondholders should not suffer. His government therefore had authorized him to recognize as part of the national debt the £163,300 in bonds in circulation, which he requested be presented at his 31 Manchester Street residence so that they might be 'stamped, authorized and recognized as legitimate and valid for the future'.[10]

The following day The Times commented that Guatemala should be grateful that Barclays had failed to raise the full amount of the loan. Guatemala only owed £163,300 and so should congratulate itself for not placing a terrible strain upon its resources like other Latin American borrowers had done.[11] Although thanks to Zebadúa's efforts the bonds rose slightly, in early April bondholders must have been discomforted to learn that the civil war was still raging. Guatemala City was secure from the rebels, but the countryside remained unsettled. Moreover, casual violence persisted even in the capital, where British Consul O'Reilly was murdered one night in his own home. A Mr Herring, son of the London merchant banker, was in the house at the time and narrowly escaped assassination himself.[12]

While Zebadúa was weathering the latest bond crisis and at the same time seeking vainly to persuade the British government to recognize his country, Minister Rocafuerte and the Mexican bondholders continued their unhappy relationship. In early January Mexican bondholders anxiety had diminished when reports that $2,000,000 in bullion had been shipped by wagon from Mexico City to Vera Cruz caused the 1825 bonds to jump 3 per cent. Within a month the bonds had collapsed to 38½ when the rumours once again proved false, causing many investors to abandon all expectation of any recovery on their bonds 'as a hopeless speculation'.[13]

Mexican and Buenos Ayres bonds now were both selling at the same prices, while Colombia (1824) was on offer at 23½, Peru at 23, and Guatemala at 30. Only Brazil 1825 bonds at 61¼ – twenty-four points below issue price – seemed to offer any promise of recovery. In early February, letters arrived from Mexico asserting that far from possessing sufficient funds to transmit to London, the government had not paid its civil service for several months, and it had only been able to liquidate the arrears due to its troops by levying upon merchants. Mexican 1825 bonds then tumbled a further two points.[14]

Rocafuerte meanwhile came under sharp attack for insuring bullion shipments from Mexico, purportedly on his government's instructions. The cargoes had never arrived, but his actions had caused a brief flurry of activity on the Foreign Stock Exchange, obviously, it was alleged, to profit speculators with inside knowledge. Rocafuerte refused to comment on the accusation, causing *The Times* to conclude in most undiplomatic language that there could be no excuse 'for so unworthy and treacherous a proceeding'.[15] Bondholders were soon demanding to know what explanatation the Mexican government had offered to Rocafuerte when it ordered him to insure bullion which would not arrive. When Colombian Minister Hurtado had arranged similar insurance, the manoeuvre was had been branded 'a shameful fraud'. A similar act performed by a government deserved no better name, and, 'as the mischief is greater and less to be guarded against, so is the stain deeper'.[16]

In early March payment prospects seemed even dimmer when yet another attempt to overthrow the Mexican government was reported. Bondholders were so alarmed that 1825 bond quotations quickly fell to 32¾ – two points below Guatemala.[17] The once-supportive *Morning Chronicle* observed that most people believed no material distinction should be made between the prices of any of the Latin American issues, noting that Mexico had only eight points to fall before it reached Colombia's level.[18] Even news that the latest Mexican revolt had been suppressed failed to cheer bondholders. The failed coup reminded them all too well that in its weak, politically fragile condition, where the bulk of government resources was consumed by the military, there was not the least expectation of any remittances to pay dividends. Letters from Vera Cruz merchants confirmed that the treasury was exhausted, and that ministers who received but nominal salaries only continued at their posts out of patriotism or hopes of an improved future.[19]

Surprisingly in mid-May Mexican 1825 bonds quickly rose ten points when letters via the United States indicated that the Mexican government would soon be placed in funds through a plan to allow Vera Cruz merchants a discount if they paid certain customs duties in advance. Approximately $400,000 would be raised, which would not, of course, be sufficient to cancel the three overdue quarterly interest dividends, which now totalled £219,000. Nevertheless, this demonstration of an intention to begin repairing the nation's credit was enthusiastically received in the City.[20] Major speculators made several large purchases, boosting prices to 45.[21] Expectations crumbled the following week when a ship arrived from Vera Cruz not only empty of bullion, but bearing the sad news that while the government had indeed raised $400–500,000 from the Vera Cruz merchants, the money had been spent on pressing domestic requirements. Fifteen minutes after the Foreign Stock Exchange opened its doors, Mexican 1825 bonds shed six points to close at 38¾. One group of speculators who had bought a large block at 44¼ when the exchange first opened, soon regretted their eagerness when the price fell.[22]

During the first week in June, HMS *Scylla* arrived at Portsmouth with the disheartening news that only £20,000 of its specie cargo was for the Mexican government's account. This small amount was not for the bondholders, however, but to defray embassy expenses. While $2,500,000 in bullion had indeed been sent from Mexico to Vera Cruz as reported earlier, only $500,000 was shipped to Britain. The remainder, the property of banished Spaniards, was sent either to the United States or to Bordeaux. Over the last year trade and banking in the French port town had taken on new life and energy thanks to the stimulus provided by a number of enterprising Spanish families from Mexico who had found there a more congenial refuge than either cold, rainy Britain or the reactionary Spain of Ferdinand VII.[23]

The first half of 1828 had not brought any great relief to Colombian bondholders either, despite continued expectations that they would benefit from Bolívar's reforms of the nation's financial structure. The low quotations for Colombian bonds did not indicate widespread confidence in the City that his efforts would succeed. Scepticism was compounded in early February, when, together with news of a devastating earthquake in Bogotá, the press cautioned that however great Bolívar's efforts, even under ordinary circumstances little could have been accomplished in the brief time since he had assumed supreme power in the republic.[24]

In mid-February bonds rose quickly by two and a half points to 27½ when rumours ran through the City that in keeping with Bolívar's 'extreme desire' to restore Colombia's credit, a plan was under consideration to capitalize overdue interest by issuing a new series of bonds. Although the rumours proved false, and the bonds just as quickly fell three points, the capitalization of interest arrears would eventually become commonplace when, after years of default, Latin America would seek to restore its credit standing. Three weeks later, rumours that Bolívar was seriously ill with a lung infection provoked concern, indicating again how in Britain as in Colombia so much was perceived to depend upon one man.[25]

Meanwhile, the rejected interest-capitalization suggestion retained favour in some quarters, and was one of several solutions discussed among bondholders who, unlike the loan contractors, were not content with awaiting vague replies to their entreaties from Bogotá. In late January one Colombian bondholder in a letter to *The Times* had proposed that bondholders accept an interest reduction for all Latin American issues to 3 per cent until 1835, when the 6 per cent rate would resume.[26] In the interim the Latin American borrowers could repurchase their bonds to reestablish their credit, and investors would receive the same rate of return provided by British securities. It would be far better to accept a realistic, lower amount which could be paid, rather than insist on a higher rate and receive nothing. The writer stated that he had purchased Colombian bonds for £920, and would now gladly subscribe to an agreement entitling him to receive £30 per annum rather than £60. Although this idea, like capitalizing overdue interest, was ahead of its time, eventually it would be adopted and is even today suggested as one of the components in a package of solutions to the current debt crisis.

Not all bondholder proposals were as non-violent, however. In March, 'X. X.', presumably a bondholder, wrote to *The Times* deploring the British government's failure to interfere directly with the Latin American nations on behalf of their creditors.[27] The press was also at fault, he claimed. By first urging people to lend to the Latin American nations and exaggerating their resources, newspapers had 'done more mischief than the knavery of interested individuals'. Now the press did nothing but 'laugh and sneer' at their unfortunate victims, leading X.X. 'to wonder if these bankrupt States had found some means of silencing the press'. The correspondent was probably voicing the sentiments of other frustrated investors when he then suggested that since they could not expect any official assistance from the British government, bondholders should take the law into their own hands and fit out armed vessels to harass Latin American shipping in order to teach the defaulters 'that honesty with States, as well as with individuals, will always be found to be the best policy'.

The Times leader replied to the letter in the same issue, suggesting that anyone who armed a vessel to prey upon Latin American commerce could be hung for piracy. Moreover, the correspondent had been unfair to the press. Whenever newspapers attempted to alert the public to the dangers of Latin American loans, they risked libel actions. The Morning Chronicle, for example, had sought to expose scandals attending the Chilean loan. As a result it had been sued and incurred heavy damages after the presiding judge instructed the jury that 'the conductors of Newspapers had no recognized vocation to enlighten the public with regard to abuses'. The leader did agree, however, that the British government had scandalously neglected its duty towards those of its subjects who had purchased Spanish and Latin American bonds: 'If the creditors urge their claims on the Government, we should think the result might tell to their advantage.'

Meanwhile, Peruvian bondholders were faring even more poorly than Colombian investors since the Lima government, unlike the Bogotá authorities, seemed much less concerned with finding a solution to their difficulties. There was little direct communication with Britain, and any reports that specie was about to arrive probably originated with speculators and were not inspired by news from South America, as when on 22 May, Peruvian bonds rose from 24 to 27 following rumours that remittances to pay dividends could be expected soon from Lima.[28]

Although Chilean bond quotations during the first months of 1828 were roughly the same as those of Peru, their owners' spirits were perhaps marginally higher due to better and more frequent communication between London and Santiago, and to the enterprise of the local British consul. In late February news arrived reporting Consul Nugent's 27 October favourable interview with the Chilean president, to whom he had presented a bondholders petition. The president had regretted Chile's inability to pay, stating that the estanco established to service the loan by collecting certain duties allocated to interest payments had not performed its contract with the government. Therefore the president would agree to the appointment of two people – one by the government and the other by the bondholders – to receive the duties and remit them to Britain as the estanco should have done.[29]

The news from Santiago was warmly welcomed in the City and suggested that the new foreign office policy of allowing the local consuls to utilize their good offices on behalf of bondholders might yet bring tangible relief. As a result the bonds quickly rose four points to close at 26½ – still below Guatelmala at 34, but higher than Peru at 22½.[30] On 25 March Chilean bondholders met at the City of London Tavern to discuss Nugent's letters forwarded to the bondholders' committee through the foreign office. Among the documents was the letter to Nugent from Foreign Minister Zegers promising that new legislation would assure resumption of interest payments after 31 March, by which date four dividend payments would be in arrears. Bondholders were invited to elect – which they promptly did – someone to represent them in Chile and superintend dividend payment arrangements.

Despite the welcome intelligence in Nugent's dispatches, speculators refrained from significant new purchases. Because of the country's unenviable payments record *The Times* advised the public to exercise great caution before investing again. Moreover, while the Chilean government might in good faith intend to honour its obligations, in such unsettled countries 'a sudden revolution may destroy all the hopes thus raised' leaving creditors in worse positions than before.[31]

City merchants and bondholder committees had also been making their grievances known to parliament as well as to the foreign office. In mid-March several MPs met to discuss possible solutions, and decided to circulate a petition calling for a general meeting of all the creditors of the various defaulting borrowers. Previously bondholder meetings had been confined to creditors of a particular country. Often 'the utmost apathy and indifference' prevailed, perhaps because even those deeply involved felt their cause was too unimportant to merit government consideration. The MPs believed that if attention could be focussed upon the claims in their entirety, however, their combined magnitude would demonstrate their national importance and assure greater government support for bondholders. The petition was quickly signed by some of the most prominent City merchants, and a meeting scheduled for the following month.[32]

In early May the expected general bondholders' meeting was convened at the City of London Tavern.[33] Approximately 120 bondholders were present, and they unanimously invited MP Alexander Baring to take the chair. One of the meeting's organizers then explained that loans of over £17,000,000, which should be yielding interest of nearly £1,000,000 per annum, were now in default. It was advisable, therefore, that a committee be formed to apply to the government for assistance, and request that it urge the consuls recently appointed to Latin America at great public expense to press the claimants' cause with the defaulting nations more energetically.

Chairman Baring confessed he felt no great surprise that the loans had lapsed into default. The borrowing nations were young, and their legislatures lacked the financial expertise and information available in other countries. Given also the revolts and wars plaguing them, it was not astonishing they had suspended payments. He did not believe any of the borrowers considered repudiating their debts, but that they did not appreciate the necessity of regularity in their payments. While in Britain dividends were paid promptly, only recently had this become the rule even in a state such as France. In Spain, from which the Spanish American nations derived their notions of finance, no such regularity prevailed. Moreover, he reminded the meeting, the high interest rates and discounts at which all the bonds had been offered should have warned investors that their purchases were not without risk. Nevertheless, in view of the generality of the defaults, he felt sure the request for governmental assistance would be heeded, although to what extent remained to be seen. Any action taken, however, would, by demonstrating the British government's concern over bondholder losses, stimulate Latin American governments to make greater efforts to satisfy their creditors.

Unfortunately, the expedient of seeking a greater impact through presenting a united bondholder front against a group of defaulting nations was, like earlier suggestions to capitalize defaulted interest or reduce interest rates, premature. Not until 1873 would the different national bondholder committees combine to form the Corporation of Foreign Bondholders as a single coherent lobbying and pressure group. Nevertheless, the 1 May meeting focussed public attention on the enormity of the losses suffered by British lenders, much as Henry English's work had done regarding the total investments lost in joint stock companies.

Unfortunately the numbers of holders of defaulted Latin American bonds increased when Guatemala failed to make its 1 August dividend payment. Although Central America had not suffered from a bloody Spanish reconquest attempt as had Colombia, for example, civil dissentions within the small area had brought as much death and destruction as an invader's sword. So deep were the differences between rival political factions that any truce was sure to be of short duration. Unveiling once again that special blend of racial-cultural determinism which had replaced the earlier openness of mind with which the British had once regarded Latin America, The Times observed that 'the inherent pride of the old Spanish character makes them submit with impatience to a superior who was once an equal; and the feeling proves in almost all cases more than a match for their patriotism'.[34]

The anguish of the Mexican bondholders persisted throughout the year. More letters from Vera Cruz, written in May, arrived in mid-

July with the usual litany of ill tidings. Trade was depressed and the treasury empty. Only moderately cheering was news that President Guadalupe Vitoria had issued a decree ordering retention of one-eighth of the proceeds from the Vera Cruz customs houses, together with the duties on gold and silver exports, for servicing the foreign loans. The report was treated with great scepticism, and *The Morning Herald* predicted the plan would 'turn out like all the previous *setting asides* – namely, a delusion'.[35]

In late October earlier incredulity concerning the efficacy of Mexican measures taken to assure debt service turned out to be well-placed as more letters arrived from Vera Cruz confirming such fears. The customs receipts directed by presidential decree to be set aside for loan service had been seized to pay the local garrison, establishing a pattern which would be repeated frequently later in the century when customs receipts again were pledged to bondholders.[36] Within a few weeks bondholders frustration escalated to alarm when news arrived of a rebellion led by General Antonio López de Santa Anna. Santa Anna and his colleagues had supported the losing presidential candidate in the last elections, and, as he was to do time and again in future years, now had attempted to achieve by force what he could not obtain by constitutional means. The revolt failed, but added to the government's financial embarrassment.[37]

Although some Peruvian shareholders might have been heartened by the 1 May general meeting, the following months offered little relief. Fears persisted over the war with Colombia. Both nations strengthened their armed forces, further draining available resources. In early September copies of the 1828 report of the Peruvian Congressional Finance Committee arrived from Lima. No funds had been remitted to pay dividends due to the need to secure the nation against the designs of Bolívar, 'a warrior as fortunate as he is ambitious'. Once welcomed as a liberator, the Venezuelan leader was now considered a menace by rival factions in Peru, who used the excuse of the feared invasion to consolidate their own power, and to avoid paying either the arrears or the 1 October dividends.[38]

Indeed, since Bolívar's departure for Colombia in September 1826, Peru had lapsed into virtual anarchy. By 1836 the country would have had six constitutions and eight presidents, only one of whom was sufficiently ruthless to complete his four year term.[39] Meanwhile, the most the finance committee's report could offer was a recommendation that congress empower the executive to appropriate government-owned property either as security for the bondholders, or to sell it to obtain money to cure the arrears. Unfortunately, one letter writer observed, given the generally stagnant economy it would be extremely difficult to find purchasers.[40]

Colombian bond speculators continued to hope that Bolívar would somehow find the means with which to redeem his nation's credit. Reports of his efforts to reassert his authority over rebellious factions in Venezuela and New Granada were therefore closely followed in the press, alternately raising and lowering bond quotations by a few points. In September news was received that legislative assemblies in Bogotá and Cartagena had declared him 'Supreme Chief' of Colombia. When he entered Bogotá to an enthusiastic reception, he was conducted in triumph to 'a temporary throne' in the main plaza to receive the congratulations of leading officials, merchants and inhabitants. *The Times* noted, however, that substantial opposition still existed elsewhere in the country, and that civil war might errupt before he could achieve the complete submission of all contending power groups.[41]

But not even Bolívar could perform fiscal miracles, and his attention – never keen on financial matters – was absorbed with monitoring the nation's internal unity and by foreign affairs. In October 1828 an extract of the *Gaceta de Colombia* was published in London defending the decision to attack Peru, which had designs on Colombia's southern provinces and had blockaded Guayaquil. Therefore, despite the cost Colombia was obliged to maintain its army at full strength.[42] To support the military establishment, and generally improve finances, duties were 'cruelly increased,' and a head tax imposed of $3 a person, only a fraction of which could be collected.[43] Sadly, disputes over the frontier between the two nations would continue well into the twentieth century, leading to armed clashes as late as the 1930s.

By the end of October, Colombian bonds could hardly be sold at any price, and quotations were purely nominal. News that differences with Peru would be settled amicably had no effect. Not surprisingly, on 11 November 1825, bond quotations reached a record low of 18¾, not that far above the repudiated Spanish bonds then quoted at 11.[44] Incredibly, the 1824 Colombian bonds rose to 22 in less than a week when letters from Cartagena revealed that the government now intended to farm out the collection of the tobacco duty, which had been pledged for interest payments in the loan agreement. On 9 August Minister Estanislao Vergara wrote to bondholders telling them that commissioners appointed by bondholders to receive and transmit the funds to London would prevent the misappropriation of these funds by 'subaltern authorities', as had happened before. Bolívar, Vergara continued, was determined 'on exonerating Colombia from the reproach which, with greater or less justice, has been cast on the new States of this continent on account of their apathy in the fulfilment of their financial obligations'.[45]

By now investors should have learned that the excellent intentions evidenced in Latin American legislation were seldom carried out in practice.[46] Nevertheless, on the evening of Friday 28 November some 200 Colombian bondholders gathered at the City of London Tavern to discuss appointing commissioners to receive the duties appropriated to the loan service. MP Sir Robert Wilson took the Chair, and the meeting was informed that Foreign Secretary Lord Aberdeen had instructed the British chargé d'affairs in Bogotá to assist the efforts of any agent sent by the bondholders to settle differences with the Colombian government.[47]

After extended discussion the commissioners were appointed. One bondholder almost spoiled the atmosphere of good fellowship when he requested that Powles account for the disposal of the loan proceeds. The wily contractor evaded the request, and, in response to insinuations of insider dealing, promised in future to provide the public and the bondholders at the earliest opportunity with any information his house might obtain which might affect bondholder interests or bond prices in order 'to prevent every possibility of individual advantage being taken by a partial knowledge of the facts'. The meeting adjourned at 3.15a.m., with resolutions congratulating Bolívar on his 'late elevation to supreme power', and thanking Lord Aberdeen for the interest he had taken in the bondholders difficulties, 'so far as was consistent with the principles adopted by His Majesty's Government in respect to foreign loans'.

The following Monday bonds rose two points, but the trend reversed when letters arrived reporting a frustrated coup against Bolívar engineered by his former colleague Vice President Santander. Bolívar had barely escaped assassination, but his British aide-de-camp had been slain. One of the allegations levelled at Bolívar by the conspirators was that he had planned to suspend payment on the domestic debt in order to pay the British creditors![48]

Chilean bondholders also finished the year without receiving any dividends. Non-payment was not, however, due to lack of diligence by British Consul General Nugent or Vice Consul White. In September, White sent Minister Carlos Rodríguez a copy of the recent Chilean bondholder resolution nominating a debt commissioner. He hoped the government would appreciate the necessity of resolving the claims, since such an action would show the British government 'which is always deeply interested in the prosperity and happiness of Chile, the fullest conviction that she is at all times desirous to fulfil her engagements when not prevented by untoward and unexpected circumstances'.[49]

In early September bondholders were informed that at Nugent's suggestion the Chilean government, like the Peruvian, was planning to sell 'a former monarchical estate' to raise $100,000 for interest payments. Nugent had reminded Rodríguez that the frigate HMS *Dove* was about to sail from Valparaiso and could take the proceeds on board. Alas, replied Rodríguez, the legal formalities of the sale would not be completed by the sailing date. Nevertheless, as soon as the sale was completed 'the most efficacious measures will be adopted' by the government 'for fulfilling its promises without delay.'[50] This same pattern of promises to sell government property, followed by offers from Nugent or White to make warships available for dividend remittance, which were then countered by excuses for why sailing dates could not be met, would be repeated well into the next year and beyond.

Not even good offices could help Buenos Ayres and Brazilian bondholders. At times during the past Buenos Ayres bond quotations had been higher than Brazil's. After the Buenos Ayres January default, twenty-four points soon separated the issues. By early February, Buenos Ayres was quoted at 38, and Brazil at 61¼.[51] Although the immediate political fortunes of both nations were linked by their mutual hostility, the differences in bond quotations would continue with small variations as hopes of peace rose and fell.

Foreign nations now became ever more concerned at the seemingly endless conflict. Since the war began both the blockading Brazilian fleet and Buenos Ayres privateers had been capturing foreign merchant ships suspected of trading with the other side. By mid-1828 detained British vessels and property at Rio de Janeiro and Buenos Ayres exceeded £2,000,000 in value. Ships rotted at the wharfs, and impounded cargo perished in customs warehouses while consular protests were ignored. Opinion now grew in favour of active intervention to halt the war, which was depriving Britain of one of its best Latin American markets. Eventually, *The Times* speculated, 'it may cost Europe as much trouble as Greece now does, to put down this growing evil'.[52] Such considerations undoubtedly led the foreign office to decide once again to mediate between the two contenders.

During this difficult period the Brazilian government was further distracted by events in Portugal. In March 1826 Brazilian Emperor Pedro had succeeded to the Portuguese throne when his father Dom João died. Because of the physical impossibility of reigning in two nations so far apart, Pedro provisionally renounced the Portuguese throne in favour of his eight-year-old daughter María, appointing his sister Isabella as regent. Pedro's younger brother Dom Miguel, however, schemed to take power himself and discard the constitution which Pedro had bequeathed as a parting gift to the nation. Spain's troublesome King Ferdinand, happy to aid another absolutist, offered support to Miguel and allowed Portuguese army deserters in Spain to cross the frontier and attack loyalist Portuguese forces.

Canning had been alarmed at the turn of events, behind which he again saw the machinations of France and the Holy Alliance. In late December 1826, at loyal Portuguese request, he had dispatched 5,000 troops to support the regency, and Spanish-backed insurgents were quickly routed. Although Pedro and Miguel were reconciled, the latter continued to plot secretly. In February 1828, Dom Pedro, still trusting his brother, appointed Miguel Lieutenant Governor of the Kingdom and Regent for María. Pedro then abdicated completely as king in March. In July Miguel overthrew the regency and seized the throne.[53] Miguel's perfidy was widely denounced in Britain, and holders of Portuguese bonds became distinctly uneasy as the June dividend date drew near, lest he prove as cavalier in his treatment of bondholders as his neighbour Ferdinand.

Brazil, of course, had guaranteed the Portuguese loan in 1825 as the price of obtaining recognition of independence. Since then, despite its own financial difficulties, Brazil's representatives had regularly paid the dividends to Portugal's London agents for distribution to bondholders. Now both Portuguese and Brazilian bondholders, anxieties renewed, began beseiging Brazilian Ambassador Viscount Itabayana to confirm that payments would continue despite the differences between the two nations. By 30 April, Portuguese bonds issued originally at 87 were quoted at 60½. The ambassador nevertheless kept assuring bondholders they had no cause for alarm and that payments would be made as usual.

Thus encouraged, some speculators made large purchases, driving Portuguese bond prices up nearly three points. Within days, the ambassador was informed that Miguel was governing in his own name and no longer even pretending to act for Queen María or Dom Pedro. Itabayana then announced that he could not pay the dividends without confirming instructions from Rio. Bond prices naturally collapsed, and by mid-month were offered at 52½. Recent purchasers lost heavily, and accused the ambassador of deliberately misleading the public for his own ends. As The Times pointed out, however, although in the past diplomats indeed had 'disgraced themselves by frauds of the nature now imputed', on balance so great were the chances of detection in this case that it would be absurd to accuse Itabayana of such folly.[54] The editor of The Morning Herald was less sympathetic and later would have cause to regret his comments.[55]

Debates now raged in the Stock Exchange and in City coffee houses over whether Miguel's action justified non-payment of the dividends. Financiers and the press insisted that even though the Portuguese bondholders were not party to the Portuguese-Brazilian treaty, they had relied upon the Brazilian guarantee, and so should be paid even though Miguel had betrayed the emperor. Certainly if the dividends were delayed, Brazil's credit would be impaired, and 'the stain if once incurred, will never be eradicated' a Portuguese bondholder wrote.[56] The Times reflected many people's thinking. British creditors should not be made to suffer because Miguel had proven a knave and traitor. 'This is a debt contracted by Portugal, but transferred by agreement and for a valuable consideration to Brazil. The politics of neither country have anything to do with the question, and Brazil must pay it, or its credit is gone.'[57] All the same at the end of May the Portuguese loan agents announced regretfully that the dividend would not be paid, although they hoped the delay would be temporary.[58]

Meanwhile, in mid-May Brazilian quotations slid to 59 when a large quantity of bonds were placed on the market, some with the ink of the signatures 'scarcely dry'. Apparently they had been retained earlier by the loan contractors, and their release was interpreted to mean that even the issuing houses had no great faith in their future as investments. Across the Atlantic the war continued, with conflicting reports of victories for one side or the other.[59] Brazilian bondholders were then cheered when news arrived in mid-June that serious peace negotiations had begun. Buenos Ayres finances were, however, in a particularly deplorable state.[60] Military operations on land had been suspended, but the blockade was still nominally in force. All was not well inside Brazil either. In June several thousand foreign troops hired by Dom Pedro mutinied in Rio de Janeiro, and the government only regained control with the assistance of men from British and French naval units in the harbour.[61] Then, to the surprise of many investors, on 1 October, despite its problems, Brazil paid the dividend due on its 1824 loan. The country was still in technical default, however, as long as the dividend on the Portuguese loan which it had guaranteed remained unpaid.

At last, on 12 December, the press confirmed that the long-awaited Brazilian-Buenos Ayrean peace treaty had been ratified late in September, thanks to British mediation. Even this good news, however, could not raise Brazilian bonds beyond 64, while those of Buenos Ayres languished at 47. Nevertheless, merchants with trading interests in Brazil were delighted. Both the exhausted contending governments renounced their claims to the Banda Oriental and agreed to the establishment of a new, sovereign nation, the independence and integrity of which they both guaranteed, and which in its own name of Uruguay would itself become a borrower after mid-century.[62]

The year would have been incomplete without two more unedifying lawsuits to recall again to public attention the misfortunes seemingly inherent to the Latin American loans. In November, in *King v Thwaite*, the editor of *The Morning Herald* was sued for libel by Mexican Minister Rocafuerte over the comments printed on 12 May after Viscount Itabayana had first publicly advertised that the Portuguese dividends would be paid, and then later retracted his announcement.[63] Unlike *The Times*, the newspaper had condemned the Viscount's actions, since they had caused Portuguese bond prices to rise – enabling speculators to take a fast profit – and then to fall abruptly. The leader went too far, however, when it declared: 'Some people affected to be astonished at a Minister of a foreign state acting in this way ... but for our parts when we recollect the exploits of Hurtado, Rocafuerte, and others of the representatives of the new States, it is not difficult to imagine.'

At the trial Rocafuerte denied he had ever inserted an advertisement for his own private purposes, nor ever in his character as minister or in any other character had published any false or fradulent statement or made any wilful misinterpretation of any kind. Defence counsel replied that Rocafuerte's denial was too narrow, and that even if he had not made any announcement for his 'private purposes', he had done so for his government and, in any case, his conduct required explanation. The vice chancellor agreed, and found for the newspaper's editor, although there was no evidence that Rocafuerte had actually originated the rumours which had circulated in early October 1827. Nevertheless, the minister had not made out a sufficient case, and should have stated that he had been instructed by his government to place the advertisements, the contents of which he believed to be true, instead of merely asserting he had never published false or misleading statements.[64]

Guatemalan bondholders scarcely can have enjoyed reading the vice chancellor's 12 November decisions in *Taylor v Barclay* and *Taylor v Powles*.[65] The plaintiff had paid several instalments on Guatemalan bonds, and now sued to recover his money on the grounds of fraud. In order to obtain evidence to support his claim, he sought a bill of discovery which would require defendants to produce an accounting.

The defendants objected to the bill, stating that the plaintiff alleged he had dealt with the defendants as agents of the Guatemalan government. No such government, however, was recognized in Britain. If it were contrary to public policy to allow representatives of unrecognized governments to sue in British courts, the defendants' counsel asserted, it would also be against public policy to allow claims to be enforced against them. In rebuttal, the plaintiff's counsel argued that should his opponent's argument prevail, and Central America not be deemed recognized, then the defendants by purporting to represent a country which did not legally exist had not acted in good faith.

The vice chancellor, however, decided plaintiff's pleading was unsound since no Guatemalan government existed as far as the foreign office was concerned, and public policy indeed 'forbids the Courts to interfere with governments not recognized by the State'. He therefore allowed the objection. This consistent refusal to look behind technical niceties and thereby allow parties to profit from transactions which could not be challenged because they involved unrecognized governments surely disturbed many investors.

By December, of the twenty foreign loan issues still traded at the Foreign Stock Exchange only seven were still being serviced and repaid. Of these, six were by European nations – Austria, Denmark, Naples, Prussia and Russia. Together with Greece, Portugal and Spain, six Latin American countries were in default. Only Brazil had consistently paid interest when due throughout 1828.[66] Its ability to continue to do so was in doubt, however, due to the financial drain of the Buenos Ayres conflict and because of its burdensome guarantee of the Portuguese bonds, no dividends on which had been paid since June. For the third consecutive year bondholders throughout the nation had a less than merry Christmas.

IX
THE ONLY SURVIVOR

IF BY 1829 Latin American bonds were listed at all in the press they often appeared without any price quotations, indicating an absence of any regular trading. What little commentary there was concentrated on Brazil, reflecting the City's concern with the health of the lending boom's only survivor.

Even though the Brazilian-Buenos Ayres war had ended, instability and violence prevailed almost everywhere else in Latin America. In Mexico rivalry between federalists and centralists burst into revolution when federalists refused to accept the election of General Gómez Pedraza in December 1828. After a brief, successful coup in the capital, he was replaced in January 1829 by the rival contender, General Vicente Guerrero. The new president promptly expelled those Spaniards who had managed to remain in Mexico.[1] The expulsion, which deprived Mexico of yet more scarce commercial talent, combined with the collapse of Mexico's first attempt at constitutional government to depress British bondholders completely. Even satisfaction over the defeat at Vera Cruz of the long-awaited Spanish invasion could not counterbalance earlier disheartening news that the Mexican government was 'all but bankrupt' and unable to meet even a quarter of its domestic financial engagements. How assurances given to the foreign bondholders were to be fulfilled 'remains to be seen', mused *The Morning Chronicle*.[2]

While Mexico headed for yet more turmoil, the City was disturbed by rumours of renewed armed conflict between Colombia and Peru. Little faith was now placed in Bolívar's plan to redeem Colombia's credit by allocating specific revenues for debt servicing. Nor were bondholders reassured by the leniency with which Bolívar had treated the ringleaders of the recent conspiracy to unseat him. Colombian bonds fell 2 per cent on receipt of news that their lives had been spared, thereby assuring them the opportunity to strike again on some future date at Colombia's fragile unity.[3] Moreover, dissatisfaction felt by some bondholders with Powles' stewardship of the defaulted Colombian loans continued, and consequently City stockbrokers Morgan & Co., on its own behalf and representing other bondholders, contacted the Colombian government directly to explore settlement possibilities.

At a turbulent bondholders meeting at the City of London Tavern in early June, Powles explained defensively that his agents had delivered the settlement proposal resolutions taken at the 28 November 1828, meeting to the Colombian government. Unfortunately Bolívar had been too distracted with the Peruvian war and Santander's conspiracy to reply. Powles then urged the bondholders to refrain from making separate, divisive proposals to the government as Morgan & Co. had done, and persuaded the majority to agree that future settlement negotiations should be conducted only through himself.[4] Although the argument in favour of maintaining a united front against the debtor was reasonable, Powles' opposition to Morgan's proposal was perhaps more influenced by its suggestion that dividends be paid directly to the bondholders rather than through Powles, who would thereby lose his commissions.

Mr Morgan then vigorously demanded that Powles reveal how 'accounts stood' between the Colombian government and the contractors. Powles refused, asserting that the inquiry was improper and would only produce 'unnecessary and unpleasant discussion'. The chairman, Sir Robert Wilson, stated he was sure that with Bolívar back in control the country would continue to enjoy internal tranquility. He then recommended that instead of selling their bonds, bondholders keep them locked away in their drawers until the day came when they would be reimbursed in full. The meeting did little to raise bondholders' hopes.

Nor was all well in Buenos Ayres. Although the blockade had been lifted and large shipments of British merchandise were on the high seas to the Río de la Plata, peace had not brought internal stability. In late November 1828, disaffected army officers overthrew the Buenos Ayres government. Colonel Manuel Dorrego, who had led the nascent republic since August 1827, fled, was captured, and summarily shot in front of his troops. A new military government was established on the ruins of the last, causing bondholders even greater concern and erasing any hopes entertained for economic recovery which might have been raised by the recent peace treaty. As The Courier commented gloomily, 'we can scarcely predict, that a Revolution brought about by such means, is likely to lead to a state either of tranquility or freedom'.[5] Civil war seemed certain once Dorrego's followers recovered from their defeat.

The brutal overthrow and execution of Dorrego was considered as yet further proof that the Latin Americans were 'too imperfectly civilized' for responsible self-government. The revolutionary chaos which was afflicting all Spanish Latin America was bitter evidence of the failure of the Spanish colonial system. Had the people been allowed to participate in the management of their own affairs, wrote *The Times*, and 'had a well-organized system of civil government existed, in which the colonists had their proper weight under a viceroy or governor from Europe – the mere removal of that high officer, with his train of subordinate agents, would not have left them a prey to the anarchy in which they have existed since independence'. In contrast, *The Times* observed, when the United States became independent they found themselves fully prepared for the full enjoyment of the freedom which their spirit and perseverance had secured.[6]

Nearly fifteen years before Simón Bolívar had voiced similar opinions on Latin American incapacity for self-government. In his famous *Letter from Jamaica*, written in 1815 ostensibly in reply to a request for information on the Latin American independence movements, the Liberator had concluded that the Spanish colonial regime 'kept us in a sort of permanent infancy with regard to public affairs. If we could at least have managed our domestic affairs and our internal administration, we could have acquainted ourselves with the processes and mechanics of public affairs.'[7] Now, he explained, without any previous experience in self-government Latin Americans were required 'to enact upon the world stage the eminent roles of legislator, magistrate, minister of the treasury, diplomat, general, and every position of authority, supreme or subordinate, that comprises the hierarchy of a fully organized state'.[8] Not surprisingly, experiments with democratic government had been unsuccessful. The colonists had not been able to acquire the abilities and political virtues of the North Americans, and consequently were still 'dominated by the vices that one learns under the rule of a nation like Spain, which had only distinguished itself in ferocity, ambition, vindictiveness and greed'.[9]

True to *The Courier*'s predictions, the new Buenos Ayres regime did not usher in an era of tranquility and freedom. By the end of June, Buenos Ayres bonds collapsed to 22 at news of another civil war. Insurgent troops were poised to attack the city of Buenos Ayres itself, where all inhabitants able to bear arms, with the exception of the British and North Americans, had been drafted into the militia.[10] The eventual outcome would be disastrous. General Juan Manuel de Rosas, Dorrego's former colleague, would emerge as governor and begin a thirty-year dictatorship of repression and terror during which bondholders would receive very little on their investments.

In Central America civil war continued to sap the economy. Although there would be occasional respites from the violence, discord would persist for another eight years until the federation finally disintegrated. Central American bonds were unsaleable at any price, even when, in late May, the City heard via Belize that Guatemalan forces had won a great victory over the Salvadoreans.[11] Central American bondholders considered the time opportune to renew their efforts to persuade the defaulting government to resume debt servicing. On 15 September they passed a resolution which noted that three semi-annual dividends were now in arrears. Although they were aware that the failure to pay was due 'to the lamentable state of civil contentions in parts of the Republic', now that the situation had improved the time had arrived to call on the republic to fulfil its obligations according to the true spirit of the contract.[12]

A copy of the resolution was sent to Foreign Secretary Lord Aberdeen, along with a letter from Reid, Irving claiming £12,000 from Guatemala for dividends they had advanced bondholders at Minister Zebadúa's request. Lord Aberdeen was requested to allow Consul Dashwood in Guatemala to take charge of the bondholders' claim in his private capacity and 'to use his influence toward recovery of a Debt which had rendered important service to the Government to which he is to be accredited.' So, on 24 October Aberdeen instructed Dashwood to second by his good offices any proper representation made by the British claimants through their agents in Guatemala. At the same time he was cautioned against a more formal interference, since the claims arose from private speculations which 'have never been held to entitle the claimant to ask as a matter of right the official intervention of this Government, nor with respect to which could this Government properly attempt to exercise any authoritative Interference with the Government of Guatemala'.[13] The Guatemalan government resisted Dashwood's entreaties, however, and postponed any decision regarding resettlements.

In Chile Vice Consul John White continued to suffer frustrations similar to those Dashwood experienced in Central America. In February he again wrote to Foreign Minister Rodríguez, reminding him of the bondholders' memorial which White had sent him the previous September, and of the bondholders 'extreme anxiety ... for a remittance'. In case the Chilean government wished to make a payment on overdue dividends they could load the specie aboard the HMS *Lord Wellington*, about to sail from Valparaiso for England. The longer payment was delayed, the more depressed Chilean bonds would become. Moreover, nothing short of an actual remittance would convince the bondholders of the Chilean government's sincerity and good intentions.[14] Over the next months the vice consul continued to suggest convenient ship departure dates, but without any tangible results. In May, White again informed Rodríguez that a British ship, HMS *Menai*, would be available to convey remittances to Britain. The minister replied that his government had already shipped 2,000 quintals of copper (approximately 200 tons) in a British merchant ship as a partial remittance, and could not obtain more in time for the *Menai's* departure.[15]

The Mexican bondholders committee also continued to request more vigorous foreign office intervention. On 8 April hard-pressed Under-Secretary Backhouse, on behalf of Lord Aberdeen, once again reminded Mr Ewing of the bondholders committee that 'the grievances of which you complain arise out of speculation of a purely private nature, for the success of which His Majesty's Government is in no way responsible, and upon which they cannot, as a matter of right, claim to exercise any authoritative interference with foreign States.' Of course, the government was ready 'so far as they can properly interfere, to second, by their countenance and good offices . . . any representation which bondholders may address to be respective Governments to obtain the early and complete satisfaction of their claims.' Eventually the unofficial pressure would partially achieve the desired results, but only almost two years later.[16]

In early March *The Morning Chronicle* perhaps unwittingly pronounced the obituary of all the Latin American bond issues when it noted that 'scarcely a bargain has been made all day in the Republican Securities, which are now a complete drug on the market'.[17] By the beginning of April *The Times* reported 'a perfect panic' among Latin American bondholders because money advances could no longer be obtained against the security of the bonds, and their holders were now selling almost at any price. From blind faith in the resources of the new states, 'people are falling into the extreme of distrust'.[18]

Some investors attributed the collapse of their dreams to the still unsettled relations between Spain and the new nations. In a memorial addressed to Lord Aberdeen, 'the most respectable' London merchants noted that continuing hostility between Latin America and Spain was encouraging privateering and piracy, endangering even neutral trading vessels. The large standing armies required to protect the new states against their former colonial overlord consumed the resources of the Latin American nations, and were 'the constant object of intrigue for factions' purposes.' Groundless rumours of Spanish invasion interrupted peaceful commerce and industry, and led to arbitrary and oppressive exercise of authority. Without peace the loans could never be repaid. The authors of the memorial concluded by suggesting the British government interpose its friendly offices and counsel with Spain to terminate the fruitless conflict. If Spain had been unable to regain its colonies when it had a large army in their midst, it was doubly incapable of doing so now.[19]

The memorial was enthusiastically supported by *The Courier*, which also urged a formal end to hostilities and Spanish recognition of Latin American independence.[20] *The Times* was more reflective. The loans should now be considered doubtful, if not bad, debts. The British government had helped as far as it could, instructing consuls and ambassadors to explain to the new nations the importance of re-establishing their credit. But in no instance had their efforts resulted in any actual transmission of money for dividends. In Chile, for instance, Consul General Nugent had persuaded the government to order a sale of state property in order to be able to make a dividend payment. The proceeds, however, recalled the leader, were paid into the treasury for local expenses rather than remitted to Britain as agreed. The deviation from the original agreement had made a bad impression in Britain, 'and inspired distrust in the promises made in regard to the future'.[21]

In Buenos Ayres the Brazilian conflict and civil war at home also delayed payment resumptions. Peru's congress had acknowledged its debt but taken no measures to liquidate it. In Colombia, Santander's plotting and now the Peruvian war presented other obstacles. Mexico meanwhile was distracted by the bitter rivalry between the two major political parties which made necessary the maintenance of an army 'sufficiently numerous to absorb all the revenues of the country', *The Times* observed.

It was, therefore, fallacious to assume that with Spanish recognition of Latin American independence the new nations would no longer need costly defensive military establishments, and that the money saved could be utilized to liquidate the foreign debt. Even in the unlikely event of Spain consenting to the proposal, the armies would be retained due to 'the utter aversion the American-Spaniards feel to the assumption of supreme power by any individuals among them'. The rulers, therefore, conscious that this antipathy exposed them to constant plots and conspiracies, required large standing armies to protect their positions. While recognition by Spain would be desirable, unless it were accompanied by the formation of governments which could maintain peace at home, the lot of the British creditors would not significantly be improved. It was a prophetic and unsettling conclusion.

Brazil's internal political situation, although not free from stress, was far less worrisome to creditors than the nation's economic problems. While dire predictions had been made that failure to pay the Portuguese dividends would irreparably damage Brazil's credit standing, Brazilian bond prices were affected either only marginally or not at all, and remained in the mid-to-upper fifties. Correspondence exchanges in the press continued to debate whether Portuguese bondholders could look to Brazil for payment.

Although the Portuguese bondholders were not party to the agreement by which Brazil had guaranteed the Portuguese loan, 'A British Bondholder' argued in the press that the bondholders nevertheless had in effect ratified the 1825 agreement by receiving the dividends due under it. The convention, moreover, had been approved by the Brazilian congress, and dividends for the British bondholders had been sent regularly from Brazil. There was no legitimate way in which Brazil could refuse to make further payments under this agreement made for the benefit of third parties.[22] Brazil nevertheless still did not pay.

While the debate continued over the extent of Brazil's obligations under the convention, holders of Brazilian bonds became increasingly fearful that their next dividend would not be paid. At the end of March Brazilian bonds fell 5 per cent to 56 due to the 'understanding' that between £400–£500,000 in bonds retained at the Bank of England by the contractors of the previous loans had been suddenly placed on the market in order to raise money for dividends. Although prices recovered within a few days, there were now so many Brazilian bonds for sale that they partook 'to a certain extent, of the taint with which all other trans-Atlantic Bonds are affected'.[23]

Tainted or not, Brazilian dividends were paid promptly on 1 April together with Danish and Russian dividends also then due. Payment did not improve Brazilian quotations, however, perhaps because the City immediately began to worry about the October interest payment. Virtually no trading was done in other Latin American issues. Mexico was at 17½ (1824) and 21 (1825), Peru at 11½, Buenos Ayres 25, Chile at 20½ and Colombia at 15¾ (1822) and 16½ (1824).[24] By the end of the month City brokers were placing bets on whether or not the October Brazilian dividends of approximately £200,000 would be paid. Odds ran ten to one against, and Brazilian bonds were quoted at 52¾. The exchange rate now was so unfavourable that it would have been three times cheaper to borrow rather than remit specie or other products. Consequently it was soon rumoured that a loan proposal had been submitted privately to an as yet unnamed banking house.[25] Such a transaction could expect little support, however, from the general public 'who have suffered too severely from foreign loans to engage in them again for a long time to come', opined one editor. Any new Brazilian issue therefore would have to be a private placement restricted to the banks and their wealthier customers, similar to those then being arranged for canal and turnpike companies in Pennsylvania, Ohio and Louisiana.[26]

In mid-May a large sale of Brazilian bonds depressed prices to 52.

News of a miliary revolt in Pernambuco the preceding June sent them down further to 50¾ as bondholders feared Emperor Pedro's lack of funds would prevent him reasserting his authority. The bonds recovered a few days later on news that the magnitude of the revolt had been exaggerated.[27] Even more welcome was the report carried in morning newspapers on 21 May that 'an eminent capitalist, in conjunction with a mercantile house of high standing' had offered to arrange a small loan to pay the October dividends and thereby give Brazil time to reform its financial system. The bonds promptly rose from 51 to 55, but closed at 53¾ when the story was denied. It was confidently believed, nevertheless, that negotiations on the loan were in fact proceeding. The contractor's identity could not be confirmed, but Rothschilds seemed an obvious candidate.[28]

In fact, more than one Brazilian credit proposal was under discussion. Some opinion favoured a loan to which the public at large could subscribe in the usual way. Given the existing prejudice against foreign loans, however, others feared the bonds might not sell. A private placement was another alternative. The amount of the loan was also debated. A smaller credit might sell better than a large issue, one strand of opinion maintained. Therefore, the amount should be limited to a sum which would cover Brazilian bond dividends over the next two to three years, during which the country might complete its financial 'regeneration'. Other Stock Exchange experts believed that additional new money should be made available to attack the root of Brazil's financial problems, the adverse exchange rate. The debate continued several days, and Brazilian bonds rose to 55.[29]

Gradually the new loan took shape and more details became available to the public. At first the amount was said to be limited to £400,000, not an exciting sum but more than enough to cover the October dividend. The loan's particular novelty, which excited considerable talk, was its being raised specifically and solely to pay a prior credit's interest. This concept was new in 1829 and elicited great criticism. As *The Times* remarked primly, borrowing for such a purpose was objectionable in principle and amounted to permitting the debtor to repay a creditor with his own money. The loan's proponents, however, contended that Brazil's circumstances were sufficiently exceptional to justify departure from usually accepted practice.[30] Today, of course, such a proposal would not seem at all unusual or strange.

By the end of May it was revealed that a five per cent loan had indeed been arranged by Rothschilds and Thomas Wilson & Co. at 54, and entirely subscribed by them and their friends. It was said that when the Brazilian ambassador had first offered the loan to Rothschild he had rejected the proposal. The financier changed his mind and accepted the offer – and a two per cent commission – when he heard Barings was bidding for it.[31] No prospectus was published, and no instalment payments requested. The actual amount issued was £769,000, almost twice what had been expected, since Dom Pedro's financial requirements were reported to be so great that he was selling the family heirlooms and diamond collection. Bonds reached 59 at one stage, causing some brokers and investors to wish they had been invited to form part of the inner management group. Instead, they could only purchase bonds at current market prices.[32]

The loan was in effect an admission that without new financing Brazil could not have paid the October interest, and caused investors to wonder whether it would be in any better financial condition when the proceeds were exhausted at the end of 1830. In addition, the contractors' motives were at best ambiguous. While they may have wished to provide Brazil with a respite in which to mend its economy, suspicions lingered that they had taken the opportunity to refinance or liquidate earlier investments, possibly through exchanging old bonds for new. Hopefully, The Times conjectured, the country would make good use of the breathing space afforded by the new funds to reorganize its financial system 'as to be enabled ultimately to do full justice to the English creditors'. Nevertheless, the public hesitated to purchase the issue. But for the moment, at least, Brazil had retreated from the brink of default and by 30 December its bonds would be quoted at 72½, which was still over 2 points lower than the price of the 1824 issue, and over 12 points less than the offer price of the 1825 loan.[33]

Brazil's continued solvency, made possible by the Rothschild-sponsored rescue, affirmed once more the basic differences between that vast country and the former Spanish colonies. The Portuguese colonial regime in comparison to its Spanish counterpart had in practice been more benign, probably less corrupt, and certainly less centralized. Its establishment in the New World had not been attended by the deliberate, violent destruction of well-developed aboriginal civilizations and the virtual enslavement of their populations. Because of the special manner in which it had achieved its independence with British mediation, and the form of government it subsequently had adopted, Brazil had not been ravaged by the terrible fratricidal civil wars which had scourged its neighbours before they could free themselves from Spain. At the same time, because the Brazilian population was clustered along the coast and were connected by sea, powerful and disruptive regional, economic, and political interests fostered by physical isolation could not develop to the same degree as in, for instance, Colombia. Consequently, Brazil had no comparable legacy of militarism, and possessed no cliques of greedy generals and provincial *caudillos* demanding rewards for their years of campaigning and eager to collaborate with civilian autocrats in fastening a new absolutism on their countries in republican disguise.

Spanish Americans did not, however, envy the Brazilians the undeniable advantages with which they had begun independent existence. Rivalries between Spain and Portugal during the colonial era had been intense, if not overtly hostile. Mutual suspicion did not evaporate with independence. Brazil's slave-based economy, its imperial form of government, and its ties to the Portuguese ruling houses were viewed with great dislike and mistrust by many Spanish American republicans. Bolívar even considered Brazil's war with Buenos Ayres as the beginning of an attempt by the Holy Alliance, with Brazilian Emperor Pedro as their agent, 'to subjugate Spanish America by force, in order to consecrate the principle of legitimacy and to destroy the revolution'. After all, Dom Pedro had close personal ties to the Holy Alliance through his Austrian wife Leopoldina.[34] At one point in late 1825 Bolívar was almost persuaded by Buenos Ayres politicians to lead a joint invasion of Brazil and destroy the last monarchy in the New World. The opposition of Santander and most Gran Colombia leaders, and the certainty of British opposition, persuaded him to drop the project.

Brazilian policy-makers meanwhile became wary of being manoeuvred into situations where they might be outvoted by the more numerous republican States. Although Brazil had accepted an invitation to the 1826 Panama Conference and had designated a minister to attend, the appointment was considered no more than a public relations exercise. The nominee declined the honour, and no replacement was made. The emperor had no desire to participate in discussions where Spanish American delegates would surely unite to support Buenos Ayres in the Banda Oriental dispute. One recent commentator has observed that 'as the largest country in South America, Brazil's advantage lay not in promoting an institutionalized system of international relations but in pursuing a divide-and-rule strategy'.[35] This pattern established in those early years survived throughout much of the century. Based upon a perception of diverging interests if not ideologies, it accounts for the occasional reluctance to include Brazil in the inter-American conferences convened in Latin America prior to the First Inter-American Conference in Washington in 1889, the year in which Brazil became a republic.

Just as the loan crisis had wound down to its conclusion by 1829, so most companies formed for Latin American mining and other operations either had ceased to exist or had greatly curtailed operations over the last two years since publication of Henry English's study. The news of their demise had done little to inspire confidence in the economic future of their countries of operation, let alone in their bonds.

Although many companies had been moribund since the beginning of 1827, some had remained operational even if their share prices were depressed. Mexican mining companies at first appeared to be the strongest. On 3 January 1827, the chairman of the board of directors of the Anglo-Mexican Mining Association had reported to the shareholders that £70,000 in silver had been coined up to last November, thanks largely to the introduction of stamping and ore-dressing techniques from Saxony.[36] In contrast, a week later the Chilean Mining Association, and the Chilean and Peruvian Mining Association shareholders resolved at the City of London Tavern to abandon their hopes of mining precious metals and merge in the interests of economy into a company to mine and smelt Chilean copper.[37]

In mid-January 1827 *The Morning Chronicle* had printed a table comparing current mining company share prices with their par value and the amounts paid in.[38] In some few cases the results were still encouraging:

	PAR	PAID IN	CURRENT
Colombian	100	15	17
Brazilian	100	20	24
Potosí, La Paz	50	5	3
Real del Monte	400	400	500
Tlapuxahua	400	150	197
United Mexican	40	27½	19

By the end of January Anglo-Mexican and Tlapuxahua mining shares had risen following news that $300,000 in specie had been shipped from Vera Cruz.[39] In general, however, South American west coast mining companies would continue throughout 1827 to have greater difficulties than their Mexican counterparts. The Pasco Peruvian Mining Association, for example, was an early casualty.[40]

Meanwhile during 1827 the marginal if not slighty fraudulent concerns continued to collapse, including Herman Hendriks' Haytian Mining Association. At an acrimonious meeting at the company's offices at 35 Finsbury Circus, shareholders accused directors and Hendriks of misrepresentation in the prospectus, which had stated 'that in order to procure gold of the most pure and rich description it

would only be necessary to wash a handful of earth taken up indis-
criminately over a space of sixty square leagues'. Deposits of £5 per
share had been collected for a total of £32,905, but the directors were
accused of improperly advancing Hendriks £8,000 from this amount
to purchase the grant he had obtained from the Haytian Government. The directors replied that they had only paid the £8,000 to
Hendriks 'for the purpose of getting rid of him', which only made
the situation worse. In mitigation, the directors also claimed they
had relied on the testimony of every writer who had ever 'treated of
the Island of Santo Domingo', and had been 'strongly impressed
with the hope that they could encourage the free labour of the
negroes, and successfully cultivate commercial relations with a new
State, which had already attained not only a high degree of opulence,
but of personal liberty'.[41] The shareholders were unimpressed.

Although other mining companies might not yet be forced to
merge or be liquidated, some began to reduce authorized capital
in recognition of the futility of further calls upon shareholders.
Thus, at an Extraordinary Meeting at the City of London Tavern on
Bishopsgate in March 1827, Peruvian Mining Company shareholders resolved to amend their Articles of Settlement to reduce the
par value of their stock from £100 to £40.[42] The City of London
Tavern was also the venue in early May for a Mexican Mining
Company shareholders meeting. Although the past year had shown
a net revenue of but £21,000 and the company had produced only
twenty bars instead of the 200 projected, the directors reported that
the recent acquisition of German miners and engineers would assure
the company's future prosperity. Nevertheless it was resolved to
reduce the nominal value of the shares from £100 to £50, presumably
to encourage the uneasy holders of 440 still unpaid shares to meet the
last call.[43]

By the end of November 1827, Imperial Brazilian Mining Association share prices were rising rapidly at reports of new discoveries.
During the first week of September, 142 lb. of gold had been produced, and nearly the same amount in the second week. In light of
past experience *The Morning Chronicle* cautioned the public 'against
placing credit in what is said respecting the mines'. Nevertheless, so
great was the demand that Brazilian Mining Association shares,
which had a par value of £35 and on which £20 had been paid, were
soon selling at £80. Within two weeks they had risen to £102. With
the exception of Mexico's Real del Monte Mining Association,
whose fully paid-in shares of £440 were commanding £450, by the
end of 1827 all other non-Brazilian mining company shares were
selling below their paid-in value – in some cases far below, as *The
Morning Chronicle* informed its readers:[44]

	PAR	PAID IN	CURRENT VALUE
Anglo–Mexican	100	85	26½
Anglo–Chilean	100	8	3
Bolanos	300	200	155
Colombian	100	20	14
Mexican	100	23	5½
Potosí, La Paz and Peruvian	50	5	1½

Apparently the war did not depress Brazilian mining share prices as it had the nation's bond quotations. Even though *The Morning Chronicle's* financial correspondent suspected that the flattering accounts of the productivity of the Brazilian mines had been written to mislead British investors, he ventured in early December that it would be unfair 'not to admit that the prospect of the undertaking succeeding is much less distant than supposed'.[45]

Paralleling the declining fortunes of most mining and commercial companies, the colonization ventures had been utter failures. Following the well-publicized misfortunes of the Rio de la Plata Agricultural Association, news of the fate of John Powles' Colombian Agricultural Association confirmed that just as the new states would produce no immense mineral wealth for British investors, neither would they provide suitable outlets for Britain's unemployed. While the association was included among Henry English's companies still 'existing' as of 31 December 1826, its finances were precarious. Only £5 had been deposited on each £100 share, leaving the company with a total paid-in capital of £65,000. There was little realistic hope that the additional £95 still due on each share could be obtained.

News trickled back to Britain that all was not well with the 200 Scottish men, women and children who had arrived at La Guayra in December 1825 to settle at El Topo, nine miles west of Caracas. At first all had gone according to plan. The new arrivals were lodged in a large building erected by the association in advance of their arrival and allocated individual parcels of land. According to diary entries by Sir Robert Ker Porter, the British consul in Caracas who visited them just after their arrival, all seemed healthy and contented.[46] Soon, however, the colonists began to quarrel with association representatives over the distribution of land, and at being obliged to grow coffee, cotton and indigo instead of wheat and vegetables as the association had promised. By October 1826 the situation had become so bitter that the association stopped the supply of provisions, and the despairing colonists – even the children – took to drink. All work halted and starvation seemed a real possibility.

Porter and the educator Joseph Lancaster, whom Bolívar had invited to Caracas to reform the school system, sponsored a subscription on the immigrants' behalf. Bolívar himself donated 500 pesos. Nevertheless, the settlement began to disintegrate as the more enterprising of the emigrant Scots left for North America, assisted financially by Porter, often out of his own pocket. He noted in his diary on 31 January 1827, that as a result of the settlement's failure the settlers were 'let loose upon the world, some starving, others idling, drunk, and disgracing both themselves and Gt. Britain'. Fortunately, he wrote, 'the British Govt. have at length taken into consideration the deplorable state of the effects of those thus spread abroad by the bursting of the speculative bubble – I am instructed to find passages for those who wish to go home.' This first attempt at colonization would, he concluded regretfully, discourage emigration from Britain for many years.[47]

By mid-April 1827 only 127 Scottish settlers were left at El Topo. Although they had been 'cruelly deceived' by the association, they were, Porter confided to his diary, 'a worthless, drunken set, mostly weavers, and mechanics. Scarcely ten out of the whole know any thing of agriculture.'[48] By late July 1827, Porter had arranged passage for the remaining 56 colonists – 32 adults and 24 children under 12 – on a ship sailing from La Guayra. The consul was delighted 'to be rid of restless and tormenting beings', few of whom had evinced any gratitude to him or the British government for their rescue.[49]

Some settlers returned to London where, like the earlier Poyais victims, they complained publicly and loudly of their treatment. In September 1827 a 'poor, weatherbeaten man' came before the lord mayor at Mansion House to denounce the association's directors and request 'some recompense for the injury he has sustained in going over to Colombia as a settler'. Although sympathetic, the lord mayor said he could do nothing to help, and that the applicant was not the only person to have been duped by company organizers.[50] In addition, the Parliamentary Select Committee on Emigration had received several petitions from the former colonists which were reported in the press. They alleged that the association had failed to perform their side of the contracts they had entered into with the emigrants by providing them with poor, infertile land and stopping their provisions after the first crop had failed. Alternative employment was difficult to find, so the emigrants had been left to starve in a strange land where they would 'have perished but for the generosity of several merchants of La Guayra and Caracas'.

Powles, invited to testify before the committee in October 1827, refuted the allegations vigorously. According to him, the association had more than fulfilled its bargain by supplying settlers with rations for eleven instead of the eight months for which it had contracted. Supplies were only stopped when it became obvious that the settlers were 'giving themselves up to intemperence and indulgence'. Moreover, after the supplies had ceased the Mayor of Caracas had offered all the colonists employment 'if they were disposed to work, and would be satisfied with the fare of the country'. No settlers accepted the offer.[51]

Powles asserted that the real defaulters on the contract were the settlers themselves who, as the company superintendent in Venezuela had stated, 'were such a set of people, with a very few exceptions, as could not have been procured in any country'. They had had every advantage but availed themselves of none, and had only themselves to blame for their impecunious state. By their misconduct they had caused the association to incur heavy financial losses, and 'greatly retarded the progress of an undertaking calculated to produce the most extensive advantages both to Colombia and Great Britain'. Although Consul Sir Robert Ker Porter was occasionally short-tempered and impatient, his assessment, blaming both the colonists and the association, undoubtedly provides a more accurate insight into why the venture failed.

Nor did 1828 brighten the lives of company investors as trends to terminate or restructure continued. In early January, Anglo-Mexican, Real del Monte, Bolívar, Colombian, Mexican, Tlapuxahua and United Mexican mining association shares were still quoted in the press, but generally at much depressed prices. Speculators continued to spread false reports, as they did with bond issues, to add artificial lustre even to Brazilian mining shares. Although high hopes for Brazilian mines had been entertained a few months previously, on 7 February investors were informed that a British warship just arrived from Brazil had brought letters 'fully confirming the suspicion previously indulged, that the accounts of the prolific supplies of gold from the Brazilian mines have been much exaggerated, for the express purpose of forcing up the premium on the shares extraordinarily high'. Not surprisingly, within days the shares fell from their peak of 102 to 63, but presumably not before some speculators had lined their pockets at the expense of more credulous colleagues.[52] In late February a special shareholder meeting of the Anglo Chilean Mining Association at the City of London Tavern voted to dissolve the company, and appointed a committee to superintend the winding up of its affairs.[53]

On 3 April shareholders of the Tlapuxahua Mining Association met at the company's 38 Broad Street offices to receive the directors' most recent report. The last call for new capital had elicited a poor response, short of its goal by £7,600. The directors opined that the company 'had grasped at' too many mines and advised that it should either dissolve or concentrate on a smaller number of mines in order to utilize its resources more efficiently. The shareholders decided to continue, but resolved that the directors consider dividing the shares into one-quarter parts in order to encourage holders to comply with future calls. Sadly their efforts to rescue the company were foredoomed to failure since shareholders could not be convinced to pour in more money. Three weeks later *The Times* announced that 'one of the most extraordinary instances ever known of the depreciation of property has just occurred in the foreign market' when Tlapuxahua shares on which £270 had been paid were priced between 20s. and 25s.[54]

Other Mexican-based mining ventures continued to operate – apparently at a profit – because of a fortunate combination of prudent management and good luck. Bolaños Mining Association shares rose in early September when news reached London of important new discoveries. Initially *The Times* was doubtful, noting that the reports did not indicate when a dividend would be paid. Moreover, 'prospects as splendid as those are now, have, on former occasions, wholly disappeared on investigation'.[55] Yet within three weeks *The Times* was noting that Bolanos was reputedly yielding a £20,000 monthly profit. Ironically, a few years previously the directors had concluded that the mines were unproductive and suspended operations but their employees in Mexico had kept working and hit a rich new vein. Shares now rose from £155 the previous December to a premium of £200 each.[56] Apparently the reports were genuine, for the company was still in existence in 1839.

Of the companies formed during the 1820s to work the Mexican mines, only four others survived as long.[57] Most were inactive paper shells, but outstanding among them, of course, was the Real del Monte, which after three years spent repairing and developing its rich mines did not begin production until 1827. The company's failure to produce the expected returns led one disappointed shareholder to complain that 'I do not know of any other speculation attended with more public delusion, or more unfortunate management'.[58] After a series of further mishaps, chronic cash flow problems and reorganizations, it developed into a profitable venture. The Real del Monte mines, which had first yielded up their silver in 1521, still operate today.[59]

Lack of capital remained a terminal problem for most mining concerns, however, because of shareholder reluctance to honour call agreements. In late October an Anglo-Mexican shareholder meeting was convened to consider means of raising additional funds, while Bolívar Mining Association shareholders also met to decide their company's future.[60] The Colombian Mining Association was in even direr straits. After two years of existence it had produced no silver or gold and by 26 October its shares were selling at discounts of £7 to £8. Even the Imperial Brazilian Mining Association, the shares of which were quoted at £70, a premium of £50 over their paid-in value, had yet to declare a dividend. The specie flow had been east to west, not vice versa. While without exception the companies 'have taken silver, or its equivalent, out of the country . . . not one of them has brought any into it'.[61]

In late November 1828 several mining companies encountered further misfortunes due to the unexpected failure of one of their London bankers, Fry and Chapman, which had never fully recovered from losses sustained in 1826 when it had been rescued by several stronger banks. A small institution, it had not been well known prior to 1824 when it acquired a certain notoriety through its promotion of, and connections with, a large number of the new joint stock companies then being organized, as well as by acting as paying agent for a portion of the Peruvian loan.

At first the City was alarmed lest the suspension of payments trigger a general run on all other banks, as in 1825–6. While financiers and merchants were no longer willing to aid Fry and Chapman directly, they nevertheless increased their deposits with other institutions and thus helped instil a general confidence. At the same time City banks averted a run on the country banks for which Fry and Chapman had been agents by distributing the various agencies among themselves. It soon became apparent that the failure was an insolated incident, and that no panic would ensue. The owners of the £500,000 in deposits at Fry and Chapman were not so fortunate, however, and their losses were heavy. Along with several domestic companies, they included the Real del Monte, the Pasco, Peruvian, and Famatina Mining Associations, and the Imperial Brazilian Mining Association which had £680 of its shareholders' funds on deposit.[62] The year 1828 thus ended with Tlapuxahua and United Mexican Mining Associations reminding shareholders that they must pay the new calls upon their investments before mid-January.[63] Although United Mexican would survive the new year, the Tlapuxahua – and several others – would not.

Just as it maintained its credit standing through the 1829 loan, Brazil also managed to retain limited investor interest in its mining prospects. Two new companies were formed during 1829 to mine gold in Minas Gerais – the Brazilian Mining Company, capitalized at

£450,000 and not to be confused with the Brazilian Mining Association formed in 1825, and the Barra and Castro Mining Company. The latter was capitalized at only £100,000, represented by 5,000 shares of £20 each. Its prospectus noted that the Imperial Brazilian Mining Association had been eminently successful, even though it had had to deposit £20,000 with the Brazilian treasury, pay a tax of 25 per cent on gold extracted, and purchase slaves and mines – for a total outlay of £150,000. The new company expected to be even more profitable, since it had received a 20 per cent tax concession through the influence of its president, the Brazilian ambassador in Vienna.[64]

The occasional press item concerning a new discovery or production increase could still cause Brazilian shares to jump. On 23 April 1829 Brazilian Mining Association shares were selling at a £49 premium. In May *The Morning Chronicle* informed its readership that Brazilian gold mining production had risen from 24 to 81 lb. a day in less than three weeks. The news lifted the association's shares to £15, leading shareholders to anticipate they would soon be back to £100.[65] By the end of 1828, Anglo-Mexican shares were up to £41, still well below their paid-in figure of £85. Brazilian Imperial Mining Association shares on which £20 had been paid were selling, however, at £96.[66] Few non-Brazilian companies were now even mentioned in the press, although there is evidence that a few small mining ventures were still being launched for Colombia and Chile. Like the bond issues, the prices of which it had done much to influence, by 1829 the Latin American company share boom had run its course. To be sure, in late 1829 the shares of the Imperial Brazilian Gas Light Company, formed to illuminate the city of Rio de Janeiro, were offered on the Stock Exchange. The era of large-scale British investment in Latin American public utilities was still some years in the future, however, and interest in direct investment was by now virtually nonexistent.

It is tempting to ascribe the failure of the mining companies principally to their inability to raise more capital during the panic of 1825–6 and its aftermath, as suggested by two recent commentators.[67] The economist Charles McCulloch, writing in the early 1830s much closer to the event, suggests other reasons, equally if not more important. The British entrepreneurs had had little idea of the damage suffered by the mines in the civil wars: 'nor were they aware of how little useful information they could expect from the natives; the working of the mines, like every operation requiring skill and intelligence, had been superintended by natives of Old Spain, who had either fallen in the civil war, or been expelled by the laws passed against them'.[68]

Moreover, in England there was a shortage of good mining superintendents and engineers. Consequently the association often had had to appoint as their agents abroad army and navy officers on half-pay, who, whatever their merits, did not have the abilities or working habits of 'merchantile men.'

One of the chief causes of the Mexican company failures, McCulloch believed, was 'the non-existence of silver mines in England', unlike in Germany. As a result, the British were not familiar with the most modern extraction processes, and the yields of silver per ton of ore were consequently disappointing. Other difficulties according to McCulloch included 'the various disadvantages of distant management'. These, however, could be reduced by selling the ore as soon as it was raised, allowing others to do the extraction for their own account as was done in Cornwall for tin. Also, the miners should not be paid fixed wages, but a portion of the proceeds.

No amount of additional investment, however, could overcome the problems presented by 'the half-civilized state of the inhabitants, their unsettled political condition, and the probability of changes of the parties in power. For this there seems to be no remedy, except the ascendancy of an eminent political leader like Washington, or a close connection with one of the great powers of Europe.'

Nevertheless, McCulloch was basically still optimistic due to the likelihood of continued peace in Europe, and 'of an abundance of monied capital'. Future 'adventurers' would, he was certain, come forward with 'more judicious' plans and succeed in developing the mines.[69] Although McCulloch's comments were principally directed to Mexico, they were applicable to the other mining areas as well.

The problems described by McCulloch, Captain Head and other contemporary observers – including the fact that some of the better lodes worked in colonial times were almost exhausted – could not all be cured simply by injecting more money. And, indeed, funds still existed in the late 1820s for mining investment, as is shown by the continued formation from 1829 into the 1830s of companies for Brazilian and other ventures, where apparently some of the non-pecuniary obstacles presented to operations elsewhere in Latin America did not prevail.

X
RESCHEDULINGS AND NEW BORROWINGS

INTERNATIONAL LENDING AND investment did not cease after the Latin American defaults, but instead was quickly diverted into other areas, notably the United States where British capital poured into canals, banks, roads and bonds issued by the individual states of the Federal union. European – principally British – investment in state and corporation bonds and stocks in the United States had risen from US$12,790,728 in 1820, to US$26,470,417 in 1830, to US$200,000,000 by 1840.[1] The halt in new lending and investment in Latin America was not, therefore, caused by a lack of funds, but instead was attributable to a reluctance – for over a generation at least – to throw good money after bad.

In the interim Latin American bonds continued to trade at steep discounts while bondholder committees utilized a variety of techniques and formulae to salvage what they could from the massive wreckage of dashed expectations. Throughout the rest of the nineteenth century British bondholders, despite discouraging responses, never ceased requesting their government to intervene officially with defaulting states. Nevertheless, the foreign office continued the policy initiated by Canning and Aberdeen, and would only authorize its representatives abroad to provide good offices to bondholder committees. Bondholders had known, as Alexander Baring had stated in 1828 at a general Latin American bondholders' meeting, that their investments entailed a risk of non-payment, reflected in the high interest rates and the discounts at which the bonds were sold. They could not expect the government to act as an insurer for what were, in essence, gambling losses.[2]

By July 1836 the Latin American states, with the exception of Brazil, owed British creditors £18,542,000 in unpaid principal, and a staggering £8,023,008 in interest arrears.[3] Economist Charles Fenn surveying the unhappy economic picture commented disparagingly on Latin American repayment capacity. In Buenos Ayres, he wrote, 'the revenue is seldom sufficient to meet the expenditure', and in neighbouring Chile 'the revenue of the republic amounts to about

£320,000 annually, but the expenditure generally exceeds the income'. In Central America revenues 'are unequal to defray the expenses of government', while in Mexico, due to 'the late civil wars', government annual expenditure exceeded £10,000,000, nearly all of which was spent on the armed forces. Nothing was left for bond servicing. Peru was in no better condition, with a total public debt of $25,000,000 and an annual revenue of but $5,000,000.[4]

Sadly even if government expenses could have been curtailed, the Latin American countries had little that they could sell to Britain to generate the foreign exchange necessary to resume debt servicing. A certain amount of hides and tallow were exported from Buenos Ayres, and sugar and coffee from Brazil. However, the other countries, with their credit exhausted, had nothing to offer except, in some cases, limited amounts of silver and gold with which to redress their persistent unfavourable balance of trade with Britain.[5]

Bondholders were so exasperated that in September 1836, a special delegation visited Lord Palmerstone to urge more vigorous government action. The delegates argued there was no difference between situations where foreign governments seized or damaged British property within its jurisdiction, and when they fraudulently refused to perform engagements into which they had voluntarily entered with British subjects abroad. The injury was the same, and the British government was under an equal duty to protect them. Palmerstone was not convinced and at the end of the hour-long interview would do no more than agree to order British diplomatic representatives abroad to make even more 'vigorous representations' than they had hitherto done.[6]

The foreign office continued to resist bondholders' pressure over the next twelve years, until in January 1848, Palmerstone would attempt to clarify official British policy. Through a circular to all British representatives abroad he hinted strongly that the government's patience with defaulting states was not endless. Although in the past the government had declined to intervene officially on behalf of bondholders, he emphasized that the decision whether or not to intervene remained at the government's discretion, the exercise of which 'turns entirely upon British domestic considerations'. The British government up to 1848 had sought to discourage its subjects from investing capital in 'hazardous loans to foreign governments' which might be better employed at home. Therefore, the government had abstained from taking up as international questions complaints by British subjects against defaulting foreign governments. In the future this policy of restraint might change, Palmerstone admonished, if losses on foreign loans became 'so great that it would be too high a price for the nation to pay for such a warning as to the future'.[7] The veiled threat did not go unnoticed in Latin America, where, because of the great power disparity between Great Britain and the debtor states, the borderline between good offices and official interposition must have seemed blurred anyway.

The effectiveness of appeals to the foreign office was so unpredictable, however, that bondholders turned increasingly to 'self-help'. Since 1827 they had been meeting on a regular basis at City hotels and taverns to discuss grievances and appoint committees to draft letters of protest to loan contractors and the diplomatic representatives of the debtor states, and, later, to prepare formal memorials which they either sent to the foreign office or directly to the governments of the offending states. At first organized on a country-by-country basis, the various bondholder committees united in the 1830s to form an umbrella organization, the Spanish-American Bondholders Committee. On behalf of its country sub-committees the new entity sought to obtain redress by pressuring defaulting states in the press, lobbying parliament, and persuading London and continental stock exchanges to refuse listings to any new issues of defaulting nations. By 1868 various non-Latin American nations were also in default, so it was decided to centralize the activities of national and regional committees into a single, permanent organization, the Council of Foreign Bondholders Association.

Business was so brisk that in 1872 the council circulated a prospectus to raise funds to cope with increasing demands for its services. The document noted that after three years of operations the council's duties 'have assumed such large and constantly increasing dimensions that the existing offices, staff, and revenues, derived from a few bondholders' committees and occasional fees, no longer suffice for the due performance of its functions'. It was therefore proposed to form an association of 1,000 members who would each purchase a £100 bond. Future revenue would be derived from interest on invested capital, contributions from bondholders, from commissions on claims settled, and from other fees. The following year the association was incorporated as the Corporation of Foreign Bondholders.[8]

The corporation's brief extended well beyond lobbying in parliament and in the press, and negotiating rescheduling agreements with recalcitrant borrowers. The corporation and its subsidiary committees, and indirectly the British government, became involved in supervising customs collections, managing banks and railroads, and overseeing other economic sectors of debtor states. Its activities thus anticipated in a modest fashion the more comprehensive intervention today by the International Monetary Fund in the economies of debtor nations, as well as prefiguring the bank steering committees which since 1982 have been negotiating the restructuring of Latin American debt on behalf of hundreds of other creditors. The combination of bondholder committee pressure and diplomatic good offices in the nineteenth century did at least compel creditor nations to agree to reschedulings and restructurings which cured the defaults on paper and thus persuaded a new generation of investors and bankers, unscorched by the experiences of the 1820s, to resume lending. Although some small returns reached bondholders, often the new agreements seemed but to provide opportunities for further default.

Mexico was the first Latin American debtor nation to reach an accommodation with its creditors when in 1830 it was encouraged by Britain's local diplomatic representatives to agree with the Committee of Mexican Bondholders to capitalize over £1,000,000 in interest arrears. Holders of 1824 bonds would receive new 5 per cent bonds at the rate of one £100 bond for every £625 in interest owed, while owners of the 1825 bonds were given 6 per cent bonds at the rate of one £100 bond per £75 of interest capitalized. Interest payments on the new bonds would not begin until 1 April 1836, however, and would be paid by issuing new bonds and from one-sixth of the customs collections at Vera Cruz and Tampico. At the bondholders' request, Lord Aberdeen gave limited permission to the British consuls at those ports to receive and remit funds segregated from customs duties for bond dividends. Such action did not, Lord Aberdeen noted, signify direct British government involvement, since the consuls were to undertake the business entirely on their own responsibility and were free to accept or decline the bondholders' petition for their services. Unfortunately revolutionary disturbances meant the arrangement was doomed. Although some customs proceeds were successfully remitted to London, they never equalled the amounts due, and the new bonds were never issued.[9]

When in 1836 Mexican customs duties reserved for debt servicing were seized by rebellious troops, angry bondholders requested Lord Palmerstone's permission to send 'armed vessels to make reprisals on the Mexican Government to the amount of the property which is stated to have been unlawfully seized'. Under Secretary Backhouse answered on Palmerstone's behalf rejecting the plan, but assuring bondholders that the British chargé in Mexico would exercise his influence 'in an unofficial manner, to point out to the Government of that country the hardship and injustice and impolicy of the course they have pursued'.[10] The following year a despairing committee approved a further renegotiation by which more 5 per cent bonds were issued in exchange for the defaulted 1831 issue.

In 1846 yet another consolidation attempted to merge the rescheduled loans into a new 5 per cent issue. The arrangement did not prosper, and by 1850 long-suffering London bondholders had agreed to reconsolidate the consolidation and to accept a stock paying a reduced 3 per cent semi-annual interest. Claims for overdue interest on prior issues were to be satisfied by payment of US$2,500,000 from the indemnity Mexico expected to receive from the United States for territory seized in the recent war. Future interest payments would be secured with 25 per cent of Mexico's total import duties, 75 per cent of the export duties levied at Pacific ports, and 5 per cent of the export duties collected at Tampico and Vera Cruz on the Gulf of Mexico.[11]

But bondholders waited in vain for repayment as Mexico again tore itself apart in civil war. Finally in 1861 Liberal leader Benito Juárez re-asserted centralised control but inherited an empty treasury. He therefore felt compelled to retract an earlier pledge to honour bondholder claims and declared a two-year moratorium on foreign debt payments.

Although Juárez insisted his action was not a repudiation but simply a temporary suspension, nevertheless it helped precipitate the landing of British, Spanish and French troops at Vera Cruz, which in turn led to France placing Archduke Maximillian of Austria on the throne of Moctezuma.[12] Maximillian's French-sponsored empire was short-lived. Juárez was ultimately victorious, and in retaliation for the Vera Cruz landings broke off diplomatic relations with Britain. Now not even diplomatic good offices were available to bondholders, who made several fruitless attempts to reach a settlement all the same. Although in 1874 the Corporation of Foreign Bondholders persuaded the London and European stock exchanges to refuse listings to any new Mexican issues, not until after Porfirio Díaz became president in 1877 were diplomatic relations restored. A new arrangement was made with the bondholders and a loan floated to redeem the Goldschmidt and Barclay bonds. The interest received by original holders, however, due to years to reschedulings averaged but 2.3 per cent per annum on 1824 bonds, and 1.1 per cent on those issued in 1825. This was a far smaller return than originally expected by eager investors.[13]

The post-1828 saga of the Colombian loans was also disappointing. On 17 December 1830, about the time the Mexican bondholders' committee was completing its first loan renegotiation, Simón Bolívar died near Santa Marta in Colombia, aged forty-eight. Although reports of his illness had been circulating in London, not until the arrival of the Jamaican mail in mid-February 1831 did the City learn of his death.[14] The news disheartened Colombian and other Latin American bondholders, who now saw the end to any expectations of administrative reform or political stability in the nations the Liberator had called into being. Bond quotations were so low anyway, however, that there was no latitude for dramatic falls. Colombian bonds closed slightly lower at 16¾ and 17, Chile down to 20½, Mexico (1825) at 36¼, Peru at 14¾, Brazil 57¾.[15] Indeed, Gran Colombia was already disintegrating due to the centrifugal impulses of military ambition, faulty communications, geographical isolation and strong provincial identification. The three republics which emerged from the wreckage of Bolívar's dream were impoverished, fragile, and dependent for foreign exchange upon a few primary exports, such as coffee in Venezuela, cacao in Ecuador and precious metals in New Granada.[16]

Poverty and political violence left little margin for debt servicing, as demonstrated when tobacco set aside for shipment to Britain for interest payments was seized and sold by Venezuelan General José Antonio Páez to prepare for war with the pro-Bolívar Bogotá government.[17] By early 1832, however, the political uncertainty had abated. New Granada had followed Venezuela's example and declared itself an independent republic, and hopes were entertained in official circles in London for a treaty of perpetual amity, league and confederation which would also provide for payment by the three countries of their common debt.

In September 1832 Sir Robert Ker Porter in Caracas was instructed by the foreign office that Powles & Co. of La Guayra were to be the bondholders' agents in Venezuela, while their sister office in Bogotá would act for New Granadan bondholders. The following month Ker Porter presented the minister of foreign relations with the first official statement of bondholders' claims, hoping to accelerate negotiations for allocating Gran Colombia's debt. Not until 1837, however, would the heirs of Gran Colombia ratify the 1834 convention by which New Granada assumed 50 per cent of the total obligation (£3,312,975), while 28.5 per cent was allocated to Venezuela (£1,888,396) and 21.5 per cent to Ecuador (£1,424,579). Interest arrears of over £3,000,000 were similarly apportioned.[18] Recognition and division of the indebtedness unfortunately did not mean payment was imminent, and Palmerstone ordered Ker Porter to take a stronger line with the Caracas government.

Eventually in 1840, thanks in great part to Porter's efforts, the Venezuelan government accepted a proposal to convert the principal it owed under the allocation into 'Active' Bonds bearing 2 per cent per annum interest from 1845, and increasing gradually over seven years to 6 per cent. Interest arrears were capitalized into 'Deferred' bonds yielding 1 per cent interest, increasing annually from 1852 by ¼ per cent to 5 per cent. Some £3,800,000 in both types of bonds

were issued before Venezuela defaulted in 1847 following more revolutionary disturbances.[19] The 1840 settlement had been unpopular
in Venezuela, however. The new British minister in Caracas, Belford Hinton Wilson, commented discouragingly to Lord Palmerstone on 'the illiberal views prevalent in Venezuela as respects the
sacredness of Debts contracted by the Republic with foreigners, and
the apparent determination not to consent to the adoption of bona
fide steps for effecting the gradual redemption of the Capital of the
Anglo Venezuelan Loan'.[20]

Bondholder relations were further exacerbated three years later
when Venezuela's congress refused to ratify a rescheduling agreement. Although yet another agreement was signed with the London
Spanish–American Bondholders Committee in 1859 and more 'active'
and 'deferred' bonds issued, these also went promptly into default
when a further round of civil war errupted.[21] In 1862 Baring Brothers
proposed to arrange a new 6 per cent loan of £1,000,000 at 63, the
proceeds of which would be allocated partially to liquidate the unpaid coupons on the restructuring bonds issued in 1859. The remaining proceeds would be used to re-establish the currency on a sound
basis and 'to restore financial order and regularity in the Republic'.[22]

In 1864 a further £1,500,000 6 per cent Venezuelan credit was
launched at 60 by London's General Credit and Finance Company to
repay earlier borrowings and finance infrastructure and agricultural
development. It was to be funded by export duties collected at four
ports where British consuls had been authorized to transmit revenues
to the loan's London agent.[23] Despite such elaborate precautions,
neither the loan nor Venezuela prospered as a new stage in the
bloody internecine Federal Wars promptly drained the treasury. On
3 December 1864, a government decree suspended payment of the
custom proceeds required by the 1862 loan agreement, and forced
bondholders' agents to return the customs fees already collected.

Edward Eastwick, a special commissioner sent by the bondholders
to Venezuela, was thoroughly disillusioned. He deplored official
British reluctance to support bondholders' claims more firmly, and
complained 'that the English Government gratuitously parades its
determination not to enforce the claims of its subjects ... It is like
putting up a board to warn trespassers that they will *not* be pro-
secuted.'[24] Venezuela remained in default until 1880 when strong-
man Antonio Guzmán Blanco forced congressional approval of a
£2,750,000 consolidated bond issue. This new proposal was ratified
by the bondholders, and Venezuela did not default again until 1892.[25]

Although in 1834 New Granada – as Colombia was then known –
agreed to assume half of the defaulted principal of the Gran Colombia debt and half of the accrued interest for a total of £4,903,203,

bondholders waited eleven years without relief. In 1842 Powles again wrote to Lord Aberdeen requesting him to instruct the British chargé in Bogotá to interfere on the bondholders' behalf. Under Secretary Addington sent Powles the familiar reply that the bondholders' case would not justify interference of an authoritative or compulsory nature. Nevertheless, Aberdeen would authorize consuls at New Granadan ports to receive customs duties proceeds retained for debt service and to remit them to London. 'It must, however, be understood that the Consuls will be left entirely at liberty to accept or refuse the agency, if it should be offered to them by the parties interested.'[26]

Finally, in 1845 an acceptable arrangement was agreed to restructure the country's indebtedness by issuing £3,312,975 in 'New Active Bonds' paying interest on a sliding scale rising from 1 to 6 per cent over several years.[27] Overdue interest of £3,776,791 was capitalized into deferred bonds with interest rising by annual increments from 1 to 3 per cent. Payments were secured by government tobacco monopoly revenues and by one half of customs' proceeds, the collection and remittance of which would be arranged by British consular representatives. The nation defaulted again in June 1850, however, and three years later the government sought unsuccessfully to lighten its debt burden by offering public lands to foreigners. Bondholder negotiating committees persisted, and in 1861 New Granada agreed to issue additional bonds to cover accrued interest on the 1845 active bonds, while percentages of customs revenues were assigned for redemption.[28]

New Granada's general economic prospects assumed a rosier hue upon completion in 1855 of the railway across its Panamanian isthmus. In view of the railroad's profitability, in 1863 the London and County Bank decided to test the market for the United States of Colombia (as New Granada had then become) obligations with a small £200,000 6 per cent loan at 86 to finance road construction, 'improvement of navigation on the Magdalena River ... and the development and promotion generally of the commercial resources of the Republic'.[29]

Sadly, despite the efforts of the bondholders' committee by 1879 all New Granadan/Colombian obligations, including the renegotiated 1822 and 1824 credits, the 1863 loan and a further consolidation attempt in 1873, were in default.[30] Mineral wealth and the promise of an effective Panamanian interoceanic route could not compensate for political instability which frightened investors and rendered illusory the rescheduling agreements so laboriously and hopefully drafted in London and Bogotá. Between 1840 and 1885 the

11. New Granada Wasteland Certificate, issued in 1861 as part of the restructuring arrangement for New Granada's (now Colombia) portion of the debt incurred by Gran Colombia in 1822 and 1824.

country was torn by four full-scale civil wars and at least fifty local revolutions, an appalling record even by Latin American standards.[31]

Ecuador was the last of Gran Colombia's three successor states to seek to appease its creditors. In 1834 it had assumed responsibility for £1,424,579 of the original Colombian debt, with interest arrears of £683,798. Not even interest was paid on its share for over fifteen years, however. In 1853 a tentative renegotiation agreement between the bondholders' committee and the Ecuadorean executive branch was rejected by the senate, which opposed capitalization of interest arrears. As a result, a mid-century economist commented that 'the same system of delay and duplicity which has been practised by some of the other South American States, under the delusion of some remote advantage being held out to the bondholders, has been practised by the Republic of Ecuador'.[32]

Two years later, however, a settlement was finally negotiated and approved. Counting twenty-eight years of interest arrears, the debt now totalled £3,817,871, but was reduced by agreement to £1,824,000. Of this, £400,000 represented capitalization of interest arrears, and would yield interest of 1 per cent per annum. An additional £400,000 of arrears was cancelled and land warrants issued against another £566,120. The remaining overdue £516,000 was satisfied by delivery of $860,000 in Peruvian 4½ per cent bonds which had been issued by Peru to settle its portion of the debt owed to Colombia for Bolívar's expenses in liberating the nations from Spanish rule.[33]

The rescheduling arrangement lasted until 1868 when Ecuador stopped payment. Attempts to renegotiate failed, causing the Council of the Corporation of Foreign Bondholders to comment in 1874 that it was not 'able to report the removal of the stain of repudiation from the Republic of Ecuador'.[34] Subsequent negotiations collapsed, even though the Council sent a representative to Quito to re-open discussions. Unfortunately when he arrived the country was in the midst of yet another revolution, and no agreement was possible. Not until 1890 did Ecuador agree with the Corporation of Foreign Bondholders on a new consolidation.[35]

Nor were the five successor states to the United Provinces of Central America any less reluctant than Gran Colombia's progeny to accommodate bondholder creditors. After years of futile protest, in February 1835 Lord Palmerstone forwarded Chargé d'Affaires Frederick Chatfield a bondholders' memorial for transmission to the Central American federal government. Palmerstone ordered Chatfield, a headstrong man less concerned than his predecessor Dashwood with diplomatic niceties, to urge the case upon the government's attention 'in a friendly but firm tone, stating that His

Majesty's Government confidently anticipates that the Government of Central America will see the propriety of taking speedy and effectual measures to satisfy the just claims of the bondholders'. Otherwise, Palmerston threatened, European governments might be reluctant to enter into 'closer Relations' with Central America.[36]

Chatfield pressed the Central Americans for payment, forwarding the additional plaintive memorials with which bondholders bombarded the foreign office. In 1836 the bondholders' committee, through Chatfield, reminded the Guatemalan government officials that in 1828 Minister Marcial Zebadúa in London had specifically recognized his nation's responsibility for £163,300 after examining and endorsing bonds already issued to that amount. Despite a reply from Zebadúa, who had since returned to Guatemala and was now a senator, in January 1834 that measures would be taken by the government to satisfy its creditors, internal dissentions had prevented any action from being taken. Now that the civil wars had abated, the bondholders ventured, surely settlement negotiations could recommence.[37] If the Central Americans could not afford to repay overdue interest, Committee Chairman Alexander Read wrote to Palmerstone, Chatfield might suggest that the government consider, as had been done by Mexico, capitalizing overdue interest by issuing new bonds with a five year interest grace period.[38] The Central American government's resistance to settling the relatively small amount of bondholder claims was based not just on its poverty and concern over its own forthcoming disintegration, however. Payment had become a sensitive political issue due to assertions that the party in power in 1825 had squandered the proceeds.[39]

Finally, in 1838 the Central American federation, after fifteen years of internal squabbles, collapsed into its five component units of Guatemala, El Salvador, Honduras, Nicaragua and Costa Rica, just when Chatfield has prevailed upon the federal government to apply half the tobacco duty revenues to servicing the debt.[40] The union had always been fragile. Mountains and jungles had isolated population centres from each other and encouraged development of local political and economic interests at the expense of any wider awareness. The federal form of government adopted in 1824 could not alter physical reality. Each state or province had its own constitution and its own executive and legislative branches within a federal umbrella organization centred in Guatemala City, where the federal executive and legislature sought to harmonize legislation and impose order upon their provincial counterparts. It was a formula which could have succeeded only in a more closely-knit, homogeneous setting with adequate interregional communication links and economic ties. Instead, under pressure from the rival warring partisans of stronger central government and the adherents of a looser confederation, the new nation fragmented as Colombia had done eight years before.[41]

The collapse of the United Provinces made Chatfield's task of obtaining satisfaction for British claimants physically more difficult, since he now had five nations with which to negotiate instead of one. Undiscouraged, however, he began lobbying anew and persuaded, threatened and cajoled the federation's successor states to apportion the principal of the £163,000 foreign debt among themselves. At first he insisted upon an equal division among them. The Costa Rican government objected, stating that the debt should be allocated on the basis of population, with Guatemala paying the largest amount. Eventually the outstanding principal was shared so that Guatemala assumed £67,900, Nicaragua £27,200, Honduras £27,200, Costa Rica £13,500 and El Salvador £27,200. Interest arrears of £93,333 were similarly divided, using the Colombian settlement as a precedent.[42] As in Colombia's case, however, recognition of indebtedness did not mean prompt payment.

Costa Rica, which had the smallest share of the debt, was the first of the five to succumb to Chatfield's entreaties to honour its commitment to pay. In 1840 it liquidated 85 per cent of its portion with cash proceeds of tobacco sales arranged by Chatfield, although apparently the payment did not include the nation's share of interest arrears.[43] With its credit thus somewhat restored, Costa Rica came to market in 1871 with two 6 per cent loans of £500,000 each. Another £2,400,000 7 per cent issue was launched shortly thereafter. The loans quickly went into default. So great was the corruption which attended their issue that the Parliamentary Select Committee formed in 1875 to investigate foreign loan frauds found that except for some funds retained in England from bond sales, bondholders had received no interest or principal payment.[44] Apparently investors had learned nothing from the disasters of fifty years before.

The other Central American nations continued to sidestep Chatfield's demands, leading him in 1849 to urge Palmerstone to seize Honduran and Salvadorean islands in the Gulf of Fonseca on the Pacific coast as security for outstanding claims by bondholders and by British subjects who had been injured or had had their property damaged in revolutionary and other civil disturbances.[45] Palmerstone refused, replying that parliament would never agree to accept the islands in settlement of the claims. The headstrong proconsul was nevertheless undeterred. Assuming Palmerstone might yet approve a *fait accompli*, Chatfield summoned the British Pacific squadron to occupy Tigre Island. This was too much even for Palmerstone, who, when he learned of the event some weeks later, promptly ordered the British flag lowered and the island restored to Honduran sovereignty.[46] Perhaps impressed by this example of naked force, El Salvador finally capitulated, and in 1860 attempted to settle its £27,200 portion of the defaulted loan by paying 90 per cent of the principal in cash, but without accrued interest. When in 1863 the country sought unsuccessfully to float a £400,000 8 per cent loan in London, the prospectus claimed in an amazing half-truth that 'Salvador has neither an Internal nor an External Debt'.[47]

Honduran attempts to pay its share of the Central American debt led that nation into even deeper financial disaster. In 1866 the Honduran minister in London, Carlos Gutíerrez, and Víctor Herrán, minister in Paris, decided to capitalize on the British public's persistent faith in the rich potential of a Central American interoceanic route. They wrote to the Honduran minister of foreign relations that European investors were prepared to advance £1,000,000 to construct an interoceanic railway, and obtained a broad power of attorney from their government authorizing them to arrange the loan.[48] In order to assure market acceptance, however, Gutíerrez and Herrán first decided to make a gesture towards settling the Honduran share of the Central American Federation loan, which with interest arrears now amounted to £90,075. Accordingly, in mid-1867 a 5 per cent conversion loan for £90,000 secured by customs duties at the Pacific port of Amapala was arranged, pursuant to which Central American bondholders were promised new bonds in full settlement of their claims. Thus began one of the more blatant swindles since the Poyais episode.

Between 1867 and 1872 the two diplomats arranged three 10 per cent bond issues in London and Paris with a face value totalling nearly £6,000,000 to fund the 1867 settlement and finance construction of a 236 mile railway linking the Gulf of Fonseca on the Pacific with Puerto Caballos on the Caribbean. Only £689,700 was ever paid to the railway contractors, however, who after building but 53 miles suspended work in May 1872. When news reached Europe that the project had been abandoned the bonds plunged since without an operating railway there were little hope of receiving even interest payments.[49]

The outcome of the loans was disastrous for Honduras and for the investing public. The 1875 Parliamentary Select Committee investigating loan swindles found that out of £2,051,511 received by the trustees, the Honduran government received but £58,930 while only £2,700 was ever paid on the federation debt. The rest lined the pockets of Gutíerrez, Herrán and their Anglo-French broker friends.[50] By 1875 Honduras had contracted a principal obligation of £5,990,108, with interest in arrears of £1,230,134, while thousands of investors had lost their savings through a complex fraud. Although the principal villains in the drama escaped justice by fleeing to Europe, disputes over the indebtedness they had created marred relations with Great Britain until a final settlement was agreed in 1923. Even today there is no rail link between the Honduran Atlantic and Pacific coasts.

Meanwhile in 1839 neighbouring Nicaragua had accepted responsibility for £27,200, representing one-sixth of the 1825 loan. Despite 'unofficial' remonstrations by Chatfield and other British Central American diplomatic representatives, no payment was forthcoming. Nicaraguan recalcitrance was attributable not only to its own endemic poverty, but also to resentment at Great Britain's support for the Mosquito King's pretensions to sovereignty over a large extension of Nicaragua's Caribbean coast. Whitehall's policy was largely motivated by desires to secure for Britain the transoceanic canal route via the San Juan River and across Lake Nicaragua, and in 1848 this resulted in armed confrontation between British and Nicaraguan forces. Eventually in 1850, as the price for improved relations with the United States, Britain renounced by treaty with Nicaragua its protectorate over the Mosquitos, who were thenceforth confined to a semi-autonomous reservation. At last the moment appeared ripe to negotiate settlement of British bondholder claims.[51]

Despite the joint efforts of British diplomats and bondholder committees, however, no payment was made until 1874. In that year Nicaraguan government agents sailed to London where they offered a private meeting of Central American bondholders 5 per cent four-year government bills at an exchange rate of £14 of bills for each £100 Central American bond assumed by Nicaragua. The Council of the Corporation of Foreign Bondholders protested that the terms 'besides being utterly inadequate and not calculated to satisfy the Bondholders, were not of a nature to maintain the credit of the Republic'. Nevertheless, some bondholders accepted the offer. No new credits were obtainable, however, until 1886.[52]

Guatemala, recipient of most of the 1825 loan, had been pressured by Chatfield to assume the lion's share of federation indebtedness. In 1856 it finally agreed to settle its £67,900 portion, with accrued interest reduced to £45,567, by issuing £100,000 in 5 per cent bonds secured by 50 per cent of the customs proceeds at the Caribbean port of Izabal and at Guatemala City. With credit temporarily at least restored, in 1869 Guatemala floated a 6 per cent £500,000 issue in London. Principal and interest payments were guaranteed by pledging import duties, and in order to stimulate further investor confidence the prospectus promised bondholders' representatives the right to appoint a special receiver for the receipts.[53]

The loan was intended to repay the 1856 bonds and also to finance Guatemala's share of constructing a road to the British Honduran coast. Since colonial times the frontier between Guatemala and Belize had been bitterly disputed. In 1859 British and Guatemalan negotiators signed a treaty in which Britain renounced its claim to the contested area. In addition, the parties were required to use their best efforts to open a route by 'cart road or employing the rivers, or both united ... between the fittest place on the Atlantic coast, near the settlement of Belize and the capital of Guatemala'.[54] Back in London the foreign office doubted if parliament would vote the necessary appropriations for the road, and so proposed a compromise cost-sharing convention to the Guatemalan government. When Guatemala did not accede to the convention until after the expiry of the ratification period, the new foreign office functionaries, who were not as favourably inclined to the arrangement as Lord Palmerstone's government had been, themselves now declined to ratify the proposal. The British government had obtained the frontier demarcation it desired and now saw no reason to incur the expense of the road. Moreover, the foreign office argued, the treaty had only spoken of 'best efforts' and so did not impose a binding obligation upon Great Britain to participate in the road construction.

In 1869 the Guatemalans tried again to persuade the foreign office to divide construction costs, noting that the loan raised that year would fund Guatemala's portion. The foreign office replied there was not the 'smallest expectation that the question would be reopened'.[55] The 1856 and 1869 loans went into default, and not until 1888 could bondholders and the Guatemalans agree to convert them into 4 per cent consolidated bonds. Even this arrangement collapsed.[56] Today disputes over the frontier and Guatemala's claims to access to the Caribbean across a now independent Belize continues to strain relations between the three countries.

Investors in Chilean, Peruvian and Buenos Ayres bonds fared better than other Latin American bondholders in post-default reschedulings. After 1830, under the conservative regime of Diego Portales Chile entered a long period of relative stability, with far fewer attempted coups than in its neighbouring republics. Economically the country also made great progress as exports of silver, copper and nitrates brought new prosperity.[57] Investor confidence in the country revived further when in 1842 through the agency of Baring Brothers Chile agreed to resume interest payments on its 1822 loan and to capitalize £756,000 in interest arrears with new 3 per cent bonds. Although the rescheduled payments were duly made, over a decade would elapse before any new money would be available for Chile in London. Then, in 1858 the pricing of a

£1,544,800 issue managed by Barings to finance railroad constructions reflected Chile's new-found market respectability. The bonds
bore interest of 4½ per cent and were offered at 92.

Over the next two decades additional loans totalling over £7,500,000
were floated in the City for Chile, principally for railway construction, before the War of the Pacific with Peru and Bolivia broke out
in 1879.[58] On 10 March of that year the Chilean finance minister
wrote to the London Stock Exchange Chairman that despite the last
abundant harvest, a thriving nitrate industry and increasing customs
duties, 'the armed rupture of our relations with Bolivia, has placed
the government with the painful necessity of stopping payments
into the sinking fund out of which the principal of the national debt
was to be repaid.' He requested that Baring Brothers and Chile's
other bankers be informed that as from 1 May the government 'will
only provide – in consequence of the reasons explained – for the
payment of the interest of the National Debt'. Not until after the
1883 peace treaty could Chile return to London for further credits.[59]

After the general mid-century lending revival Peru also became
an outstanding market favourite, and by 1880 had placed approximately £30,000,000 in new issues in London, more than any other
Latin American nation including Brazil. For over twenty years,
however, bondholders had despaired of receiving principal or interest. Before his posting to Caracas, the British consul in Lima was
Belford Hinton Wilson, who in 1833 complained to the Peruvian
foreign minister of 'the misery and ruin' which had afflicted 'a considerable body of British subjects' as a result of Peru's default. He
suggested a settlement modelled on that recently negotiated with
Mexico whereby portions of customs duties were deposited with
bondholders' local agents for remittance to Britain.[60] Wilson's plan
was never implemented, and the country soon lapsed into near
anarchy. Uprisings, coups and counter-coups then dominated
national life for the next forty years.

Within such a maelstrom of violence foreign investors could expect little relief. Bondholders were saved, however, not by silver,
copper and nitrates as in Chile, but by seabird droppings called *guano*.
Although guano had been used as a fertilizer since pre-Colombian
times, it had never been a significant export. With the increasing use
of fertilizers in Britain and Europe after the mid-century, however,
the large guano accumulations on Peruvian coastal islands suddenly
became valuable. The discovery in the 1840s of particularly rich
deposits on the Chincha Islands converted bondholder despair to
optimism.[61]

In 1849 Peru's new source of wealth encouraged it to agree to a
restructuring plan with its bondholders so that its credit standing

in Europe would be restored. 75 per cent of interest arrears of £2,615,000 were capitalized into deferred bonds bearing interest on a sliding scale from 1 to 5 per cent per annum. Unpaid capital of the 1822 and 1824 6 per cent issues was refinanced with new bonds, the 4 per cent interest on which would increase by yearly ½ per cent increments up to 6 per cent. The loan was secured and serviced by the Peruvian government's net income from guano exports to Britain and Ireland, a portion of sales proceeds of which would be deposited in the Bank of England by Anthony Gibbs & Sons, the government's guano consignees, so that principal repayments could begin in 1856.[62]

Unfortunately, much of the guano sales proceeds would be squandered on a non-productive military establishment and a massive expansion of the bureaucracy. Guano also provided collateral for more bond issues to construct railroads and develop ports and other infrastructure.[63] By 1872 bondholders were concerned that Peru had pledged more guano than could ever be produced from its dwindling supplies. National finances were so overstretched that yet another consolidation loan was proposed, by which holders of bonds issued in 1865, 1866 and 1870 could exchange their old paper for the new issue at preferential rates.

Despite high expectations and elaborate precautions, railway construction costs were so great that in 1876 Peru defaulted, promising, however, to resume interest payments in January 1879.[64] Then, like Chile, the nation suffered a crippling economic blow when the War of the Pacific errupted and Chilean forces occupied the Lobos Islands, the guano of which had been pledged to British bondholders as security for various Peruvian loans. The bondholders then approached the Chilean minister in London requesting permission to load the guano hypothecated to them. After protracted negotiations the Chileans eventually agreed to allow the bondholders to remove the guano, but only 'in consideration of a payment of thirty shillings per ton'![65]

Meanwhile Buenos Ayres bondholders' expectations had remained at a low ebb since the January 1828 default. Bondholders had become increasingly frustrated, and in 1831 Minister Mariano Moreno reported from London to the Buenos Ayres foreign ministry that bondholders were particularly angry at the government's failure to reach a settlement capitalizing overdue interest. A press campaign instigated by the bondholders vilified the Buenos Ayres government, and perhaps it was no coincidence when in the following year Britain occupied the Falkland Islands.[66]

Juan Manuel de Rosas, Governor of the Province of Buenos Ayres since 1829, was aware of the importance of keeping creditors at bay, however, and in 1838 suggested that Moreno hint to the foreign office that Buenos Ayres might surrender its claims to the Falklands if Britain would reimburse the bondholders.[67] Finally, in 1844 Baring Brothers, aided by the good offices of the British diplomatic representative, persuaded the Buenos Ayres dictator to make a monthly token payment of £1,000 until a final settlement was agreed.[68]

After Rosas was overthrown in February 1852, bondholder hopes rose. Barings had by now received £14,655, which it divided among 1,954 bondholders at £7.10s. per £500 bond.[69] Even this miniscule repayment was sufficiently encouraging, coupled with Rosas' fall, to push quotations up to 73. Over the next three years Barings twice sent representatives to Buenos Ayres to persuade the new government to reach a settlement with the bondholders. Both missions failed, and in December 1853, £977,000 in principal was still outstanding, as well as £1,480,155 in overdue interest. Nevertheless observers in London remained hopeful. One financial commentator remarked in 1855 that 'now the reign of terror that existed under the despotic power of Rosas has been brought to a termination, the future prospects of this province hold out greater hopes of improvement.'[70]

Eventually Barings' and the bondholders' persistence, combined with increasingly less subtle applications of diplomatic good offices, produced a mutually satisfactory settlement in 1857, by which time the group of provinces led by Buenos Ayres had become the Republic of Argentina. Outstanding principal would be repaid in annual instalments rising from £36,000 in 1857, to £60,000 in 1860 and thereafter to £65,000 until complete redemption. Barings, of course, acted as agents for the £1,641,000 credit which capitalized the 1824 interest arrears by issuing new bonds initially yielding 1 per cent interest until 1886, then rising to 2 per cent until 1871, and to 3 per cent thereafter. With the nation's credit thus restored, in 1866 Barings marketed £550,000 in London at 75 as the first portion of a £2,500,000 6 per cent bond issue repayable over thirty-three years. Additional, larger credits followed. Despite a severe crisis in the early 1890s, until the end of the century Argentina proved the most consistently creditworthy of the Spanish American borrowers.[71]

To the north, Argentina's old rival Brazil maintained its high credit rating in London. Despite its enormous size, the nation had not suffered from the separatist movements, coups and civil wars which plagued the former Spanish colonies. It survived the economic shambles caused by the War of the Triple Alliance (1864–70) in which Brazil, Uruguay and Argentina became locked in a prolonged, sanguinary struggle with Paraguay, and even the transition from monarchy to republic was achieved peacefully.

Nevertheless, after its 1829 loan, Brazil could not approach the

London market until the 1834 restoration of Queen María to the Portuguese throne, when interest payments on the guaranteed Portuguese loan were resumed. In 1839 a small £312,512 5 per cent credit was obtained, followed in 1843 by a £732,000 issue. In 1852 Rothschilds managed a 4½ per cent £1,040,600 loan at 95 for funding the outstanding Portuguese loan, which had been reduced to £954,250 by agreement with the bondholders. By mid-century coffee and sugar had brought new prosperity, and in 1855 a London economist assured readers that Brazil's credit 'is inferior to no country in the London Money Market, the 5 per cent bonds having been for some time quoted at par'. Between 1860 and 1875 the British investing public happily purchased an additional £20,950,000 in Brazilian bonds.[72]

By the 1870s new lending to Latin America, at first an adjunct to refinancing packages, had become an end in itelf as a new generation of financiers and investors ignored the lessons of the past. The dramatic expansion of industry in Europe led to a massive demand for minerals, wheat, fertilizers, wool and other Latin American primary products. As one commentator wrote in 1878, 'the emancipation of industry ... strengthened the general spirit of enterprise, and forgetfulness of the old repudiatory tendencies of our American correspondents, and the manifold material progress of our kinsmen, rendered it possible again to appeal for funds for various loans and undertakings.'[73] Borrowers who had not approached the market in 1822–5, either as independent states or as components of larger entities such as Colombia, now obtained listings in London. Bolivia, Santo Domingo, Paraguay, Uruguay, and even administrative subdivisions such as the Argentine provinces of Buenos Ayres, Entre Ríos and Sante Fé, had all tapped the London bond market by 1881.

The Latin American loans were, however, but part of the general surge in foreign lending which accompanied the upswing in global trade and overseas investment. Between 1860 and 1876 over 150 foreign loans were issued in the City with a nominal value exceeding £720,000,000. Recipients included not only the Latin American states, but also Austria, Belgium, Egypt, France, Holland, Hungary, Japan, Liberia, Morocco, Norway, Roumania, Russia, Sardinia, Spain, Turkey and a number of states and cities in the United States of America.[74]

The saga of the repeated, frustrated attempts of bondholder committees to recover defaulted interest and principal due on the 1824–5 Latin American loans and their successors suggests that the old adage that countries do not go bankrupt like private companies is at best misleading. While the borrowing nations did not go out of existence like liquidated companies, the first Latin American loans were written down, repayment periods extended, interest rates reduced, and arrears converted into more paper which again often when into default. Original bondholders who kept their investments eventually did realize a small return, but nothing like what they had initially expected or been led to expect. In the meantime they and their families had undergone privation, anguish and stress. In Britain the loans generally had profited only bankers, brokers, middlemen, lawyers and, latterly, speculators who had purchased the bonds at steep discounts, and then sold them when news of a renegotiation made them rise again.

Company investors fared even worse, receiving on liquidation only ludicrously low fractions of the paid-in value of their shares. A few mining companies survived into the 1830s but, with the exception of those in Brazil and one or two in Mexico, they functioned principally on paper. At least eighteen Latin American mining associations had evaporated, and with them the dreams of hundreds – perhaps thousands – of investors. Although in 1835–6 the City experienced a minor repetition of the first company formation mania, perhaps only five of the three hundred new enterprises floated were created specifically to conduct business in Latin America, doubtless a reflection of unhappy memories still retained by the investing public.[74]

After mid-century, however, British investment poured into all of Latin America. By 1881 the British public had put over £34,437,000 into Latin American railways, £11,000,000 into its public utilities, and £3,398,000 into the continent's mining enterprises. Unlike in 1824–5, this later direct investment was profitable and, one commentator has calculated, yielded an average return of at least 6 per cent per annum. Transoceanic cable communications, more efficient maritime transport and other technological advances had combined with relatively greater local political stability to render exploitation of the economic potential of the former Spanish empire more feasible than in the 1820s. In contrast, by 1881 income from the £123,000,000 in Latin American government bonds held by the British public averaged only 2 per cent of their total face value because only £52,000,000 was being serviced. Only Argentina, Brazil and Venezuela, out of thirteen Latin American borrowers, were not in default.[74]

The first Latin American loan crisis thus seemed to have been forgotten within forty years, if not replaced and obscured with a new cluster of problem loans. However, the underlying social, legal and political effects of the 1822–25 boom were more pernicious and longer lasting.

XI
THE HUMAN AND
POLITICAL TOLL

IN THE ENTHUSIASM of post-1850 lending and investing it was easy to forget the unhappy fates of those hopeful individuals who in 1822 literally had fought each other at the Royal Exchange for the privilege of purchasing Peruvian government bonds, or who had subscribed eagerly for shares in the new companies formed to profit from Latin American mining and other commercial opportunities. Although early financial commentators attempted to assess the damage inflicted on the British economy by the profligacies of the lending and company boom, their cold statistics could but hint at the scope of the underlying human catastrophes caused by the events of 1822–5.

It is impossible to calculate precisely the number of individuals seduced into parting with their savings. The bonds were bearer instruments so no ownership records were kept. Shareowners in companies also remain anonymous since although their certificates generally were nominative, most have long vanished, together with any shareholder registers. Reliable data is therefore scarce. Nevertheless, rough conjectures suggest the extent of investor involvement.

In 1852 Barings made a partial distribution of interest arrears to 1,954 bondholders of the 1825 £1,000,000 Buenos Ayres loan.[1] To be sure, bondholder meetings as recorded in the press in the 1820s generally had an attendance of under a 150, but this low figure may be due to the limited space available at the City taverns and coffee houses, rather than indicate the total number of bondholders affected by a default. Also some bond issues were more popular and successful than others and therefore had more subscribers. Assuming, however, that the Buenos Ayres figures are representative, and using a conservative factor of 1,500 holders per £1,000,000 in bonds, it seems probable that even allowing for investors owning bonds of more than one issue, the £21,000,000 Latin American debt was owned initially by at least 25–30,000 bondholders. Because many bonds changed hands several times over forty to fifty years before settlements were made with debtor nations, the total number of people who at one time or another held them was much higher. The individuals affected by the defaults increased even more dramatically if one considers the bondholders' families and dependents, as well as the tradesmen, bankers and others with whom they were financially involved.

Company shareholders undoubtedly greatly exceeded bondholders in number. At least forty-six companies were formed or projected in 1823–5 for Latin American operations with a nominal capitalization of over £36,000,000, as compared with Latin American bond issues totalling some £20,000,000. The minimum bond denomination was £100 with discounts ranging from 75 to 89 per cent. As a result only fairly affluent people could afford to purchase them. In contrast, company share par values could be as low as £25 each for the 10,000 shares of the Anglo-Mexican Mint Company, for example, and could be purchased for a £5 downpayment. Even mining shares with par values of £100 such as the Colombian Mining Association could be obtained by paying in only £15, subject of course, to calls for up to the full subscription. Consequently Latin American company shares were attractive to a wider range of personal income levels than bonds.

Some company share investors like Benjamin Disraeli could afford to bear the inevitable losses. By April 1825, he owned mining shares worth £6,000, which, he told his stockbroker, would be worth £12,000 by the end of the year. 'On the Mexican mines I rest my sheet anchor.'[2] The anticipated profits did not materialize, and three years later his stockbroker was still writing dunning letters requesting payment for the shares he had purchased for Disraeli and his partner. In 1834, a sadder but wiser Disraeli would sigh: 'We have no hope of Del Montes: we try to forget such things'.[3]

Other share purchasers were not as fortunate as Disraeli, who at least was a salaried clerk in a solicitors office. Generally these human tragedies were not considered sufficiently newsworthy to merit press mention. One case in early December, 1826 was so sad, however, that *The Morning Chronicle* could not refrain from comment. On 1 December shares and debentures belonging to a 'highly respectable' deceased ham-and-provision merchant of St Nicholas Lane, Lombard Street, were auctioned for the benefit of his widow at Garroway's Coffee House. Their late owner had 'destroyed himself in a fit of temporary derangement caused by the depreciation in value . . . of some Spanish bonds'. The low prices which his Latin American mining shares realized suggest the extent of losses incurred by other small speculators as well. Ten Peruvian Mining Company shares on which the merchant had paid £15 per share sold for £1.3s. each. Ten Anglo-Chilean Mining Association shares on which £8 had been paid brought but £2 per share, while twenty Potosí, La Paz and Peruvian Mining Association shares, with £5 paid, produced only £1.4s. each.[4]

Stockbrokers were quickly singled out by the press and public opinion as principally to blame for the ruin of so many lives. Historian, essayist and critic Harriet Martineau was perhaps more accurate when, rather than blame brokers exclusively, she suggested that many victims had contributed to their own downfall. With some investors,

the charm was in the excitement, – in the pleasure of sympathy in large enterprises, – in the rousing of the faculties of imagination and conception, when their field of commerce extended over the Pampas and the Andes, and beyond the farthest seas, and among the ice-rocks of the poles. When the grey-haired merchant grew eloquent by his fireside about the clefts of the Cordillera, where the precious metals glitter to the miner's torch, it was not his expected gains alone that fired his eye, and quickened his utterance; but that gratification of his conceptive faculty to which his ordinary life had ministered but too little.[5]

Miss Martineau was particularly well-qualified to pass judgement since her own life had been indelibly scarred by the boom and crash. Her father, a Norwich cloth maker, was nearly ruined. Although the elder Martineau was no speculator, his inventory was larger 'than it would have been in a time of less enterprise; and week by week its value declined, till, in the middle of the winter, when the banks were crashing down all over England, we began to contemplate absolute ruin'.[6] Straightened circumstances forced him to alter his will, 'reducing the portions left to his daughter to something which could barely be called an independence', and thereby strengthening young Harriet's determination to earn her living by the pen. Had it not been for the 1825–6 crisis, posterity might never have been able to enjoy her prodigious literary output, which included poetry, short stories, novels, book reviews, essays on economics, travel and religion, and a history of contemporary England. One of her short novels, *Berkeley the Banker*, was particularly well received because, she admitted, it had been based upon those dramatic events in 1825–6 which had blighted so many lives. Indeed, she later recalled, 'the story was, in a great degree . . . our own family history of four years before'.[7]

Few early investors left written records. Most were fated to remain forever nameless. Nevertheless, the vicissitudes of the grandfathers of the post-1850 investing generation and the schemes in which they had lost their savings became part of popular folklore and were commemorated by best-selling novelists and storytellers. Unknown investors thus achieved an immortality which persisted long after the bond and share certificates, into which they had poured their dreams, had crumbled to dust or been devoured by insects.

During the closing days of the general loan and company boom, Disraeli captured the intoxicating, contagious spirit of the times in his first novel, *Vivian Grey*, which the precocious twenty-one-year old published anonymously in July 1826. The book was a resounding success, particularly because of its ill-disguised caricatures of prominent political and social figures. The protagonist, clearly based on the author, is a young man without fortune or connections who ascends in society through intelligence and charm. Like Disraeli, Vivian Grey began as a clerk in a solicitor's office, and experienced at first hand the Latin American lending and investing boom. A friend writes to Vivian describing a dinner party at the home of Mr Premium 'the celebrated loan-monger', for whom John Diston Powles was probably the model. The drawing-room was crowded with bankers, merchants, speculators and

> members of the different embassies, or missions of the various Governments, to whose infant existence Premium is foster-father . . . In one part of the room was a naval officer, hot from the mines of Mexico, and lecturing eloquently on the passing of the cordillera . . . Here floated the latest anecdote of Bolívar . . . and then the perpetual babble about 'rising states' and 'new loans' and 'enlightened views' and 'juncture of the two oceans' and 'liberal principles' and 'steamboats to Mexico' . . . Everyone at Premium's looked full of some great plan, as if the fate of empires was on his very breath.

When those assembled were finally seated, the narrator noted that the walls of the spacious dining room were hung with portraits of Latin American revolutionary leaders, and over Mr Premium was suspended a magnificent portrait of Bolívar.[8]

A Disraeli contemporary, Reverend Richard Harris Barham, was a humourist who wrote under the name of Thomas Ingoldsby. Today he is remembered chiefly for his *Ingoldsby Legends*, a collection of parodies on ghost stories, pious legends, and even Shakespeare, which when published in 1840 enjoyed widespread popularity. In his version of 'The Merchant of Venice' the whimsical clergyman celebrated the early loan and company boom, as the young entrepreneur Antonio explains the temporary lack of liquidity which prevents him from lending a few Ducats to his friend Bassanio:

'The bulk of my property, merged in rich cargoes, is
Tossing about, as you know, in my Argosies,
Tending of course my resources to cripple –
I've one bound to England – another to Tripoli –
Cyprus – Masulipatam – and Bombay; –
A sixth, by the way, I consign'd t'other day
To Sir Gregor MacGregor, Cacique of Poyais,
A country where silver's as common as clay;'[9]

Bassanio needed the loan to finance his suit for the hand of the fair
Portia, who besides 'vast estates, a pearl fishery and a gold mine' and
an iron strong box stuffed with company shares, also had money in
French, Danish, Brazilian, Colombian and Chilean bonds.

William Makepeace Thackeray in his *History of Samuel Titmarsh
and the Great Hoggarty Diamond* also relied upon the lending and
company boom to provide a backdrop for a humorous moral tale.[10]
Sam, the protagonist, is seduced by the easy money to be made in
the City, particularly through his employer Mr Brough, chief shareholder and director of the Independent West Diddlesex Fire and
Life Insurance Company, which had a 'splendid stone mansion' on
Cornhill, facing down Birchin Lane. Mr Brough, it develops, was a
scoundrel and promoter of such worthy enterprises as the Jamaica
Ginger Beer Company and the Consolidated Baffin's Bay Muff and
Tippet Company. His enterprises all came to grief in the 1825 panic,
their fate hastened by mysterious fires at premises the West Diddlesex
had insured for a sealing wax concern and a clothing warehouse.
The fires had been proceeded by a conflagration at the Waddingley
Cotton Mills and an explosion at the Patent Erostratus Match Manu-
factory – although rumours alleged the two disasters had been engineered by the West Diddlesex 'as advertisements for themselves'.
Fortunately young Sam survived the accusations of fraud incorrectly
levied at him as the West Diddlesex chief clerk, and after a short spell
in prison emerged a stronger and better young man. Mr Brough,
who lived in Fulham in a mansion appropriately called 'The Rookery',
escaped his creditors and the law by fleeing to France, thus following
the earlier examples of Beau Brummel, Gregor MacGregor, and
other impecunious men of fashion and finance.

Charles Dickens also utilized the company boom as a literary
backcloth in 1848. In *Dombey and Son*, Mr Dombey decides to seek a
nursemaid for his infant son, and his sister Louisa suggests he retain a
respectable widow named Mrs Pipchin.

'Who is Mrs Pipchin, Louisa?' asked Mr Dombey...
'Mrs Pipchin, my deal Paul', returned his sister 'is an elderly lady

... who has for some time devoted all the energies of her mind, with the greatest success, to the study and treatment of infancy ... Her busband broke his heart in – how did you say her husband broke his heart, my dear?'
'In pumping water out of the Peruvian Mines, replied Miss Tox. 'Not being a Pumper himself, of course,' said Mrs Chick, glancing at her brother; and it really did seem necessary to offer the explanation, for Miss Tox had spoken of him as if he had died at the handle; 'but having invested money in the speculation, which failed.'[11]

The fates and adventures of some of the real life counterparts of Mr Premium and his colleagues however, were as intriguing as those of any literary creations. With the exception of Colombian patriot José Antonio Zea, who mercifully died before he could witness the complete collapse of his country's credit, most leading participants of the lending and company boom lived well into the century. Some would continue to exercise their persuasive talents upon human credulity. A few returned to their native lands to lead lives of varying degrees of respectability. At least one – Andrés Bello – became famous. Others died in obscurity.

James Paroissien of Peruvian loan renown had but a few years left on earth after he was replaced, as we have seen, as Peru's London envoy by John Parrish Robertson. Paroissien then sailed from London for South America in late 1825 as a shareholder and director in the Potosí, La Paz and Peruvian Mining Association. He landed at Buenos Ayres, and after a long overland trip reached Potosí, once the silver-mining capital of South America.

Unfortunately for Paroissien, soon after he arrived the speculative bubble burst in London. The association, on the £1,000,000 capital of which only £54,000 had been paid, was financially overextended, and the bills of exchange Paroissien drew for supplies and other expenses in Buenos Ayres were dishonoured when presented. The large and valuable cargo of mining machinery and supplies the association had sent to Peru was attached by creditors soon after arrival. The miners and other employees had to be dismissed, and the association's Potosí office closed amidst bitter and protracted litigation. Paroissien then determined to return to England to appeal to the directors and rectify the association's financial affairs, but was too ill with dropsy to travel. Finally, he recovered sufficiently to sail on 4 September 1827 for Valparaiso, en route to Europe. Three weeks later he died and was buried at sea, a ruined man aged but forty-three.[12]

In contrast to Paroissien's sorry tale, John Diston Powles continued to scheme and thrive. Although he apparently entertained political ambitions in Britain, his main area of interest until his death around 1865 continued to be Latin American, particularly Colombian, mining ventures. Shareholders in his projects were not always pleased with his stewardship, and one published a slashing attack on Powles's dubious business management practices.[13] In April 1840, at a meeting of the Colombian Mining Association of which he was a director, Powles informed the shareholders that because too much further money would be needed for the company to survive, the directors believed it would be better to liquidate the concern. The meeting acquiesced and Powles sold the association's Colombian assets, including a mine in which it had already invested £200,000 and which allegedly was 'on the very verge of prosperity'. The shareholders were not aware that the new purchasers who had paid but £6,000 for the company's property were Powles' agents, or that the mining properties would be transferred by them to his New Granada Mining Association, which was operative well into the 1850s. Although Powles was said to have extracted over £500,000 from Colombian Mining Association shareholders, throughout its nearly twenty-year life the company paid only one dividend of ten shillings per share.

Antonio José de Irisarri also was a remarkable survivor. After his victorious libel action against *The Morning Herald*, he sought unsuccessfully to excite interest in his Central American Mining Association. Finally realizing that London offered no more scope for his talents, he returned to his native Guatemala, where presumably no one would have heard of the disastrous Childen loan and where he could begin anew. The former loan promoter prospered, founded a newspaper, and served as Guatemalan and Salvadorean minister to the United States. He died in Brooklyn, New York on 10 June 1868, aged 82, still grumbling that an ungrateful Chilean government had never reimbursed all the personal expenses he had incurred on their behalf over forty years before in London and Paris.[14]

Zea's predecessor, Luis López Méndez, who had made the first pioneering effort to finance Bolívar's efforts to liberate half a continent, also survived to survey the destruction of Latin American financial credibility. His own personal sacrifices had been considerable, and had included periods as guest of His Majesty in Kings Bench Prison for debt. After his powers of attorney were revoked, López Méndez also became involved in mining company promotion, and in March 1825, embarked for Chile as a representative of the Anglo-Chilean Mining Association. He landed in Buenos Ayres, crossed the Andes to Santiago, and then travelled north to Peru where he remained for three years. After supporting the losing side in a revolution, he was forced to return to Chile in 1829. He meddled again in local politics, was jailed briefly, became a school teacher and died in obscurity and poverty near Valparaiso in November 1841. It was a sad end for a man whom Bolívar once had described as 'the true Liberator of Colombia', since his victorious 1819 campaign would have been impossible without López Méndez's efforts in London.[15]

Despite the ignoble collapse of the Central American loan, Minister Marcial Zebadúa continued to press the foreign office to agree to the commercial treaty he had drafted and by which Central American independence would be recognized. After Canning died, Zebadúa reopened talks with Lord Aberdeen, the new foreign secretary. In an exchange of correspondence during late 1830, Under-Secretary John Backhouse wrote to Zebadúa saying that Lord Aberdeen had no objection to reviving the discussions on the proposed Central American treaty provided Zebadúa 'could demonstrate that the Government of that country is now so stable as a treaty can be made, with a reasonable probability that it will be fulfilled'.[16] Soon thereafter the Wellington administration fell, Aberdeen left, and Zebadúa had to begin anew with his successor, Lord Palmerstone. Before negotiations could progress, the Guatemalan senate for reasons of economy decided to close the London legation. Zebadúa was ordered to return home with the legation archives, and sailed for Central America in January 1832, disillusioned and sad.

Zebadúa insisted subsequently in a published vindication of his conduct that within another two months at most he could have completed the treaty negotiations. Instead, he wrote, all his sacrifices – including a six year separation from his wife and children – had been in vain. The informal but cordial relations he had established with the foreign office would now wither from neglect, he feared.[17] The former minister was of course unduly optimistic. Palmerstone probably would never have recognized the Central American federation because of the nation's chronic instability and its failure to service the 1825 loan or compensate local British nationals for damages to their property.[18]

Zebadúa was nevertheless well received in Guatemala upon his return, and appointed minister of foreign relations. Before he died in April 1849, eleven years after the United Provinces of Central America had fragmented violently into five quarrelling mini-states, he must frequently have recalled with nostalgia the more peaceful years he had spent in London at his comfortable Manchester Street home.

A more exotic fate awaited Gregor MacGregor. In 1827, after a short spell in prison in Paris, he sold his remaining Poyais bonds to another group of British speculators and moved to his native Edinburgh, where he concentrated his energies on selling Poyaisian land grants. These were large, impressive documents in denominations ranging from 100 to 10,000 acres, with parallel texts in English and French. Realizing, however, that despite all his efforts his future no longer lay in Poyais or Scotland. MacGregor petitioned the Venezuelan government several times to allow him to return to the happier scenes of the military exploits of his youth. His requests for a passport were repeatedly refused, and his offers to serve the republic ignored.

In 1838 the ex-cazique's fortunes improve. Bolívar and his other enemies were by now dead. Former comrades-in-arms were in power and granted the long-sought permission to return. In Caracas, MacGregor was restored to his former rank and awarded a small pension for his valuable services during the wars of independence. Although the British Minister Sir Robert Ker Porter consistently cut him dead at parties, the Scotsman was a popular figure in the small foreign community. On 4 December 1845, the old swindler died peacefully in bed after receiving the last sacraments of the Catholic Church. His burial in the cathedral was attended by the President of Venezuela, the Cabinet and the diplomatic corps.[19] Visitors to Caracas today will see MacGregor's name inscribed with that of the nation's other independence leaders on the gigantic obelisk memorial erected on the Avenida de los Próceres.

Sir Robert Ker Porter, who had aided the unfortunate settlers of the Colombian Agricultural Association, remained in Caracas until 1841, and helped work out the division of the defaulted Gran Colombia debt between Venezuela, New Granada and Ecuador. In his younger days Porter had travelled widely in many countries, including Persia and Russia, where he had become a favourite painter of the Czar. While in Caracas he finished several large landscapes and religious scenes, and even a portrait of Bolívar. He returned to England after over 21 years in Venezuela, and the following year went to St Petersburg to visit his married daughter. Unfortunately on 4 May 1842, the eve of his return to England, he died of apoplexy as he was returning home in his droshky from a farewell visit to Czar Alexander I. It was a stylish ending to a colourful and eventful career.[20]

Andrés Bello, unlike Luis López Méndez, his former colleague and fellow Venezuelan, found a congenial home in Chile. For years while in London Bello had written to friends in Caracas, including Bolívar, requesting employment in his native land. His pleas had either been ignored or evaded. Fortunately, Chilean Minister Egaña, who had engineered Bello's resignation from the Chilean legation and his departure to work in the Colombian mission, soon realized his error and persuaded the Chilean government to offer a position to the diligent, brilliant scholar. Despairing of ever receiving an offer of employment from Bolívar, in February, 1829 Bello and his family sailed for Santiago.

In Chile Bello soon became the chief legal adviser to the foreign ministry and began a long career in public service. He was a senator for many years, first rector of the University of Chile, and editor of the semi-official newspaper *El Araucano*. He drafted the Chilean Civil Code which was widely copied through Latin America, negotiated treaties, and was invited to arbitrate international disputes. When he died in October 1865, the government declared a national day of mourning.[21]

Among Bello's many outstanding accomplishments was his celebrated work on international law, *Los Principios de Derecho de Gentes*, published in 1832. Enlarged and reissued in 1844 and 1864, the *Principios* became a standard law school text-book in Latin America and an indispensable reference manual in chanceries throughout the continent. In one passage in the 1864 edition, Bello, undoubtedly remembering his London years when he saw Latin America's credit standing destroyed by defaults, insisted that states should scrupulously honour their obligations to foreign creditors in order to forestall claims for breach of contract. It was irrelevant if the money lent had been dissipated or spent wisely: 'Loans contracted for the service of a State and the debts created in carrying on public business ... are binding on the entire nation. Nothing can excuse it from paying these debts.'[22] Forty years after Bello's death the celebrated Argentine publicist Carlos Calvo, who had relied heavily on Bello for his own monumental seven-volume treatise on international law, described him as 'one of the most remarkable men Latin America has ever produced'.[23]

Back in England, Rudolph Ackermann, who had engraved the bonds for the 1822 Colombian loan, went on to further fame and fortune as a publisher of books on fashion, technical subjects, drawing and decorative prints. The most famous of his numerous publications was the monthly *The Repository of Arts, Literature, Commerce, Manufacture, Fashion and Politics*, a collection of articles and prints on furniture design, scientific achievements, new inventions, medicines, law and fashion. His illustrators were among the great artists of the day, including Thomas Rowlandson and Augustus Pugin.

At the same time Ackermann also became the leading publisher of books in Spanish for distribution in the infant Latin American nations. In 1823 he began the series *Variedades*, a magazine in Spanish modelled closely on *The Repository of Arts*. This was followed by translations of *Ivanhoe* and *The Talisman*, and a magazine in Spanish devoted to applied science. Believing that with the demise of the Inquisition after independence fresh markets for his publications would emerge in Latin America, he sent his son with a cargo of books to Mexico, and soon had book-selling outlets in Lima, Buenos Ayres, Bogotá and Guatemala. Meanwhile, not content with the Colombian bonds he had received in partial payment from John Diston Powles, Ackermann invested £800 in Mexican bonds, a further £600 in the second Colombian loan, and then £540 in Brazilian bonds. Tempted by the glittering rewards promised by the mining companies, he also purchased shares in the Chilean Mining Association, the Chilean and Peruvian Mining Association, and the Tlapuxahua Mining Association. So great was his commitment that he even invested £165 in Rio de la Plata Agricultural Association shares.[24]

Fortunately for Ackerman, his publishing business in The Strand enabled him to absorb the losses of his Latin American ventures. He died honoured and prosperous in March 1834. The high standard of engraving and design he had used on the 1822 Colombian bond remained unsurpassed throughout the nineteenth century. Indeed, the only bond whch seems to have approached Ackermann's product in artistry was the 1823 Poyais certificate, clearly modelled on the work of the master engraver. Unfortunately for investors, of course, in both cases the technical and artistic quality of the certificates far exceeded the quality of the loans for which they were printed.

Captain Francis Head had a long and successful career as an author and colonial administrator after he quit the Rio Plata Mining Association.[25] Known as 'Galloping Head' for his swift crossings of the Pampas, he won his Majority in the Royal Engineers for his efforts to introduce the South American lasso into the British cavalry. He published an impressive list of travel essays and fictional works, and in late 1835 was offered the post of lieutenant governor of Upper Canada. While in office he put down an insurrection against British rule, in the course of which his troops crossed to the American side of the Niagara River to sink an American vessel, *The Caroline*, which had been supplying arms to the rebels. The incident provoked a series of heated exchanged between US Secretary of State Daniel Webster and the British government which have found their way into the law books as classical expositions of the competing doctrines of self-defense and non-intervention. Head was created a baronet in 1836, and became a member of the privy council in 1867. In addition to writing, he was a keen sportsman and rode to hounds until his mid-seventies. He died in 1875, aged eighty-two, at his Croydon residence, one of the last surviving participants of the first Latin American debt and investment crisis.

Due to the relatively small amounts received by the borrowers, the positive economic effects upon the Latin American nations of the 1820s loans were not nearly as great as had been anticipated. The ambitious infrastructure and other productive projects – canals, roads, port facilities – were never built, while agriculture and mining were left to recover and progress with locally generated finance. The funds, ships, and military stores which did arrive, however, were sufficient to cause significant moral and political damage to the war-torn, impoverished and fragile new states.

Loan proceeds and military supplies were used not just to defeat the common Spanish enemy, but also for adventures against neighbours, as in the prolonged Brazil-Buenos Ayres conflict, to suppress internal opposition, and to support bloated army and naval establishments. The loans thus encouraged militarism and the institutionalization of political change by violence rather than through the orderly procedures provided in the nations' new constitutions. The easily available revenues in London were also an irresistable temptation to leaders who had inherited a Spanish bureaucratic tradition which tolerated financial irregularities in order to offset low or nominal salaries for holders of public offices. The more corrupt characteristics of the colonial regime were thus preserved through injections of British capital, and instead of stimulating a new prosperity the loans encouraged violence and financial irresponsibility.

In Colombia political bickering and charges of waste and corruption in the use of loan proceeds were particularly vicious, and were used by Santander's enemies to undermine his authority. Nearly £200,000 of the proceeds of the 1824 loan were spent on sending reinforcements to Bolívar in Peru. Other large amounts were used to purchase additional war material and ships in Britain and in the United States. Some £600,000 was also expended liquidating internal government drafts and notes, many of which had been first issued for military expenses and salaries, and were later purchased by speculators from their holders at steep discounts. Pledges to use the loans to stimulate agriculture and mining were quickly forgotten.[26] One Latin American writer even persuasively cites the general misuse of public funds, including the foreign loans, as one of several reasons for Gran Colombia's disintegration. The loan proceeds had been

the subject of the most criminal peculation and this deeply angered the people who had hopes of government help for their agriculture and industry. Above all, the people of Ecuador and Venezuela, far from the principle centre of government and the influence of superior authorities, each day became increasingly irritated with the inadequate laws and fiscal disorder.[27]

The impact of the general lending and company boom upon the British economy was less drastic. To be sure, the hectic speculation in Latin American ventures contributed to the general overheating which preceded the financial panic of 1825–6. Of the net amounts actually placed at the disposal of the borrowers after deductions, approximately two-thirds was remitted as merchandise – military equipment, naval stores, textiles and hardware. The relevant export industries thus received some stimulus. By 1825 British exports to Latin America had risen from £2,800,000 per annum in 1818 to £6,425,715. How much of this was loan-related, and how much due to general trade expansion, is difficult to ascertain. It is significant, however, that this export volume was continued after 1825, with Brazil accounting for between one-third and one-half.[28]

In justice to the Latin Americans, reluctance to service the loans was partly motivated by legitimate anger at what they perceived as their onerous terms – especially the high commissions exacted by financial intermediaries. On average only 60 per cent of loan proceeds reached Latin America, much of it in goods rather than money. In return the borrowers assumed an indebtedness which they could only hope to service at great sacrifice. Nowhere even with the best intentions could Colombia have found the £405,000 required for annual debt servicing. Nor could unstable Mexico realistically have been expected to pay £192,000 in annual interest. Impoverished Peru could not find the £108,900 per annum it needed, and the vicissitudes of the Central American federation made even a £10,000 annual payment impossible.

At least one commentator suggests that the defaults may be largely ascribed to a turn-down in British trade with some countries after the 1825–6 crisis, which would have accounted for a decrease in Latin American customs revenues, a vital source of government income.[29] The loans, however, were doomed from the start. The borrowers simply did not possess the economic and relatively efficient administrative structures of European borrowers like France, Prussia, Russia and Denmark. Moreover, large areas had been devastated by civil war, which depopulated the countryside and ruined agriculture and mining. Poor statistical information and lack of macro-economic data available to the lenders, combined with greed, were major contributors to the disaster.

Worse, in the initial rosy glow of optimism pervading Britian and

Latin America, few investors or bankers could – or were willing to – foresee the years of political misrule and violence which would follow independence, and which made necessary the maintenance of large military establishments. Spending the limited available funds, often obtained by forced or usurious loans from local moneylenders, on national survival naturally had a higher priority than paying investors in Britain. Not surprisingly, despite official protestations of goodwill and willingness to pay, factions in the borrowing states preferred to incur the opprobrium of default rather than remit to foreign creditors resources they felt, rightly or wrongly, could be better applied at home. Over 165 years after Francisco Zea signed the contract for the first Latin American loan, Latin American leaders and their central bankers are again weighing against the consequences of default, the economic and political cost of continuing to transfer substantial portions of national income to the developed countries which are their creditors.

The fates of the companies formed to extract Latin American minerals, to navigate the continent's rivers, to produce paper, mint coins, and bring European manufactures to the new nations were disillusioning both to Latin Americans and to British shareholders. Although profits from the mining and other ventures would, except for taxes, be remitted abroad, initially the economies of the host countries were stimulated at least temporarily by their activities. For example, the newcomers needed food, mules, saddles, timber props for mine shafts, and artisans and labourers to help repair roads and trails so the heavy machinery imported from Britain could be transported from ports to the pit heads. The companies' collapse naturally depressed these local economies.

In Britain, the failure of the enterprises to achieve instant success in Latin America, and the well-publicized derogatory reports of individuals like Captain Head and James Beaumont who had actually been to Latin America, gave lie to glowing prospectuses circulated by desk-bound company directors. Worse, in many bondholders' minds the continued safety of their own investments was linked to the health of the mining companies. Those enterprises, employing British capital and the much vaunted British technology and energy, had been expected to provide a source of income for the borrowing states which could have been utilized to help service the loans. For example, the Pasco Peruvian Mining Company in order to obtain its concessions had agreed to pay the Peruvian government an annual rental of $15,000 plus a duty for 30% on exported silver bars.[30] Now not even these amounts would supplement the scanty governmental revenue available for interest payments to foreign creditors. At the same time, the harrowing tales of primitive local conditions, economic chaos and corruption in which the mining and other companies had been expected to operate further undermined bond-holder faith in the viability of the countries to which they had lent their savings. Alarmed bondholders hastened to sell before their investments became totally worthless, thereby driving down bond prices even more.

The immigration associations had only a scant perceptible impact. Some emigrants who did not return home lived to attain prominence in their adopted countries. Most, however, merely merged their modest British life-styles into their new surroundings. Among the latter was a carpenter from London named Hughes, who had landed in Buenos Ayres in 1825 under the auspices of the Rio de la Plata Agricultural Association. In 1832 his daughter Ana married Tomás Mario Perron, a young man recently arrived from Sardinia. In 1946 their great-grandson, Juan Domingo Perón, would become the most powerful Argentine leader since Juan Manuel de Rosas.[31]

Aside from the human and economic damage it wreaked, the worst and longest lasting effect of the loan debacle and its aftermath of frustrated reschedulings was the destruction of the mutual good-will which had characterized British-Latin American relations in pre-independence and early post-independence years. Press reactions to the news of Bolívar's death in 1830 illustrate vividly the change in attitude. According to *The Times*, had Bolívar expired a few years previously his death would have created a sensation in Europe and in the Americas. Now, however, 'his exit will scarcely compose an article in the common obituary of warriors and statesmen'.[32] In the nine years since he had crushed the Spanish at Carabobo, it had become evident that Bolívar's efforts to create a permanent, secure and stable Colombia and Peru had failed. It was his misfortune to have remained too long in power, and the intrigues, rebellions and disorganization of his new states had undermined fatally his reputa-tion as leader and administrator.

Sadly, the Colombian loan fiasco also contributed to Bolívar's fall from grace in European eyes. By authorizing Zea to seek financing in Europe he had set an example for the other Latin American coun-tries and thus could be considered the author of the disastrous lend-ing boom. Therefore, despite his other achievements, *The Times* concluded that 'in this country we can never pardon a Government which contracts debts without paying dividends, and on the Stock Exchange we are afraid that the glory of the Liberator is now at a discount'. *The Morning Post* leader was more charitable. The 'brave and noble Bolívar' had died of a broken heart from the ingratitude of his countrymen. Although he had had the opportunity to acquire great riches, he had died a poor man. 'Of him let it may be said what was so justly observed of our own pure and immortal Minister William Pitt: "Who governed nations left no wealth behind."[33]

In an era in which politicians, bankers and the respectable middle-classes at least publicly preached high standards of business morality, Latin American failure to honour legal obligations was unforgiveable. The generally favourable attitude of the press towards Latin America had undergone a complete change since 1822 when *The New Times* could exclaim 'we may indulge the brightest hopes of these Southern Republics. They have entered upon a career of almost endless improvement. And though much disorder and confusion may attend the beginning of their course, they will soon attain the knowledge and freedom and civilisation of the happiest States of Europe.'[34] Public opinion now, however, came to view Latin American nations – like Spain – as hopelessly feckless and financially irresponsible, a stereotype which, with some justice, the intervening years have not totally dispelled.

While company failures contributed to the general bad feeling and mistrust, shareholder memories faded with time. Recollections of the unhappy experiences of investors in the first Latin American loans were better preserved. Constant reschedulings and new defaults were not only persistent reminders of the collapse of the earlier relationship of trust, but themselves provided new reasons for irritation. Failure to service bonds was, however, but one cause of a more general disillusion in Europe with Latin American institutions which clearly did not function as their creators had intended.

Political realities had made a mockery of the elaborate constitutional guarantees of free expression, freedom of assembly, freedom from arbitrary imprisonment and the impartial administration of justice. All these freedoms and guarantees could be and were suspended under executive emergency powers enshrined in the same constitutions. In fact, these carefully crafted constitutions, which like that of the United States provided for republican forms of government allocated between executive, legislative and judicial departments, centred real power in the executive branch. The documents thus perpetuated familiar earlier authoritarian patterns in fashionable republican dress, and, with the army and the Church, assured the survival of the Spanish colonial heritage well into the nineteenth century, if not to the present day.

At the same time, constitutional and treaty pledges of special protection to aliens and their property, together with other privileges promised by additional legislation and contracts, were revealed as illusory and deceptive. The inability of nineteenth-century Latin American governments to prevent injuries to British subjects and their property by brigands, revolutions and civil war was notorious.

Access to courts on the same basis as nationals by foreigners seeking redress was meaningless where the judiciary was corrupt or subservient to other government branches. Equality of treatment with nationals – once considered a highly commendable innovation – now seemed to mean that British immigrants and other foreigners living and working in Latin America had equal rights with nationals to be pillaged, victimized by forced loans, unjustly imprisoned and even killed in revolutions. As one British merchant in Central America complained to the foreign office in 1828, 'British subjects have been invited to this Republic and promised protection to their persons and property. This is a strange way of realizing such a promise.'[35]

By 1860 there was not a single Latin American nation against which some British claim arising out of injury to person or property was not outstanding, and the review and presentation of claims had become a major preoccupation of British diplomats in Latin America. The foreign office consistently attempted to differentiate between the remedies available for claims arising out of direct injury to persons or property, and the relief to which frustrated bondholders were entitled. The British government felt entitled to intervene with force, if necessary, to obtain settlement of the former, but not where the claim arose out of bonds purchased on the market. Fine distinctions were not always possible, however, particularly where, patience exhausted, attempts were made to resolve a large backlog of unsettled claims for personal and property loss by some drastic, forceful government action. In such situations bondholders sometimes were able to insinuate their own claims into the settlement efforts.[36]

In the nineteenth century failure to honour loan obligations did not in itself under international law entitle a state to intervene forceably on behalf of its creditor-subjects. States had, after all, been defaulting on their obligations for centuries and mere inability to pay was not considered an international delict. International responsibility could arise, however, if foreign creditors were not treated on at least the same basis as domestic creditors, or if the default violated an international agreement. In such cases a creditor's state might legitimately decide to champion its subject's claim, using force, if necessary, to extract compensation. Although instances of forceable or official intervention purely to enforce bondholder claims were rare, the constant, repeated irritant of recurring defaults and broken rescheduling agreements must have made British policymakers more prone to intervene with armed force in other less clearcut situations, as occurred in Mexico and in Venezuela.

In 1861 British ships and troops participated with French and Spanish forces in a joint attempt to force Mexico to settle a number of outstanding claims by seizing customs houses at Vera Cruz and Tampico. Among British complaints was the default on bonds issued pursuant to a diplomatic convention in 1851 to compensate British subjects for personal and property injuries suffered in the numerous civil disturbances which had wracked the nation since independence. These bonds had not been acquired on the open market as speculations, but had been issued as compensation in lieu of money damages, and were to be serviced by amounts withheld from customs duties. Interest payments fell into arrears on the convention bonds, as well as on those issued on the London market. In 1859, the commander of a British naval unit pressured the Mexican government into signing a new convention, pursuant to which increased customs revenues were set aside for both the 1851 convention bonds, as well as for those which had been issued in London following various conversion plans. Still, by 1861 the total British convention debt was but the equivalent of US$12,000,000, whereas the debt represented by the bonds floated in London, plus accumulated interest, exceeded US$60,000,000.

Meanwhile, the Spanish and French governments signed similar conventions with Mexico to secure payment of claims and bonds held by their citizens, issued either for services or as compensation. The French government in particular was less scrupulous than the British in espousing the claims – often inflated – of its nationals. Nor did the French attempt to distinguish, as did the British, between claims arising out of injuries to persons and property, and those resulting from defaults on bonds purchased as speculations.[37]

Other outstanding grievances for which the Mexican government was held accountable under international law included uncompensated injuries to British subjects and their property, the looting from foreign legations of dividends due bondholders, the theft by both insurgents and government forces of foreign-owned silver shipments on the roads from the mines to the ports, and the appropriation of customs proceeds earmarked for loan servicing. While the use of force by protecting states to vindicate aliens' rights was then justifiable under prevailing international law, permanent occupation of another nation's territory was not, even by permissive nineteenth-century state practice standards. Indeed, before they began landing their troops at Vera Cruz, France, Great Britain and Spain had agreed in London that they would not utilize the intervention as an excuse for territorial aggrandizement. Therefore, when French intentions to prolong their presence in Mexico became clear, the British and Spanish withdrew in protest.[38]

Similarly, British participation with Germany and Italy in the 1902 naval blockade of Venezuela was not dictated principally by desires to assist bondholders, although they certainly benefited. The imme-

diate cause of this intervention was the Venezuelan dictator Cipriano
Castro's stubborn refusal to submit to international arbitration
a large accumulation of unsatisfied claims. These ranged from revolutionary damages to aliens and their property, to forced loans
exacted from foreign merchants, seizure of foreign ships and the
confiscation of their cargoes, and the imprisonment and mistreat-
ment of foreign nationals. Castro instead insisted that the claims be
adjudicated by a commission composed exclusively of Venezuelans.
Ultimately, patience exhausted, European naval units sailed to
Venezuelan waters, where they captured or sank several naval
vessels. Only, however, after the decision to intervene had been
taken by the foreign office were bondholder claims added to the list
of grievances.[39]

Although Venezuela soon capitulated, the British government did
not require that bondholders' claims be submitted to arbitration
along with the other claims, but merely that the Venezuelans agree
to negotiate a settlement with the bondholders. The foreign office
pointedly refused to become involved in these new negotiations, to
the dismay of the bondholders' committee. Nonetheless, even such
limited interventions, when combined with the aggressive employment of good offices by diplomatic representatives, and the recruit-
ment of consular representatives to remit customs duties allocated
for debt servicing, must have seemed to debtor nations to evidence a
definite official British policy in support of its bondholders, whatever
the public declarations to the contrary. Moreover, both interventions
and good offices surely helped confirm some Latin Americans' fears
that the British and Europeans – and later the North Americans –
intended to monopolize their resources and commerce, and possibly
even entertained designs on their independence and territory.

In fact, however, the perceived political disorder and fiscal irresponsibility of the Latin Americans was not used even by aggressive
British policy-makers to justify the type of commercial and territorial concessions imposed upon governments elsewhere, as in China,
Egypt and Turkey. This was due not so much to British altruism or
carelessness, as to the fact that Latin America never had the strategic
importance of other areas closer to India and to the communication
routes linking the Empire. Also, British statesmen preferred to avoid
open confrontation with the United States, whose sphere of influence spread rapidly southwards following the Civil War. Trade
and investment on equal terms with other nations, not territorial
domination, became British policy objectives in Latin America,
although this was not always apparent to Latin Americans.

Nevertheless, by the mid-century Great Britain had come to
inspire in some parts of Latin America a resentment similar to that
with which the United States would be regarded not too many years

later. The Salvadorean *Gaceta Official* probably spoke for many when in 1856 it bitterly condemned a draft treaty between Great Britain and Honduras. Under one article, in exchange for Britain surrending its claim to the Bay Islands off the Honduran Caribbean coast, Honduras agreed to build a railway connecting Atlantic and Pacific coasts which the British would be entitled to use free of charge. The *Gaceta*'s editor, objecting strenuously to the clause, concluded that Mexico or any Central American country with rich or fertile territories or islands attractive to British commerce

> has received from nature an evil worse than the most terrible pestilences and most destructive plagues. A thousand times happier are those men who live in the most out-of-the-way places, the most unhealthy, the poorest, the most remote spots in the centre of their land. Thus they are free from the rapine of the Anglo-Saxon race, that race which believes that all others should be extinguished so that their own commerce will become more productive.[40]

The aftermath of the 1822–5 lending and investing fiasco also affected the development and application of international law. In the 1820s courts had denied bondholders relief because public policy prevented them from entertaining actions based on contracts with unrecognized governments. As the century wore on and Latin American nations received *de facto* if not official recognition, this argument became less tenable. Recovery then came to be denied on the theory of absolute sovereign immunity. Consequently, even though a loan agreement might be governed by British municipal law, a defaulting government could not be sued in British courts nor its property attached without an express waiver of the immunity which, as a sovereign state, it possessed against suit in the courts of another nation.

In 1878, for example, exasperated Peruvian bondholders sought in the Court of Chancery to attach sales proceeds of guano shipments which had been designated to secure the various Peruvian loans and which were in the hands of Peru's commercial representatives, Dreyfus Brothers & Co. The court rejected the bondholders' petition. The Master of the Rolls found that Peru had not surrendered title in the guano to Dreyfus, which was acting merely as a government agent and entitled therefore to raise the defense of sovereign immunity just as Peru could have done had it been before the court:

> [T]hese so-called bonds amount to nothing more than engagements of honour, binding, so far as engagements of honour can

bind, the government which issues them, but are not contracts enforceable before the ordinary tribunals of any foreign government, or even by the ordinary tribunals of the country which issued them, without the consent of the government[41]

The Dreyfus decision and similar holdings led one late nineteenth-century economist in 1878 to comment with some asperity on the basic inequity of a situation where 'a State as a creditor can sue as a plaintiff in Europe or the United States, but no citizen, being a creditor, can sue it as a defendant'.[42] The refusal of courts in Great Britain and in other jurisdictions to allow defaulting countries to be sued for breach of contract persisted until the 1970s. Now the British State Immunity Act specifically denies defaulting borrowing nations the privilege of invoking sovereign immunity in order to block suits by creditors. The United States has enacted similar legislation.[43]

Ironically, however, now that bondholders may sue sovereign debtors, the large bulk of private international lending is no longer channelled to borrowers through the bond market, but by massive bank loans. So large are the credits that in the case of default banks are reluctant to use the courts lest they imperil the global financial structure by triggering cross-default clauses in other loan agreements. Banks prefer negotiation to litigation, and, in a sense, have become hostages to their borrowers. Meanwhile, borrowing states, however, cavalier their attitudes towards bank creditors, generally avoid defaulting on bond issues.

The repeated use of good offices by local British diplomatic and consular representatives in the nineteenth century to support bond-holders' claims increasingly fueled Latin American complaints over the use under international law of diplomatic pressure and intervention to obtain pecuniary redress. Leading the chorus of opposition to so-called diplomatic interposition or intervention was Argentine diplomat Carlos Calvo, whose monumental *Le Droit International Théorique et Pratique*, published in 1896 in large part as a reaction to foreign interventions in Latin America, has had a lasting influence on international law. Calvo declared that sovereign states, being internationally equal and independent, enjoy absolute freedom from interference by other states through force or diplomacy. Moreover, he asserted, while aliens should be accorded equal treatment with nationals, they are not entitled to rights and privileges not accorded nationals and must seek redress for any grievances exclusively in local courts. Therefore, aliens could not appeal to their own states for diplomatic intervention except in the event of a narrowly-defined denial of justice, such as refusal of access to local courts.[44]

Calvo also argued that European nations applied a double standard of international morality and responsibility. They only intervened in each other's affairs when there was at stake

> some important principle of internal politics, such as the balance of power, or some great moral or religious interest favourable to the development of civilization; while in the New World the interventions of European States have rested upon no legitimate principles, being based upon mere force and a failure to recognize the complete freedom and independence of American States.[45]

Calvo was aided in the struggle against diplomatic and other forms of intervention by Argentine Minister of Foreign Affairs Luis Drago. In December 1902, Drago became particularly alarmed at what he saw as the armed intervention by Great Britain and Germany to exact payment of Venezuela's foreign borrowings, which he regarded as a dangerous precedent by which physical occupation of Latin American territory might at some future date be justified. In a letter to the Argentine minister in Washington, Drago admitted that while a state must honour its just debts, it should be entitled to choose the manner and time of payment. Forceable collection of public debts would lead inevitably to territorial occupation, he argued, if only to secure customs houses and thereby control trade revenue. Although protection of foreign bondholders was not the main occasion for the Venezuelan intervention, Drago hoped the United States would support the proposition, possibly as a corollary to the Monroe Doctrine, that 'the public debt [of an American state] cannot occasion armed intervention, nor even the actual occupation of the territory of American nations by a European power'.[46]

In 1906 Drago's proposition was discussed by the Third Pan American Conference in Rio de Janeiro, which resolved to request the Second Peace Conference at The Hague 'to examine the question of the compulsory collection of public debts, and, in general, the best means tending to diminish among nations conflicts of purely pecuniary origins.' The 1907 Hague Conference, however, decided to treat the matter within the context of arbitration, which in the years preceding World War I enjoyed an exceptional degree of international support as a means of resolving differences between nations. The resulting Convention for Limiting the Employment of Force for the Recovery of Contract Debts rejected resort to armed force to recover contract obligations except where the debtor state refused to arbitrate, obstructed formulation of an agreement after arbitration was accepted, or after arbitration refused to submit to the award.[47]

The reaction of the Latin American states at the conference to the watered-down version of Drago's original proposal was mixed. Venezuela refused to sign, maintaining that arbitration should only be invoked after exhaustion of local remedies and a denial of justice. Other Latin American nations signed with reservations similar to those of Drago himself, feeling that 'public loans with bond issues constituting the national debt cannot in any case give way to military aggression nor to the occupation of the soil of the American States'. Today, of course, the use of armed force and other types of coercive intervention to collect debts would contravene the Charters of the United Nations and of the Organization of American States. Thus, the teachings of Carlos Calvo and Luis Drago, both of whom were at least partially influenced by perceived examples of the threat or use of force to collect foreign bonded debt, have at last attained formal recognition as principles of international law.

Regardless of the quite understandable reasons behind the first loan defaults, the disappointments and frustrations experienced by lenders and borrowers alike caused an era of misunderstanding and confrontation to replace earlier years of goodwill and trust. Just as Europeans had overestimated the ease with which they could reap profits in Latin America, so Latin Americans had miscalculated their own ability to maintain the fiscal and general public order vital to attracting and maintaining the flow of foreign capital and investment necessary for economic development. Because expectations on both sides had been raised to such a high pitch, the subsequent disillusionment was all the deeper and more dramatic. Even though investment and lending eventually resumed, the optimistic, confident spirit of that earlier age was never completely recaptured.

XII
A POST MORTEM

THE SEMI-COMIC, SEMI-TRAGIC first Latin American debt crisis and its aftermath demonstrate that when financiers and investors choose to ignore history, they are destined to repeat the disasters of the past on an even grander scale.

Although by 1880 ten Latin American states were in arrears, investors kept providing new money and the defaults again were cured or refinanced. At the same time, the number of borrowers increased as more Latin American cities and political subdivisions joined their central governments in raising capital abroad. The funds available for lending also grew after World War I when New York became an important international finance centre in its own right, and US investment and commercial banks became increasingly involved in bond placements for Latin America and the rest of the world. Predictably, the totals in defaults and arrears then expanded to match the increasing number of obligors and creditors.

By 1935, following an intense borrowing spree, Latin American states and political subdivisions had stopped payment on loans totalling over US$3 billion. Only the Soviet Union owed its bondholders more money than Brazil and Mexico.[1] One financial commentator reviewing the wreckage wrote pessimistically that

> our prophetic soul tells us what will happen in the future. Adjustments will be made. Debts will be scaled down and nations will start anew. The investor will receive sufficiently satisfactory explanations as to how it is to his advantage to accept new promises in place of old ones which were repeatedly broken ... New foreign loans will once again be offered, and bought as eagerly as ever ... And the process known for more than two thousand years will be continued. Defaults will not be eliminated. Investors will once again be found gazing sadly and drearily upon foreign promises to pay.[2]

Although the comment was a reaction to total global defaults of over US$22 billion by governments, states and cities throughout the world – not counting interest – the general prediction proved all too true for Latin America. Following a thirty-year pause during which the defaults of the 1930s were cured or forgiven, by the late 1960s a new generation of commercial bankers was again lending to Latin American States, having 'rediscovered' the continent first seen by Columbus in 1492. The subsequent lending boom differed from its predecessors both in the size of the borrowings and in the structure of the Eurocurrency market upon which it relied.[3] Banks now could not satisfy the burgeoning demand for funds by underwriting and issuing bonds on behalf of their sovereign clients. Not only were the amounts required by the developing nations immense, but US commercial banks were now prohibited by post-1930 investor-protection legislation from selling bonds to the general public. If they wished to take advantage of the new financial opportunities offered by the Eurocurrency market they had to become principal creditors themselves, either by relying on their own deposit bases or by borrowing on a short-term basis from other banks to on-lend to Latin America for terms up to ten years.

The risk of a rise in interest rates was passed on to borrowers. They paid not only the banks' cost of the funds borrowed from other banks, which was recalculated every six months, but also a fixed percentage 'spread' on top. As competition for loans increased during the 1970s this spread would drop. Banks' profits were, however, still impressive due to the high front-end managerial and syndication fees charged to the borrowers. After 1974, the funds available for interbank borrowing increased dramatically when the OPEC nations deposited with the major banks in London the funds they had earned as a result of the decade's first oil price increase. Absent demand in the developed countries, the banks happily 're-cycled' these funds to Third World – particularly Latin American – borrowers. London, as in the 1820s, once again became a major source of funds for Latin America as US and other banks set up in the City to tap the pool of funds available in the unregulated Eurocurrency market, and to avoid credit restriction legislation at home.

So, instead of passing on the risks of non-payment to individual investors through bearer bonds as before, banks now kept the loans in their own portfolios, thus themselves assuming the risk of non-payment either individually or as members of lending consortia. Therefore, unlike in the 1930s, if a major default occurred the consequences could not be diluted among thousands of individual bond-holders. The banks themselves would have to shoulder any loss. Many major institutions due to poor capital to loan ratios could find it difficult to survive such a disaster, which might then spread to imperil the entire international financial system. Some financiers saw the dangers inherent in violating the basic banking rule against borrowing on a short-term basis from other banks for the purpose of re-lending the money on a medium to long term basis, especially in a politically unstable area. Most lenders, however, continued to compete fiercely to become managers of loans to Latin American borrowers, portions of which they would then syndicate among other institutions while retaining the bulk of the lucrative front-end fees for themselves. Over 1500 US banks alone were involved. Any doubters were instructed to take comfort from the hoary dictum, later dusted off and repeated by the chairman of a major New York bank, that states cannot go bankrupt.

Believers in such conventional wisdom received a severe jolt when in August 1982, Mexico informed her creditors that she could no longer service her foreign indebtedness. Brazil and other Latin American nations soon emitted similar distress signals. The combined impact upon Latin American economies of high interest rates in the developed countries, which raised the cost of debt servicing to unforeseen levels, oil price increases in 1974 and 1979, and slackened international demand for Latin American products and commodities, could no longer be ignored. The latest Latin American lending boom was over, and the newest, most dangerous phase in the long cycle of crises which had characterized Latin America's relations with its creditors began. Hoping to stave off mutual disaster, bankers and borrowers embarked on a series of loan reschedulings and renegotiations which so far have averted major financial collapse by pushing back and postponing payment dates for overdue interest and principal. In contrast to earlier *laissez faire* policies, governments now demonstrated a decided concern in the problem which, if left unresolved, would upset the international financial structure instead of, as in the 1820s and 1930s, merely affect the bank balances of unfortunate individual bondholders. Since 1982, governmental, central bank, International Monetary Fund and World Bank credits have been extended to support and supplement the renegotiated agreements, and even to enable states to purchase back their debt at secondary market discounts. Meanwhile, Latin American indebtedness has not stopped growing because the renegotiations, again as in the nineteenth century, generally have also involved flows of additional money to the borrowers, much of it to refinance and service earlier loans.

As a result, today Latin America owes its creditors – governments, international lending institutions and commercial banks – US$416,000,000,000, a quantum increase over the £19,000,000 in defaults which so alarmed British investors and statesmen in 1828–9,

and nearly half a billion dollars more than it owed eight years ago
when the latest lending bubble burst. Perhaps somewhat unfairly,
once again, as in the nineteenth century, the Latin American debtor
nations have become bywords for financial profligacy. Recently the
London press revealed that Lambeth Borough Council had sought
to evade government spending curbs by borrowings from foreign
banks at excessively high interest rates and secured by mortaging
public buildings. An opposition Tory spokesman was moved to
accuse the Labour Council of reducing the borough 'to the level
of a South London equivalent of Mexico by arranging this type of
desperate finance'.[4]

Various comprehensive regional plans have been proposed to
defuse the crisis and reconcile the long-term interests of both
borrowers and lenders. To date, in practice, they have been rejected
in favour of a piecemeal, case by case approach to the problem
which, it has been alleged, allows creditors to reward or punish
individual debtors, and forestall their organization of a united,
common front or policy.

Ironically, many of the solutions bankers have suggested or have
invoked since 1982 would have been familiar to nineteenth-century
financiers and bondholder committees who sought to deal with the
financial disarray created by the first Latin American debt crisis. For
instance, borrowing new money specifically in order to service earlier credits and thereby prevent their going into default was first
attempted in 1829 when N. M. Rothschild and Thomas Wilson &
Co. sponsored a £800,000 Brazilian issue. One of the avowed purposes of the credit was to finance interest payments on the 1824 and
1825 loans, causing *The Times* to assert critically that borrowing
for such a purpose was 'objectionable in principle' and meant that
creditors were paying themselves with their own money. The loan's
backers asserted that the circumstances were exceptional, and that
the credit would give Brazil time to put its financial affairs in order.[5]
This argument has, of course, become commonplace in recent years.

Once loans were in default, nineteenth-century bondholder committees would, as we have seen and as their successors do now, negotiate new agreements extending repayment and maturity periods,
and offering other concessions. Indeed, repayment periods were
sometimes stretched to up to thirty-five years or more, much longer
than is the current fashion. Pursuant to the renegotiated agreements,
new bonds would be issued to be exchanged for earlier issues in
much the same way as today's new loan agreements, containing the
renegotiated terms, are signed to amend earlier agreements. The
three debt consolidation agreements exchanging new debt for old,
negotiated with Venezuela by 1864 in order to work out its share of

the 1822 and 1824 Colombian loans, as well as to supply new financing, provide early examples of renegotiation. So too do the 1846 and 1851 Mexican consolidations and post-1850 Peruvian and Chilean arrangements.[6] Recently, a London financial publication reported discovering a precedent for Mexico's 1988 refinancing programme in a still-born plan mooted by J. P. Morgan & Co. in 1930. In this, defaulted Mexican central government and National Railways obligations would be exchanged for participations in a new loan, secured by a sinking fund linked to customs revenues.[7] If the publication's researchers had delved further they would have concluded that neither the 1930 refinancing scheme or the more recent Mexican plan were as innovative as they had assumed, and had been attempted – without lasting success – many years before.

Interest rate concessions are often a feature of post-1982 renegotiations. This device was first suggested by a Colombian bondholder in 1828, who proposed that interest be reduced from 6 to 3 per cent per annum until the borrower's financial affairs improved. It would be far better, he had argued, to accept a lower, more realistic interest rate which could be paid, than insist on the original higher rate and receive nothing.[8] Although at first the proposal was scorned, the principle was later adopted in renegotiated settlements with Mexico (1831), Peru (1849) and Buenos Ayres (1857), which on average reduced interest rates by over half.[9]

Nor is the concept of interest capitalization of recent origin. Although until recently steadily resisted by many banks, in the nineteenth century it was a common technique, utilized, for example, in the 1831 Mexican renegotiations when over £1,000,000 in interest arrears was converted into new bonds yielding 5 and 6 per cent per annum. A similar solution was negotiated with New Granada in 1845, when £3,700,000 in overdue interest was capitalized into so-called 'deferred bonds', initially yielding 1 per cent interest and then rising over sixteen years to 3 per cent per annum. Interest capitalization arrangements were also agreed with Ecuador (1853), Chile (1842) and Peru (1849), among others.[10]

In September 1987, a British clearing bank signed an agreement with Peru entitling it to cancel part of its Peruvian loan exposure in return for arranging the marketing of US$23,000,000 in Peruvian goods, including iron and iron-ore pellets, copper-coated wire and oil filters. Of the total receipts, US$8,800,000 would be retained by the creditor bank, with the remainder reverting to Peru.[11] The banking community was incorrect, however, in hailing the arrangement as a 'new technique in managing the debt problem'. In 1829 Peru had shipped copper to its British creditors in lieu of interest payments,[12] and Costa Rica in 1840, with the assistance of the British

Central American chargé, satisfied the greater portion of its share of the Central American federation debt by the proceeds of tobacco sales.[13]

Even the exchanges of debt for equity participations in companies and industries in the borrowing nations now currently being arranged with Latin American debtors are prefigured in nineteenth-century efforts to work out defaulted loans. One of the original purposes of the three 1869–72 Honduran railway bond issues, for example, had been to cancel Honduras' share of the 1825 Central American federation loan. When the later loans also went into default, a group of bondholders formed the Honduras Interoceanic Railway Company to complete the railroad project. It was capitalized at £5,347,720, to be raised by converting the defaulted Honduran government bonds for shares in the projected company on a one-to-one basis. The Council of the Corporation of Foreign Bondholders feared that the project would impair collateral already pledged to bondholders in Britain and France, however, and the company never proceeded beyond the prospectus stage.[14]

In an attempt to recoup bondholders' investments, a highly original variant of a debt for equity swap was attempted in 1876 with the approval of the Council of the Corporation of Foreign Bondholders when Paraguay defaulted on a £1,000,000 bond issue. A prospectus soliciting share subscriptions then was circulated in the City for the National Bank of Paraguay, which with a capital of £300,000 would obtain a variety of exclusive financial concessions from the government, as well as a 45-mile operating railway with strips of land one mile wide on both sides. Defaulted bonds could be exchanged for shares in the bank, which would become the receiver general of all government revenues, act as Paymaster General, and enjoy the exclusive right to any loan commissions. The Paraguayan government undertook to furnish the bank with suitable premises in either 'the palace of the former dictator' or in another 'National Building'. The project collapsed when it failed to excite sufficient bondholder and other investor interest in London.[15]

The most extreme remedy of all the solutions discussed today – voluntary overall debt forgiveness or reduction of outstanding principal or arrears – was also implemented in the nineteenth century. Ecuador succeeded in persuading its creditors to accept a reduction of £2,000,000 in interest arrears in 1855, while Costa Rica in 1840 managed to negotiate an arrangement whereby outstanding principal was reduced by 15 per cent. Nicaragua seems to have fared even better when in 1874 it persuaded some London bondholders to accept 5 per cent government bills redeemable over four years at an exchange of £14 for each £100 Central American federation bond assumed by Nicaragua.[16] To be sure, such debt 'forgiveness' was hardly voluntary, but the product of intransigence on one side and desperation on the other.

The pre-1982 remedies, however, were never particularly successful as far as bondholders were concerned. Nineteenth-century bankers and lawyers basically had sought to apply to sovereign lending problems solutions designed for commercial bankruptcy or default situations. These devices seldom – even if supplemented by foreign office support – produced completely satisfactory results. Their adequacy for coping with the present crisis is even more questionable. The size, structure, complexity and disastrous implications of today's debt problems demand more intricate, co-ordinated and far-reaching problem-solving exercises at an international level than those which were developed *ad hoc* over a hundred years ago.

Since 1982 the banks, the International Monetary Fund and the World Bank have been collaborating in an on-going joint exercise in crisis management. Their efforts have been largely successful. Although there have been suspensions of payments, interruptions in debt servicing and attempts by borrowers to limit interest payments to a specific portion of export earnings, the continuing rescheduling process has prevented any of the massive unilateral repudiations and defaults which occurred in the 1930s.

Indeed, the banks are less vulnerable than they were in 1982 thanks to increases in capital and reserves, and the reduction of Latin American exposures by discounted debt sales in the secondary market, equity for debt swaps, and the exchange of medium term debt for long-term bonds. The Third World debt overhang is still a matter of grave concern for banking executives and their shareholders, however, particularly because unfortunately, to date no broad, long-term initiatives to cope with the crisis have been successful. Perceiving that the problem is getting worse, not better, major British and US banks have reacted by increasing their bad debt provisions up to 70 per cent of their leading exposure to Third World countries. These increases, other bankers fear, may be interpreted by debtor states to mean that the banks are not really expecting to be repaid, and will thus weaken their negotiating positions with their debtors.[17]

Meanwhile, the methods used to preserve the financial system, including the IMF austerity programmes required by banks as a precondition to further credit extension, have been disastrous for the borrowers, however necessary they may have been in the short run. The result has been a stagnation of economic growth, unemployment, increases in poverty, malnutrition and crime, deteriorating infrastructures and social services, ecological damage, and social and political unrest. An average of over 30 per cent of Latin American export earnings is needed for debt service. Little is left for reinvestment or replacement of capital equipment. Indeed, for eight consecutive years the region has been a net exporter of capital to the developed world as interest repayments, capital flight and remittances outstripped inflows of new funds. In such circumstances it is highly unlikely that the Latin American nations can grow their way out of debt. Even the benefits of a massive and sustained – and as yet not visible – improvement in the terms of international trade would take years to reverse the effects of what has been termed by a recent World Bank report as a decade of lost development.

While initially the focus of the rescheduling process was quite legitimately upon averting a breakdown in the international financial structure, fortunately there are now signs that international concern is turning increasingly to the plight of the debtors. Governments now seem aware that their own self-interest in preserving economic and political viability in Latin America is threatened by the continuing impasse between the banks and their borrowers. Thus, the so-called Brady Plan, presented by the US Secretary of the Treasury in March 1989, urges commercial banks to work with debtor nations to achieve reductions in debt and in debt servicing. Their efforts should be supplemented by IMF and World Bank support for debt reduction plans. Mr Brady thus legitimized for the first time the hitherto unthinkable, and opened the door to a recognition of the obvious – that the banks' official pretence that their loans are worth 100 cents on the dollar, and should be repaid accordingly, is belied not only by the existence of a secondary market in discounted debt but also by economic reality. The Latin American debt problem is not one of illiquidity but of insolvency.

Debt reductions, if the latest Mexican renegotiation is any indicator, basically could be achieved by a combination of substituting existing debt for long term bonds at fixed interest rates, as well as exchanging bank credits for bonds at a discount of their face value. Additional strategies may also be invoked, including multinational institutional financing to enable nations to buy back their debt at secondary market rates, and a continuing of debt for equity swap programmes. Whether or not the Brady Plan will prove a durable strategy, or be replaced by other 'plans', it represents an official acknowledgement that the mistakes of banks and borrowers in the 1970s should not be permitted to hinder Third World governments and their peoples in their search for growth, stability and economic well-being in the 1990s.

Whatever solutions may be proposed, continued reduction seems likely, because, as some commentators maintain, Latin America's debt now has grown so large that it will be impossible to repay anyway.[18] Whether or not these observers will prove to be correct, it is certain that the special hazards and complexities of today's Latin American problem loans make them at first seem irredeemably remote in time and space from the credits marketed in London when King George IV was still on the throne. Indeed, in our less innocent age of global, electronically linked markets it is difficult to imagine a time when good or bad news could take six weeks to arrive in London from Vera Cruz or La Guayra, or when investors' knowledge of geography was so hazy that they could be induced to lend money to an imaginary Central American country.

It is remarkable, however, that several of the factors which were identified by one observer as stimulating the 1970s lending boom were also present in more rudimentary form in the 1820s.[19] In both instances the political climate was encouraging. For example, during the 1970s there was an absence of any banking regulation in London which might inhibit portfolio investment abroad. Even in the United States the credit restrictions which had driven banks to London in the first place were gradually relaxed or abolished. At the same time low cost US government loans to Latin America dwindled as Alliance for Progress credits ended, thereby eliminating a source of competition to the banks.

While in the 1820s no official foreign aid programme for Latin America existed, the British government did not discourage its citizens from investing in foreign loans. Diplomatic recognition of the new states further encouraged lending and investment. In addition, the social climate in which the loans were launched could not have been more favourable, as evidenced by widespread popular support in Britain for Latin American independence movements.

Also during both booms an adequate institutional framework existed to support the loan placements. By 1822 London had a well-developed Stock Exchange and a merchant banking system accustomed to international transactions. In the 1970s the Eurocurrency market enabled London once again to become the world's financial centre, and provided a source of funds for lending to Third World countries as hundreds of US, Japanese and other foreign banks moved into the City.

The third necessary condition for both lending booms was an income distribution pattern which fostered the accumulation of savings and their channelling into foreign loans. Britain in the 1820s was prosperous, unravaged by war, with a burgeoning industrial base. There were numerous individuals who could afford to purchase foreign bonds which promised a better return than British government stock. Indeed, in the 1820s consol interest dropped steadily from 5 to 3½ per cent. Many holders accepted government redemption offers and cashed in their consols, thereby adding to the general liquidity. Something similar occurred in the 1970s when savings were generated by the OPEC countries' new wealth – their current account surplus rose suddenly from US$7 billion to US$68 billion, a large percentage of which was deposited with banks in London and thus became available for on-lending.

In Latin America the same factors which encouraged borrowing in the 1970s were also present in 1822, that is, a need for imports and an absence of a domestic capital market. Spanish imperial policy had inhibited the growth of local industry, so the new nations required foreign exchange to pay for European industrial products as well as military equipment. Moreover, in 1822 many of the income sources enjoyed in the colonial era were no longer available – sales taxes, Indian tribute and other duties – had been eliminated. The ranks of wealthy local merchants had been thinned as many fled or, being Spanish, were expelled. Little financing of domestic origin was thus available, and foreign loans were eagerly sought.

Although by the 1970s the Latin American industrial base was securely established, imports of capital equipment were still vital to sustain growth. Equally, even today the internal Latin American financial market is small. The stock exchanges that exist are, with few exceptions, insignificant, and the taxation systems inadequate. Latin American governments in the 1970s naturally looked to the Eurocurrency market for development finance and to repair the budget deficits caused by two large OPEC oil price increases and a decline in trade, as earlier Bolívar had turned to London to fund Colombian independence. Thus, both in the 1970s and 1820s the supply of funds in London was matched by a corresponding demand in Latin America.

There is, however, a more fundamental link between the two lending booms than a similarity in the conditions which encouraged them. The bridge which spans the chasm of time separating us from that earlier, simpler era is the enduring conviction, shared by generations of financiers and investors over the years, and articulated in the sixteenth century by the old soldier Bernal Díaz del Castillo, that in Latin America one could easily acquire the magical 'cosas de Amadís': the vast Latin American sub-continent was a cornucopia of riches awaiting exploitation either by pillage, mining, trade or money-lending. From this conviction flowed those intoxicating dreams of easy riches which in the 1820s tempted, and sometimes ruined, City financiers, Lords of the Realm, budding politician Benjamin Disraeli, fashionable engraver Rudolph Ackermann and thousands of nameless bondholders. In the 1970s those same bewitching dreams resurfaced in more sophisticated form to haunt, lure and eventually betray legions of bank lending officers who had never heard of the first Latin American debt crisis.

APPENDIX 1

The purpose of these graphs, based upon information in the *Course of the Exchange*, is to illustrate the abrupt fluctuations which took place due to speculative buying and selling, and to the impact upon the market of conflicting reports on the political and economic health of the borrowers.

To be sure, there was also considerable fluctuation in the six month intervals between the reference dates used in these graphs. Also the quotations may differ slightly from the prices reported in the press. Nevertheless the general trend shown is accurate.

Notes to graphs

1. Colombia (1822) was issued at 84. Colombia (1824) was issued at 88½.
2. Chile was issued at 70.
3. The 1822 Peruvian loan for £1,200,000 was launched at 88. Due to litigation, bond sales were suspended after only £450,000 had been placed. After settlement of the lawsuits in February 1824, the remaining £750,000 was offered on the market at 82. A second loan, for £616,000, was launched in 1825 at 78 to help service the first credit. The *Course of the Exchange* combines the two issues for purposes of its quotations.
4. Mexico (1824) was issued at 58. Mexico (1825) was issued at 86¾.
5. Buenos Ayres was issued at 85.
6. Brazil was issued at 75. A second tranche was issued in 1825 at 85. Unlike in the Colombian and Mexican cases, the *Course of the Exchange* does not list the two Brazilian loans separately, apparently because both credits were considered merged into a single transaction, having originated from the same borrowing authorization.
7. Guatemala [United Provinces of Central America] was issued at 63.

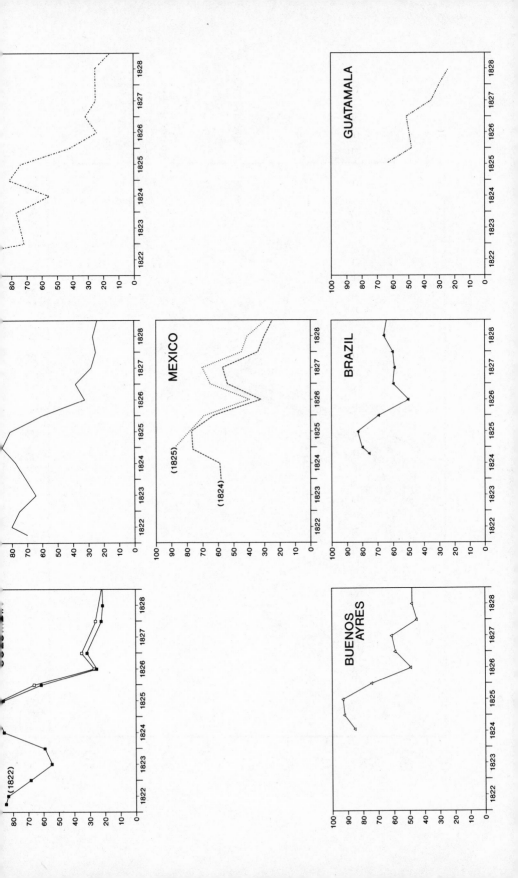

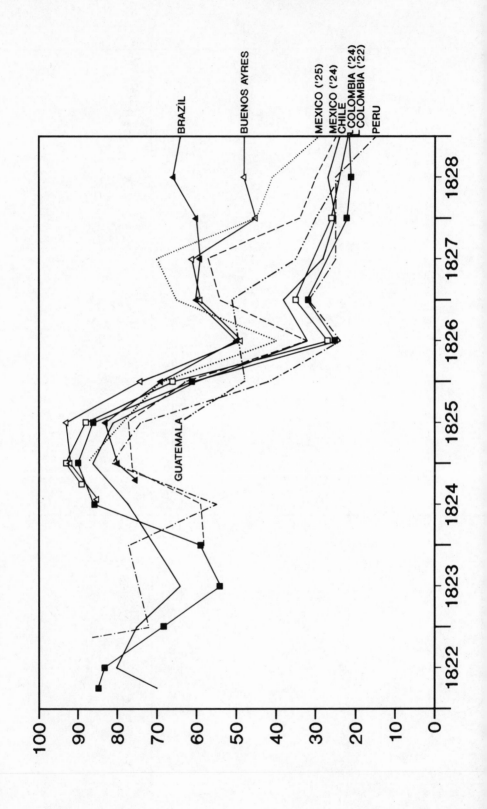

Year of Issue	Name of State	Rate of Interest per cent	Total amount of Loan contracted for in £	Amount of Loan Issue in London in £	Price of issue	Agents for Issue
1822	Chili	6	1,000,000	934,000	70	Hullett Bros. & Co.
	Colombia	6	2,000,000	2,000,000	84	Herring, Graham, & Powles
	Denmark	5	3,000,000	2,000,000	77½	A. F. Haldimand & Sons
	Peru	6	1,200,000	450,000	88	Thomas Kinder & Co.
	Russia	5	6,451,875	3,546,000	82	Rothschild & Sons
1823	Austria	5	3,500,000	3,500,000	82	Rothschild & Sons
	Portugal	5	1,500,000	1,500,000	87	Thomas & W. King
1824	Brazil	5	1,686,200★	1,686,200★	75	Baylett, Farquhar & Co., Alexander & Co., Wilson Shaw & Co.
	Buenos Ayres	6	1,000,000	1,000,000	85	Baring Bros. & Co.
	Colombia	6	4,750,000	4,750,000	88½	B. A. Goldschmidt & Co.
	Greece	5	800,000	800,000	59	A. Laughman & Co.
	Mexico	5	3,200,000	3,200,000	58	B. A. Goldschmidt & Co.
	Naples	5	2,500,000	2,500,000	92½	Rothschild & Co.
	Peru	6	Balance of 1822 Loan	750,000	82	Thomas Kinder & Co.
1825	Brazil	5	2,000,000	2,000,000	85	Rothschild & Sons
	Denmark	3	5,500,000	3,500,000	75	Thos. Wilson & Co.
	Greece	5	2,000,000	2,000,000	56½	Ricardo & Co.
	Guatemala	6	1,428,571	163,300	63	Barclay, Herring Richardson, & Co.
	Mexico	6	3,200,000	3,200,000	86¾	Barelay, Herring Richardson, & Co.
	Peru	6	616,000	616,000	78	Thomas Kinder & Co.
1828	Spain	5	600,000★★	600,000		Spanish Finl. Comn.
1829	Brazil	5	800,000	800,000	54	Rothschild & Sons and Thos. Wilson & Co.

★ Some sources give the amount as £1,000,000.
★★ These were issued as compensation for claims arising out of damage to British property during civil war.

NOTES

Chapter I

1. John Lynch, *The Spanish American Revolutions, 1800–1826* (London, 1973), pp. 34–5; 'Great Britain and Latin American Independence', in Fundación Casa de Bello (ed.), *Bello y Londres* (2 vols. Caracas, 1980), I, p. 33 (hereinafter 'Bello y Londres').
2. Lynch, *Spanish American Revolutions*, pp. 194–5.
3. Charles Haring, *Empire in Brazil: A New World Experiment with Monarchy* (Cambridge, Mass., 1958), pp. 4–5.
4. Charles Webster (ed.), *Britain and the Independence of Latin America 1812–1830* (2 vols., Oxford, 1938), II, pp. 8–10.
5. C. Mendoza, *La Junta del Gobierno de Caracas y sus Misiones Diplomáticas en 1810* (Caracas, 1936); 'La Misión de Bolívar y López Méndez a Londres', *Boletín de la Academia Nacional de Historia*, XVIII (Caracas, 1935), pp. 643, 647–51.
6. Lynch, *Spanish American Revolutions*, pp. 195–8.
7. J. Mancini, *Bolívar* (Caracas, 1935), pp. 313–18.
8. José Alberich, 'English Attitudes Towards the Hispanic World in the Time of Bello as reflected by the *Edinburgh* and *Quarterly Reviews*', in John Lynch (ed.), *Andrés Bello: The London Years* (London, 1982), p. 67. For a longer more complete analysis of the articles published in the two reviews, see José Alberich, 'Actitudes Ingleses ante el Mundo Hispánico en la Epoca de Bello', in *Bello y Londres*, I, p. 125. Other contemporary reviews which commented upon Latin American events included *The Westminister Review*, *The Monthly Review*, *The British Review and London Critical Journal*, and *The Eclectic Review*.
9. *The Quarterly Review* (London), XVII, pp. 530–1.
10. Calvin P. Jones, 'The Spanish American Works of Alexander von Humboldt as Viewed by Leading British Periodicals 1800–1830', *The Americas* (Washington DC, 1973), XXVIII, p. 442.
11. Stanley Morrison, *The English Newspaper* (London, 1932), pp. 206–7; Harold Hobson, Philip Knightly, Leonard Russell, *The Pearl of Days: An Intimate Memoir of the Sunday Times, 1822–1972* (London, 1972), pp. 4–5, 12–13.
12. *The Times* (London), 26 Dec. 1821, p. 3.
13. *The Morning Chronicle* (London), 8 Oct. 1818, p. 2.
14. *Ibid.*, 29 Oct. 1823, p. 2.
15. Paul H. Emden, *The Money Powers of Europe in the Nineteenth Century* (London, 1937), pp. 1–4; Charles K. Hobson, *The Export of Capital* (London, 1914, 1963 ed.), pp. 95–8.
16. *Kent's Original London Directory: 1822*; *Pigot and Co's London & Provincial New Commercial Directory for 1822–23*; *Critichett & Woods. The Post Office London Directory for 1822–23*.
17. E. Victor Morgan and W. A. Thomas, *The Stock Exchange: Its History and Functions* (London, 1962), pp. 71–7.
18. Morgan and Thomas, *The Stock Exchange*, pp. 42–73, 80.
19. The Times, *Tercentenary Handlist of English & Welsh Newspapers, Magazines & Reviews* (London, 1920).
20. Gavin Weightman and Steve Humphries, *The Making of Modern London: 1815–1914*, (London, 1983), pp. 16–28; Christopher Hibbert, *The Making of Charles Dickens*, (London, 1983), p.125.
21. Emden, *Money Powers*, pp. 7–10; Leland H. Jenks, *The Migration of British Capital to 1875* (New York, 1927), pp. 34–6; Charles L. Kindleberger, *A Financial History of Western Europe* (London, 1984),

pp. 219–20.
22. Jenks, *Migration of British Capital*, p. 38; *The Morning Chronicle*, 13 Jan. 1818, p. 2.
23. *The Times*, 5 Mar. 1822, p. 3; Charles Fenn, *A Compendium of the English and Foreign Funds and the Principle Joint Stock Companies Forming an Epitome of the Various Objects of Investment Negotiable in London* (London, 1837), p. 13; *The Times*, 19 Mar. 1822, p. 2; 2 Apr. 1822, p. 2.

Chapter II

1. David Bushnell, *The Santander Regime in Gran Colombia* (Newark, Del., 1954), pp. 10–14.
2. Malcolm Deas, 'Venezuela, Colombia and Ecuador: The First Half-Century of Independence', Leslie Bethell (ed.), *The Cambridge History of Latin America* (Cambridge, 1985), III, p. 507.
3. Zea's power of attorney was reprinted in *The New Times* (London) 23 Oct. 1823, p. 1.
4. For details of Zea's life, see Ramon Armando Rodríguez, *Diccionario Biográfico, Geográfico e Histórico de Venezuela* (Madrid, 1967), p. 872; Alirio Duque Sánchez, *Francisco Antonio Zea* (Mérida, 1970); R. Botero Saldarriaga, *Francisco Antonio Zea* (Bogotá, 1955).
5. Bolívar to Santander, 14 Jan. 1823, quoted in Bushnell, *The Santander Regime*, p. 114.
6. Gustavus Hippisley, *A Narrative of the Expedition to the Rivers Orinocco and Apure in South America which sailed from England in November 1817* (London, 1819), p. 3.
7. Sergio Elias, Ortiz, *Doctor José María del Real, Jurisconsulto y Diplomático* (Bogotá, 1969), pp. 54–60; Sergio Fernández Larraín, *Luis López Méndez y Andrés Bello* (Santiago, 1969), pp. 88–90.
8. Francis Maceroni, *Memoirs of the Life and Adventures of Colonel Maceroni* (2 vols., London, 1828), II, pp. 433–53; M. Rafter, *Memoirs of Gregor M'Gregor* (London, 1820).
9. *Prospectus of a Loan for the Service of the Confederated Governments of Venezuela and New Granada and Proposed in Conformity to the Express Powers and Instructions of the Supreme Government of the Same*, Microfilm Collection, Fundación Boulton (Caracas, Venezuela) Sección Histórica-Anexo, no. 147, serie C,

rollo 2.
10. For an early Colombian commentary on Zea's disastrous loan see José M. Restrepo, *Historia de la Revolución de la República de Colombia* (6 vols., Medellin, 1969), IV, pp. 377–82. Restrepo's work was first published in 1827 in Paris, followed by an expanded edition in 1858. The 1969 edition cited herein is a reprint of the 1858 edition. Also, Bushnell, *The Santander Regime*, pp. 112–14; Antonio María Barriga Villalba, *El Empréstito de Zea y el Préstamo de Erick Bollmann de 1822* (Bogotá, no date).
11. Fundación John Boulton, Sección Venezolana del Archivo de Gran Colombia, P, VII, pp. 39–40, 40–5, 41–3.
12. Fundación John Boulton, Sección Venezolana, P, VII, pp. 34–7.
13. Alexander Walker, *Colombia* (2 vols., London, 1822), I, p. xciv.
14. Aspurúa, *Hombres Notables*, p. 231.
15. Restrepo, *La Revolución*, IV, p. 376.
16. Howard Bierck, *La Vida Pública de Pedro Gual* (Caracas, 1947), pp. 237–8. Gual was particularly incensed over the expenses incurred by Zea in his hopeless trip to Spain.
17. Restrepo, *La Revolución*, IV p. 377; Villalba, *El Empréstito de Zea*, pp. 21–42; Bushnell, *The Santander Regime*, pp. 113–14. *The Times*, 19 Mar. 1822, p. 2.
18. British Library, *Prospectuses of Firms, of Applications for Shares, and Other Papers Relating to Railways, Assurances and Other Companies, 1800–56* (4 vols., London) (1881. b. 23) II, fol. 49 (hereinafter *Prospectuses of Firms*).
19. Restrepo, *La Revolución*, IV pp. 378–9.
20. John Ford, *Ackermann 1783–1983; The Business of Art*, (London, 1983), pp. 84–8. The bond certificates are illustrated and described in great detail in Villalba, *El Empréstito*, pp. 23–37.
21. 'Some Remarks on the Republic of Colombia', *Prospectuses of Firms*, II, fol. 44. The 'Remarks' appear to have been largely copied from Walker's *Colombia*.
22. See yield calculations in J. Fred Rippy, *British Foreign Investments in Latin America, 1822–1949* (Minneapolis, 1959), table I, p. 20.
23. Walker, *Colombia*, I, p. cx.
24. Walker, *Colombia*, II, pp. 728–37; *The Times*, 11 July 1822, p. 2.
25. Ricardo Donoso, *Antonio José de Irisarri, Escritor y Diplomático* (Santiago, 1966), pp. 87–92; Oscar Sambrano Urdaneta,

'Cronología Londinense de Andrés Bello', *Bello y Londres*, I, pp. 411, 416–17.
26. *The Times*, 31 May 1822, p. 3; 24 June 1822, p. 2.
27. *Prospectuses of Firms*, II, fol. 43.
28. Donoso, *Irisarri*, pp. 99–102.
29. *The Times*, 31 May 1822, p. 3; 24 June 1822, p. 3.
30. Robert A. Humphreys, *Liberation in South America, 1806–1827; The Career of James Paroissien* (London, 1952), pp. 5–6, 100–1; Michael J. Mulhall, *The English in South America* (London, 1878), pp. 170–1.
31. The battle occurred on 24 June 1821. See contemporary British and Irish press accounts of the engagement reprinted in Eric T. D. Lambert, *Carabobo, 1821* (Caracas, 1974), pp. 15–30. Also *The Times*, 23 Dec. 1821, p. 3.
32. *The Times*, 10 April 1822, p. 2; 16 April 1822, p. 3; 30 April 1822, p. 3; Charles K. Webster, *Britain and the Independence of Latin America, 1812–1830* (2 vols., London, 1938) I, p. 16.
33. *The Courier* (London), 7 Oct. 1822, p. 3.
34. *The Edinburgh Advertiser* (Edinburgh), 22 Oct. 1822, p. 3. See Also, *The Times*, 12 Oct. 1822, p. 2.
35. *The New Times*, 14 Oct. 1822, p. 2.
36. *Ibid.*, 14 Oct. 1822, p. 2; Humphreys, *Liberation in South America*, p. 122.
37. Carlos Palacios Moreyra, *La Deuda Anglo Peruana, 1822–1890* (Lima, 1983), pp. 13–14.
38. Heraclio Bonilla, 'Peru and Bolivia from Independence to the War of the Pacific', in Bethell, *Cambridge History of Latin America*, III, pp. 539–43.
39. *The New Times*, 14 Oct. 1822, p. 2.
40. Humphreys, *Liberation in South America*, p. 123.
41. Morgan and Thomas, *Stock Exchange*, pp. 84–6.
42. *The Star* (London), 25 Oct. 1822, p. 3. The general gambling craze is described in Paul Emden, *Regency Pageant* (London, 1936), pp. 209–17.
43. *The Times*, 7 June 1822, p. 3.
44. Frank Griffith Dawson, 'William Pitt's Settlement at Black River on the Mosquito Shore: A Challenge to Spain in Central America, 1732–1787,' *Hisp. Am. Hist. Rev.*, LXIII (Nov. 1983), pp. 677–706; Frank Griffith Dawson, 'People in Finance: Gregor MacGregor', *The Banker* (London, Jan. 1982), p. 27; Victor Allen, 'The Prince of Poyais',

History Today (Jan. 1952), p. 53. I have used the older term 'Mosquito' instead of the more modern usage of 'Mískito'.
45. Peter Dixon, *Canning* (London, 1976), pp. 208–11; Harold Temperley, *The Foreign Policy of Canning, 1822–1827* (London, 1925), pp. 24–34.
46. *Gaceta de Colombia*, no. 58, 7 July 1822, p. 11, Banco de la República de Colombia Facsimile Edition, I, (4 vols., Bogotá, 1973).
47. Gual to Zea, Bogotá, 15 Sept. 1822. Reprinted in *The Contractor Unmasked, being Letters to one of the Contractors of the Colombian Loan Occasioned by His Recent Pamphlet, by a Member of the Honourable Society of Lincolns Inn* (London, 1823), p. 29.
48. *The Courier*, 22 Oct. 1823, p. 2.
49. *The New Times*, 23 Oct. 1822, p. 1; *The Star*, 23 Oct. 1822, p. 2; also quoted in Walker, *Colombia*, pp. cv–cvi.
50. *The Contractor Unmasked*, p. 19.
51. *The Courier*, 25 Oct. 1822, p. 3.
52. Reprinted in Walker, *Colombia*, pp. cviii–cxi.
53. *John Bull*, 1 December 1822, pp. 820–1 (emphasis in original).
54. *The Morning Chronicle*, 30 November 1822, p. 2.
55. 'Circular of the British Cabinet ... May, 1820', accounts and Papers (36), State Papers (1847), LXIX, pp. 1, 3; also George Macauley Trevelyan, *British History in the 19th Century and After (1782–1919)* (London, 1948), pp. 207–8.
56. 'Circular Dispatch to His Majesty's Missions at Foreign Courts, laid before the House of Lords, in pursuance of an Address to his Majesty, Feb. 1821', in *The Annual Register or a View of the History, Politics and Literature of the Year 1821* (1822), LII, pt. II, pp. 737–9.
57. Canning to Wellington, London, 7 Sept. 1823, quoted in Temperley, *Foreign Policy of Canning*, pp. 64–5.
58. *The Times*, 2 Dec. 1822, p. 2.
59. John Bull, 8 Dec. 1822.

Chapter III

1. *The Courier*, 30 Nov. 1822, p. 3; *The Examiner*, 5 Jan. 1823, p. 2.
2. Walker, *Colombia*, II, p. 755.
3. Reprinted in ibid., II pp. 757–9.
4. Ibid., p. 760.
5. Ibid., p. 748.

6. Ibid., p. 755.
7. *The New Times*, 28 Jan. 1823, p. 2.
8. Ibid., 18 Mar. 1823, p. 3.
9. *Revenga v Mackintosh*, 107 Eng. Rep. 541–3 (1824); Restrepo, *La Revolución*, IV, pp. 226–7.
10. *The Morning Chronicle*, 1 July 1823, p. 2.
11. *The Morning Herald* (London), 25 July 1823, p. 3.
12. Bierck, *La Vida Pública de Don Pedro Gual*, pp. 237–8.
13. *The Edinburgh Evening Advertiser*, 27 July 1823, p. 403.
14. *The Morning Herald*, 31 Aug. 1823, p. 2; *The Morning Chronicle*, 1 Sept. 1823, p. 3.
15. *The Examiner*, (London), 31 Aug. 1823, pp. 566–7.
16. *The New Times*, 2 Oct. 1823, p. 2.
17. *The Times*, 3 Sept. 1823, p. 1.
18. *The Morning Herald*, 3 Oct. 1823, p. 2.
19. Raymond Carr, *Spain, 1808–1939* (Oxford, 1966), pp. 118–43; Temperley, *The Foreign Policy of Canning*, pp. 86–99.
20. *The Morning Chronicle*, 22 Oct. 1823, p. 3.
21. Ibid., 23 Oct. 1823, p. 3.
22. Bello to Minister of State and Foreign Relations, London, 8 May 1823, in Andrés Bello, *Derecho Internacional*, I, *Obras Completas de Andrés Bello*, X (Caracas, 1954), Appendix III, pp. 429, 430.
23. *The Morning Chronicle*, 30 Oct. 1822, p. 3.
24. The letter and its non-committal answer were printed in *The Courier*, 12 Sept. 1823, p. 2.
25. *The Morning Chronicle*, 29 Oct. 1823, p. 3
26. *The Edinburgh Advertiser*, 30 Sept. 1823, p. 212.
27. *The Examiner*, 2 Nov. 1823, p. 707.
28. *The Edinburgh Advertiser*, 4 Nov. 1823, p. 293; *The Sunday Times*, (London) 9 Nov. p. 2. Their lowest during 1823 had been 47. *The Examiner*, 2 Mar. 1823, p. 103.
29. *The Sunday Times*, 9 Nov. 1823, p. 2.
30. *The Morning Chronicle*, 30 Oct. 1823, p. 2. *The Times*, 30 Oct. 1823, p. 2.
31. *Gaceta de Colombia* (Bogotá), no. 109, 12 Oct. 1823 pp. 1, 4. Banco de la República Facsimile edition, I.
32. *Gaceta de Colombia*, no. 81, 4 May 1823, p. 3.
33. Aspurúa, *Hombres Notables*, p. 235.
34. *The Courier*, 16 Sept. 1823, p. 3.
35. Ibid., 17 Sept. 1823, p. 2. A number of pamphlets were circulated in London during 1823 by the contractors and the

opponents of the 1822 loan arguing for and against its validity. Some of these still exist in the British Library.
36. Donoso, José Antonio de Irisarri, p. 100–1.
37. *The New Times*, 12 March 1823, p. 1.
38. Ibid., 31 March 1823, p. 2.
39. *The Courier*, 15 Sept. 1823, p. 2.
40. *The Times*, 22 Sept. 1823, p. 1.
41. *The Morning Chronicle*, 23 Dec. 1823, p. 2.
42. Humphreys, *Liberation in South America*, p. 125.
43. *The Morning Chronicle*, 19 Nov. 1822.
44. *The Morning Chronicle*, 22 Feb. 1823, p. 3.
45. Carlos Palacios Moreyra, *La Deuda Anglo Peruana* (Lima, 1983), pp. 14–16; Humphreys, *Liberation in South America*, pp. 128–9.
46. *The Times*, 16 July 1823, p. 3.
47. *The Courier*, 16 Sept. 1823, p. 1.
48. Humphreys, *Liberation in South America*, pp. 130–1, Moreyra, *La Deuda*, p. 17.
49. *The Morning Chronicle*, 22 Dec. 1823, p. 2.
50. Humphreys, *Liberation in South America*, p. 131; Moreyra, *La Deuda*, p. 17.
51. Allen, 'The Prince of Poyais', pp. 53–7; Alfred Hasbrouck, 'Gregor MacGregor and the Colonization of Poyais', *Hisp. Am. Hist. Rev.* VII (1927), pp. 438, 445–9.
52. *The Morning Herald*, 26 July 1823, p. 2.
53. Allen, 'Prince of Poyais', p. 57; Hasbrouck, 'Gregor MacGregor', pp. 448–57.
54. 1823 Poyais Bond Certificate in the author's collection.
55. Hyde Clarke, 'On the Debts of Sovereign and Quasi-Sovereign States, Owing by Foreign Countries', *Journal of Statistical Society* XLI (London, June 1878), pp. 299, 313.
56. *The Morning Herald*, 14 Oct. 1823, p. 2.
57. Ibid., 3 Oct. 1823, p. 2.
58. *The Times*, 22 Sept. 1823, p. 2.
59. George Stapleton, *The Political Life of the Right Honourable George Canning* (3 vols. London, 1831) II, pp. 26–42; Temperley, *Foreign Policy of Canning*, pp. 114–21.
60. *The New Times*, 19 Nov. 1823, p. 2.
61. *The Morning Chronicle*, 2 Dec. 1823, p. 2.
62. *The Sunday Times*, 9 Nov. 1823, p. 2.
63. *The Examiner*, 30 Nov. 1823, p. 1.
64. 'Loan for £640,000 Five Per Cent Stock for the Service of the Order of St. John of Jerusalem (Commonly called the

Knights of Malta)', in British Library, *Prospectuses, etc of Public Companies,* (8223. e. 10) no. 72; *The Edinburgh Evening Advertiser,* 11 Nov. 1823, p. 311; *The Cambridge Chronicle and Huntingdonshire Gazette,* 7 Nov. 1823, p. 2.

65. *The Morning Herald,* 5 Nov. 1823, p. 2.
66. *The Edinburgh Evening Advertiser,* 11 Nov. 1823, p. 311.
67. *The Morning Chronicle,* 1 Dec. 1823, p. 2.
68. *The Examiner,* 28 Dec. 1823, p. 1.
69. *The Morning Chronicle,* 29 Dec. 1823, p. 3.
70. *The Cambridge Chronicle and Huntingdonshire Gazette,* 7 Nov. 1823, p. 2.
71. Ibid., 28 Nov. 1823, p. 2. In the early 1820s the peso was equivalent to one US dollar or one-fifth of a pound Sterling.
72. *The Morning Chronicle,* 13 Dec. 1823, p. 3; 10 Dec. 1823, p. 2.
73. *The New Times,* 19 Nov. 1823, p. 2.
74. *The Morning Chronicle,* 4 Dec. 1823, p. 2.
75. Ibid., 1 Dec. 1823, p. 3.
76. Ibid., 22 Dec. 1823, p. 2; *The Cambridge Chronicle and Huntingdonshire Gazette,* 26 Dec. 1823, p. 1.
77. The first Companies Act was not passed until 1856.
78. Reprinted in *The Morning Chronicle,* 10 Dec. 1823, p. 2.
79. Ibid., 18 Dec. 1823, p. 2.
80. Ibid., 2 Dec. 1823, p. 2.
81. *The Cambridge Chronicle and Huntingdonshire Gazette,* 26 Dec. 1823, p. 2.

Chapter IV

1. 'History of Europe', in *The Annual Register or a View of the History, Politics and Literature of the Year 1824* (London, 1825), p. 4 (hereinafter *'Annual Register for 1824'*).
2. *The Morning Chronicle,* 21 Jan. 1823, p. 2.
3. Edgar Turlington, *Mexico and her Foreign Creditors* (New York, 1930), pp. 16–21.
4. Ibid., pp. 21–2.
5. Ibid., pp. 25–7.
6. Ibid., pp. 29–30.
7. Ibid., p. 31.
8. Ibid., pp. 347–50.
9. Thomas Tooke, *A History of Prices and of the State of the Circulation from 1793 to 1837* (2 vols. London, 1837), p. 149; J. Fred Rippy, *British Foreign Investment*

in Latin America, 1822–1949 (Minneapolis, 1959), table I, p. 20.
10. *The Edinburgh Advertiser,* 6 Jan. 1824, p. 12; *The Morning Chronicle,* 1 Jan. 1824, p. 2.
11. *The Morning Chronicle,* 24 Aug. 1827, p. 2.
12. Ibid., 21 Jan. 1824, p. 2.
13. Ibid., 27 Jan. 1824, p. 3.
14. Ibid., 3 Feb. 1824, p. 3.
15. *John Bull,* 1 March 1824, p. 77.
16. *The Morning Chronicle,* 20 Jan. 1824, p. 2; British Library, *Prospectuses of Firms,* II, fol. 42; *The Morning Herald,* 13 Mar. 1824, p. 3.
17. *The Morning Chronicle,* 22 Jan. 1824, p. 2.
18. Ibid., 18 Feb. 1824, p. 3; Jenks, *Migration of British Capital,* p. 50.
19. *The Morning Herald,* 20 Feb. 1824, p. 3; William H. Wynne, *State Insolvency and Foreign Bondholders,* (2 vols., New Haven, 1951), II, p. 284, p. 2.
20. Bushnell, *The Santander Regime* pp. 114–15.
21. Restrepo, *La Revolución.,* V, p. 150.
22. *The Morning Chronicle,* 3 April 1824, p. 4. On 7 April Colombia was at 86½, Chile at 80, and Peru at 80. Ibid., 7 April 1824, p. 3.
23. 'An Ex-holder of Colombian Bonds' to Don Manuel José Hurtado. London, 2 April 1824, in *Prospectuses of Firms,* II, fol. 45.
24. *The Morning Chronicle,* 2 April 1824, p. 3.
25. Ibid., 3 April 1824, p. 4.
26. *John Bull,* 25 April 1824, p. 142.
27. *The Morning Chronicle,* 13 April 1824, p. 2; 16 April 1824, p. 3; 20 April 1824, p. 2.
28. Restrepo, *La Revolución,* V, pp. 150–1; *The Morning Chronicle,* 20 April 1824, p. 2.
29. *Gaceta de Colombia,* no. 119, 25 Jan. 1824, p. 4; no. 126, 14 Mar. 1824, p. 1.
30. *The Morning Chronicle,* 18 May 1824, p. 3.
31. Ibid., 21 May 1824, p. 1.
32. Bushnell, *The Santander Regime,* pp. 116–22; Alvarado Tirado Mejía, *Introducción a la Historia Económica de Colombia* (Bogotá, no date), pp. 131–2.
33. *The Morning Chronicle,* 23 Feb. 1824, p. 2; 24 Feb. 1824, p. 2.
34. Ibid., 14 April 1824, p. 3.
35. Ibid., 13 April 1824, p. 3.
36. Moreyra, *La Deuda,* pp. 18–20.

37. *The Morning Chronicle*, 7 May 1824, p. 4.
38. Ibid., 26 June 1824, p. 2.
39. Temperley, *Foreign Policy of Canning*, pp. 115–116.
40. *The Annual Register for 1824*, p. 4.
41. Ibid., pp. 7–8.
42. Ibid., pp. 10–14.
43. Ibid., p. 15.
44. Hubert Haring, *A History of Latin America* (New York, 1956), pp. 583–7; John Lynch, 'The River Plate Republics from Independence to the Paraguayan War', in Bethel *Cambridge History of Latin America* III, pp. 615, 632–3.
45. Michael Mulhall, *The English in South America*, (London, 1878) pp. 324–5, 403–33.
46. Robert A. Humphreys (ed.) *British Consular Reports on the Trade and Politics of Latin America, 1824–1826* (London, 1940), pp. 9, 26 et seq.
47. Humphreys, *Reports*, pp. 35, 42.
48. Ernesto J. Fitte, *Historia de un Empréstito: La Emisión de Baring Brothers en 1824* (Buenos Ayres, 1962), pp. 29–32.
49. Ibid., pp. 36–7.
50. Ibid., pp. 48–53.
51. Ibid., pp. 63–9, Harold E. Peters, *The Foreign Debt of the Argentine Republic* (Baltimore, 1934), pp. 12–13.
52. *The Courier*, 6 July 1824, p. 2; *The Times*, 7 July 1824, p. 2; *The Morning Herald*, 7 July 1824, p. 2.
53. The contract is reprinted in Fitte, *Historia*, pp. 73–81.
54. *The Times*, 6 July 1824, p. 2.
55. *The Courier*, 7 July 1824, p. 3.
56. *The Morning Herald*, 7 July 1824, p. 2; 8 July 1824, p. 3.
57. *The Morning Chronicle*, 24 July 1824, p. 2.
58. Ibid., 9 July 1824, p. 3; 10 July 1824, p. 3; 13 July 1824, p. 2; *The Courier*, 3 July 1824, p. 3; 7 July 1824, p. 3; 9 July 1824, p. 3; 12 July 1824, p. 3.
59. Leslie A. Marchand, *Byron: Letters*, VI, pp. 177, 212, 275, 232, 236, 240, 276, 279 (6 vols., New York, 1957).
60. *The Courier*, 9 July 1824, p. 3.
61. *The Courier*, 17 July 1824, p. 2; *The Morning Herald*, 19 July 1824, p. 2.
62. *The Courier*, 20 July 1824, p. 3.
63. *The Courier*, 15 July 1824, p. 2; *The Morning Herald*, 23 July 1824, p. 2.
64. *The Courier*, 22 July 1824, p. 1.
65. José F. Normano, *Brazil: A Study of Economic Types*, (Chapel Hill, 1935), p. 154. Some contemporary newspaper sources also state the face amount was £1,000,000. Other, later sources place it as £1,686,000. See, for example, *Fifth Annual General Report of the Council of the Corporation of Foreign Bondholders for the Year 1877*.
66. *The Morning Chronicle*, 18 Aug. 1824, p. 2; *The Courier*, 17 Aug. 1824, p. 2.
67. Normano, *Brazil*, p. 152; Alan K. Manchester, *British Preeminence in Brazil: Its Rise and Decline* (Chapel Hill, 1933), pp. 86–9.
68. *The Times*, 8 Dec. 1824, p. 2.
69. Clarence N. Haring, *Empire in Brazil: A New World Experiment with Monarchy* (Cambridge, Mass., 1958), pp. 15–22. The United States recognized Brazil in May 1824. Haring, *Empire in Brazil*, p. 32, n. 13.
70. This bizarre episode is recounted in great detail by Donoso, in *José Antonio de Irisarri*, pp. 105–14.
71. See for example, *The Morning Chronicle*, 30 Aug. 1824, p. 3; 1 Sept. 1824, p. 3.
72. Frank Griffith Dawson, 'The Influence of Andrés Bello on Latin American Perceptions of Non-Intervention and State Responsibility', *The British Yearbook of International Law, 1986* (Oxford, 1987), p. 257.
73. *The Courier*, 20 Aug. 1824, p. 2.
74. *The Morning Herald*'s comments were reprinted in *The Weekly Dispatch*, 4 July 1824, p. 220.
75. *The Courier*, 24 Aug. 1824, p. 3; 26 Aug. 1824, p. 2.
76. Ibid., 2 Sept. 1824, p. 2.
77. Ibid., 3 Sept. 1824, p. 2.
78. *The Morning Chronicle*, 18 Sept. 1824, p. 2.
79. Ibid., 11 Nov. 1824, p. 2.
80. *The Times*, 11 Nov. 1824, p. 2; 16 Nov. 1824, p. 2.
81. *The Morning Chronicle*, 15 Nov. p. 2.
82. *The Courier*, 1 Dec. 1824, p. 3; 22 Dec. 1824, p. 2; *The Times*, 17 Dec. 1824, p. 2.
83. *The Courier*, 17 Dec. 1824, p. 2; *The Times*, 23 Dec. 1824, p. 1.
84. *The Times*, 23 Dec. 1824, p. 2; *The Courier*, 23 Dec. 1824, p. 3.
85. *The Times* 8 Oct. 1824, p. 2.
86. *The Morning Chronicle*, 10 Feb. 1824, p. 2; *John Bull*, 1 Mar. 1824, p. 77.
87. *The Morning Chronicle*, 7 Feb. 1824, p. 3; 'Companies, Foreign Loans, Schemes, and Bubbles', Appendix to

Report from Select Committe, *Parliamentary Papers*, VII (1844), p. 334.

88. Paul Verna, 'Bello y las Mines del Libertador: Andres Bello Corredor de Minas y Bienes Raices en Londres,' in *Bello y Londres*, I, pp. 469, 471; *The Courier*, 4 Nov. 1825, p. 1; English, *A Complete View*, p. 4.
89. *Prospectuses of Firms*, III, fol. 59.
90. *The Times*, 23 Nov. 1824, p. 2.
91. John R. McCulloch, 'Mining Companies', *A Dictionary, Practical, Theoretical and Historical, of Commerce and Commercial Navigation* (London, 1832–3), p. 745.
92. *Prospectuses, etc of Public Companies*, no. 29; *The Times*, 29 Nov. 1824, p. 3.
93. Ibid., *The Times*, 29 Nov. 1824, p. 2.
94. *The Courier*, 7 Dec. 1824, pp. 2–3; *The Morning Chronicle*, 7 Dec. 1824, p. 2.
95. *Prospectuses of Firms*, III, fol. 2.
96. *The Times*, 7 Dec. 1824, p. 2.
97. Ibid., *The Times*, 22 Dec. 1824, p. 2; *The Courier*, 25 Dec., 1824, p. 3.
98. Ibid., 31 Dec. 1824, p. 2; *The Courier*, 30 Dec. 1824, p. 2.
99. Ibid., 30 Dec. 1824, p. 2.
100. *The Courier*, 31 Dec. 1824, p. 2.
101. *The Times*, 31 Dec. 1824, p. 2.
102. *The Courier*, 30 Dec. 1824, p. 3.

Chapter V

1. *The Times*, 1 Jan. 1825, p. 2; *The Morning Chronicle*, 1 Jan. 1825. p. 2.
2. Canning to Bosanquet, London, 31 Dec. 1824, reprinted in Temperley, *Foreign Policy of Canning* pp. 148, 150.
3. Ibid., p. 149.
4. *The Morning Chronicle*, 4 Jan. 1825, p. 2.
5. *The Times*, 22 Feb. 1825, p. 3.
6. *The Courier*, 12 Jan. 1825, p. 2.
7. *The Morning Chronicle*, 12 Jan. 1825, p. 2.
8. *The Times*, 12 Jan. 1825, p. 2.
9. *The Morning Chronicle*, 26 Jan. p. 3.
10. J. J. Sturz, *A Review, Financial, Statistical and Commercial of the Empire of Brazil and its Resources* (London, 1837), p. 21; *The Times*, 25 Jan. 1825, p. 2.
11. Ibid., pp. 8–10.
12. *The Times*, 8 Feb. 1825, p. 2; Turlington, *Mexico*, pp. 41–2.
13. *The Times*, 18 Nov. 1825, p. 2.
14. *The Morning Chronicle*, 10 Feb. 1825.
15. Ibid., 20 Aug. 1827, p. 1; Turlington, *Mexico*, p. 43.

16. *The Times*, 14 Feb. 1825, p. 2; *The Morning Chronicle*, 15 Feb. 1825, p. 4.
17. *The Times*, 12 Mar. 1825, p. 2.
18. *The Morning Chronicle*, 3 Mar. 1825, p. 3.
19. *The Times*, 3 Mar. 1825, pp. 2–3.
20. Ibid., 12 Mar. 1825, p. 2; *The Morning Chronicle*, 17 Mar. 1825, p. 3.
21. *The Courier*, 17 Jan. 1825, p. 3; 18 Jan. 1825, pp. 1–3.
22. *The Times*, 21 Jan. 1825, p. 2.
23. Ibid., 29 Mar. 1825, p. 3; *The Courier*, 2 Apr. 1825, p. 3.
24. *The Courier*, 7 Apr. 1825, p. 2.
25. Ibid., 11 Apr. 1825, p. 1.
26. *The Times*, 6 May 1825, p. 1.
27. *The Courier*, 5 May 1825, p. 2; 17 May 1825, p. 1.
28. *The Times*, 25 May 1825, p. 1; *The Courier*, 16 May 1825, p. 2.
29. *The Morning Chronicle*, 21 May 1825, p. 3; Moreyra, *La Deuda*, pp. 18–20.
30. *The Courier*, 25 May 1825, p. 2.
31. *The Morning Chronicle*, 11 June 1825, p. 2.
32. *The Times*, 16 June 1825, p. 2; *The Courier*, 8 June 1825, p. 2; 16 June 1825, p. 1.
33. For information on these and other companies see Henry English, *A Complete View of the Joint Stock Companies formed during the Years 1824 and 1825* (London, 1827).
34. *Prospectuses of Firms*, III, fol. 157; II, fol. 79.
35. *John Bull*, 10 April 1825, p. 118; *The Morning Chronicle*, 10 March 1825, p. 2; 3 Sept. 1825, p. 3.
36. *The Courier*, 13 May 1825, p. 1; *The Times*, 18 May 1825, p. 1.
37. *The Times*, 18 Mar. 1825, p. 1.
38. *Prospectuses of Firms*, II, fol. 67.
39. Harriet Martineau, *The History of England During the Thirty Years Peace: 1816–1846* (2 vols. London, 1849), I, pp. 355–6.
40. *The Morning Chronicle*, 10 Mar. 1825, p. 2; 21 Mar. 1825, p. 2.
41. *John Bull*, 27 Feb. 1825, pp. 69–70.
42. *The Times*, 23 Nov. 1824, p. 3.
43. *Bond and Share Prospectuses 1824–1880*, vol. Abb-Ang, Guidhall Library, London (hereinafter *Prospectuses*); *The Courier* 25 June 1825, p. 1.
44. *The Morning Chronicle*, 8 Mar. 1825, p. 3.
45. *John Bull*, 10 Apr. 1825, p. 118.

46. *Gaceta de Colombia*, no. 87, 15 June 1823, p. 1.
47. *The Times*, 16 Mar. 1825, p. 2.
48. *The Morning Chronicle*, 9 April 1825, p. 3.
49. *The Times*, 9 April 1825, p. 1.
50. Ibid., 13 Jan. 1825, p. 2.
51. See generally, McCulloch, 'Mining Companies', pp. 745–8.
52. *Prospectuses*, Vol. Can-Cit; *The Times* 14 Jan. 1825, p. 2; *The Courier*, 14 Jan. 1825, p. 2.
53. *Prospectuses*, Vol. Abb-Ang; *The Times*, 15 Jan. 1825, p. 3.
54. *The Times*, 24 Jan. 1825, p. 3.
55. Ibid., 24 Jan. 1825, p. 3.
56. *Prospectuses, etc. of Public Companies*, no. 122.
57. Ibid., no. 47.
58. *Prospectuses*, Vol. Ori-Phi; *The Times*, 25 Jan. 1825, p. 3.
59. *John Bull*, 6 Feb. 1825, p. 46.
60. *Prospectuses*, Vol. Phi-Rev.
61. *Prospectuses*, Vol. Abb-Ang.
62. *The Morning Chronicle*, 14 May 1825, p. 1; 16 May 1825, p. 3.
63. *Prospectuses, etc. of Public Companies*, no. 141.
64. B. N. Jerman, *The Young Disraeli*, (London, 1960); pp. 43–4; J. Gunn, John Matthews, Donald Schurman, and M. G. Weibe (eds.) *Benjamin Disraeli Letters: 1815–1834* (2 vols. Ithaca, 1982), I, nos. 18–21, 349, 351.
65. Rush to Adams, 18 Jan. 1825, in William R. Manning (ed.), *Diplomatic Correspondence of the United States Concerning the Independence of the Latin American Nations* (3 vols., New York, 1925), III, p. 1529.
66. 6 Geo I c. 18 (1720). It was repealed by 6 Geo 4 c. 131 (1825). See discussion in William Holdsworth, *A History of English Law* (17 vols. London 1922–72) VIII, pp. 219–22.
67. *Parliamentary Debates* (1825), XII, pp. 1048–55.
68. *The Courier*, 17 Mar. 1825, p. 1.
69. *Parliamentary Debates* (1825) XII, p. 1063.
70. *The Courier*, 1 April 1825, p. 3.
71. *The Times*, 15 Mar. 1825, p. 3.
72. *The Morning Chronicle*, 23 July 1825, p. 3.
73. *The Courier*, 19 July 1825, p. 2.
74. *The Morning Chronicle*, 16 April 1825, p. 3.
75. *The Courier*, 16 June 1825, p. 2; 2 July 1825, p. 2.
76. *The Morning Chronicle*, 30 July 1825, p. 3.
77. Haring, *Empire in Brazil*, p. 32.
78. *The Courier*, 31 Aug. 1825, p. 2.
79. *The British Review and London Critical Journal*, XXIII, May 1825, p. 179.
80. *The Morning Herald*, 22 June 1825, p. 1.
81. *The Courier*, 18 June 1825, p. 4.
82. *Gaceta del Gobierno de Guatemala*, no. 3, 16 Dec. 1824, p. 255.
83. *The Courier*, 23 Aug. 1825, p. 2; 24 Aug. 1825, p. 3.
84. *The Morning Chronicle*, 25 Aug. 1825, p. 3.
85. Jenks, *Migration of British Capital*, p. 57; William Smart, *The Economic Annals of the Nineteenth Century* (2 vols., London, 1917), II, p. 294; Tooke, *A History of Prices and the Circulation*, pp. 152–8; A. Andreades, *A History of the Bank of England: 1640 to 1903* (C. Meridith trans., 7th ed., London, 1924), pp. 248–55.
86. Andreades, *History*, p. 251–2.
87. *The Morning Chronicle*, 26 Aug. 1825, p. 2.
88. *The Courier*, 10 Sept. 1825, p. 3.
89. *The Morning Chronicle*, 30 Aug. 1825, p. 2; 1 Sept. 1825, p. 2.
90. Ibid., 15 Sept. 1825, p. 1; *The Courier*, 15 Sept. 1825, p. 1.
91. *The Courier*, 24 Sept. 1825, p. 2; 27 Sept. 1825, p. 2.
92. *The Times*, 13 Oct. 1825, p. 2.
93. *The Morning Chronicle*, 17 Oct. 1825, p. 2.
94. Moreyra, *La Deuda*, pp. 28–9.
95. *The Morning Chronicle*, 15 Sept. 1825, p. 3.
96. *The Times*, 10 Oct. 1825, p. 2.
97. *Prospectuses of Firms* III, fol. 7.
98. Martineau, *A History*, p. 357.
99. J. C. Jefferson, *The Life of Robert Stephenson, FRS*, (2 vols., London, 1864), I, p. 91.
100. *The Morning Chronicle*, 4 Aug. 1825, p. 1.
101. D. C. M. Platt, *Latin America and British Trade 1806–1914* (London, 1972), pp. 4–22.
102. *The Quarterly Review*, XXX, p. 462.
103. *The Courier*, 16 Sept. 1825, p. 1; 26 Sept. 1825, p. 2; *The Morning Chronicle*, 25 Oct, 1825, p. 2.
104. *The Courier*, 14 Nov. 1825, p. 3.
105. *The Morning Chronicle*, 14 Oct. 1825, p. 2; 9 Nov. 1825, p. 2.
106. *The Courier*, 16 Nov. 1825, p. 2.

107. *The Morning Chronicle*, 24 Nov. 1825, p. 2.
108. *The Courier*, 28 Nov. 1825, p. 3.
109. *John Bull*, 30 Nov. 1825, p. 2.
110. *The Morning Chronicle*, 1 Dec. 1825, p. 3.
111. *The Courier*, 21 Nov. 1825, p. 2.
112. *The Morning Chronicle*, 29 Nov. 1825, p. 2; 3 Dec. 1825, p. 2.
113. Andreades, *History*, p. 253; John Clapham, *The Bank of England: A History* (2 vols., Cambridge, 1944), II, pp. 75–102.
114. Tooke, *Prices and Circulation*, pp. 158–61; Jenks, *Migration of British Capital*, pp. 57–8; Clapham, *The Bank of England*, II, p. 99.
115. *The Courier*, 10 Dec. 1825, p. 2.
116. *The Morning Chronicle*, 13 Dec. 1825, p. 2; Tooke, *Prices and Circulation*, p. 161.
117. *The Aberdeen Chronicle*, 17 Dec. 1825, p. 3.
118. Clapham, *The Bank of England*, II, p. 100.
119. Andreades, *History*, p. 252.
120. *The Morning Chronicle*, 17 Dec. 1825, p. 2; Hobson, *The Export of Capital*, p. 104.
121. Tooke, *Prices and Circulation*, p. 162; *The Courier*, 31 Dec. 1825, p. 3; 23 Dec. 1825, p. 2.
122. *The Morning Chronicle*, 27 Dec. 1825, p. 2.
123. Ibid., 20 Dec. 1825, p. 3.
124. Ibid., 17 Dec. 1825, p. 3.
125. *The Times*, 20 Dec. 1825, p. 3. To its credit, *The Morning Chronicle* reprinted the decision in full. 20 Dec. 1825, pp. 1–3.
126. *The Morning Chronicle* 31 Dec. 1825, p. 2.

Chapter VI

1. *The Morning Chronicle*, 7 Jan. 1826, p. 3.
2. Ibid., 28 Jan. 1826, p. 3.
3. Ibid., 2 Feb. 1826, p. 2.
4. Ibid., 11 Feb. 1826, p. 4.
5. Ibid., 2 Mar. 1826, p. 2.
6. Henry Reeve (ed.), *The Greville Memoirs: A Journal of the Reigns of King George IV and King William IV by the Late Charles C. F. Greville* (3 vols., 3rd ed., London, 1877), I, p. 77.
7. *The Morning Chronicle*, 21 Mar. 1826, p. 4.

8. Ibid., 27 Mar. 1826, p. 4.
9. Ibid., 11 April 1826, p. 3.
10. Humphreys, *Liberation in South America* pp. 143–4.
11. Ibid., pp. 155–9.
12. *The Morning Chronicle*, 7 June 1826, p. 3.
13. Ibid., 6 June 1826, p. 2.
14. Ibid., 3 Aug. 1826, p. 1.
15. Ibid., 2 Sept. 1826, p. 2.
16. *The Times*, 5 Oct. 1826, p. 3.
17. *Prospectuses of Firms*, III.
18. *The Times*, 26 Sept. 1826, p. 2.
19. *The Morning Chronicle*, 6 Oct. 1826, p. 2; 9 Oct. 1826, p. 2.
20. The prospectus supplied by Bernardino Rivadavia, a former government minister who became president of the United Provinces of Rió de la Plata, is reprinted in Francis B. Head, *Reports Relating to the Failure of the Rio Plata Mining Association* (London, 1827), p. 143, (emphasis in original).
21. Francis B. Head, *Journeys Across the Pampas and Among the Andes* (Edwardsville, Ill., C. Harvey Gardiner ed., 1967), p. 158.
22. *John Bull*, 7 May 1826, pp. 148–9.
23. Ibid., 3 Sept. 1826, pp. 284–5.
24. Ibid., 10 Sept. 1826, pp. 293–4.
25. *The Morning Chronicle*, 23 Oct. 1826, p. 3.
26. *The Times*, 2 Nov. 1826, p. 3.
27. McCulloch, 'Mining Companies', p. 738.
28. *The Morning Chronicle*, 10 Jan. 1826, p. 3.
29. Bello to Secretary of State for the Treasury, London 11 Feb. 1826, *Derecho Internacional*, II in *Obras Completas de Andrés' Bello* (Caracas, 1981 ed.), XI, pp. 110–11.
30. *The Morning Chronicle*, 11 Feb. 1825, p. 2.
31. *The Times*, 16 Feb. 1825, p. 2.
32. *The Morning Chronicle*, 16 Feb. 1825, p. 3.
33. Mejía, *Historia Económica de Colombia*, p. 136.
34. *John Bull*, 26 Feb. 1826, p. 3.
35. *The Morning Chronicle*, 22 Feb. 1826, p. 3; *John Bull*, 26 Feb. 1826, p. 69.
36. Ibid., 20 Mar. 1826, p. 3.
37. Ibid., 4 April 1826, p. 6.
38. *The New Times*, 7 April 1826, p. 3.
39. Peters, *The Foreign Debt of the Argentine Republic*, pp. 14–16; *The Morning Chronicle*, 23 June 1826, p. 3.

40. *The Morning Chronicle*, 14 April 1826, p. 2; 15 April 1826, p. 2.
41. Ibid., 14 April 1826, p. 3.
42. Moreyra, *La Deuda*, pp. 38–9.
43. *The New Times*, 18 April 1826, p. 3.
44. *The Morning Chronicle*, 13 May 1826, p. 1.
45. Ibid., 5 June 1820, p. 3; 8 June 1826, p. 2.
46. Ibid., 3 July 1826, p. 3.
47. Bushnell, *The Santander Regime*, pp. 124–5.
48. *The Morning Chronicle*, 17 July 1826, p. 2.
49. Moreyra, *La Deuda*, p. 38.
50. *The Morning Chronicle*, 21 July 1826, p. 2. The Central American and Poyais issues were not included in the table.
51. Ibid., 25 July 1826, p. 3; Peters, *The Foreign Debt of the Argentine Republic*, p. 16.
52. Moreyra, *La Deuda*, p. 30; Bushnell, *The Santander Regime*, pp. 119–20.
53. *The Morning Chronicle*, 26 Aug. p. 2.
54. *The Times* noted, however, that 'the emigration this season has been far greater than on any other former one'. 8 Sept. 1826, p. 2.
55. *The Times*, 15 Sept. 1826, p. 2; 18 Sept. 1826, p. 2.
56. *The Morning Chronicle*, 19 Sept. 1826, p. 2.
57. Ibid., 21 Sept. 1826, p. 2.
58. *The Times*, 19 Sept. 1826, p. 2.
59. *The Morning Chronicle*, 28 Sept. 1826, p. 2.
60. Ibid., 29 Sept. 1826, p. 2.
61. *The Times*, 29 Sept. 1826, p. 2.
62. Ibid., 30 Sept. 1826, p. 2.
63. *The Morning Chronicle*, 2 Oct. 1826.
64. Archivo General de Centro América, Guatemala City (hereinafter cited as AGCA) Orden No. 199 of 21 June 1825, B 10 3, Exp. 3592, Leg. 169, fol. 1; AGCA, Orden No. 240 of Aug. 1825, B 10 3, Exp. 3592, Leg. 129, fol. 4.
65. Zebadúa to Foreign Minister, London, 20 Aug. 1826; 28 Aug. 1826, AGCA, B 10 3, Exp. 3605, Leg. 170, fol. 13 et seq.
66. Zebadúa to Foreign Minister, London, 18 Sept. 1826, AGCA, B 10 3, Exp. 3604, Leg. 170 (no folio number); Zebadúa to Minister of Treasury, London, 5 Oct. 1826, AGCA, B 10.3, Exp. 3605, Leg. 170, fol. 3.
67. Robert S. Smith, 'Financing the Central American Federation 1821–1838', *Hispanic American Historical Review*, XLIII, pp. 487–8 (Nov. 1963).
68. *The Times*, 4 Dec. 1826, p. 2.
69. *The Morning Chronicle*, 9 Oct. 1826, p.2.
70. Ibid., 12 Oct. 1826, p. 2.
71. *The Times*, 11 Oct. 1826, p. 2 (emphasis in original).
72. Ibid., 14 Oct. 1826, p. 2.
73. *The Morning Chronicle*, 14 Oct. 1826, p. 2.
74. *The Times*, 19 Oct. 1826, p. 2.
75. Ibid.
76. *The Morning Chronicle*, 19 Oct. 1826, p.2 (emphasis in original).
77. Ibid., 24 Oct. 1826, p. 2; 26 Oct. 1826, p. 2.
78. *The Times*, 30 Oct. 1826, p. 2.
79. Ibid., 1 Nov. 1826, p. 2.
80. Ibid., 27 Oct. 1826, p. 2.
81. Ibid., 18 Nov. 1826, p. 2.
82. For the unhappy story of the Greek loans, see Jenks, *The Migration of British Capital*, pp. 50–1; John A, Levandis, *The Greek Foreign Debt and the Great Powers, 1821–1898* (New York, 1944).
83. *The Times*, 3 Nov. 1826, p. 2.
84. *The Morning Chronicle*, 30 Oct. 1826, p. 2.
85. *The Times*, 4 Nov. 1826, pp. 2–3.
86. Bello and Michelena to Secretary of the Treasury, *Derecho Internacional*, II, *Obras Completas* XI, (1981 ed.) pp. 112–13.
87. Ibid., p. 114.
88. *The Times*, 16 Nov. 1826, p. 2.
89. Ibid., 17 Nov. 1826, p. 2.
90. Ibid., 18 Nov. 1826, p. 2.
91. *The Morning Chronicle*, 21 Nov. 1826, p. 2.
92. Bushnell, *The Santander Regime*, p. 116.
93. Hurtado to Bello and Michelena, *Derecho Internacional*, II, *Obras Completas*, XI (1981 ed.), p. 118.
94. *The Times*, 24 Nov. 1826, p. 2.
95. Bello and Michelena to Secretary of the Treasury, *Derecho Internacional*, II, *Obras Completas*, XI, (1981 ed.) p. 116.
96. Hurtado to Bello and Michelena, ibid., pp. 118–19.
97. *The Times*, 9 Dec. 1826, p. 3.
98. Ibid., 11 Dec. 1826, p. 2.
99. Ibid., 12 Dec. 1826, p. 2.
100. *The Morning Chronicle*, 20 Dec. 1826, p. 1.
101. *The New Times*, 12 Dec. 1826, p. 2.
102. *The Morning Chronicle*, 29 Dec. 1826, p. 3.
103. *The Times*, 21 Dec. 1826, p. 2.

104. Andreades, pp. 254–5, 262.
105. *The Morning Herald*, 30 Dec. 1826, p. 2.
106. Mauricio Mackenzie, *Los Ideales de Bolívar en el Derecho Internacional Americano* (Bogotá, 1955), pp. 21–57; Samuel G. Inman, *Inter-American Conferences 1826–1854: History and Problems*, (Washington, 1965), pp. 1–19.
107. *The Annual Register or a View of the History, Politics and Literature of the Year 1826* (London, 1827), pp. 419–20.

Chapter VII

1. English, *Complete View*, p. 33.
2. Ibid., p. 26.
3. Ibid., pp. 4–9.
4. *John Bull*, 4 Feb. 1827, p. 3.
5. *John Bull*, 3 Sept. 1826, pp. 284–5
6. English, *Complete View*, pp. 41–2.
7. Head, *Reports*.
8. Head, *Reports*, pp. v–vii.
9. *The Morning Chronicle*, 1 Jan. 1827, p. 3. On that same day the Greek 1824 loan went into default.
10. Ibid., 4 Jan. 1827, p. 4.
11. Ibid., 16 Jan. 1824, p. 2.
12. Ibid., 3 Feb. 1827, p. 3; 27 Feb. 1827, p. 3.
13. Ibid., 16 Feb. p. 2. Russia was at 90, Denmark at 62, Spain between 12 and 15, and Greece at 16½.
14. Ibid., 27 Feb. 1827, p. 3.
15. Ibid., 26 Feb. 1827, p. 3.
16. *The Times*, 1 Mar. 1827, p. 2.
17. Ibid., 29 Mar. 1827, p. 3.
18. Ibid., 6 Mar. 1827, p. 2; 9 Mar. 1827, p. 3.
19. Ibid., 5 Mar. 1827, p. 1.
20. Ibid., 20 Mar. 1827, p. 2.
21. Ibid., 27 Mar. 1828, p. 2.
22. Ibid., 4 April 1827, p. 3.
23. Ibid., 17 April 1827, p. 2; 18 April 1827, p. 2.
24. Ibid., 27 April 1827, p. 2.
25. Ibid., 30 April 1827, p. 3.
26. Ibid., 1 May 1827, p. 3.
27. Ibid., 1 May 1827, p. 3.
28. Ibid., 6 June 1827, p. 2.
29. *The Morning Chronicle*, 13 June 1827, p. 3.
30. *The Times*, 18 June 1827, p. 2; *John Bull*, 24 June 1827, p. 197.
31. *The Morning Chronicle*, 4 Aug. 1827, p. 2.
32. Planta to Powles, 27 Feb. 1827, London, in *Correspondence between Great Britain and Foreign Powers and Communications ... to Claimants Relative to Loans ... 1823–1847, Parliamentary Papers* (1847), LXIX, no. 159 (hereinafter *Correspondence*).
33. Quoted in D.C.M. Platt, *Finance, Trade and Politics in British Foreign Policy, 1815–1914* (Oxford, 1968), pp. 34–5.
34. *The Times*, 31 Mar. 1827, p. 1.
35. Ibid., 6 April 1827, p. 3.
36. Ibid., 20 April 1827, p. 2.
37. Ibid., 24 April 1827, p. 2.
38. Ibid., 25 April 1827, p. 2.
39. Ibid., 27 April 1827, p. 2.
40. Backhouse to Robinson, London, 4 May 1827, *Correspondence*, no. 305.
41. *The Times*, 24 April 1827, p. 2; 29 May 1827, p. 2.
42. Ibid., 11 April 1827, p. 3; 12 April 1827, p. 2.
43. Ibid., 7 April 1827, p. 2.
44. Ibid., 8 May 1827, p. 2.
45. Ibid., 29 May 1827, p. 3.
46. *The Morning Chronicle*, 21 June 1827, p. 1; 25 June 1827, p. 2; Turlington, *Mexico*, p. 51.
47. *The Morning Chronicle*, 2 July 1827, p. 2; 4 July 1827, p. 2.
48. Ibid., 26 July 1827, p. 2; 31 July 1827, p. 2.
49. Ibid., 1 Aug. 1827, p.2; 6 Aug. 1827, p. 3.
50. Ibid., 6 Aug. 1827, p. 2; 7 Aug. 1827, p. 2; 9 Aug. 1827, pp. 2–3.
51. Ibid., 10 Aug. 1827, p. 2; 17 Aug. 1827, p. 2; *The Times*, 17 Aug. 1827, p. 2.
52. Dunglas to Lowther, London, 8 Aug. 1827, in *Correspondence*, no. 160.
53. Zegers to Nugent, Santiago, 2 Oct. 1827, in *Correspondence*, no. 306.
54. *The Morning Chronicle*, 16 Aug. 1827, p. 2; 17 Aug. 1827, p. 3.
55. Ibid., 20 Aug. 1827, p. 1.
56. E. M. Butler (ed.), *A Regency Visitor: The English Tour of Prince Puckler-Muskau. Described in his Letters 1826–1828* (London, 1957), p. 315; R. J. White, *Life in Regency England* (London, 1969), pp. 79–80.
57. Butler, *A Regency Visitor*, p. 213.
58. *The Times*, 28 Aug. 1827, p. 3.
59. *The Courier*, 15 Sept. 1827, p. 1; *The Morning Chronicle*, 15 Sept. 1827, p. 1; *The Times*, 15 Sept. 1827, p. 2.
60. *The Morning Post* (London), 17 Sept. 1827, p. 3.
61. *The Times*, 16 Sept. 1827, p. 2; 18 Sept. 1827, p. 2.
62. *The Courier*, 15 Sept. 1827, p. 2.
63. *The Times*, 2 Oct. 1827, p. 2.

64. *The Morning Chronicle*, 11 Oct. 1827, p. 2; 12 Oct. 1827, p. 2.
65. Ibid., 25 Dec. 1827, p. 2; 28 Dec. 1827, pp. 1–2.
66. *The Times*, 28 Dec. 1827, p. 2.
67. Ibid., 31 Dec. 1827, p. 2; *The Morning Chronicle*, 29 Dec. 1827, p. 2.
68. *The Times*, 8 Oct. 1827, p. 3.
69. *The Morning Chronicle*, 6 Oct. 1827, p. 3; 8 Oct. 1827, p. 3.
70. Leslie Bethell and J. H. de Carvalho, 'Brazil from Independence to the Middle of the Nineteenth Century' in Bethell, III, *Cambridge History of Latin America*, pp. 679, 688.
71. *The Morning Chronicle*, 22 Nov. 1827, p. 3; 23 Nov. 1828, p. 3.
72. Ibid., 6 Dec. 1827, p. 2.
73. Ibid., 10 Oct. 1827, p. 3 (emphasis in original).
74. Turlington, *Mexico*, pp. 52–3.
75. *The Morning Chronicle*, 31 Dec. 1827, p. 2.

Chapter VIII

1. *The Morning Chronicle*, 9 Jan. 1828, p. 2.
2. *The Times*, 9 Jan. 1828, p. 2.
3. See Chapter V, *supra*, p. 102.
4. James A. Beaumont, *Travels in Buenos Ayres and in the Adjacent Provinces of Rio de la Plata* (London, 1828), p. 2.
5. Ibid., pp. 245–6.
6. Ibid., p. 252.
7. *The Times*, 18 Jan. 1828, p. 3.
8. *The Morning Chronicle*, 7 Feb. 1828, p. 3.
9. *The Times*, 17 Jan. 1828, p. 2; 9 Feb. 1828, p. 3; Ibid., 11 Feb. 1828, p. 4.
10. Ibid., 6 Mar. 1828, p. 2.
11. Ibid., 7 Mar. 1828, p. 3.
12. Ibid., 7 April 1828, p. 3.
13. *The Morning Chronicle*, 3 Jan. 1828, p. 2; 6 Feb. 1828 p. 3.
14. Ibid., 8 Feb. 1828, p. 2.
15. *The Times*, 4 Feb. 1828, p. 2.
16. Ibid., 13 Feb. 1828, p. 3.
17. *The Morning Chronicle*, 11 Mar. 1828, p. 2.
18. Ibid., 12 Mar. 1828, p. 2.
19. *The New Times*, 24 Mar. 1828, p. 2; *The Morning Chronicle*, 26 Mar. 1828, p. 3.
20. *The Morning Chronicle*, 15 May 1828, pp. 2–3; *The Times*, 15 May 1828, p. 3.
21. *The Times*, 22 May 1828, p. 3.
22. *The Morning Chronicle*, 23 May 1828, p. 3; *The Times*, 23 May 1828, p. 3.
23. *The Times*, 6 June 1828, p. 3; 8 Nov. 1828, p. 3.
24. *The Morning Chronicle*, 6 Feb. 1828, p. 3.
25. *The Morning Chronicle*, 13 Feb. 1828, p. 3; *The Times*, 6 Mar. 1828, p. 3.
26. *The Times*, 29 Jan. 1828, p. 3.
27. Ibid., 29 Mar. 1828, p. 3.
28. *The Morning Chronicle*, 22 May 1828, p. 2.
29. *The Times*, 28 Feb. 1828, p. 2; *The Morning Chronicle*, 28 Feb. 1828, p. 2.
30. *The Times*, 20 Mar. 1828, p. 2.
31. Ibid., 26 Mar. 1828, p. 3; *The Morning Chronicle*, 26 Mar. 1828, p. 3.
32. *The Times*, 25 Mar. 1828, p. 2.
33. *The Morning Chronicle*, 2 May 1828, p. 3.
34. *The Times*, 5 Sept. 1828, p. 3.
35. *The Morning Herald*, 21 July 1828, p. 2 (emphasis in original).
36. *The Times*, 28 Oct. 1828, p. 2.
37. Ibid., 27 Nov. 1828, p. 2.
38. Ibid., 9 Sept. 1828, p. 3.
39. Heraclio Bonilla, 'Peru and Bolivia from Independence to the War of the Pacific', in Bethell, *Cambridge History of Latin America*, p. 548.
40. *The Times*, 15 Sept. 1828, p. 2.
41. Ibid., 1 Sept. 1828, p. 2.
42. Ibid., 2 Oct. 1828, p. 2.
43. Ibid., 17 Oct. 1828, p. 2.
44. Ibid., 12 Nov. 1828, p. 3.
45. Vergara to Campbell, Bogotá, 9 Aug. 1828, *Correspondence*, no. 162.
46. *The Times*, 18 Nov. 1828, p. 2.
47. Ibid., 29 Nov. 1828, p. 2; Dunglas to Messrs Herring, Graham & Co., London, 8 Aug. 1828, *Correspondence*, no. 161.
48. *The Times*, 9 Dec. 1828, p. 2.
49. White to Rodríguez, Santiago, 13 Sept. 1828, *Correspondence*, no. 307.
50. *The Times*, 9 Sept. 1828, p. 3; 13 Sept. 1828, p. 3.
51. *The Morning Chronicle*, 8 Feb. 1828, p. 2.
52. *The Times*, 12 Mar. 1828, p. 3.
53. Peter Dixon, *Canning, Politician and Statesman* (London, 1976), pp. 245–51; *The Times*, 13 May 1828, p. 2.
54. *The Times*, 13 May 1828, p. 3.
55. *The Morning Herald*, 12 May 1828, p. 3.
56. Letter to the Editor, *The Times*, 27 May 1828, p. 3.
57. Ibid., 13 Oct. 1828, p. 2.
58. Ibid., 2 June 1828, p. 2.
59. Ibid., 16 May 1828; 27 May 1828, p. 2.
60. Ibid., 12 June 1828, p. 2; 14 June 1828, p. 2; 25 June 1828, p. 2.
61. Ibid., 28 Aug. 1828, p. 2.

62. Ibid., 12 Dec. 1828, p. 3; 20 Dec. 1828, p. 3.
63. *The Morning Herald*, 12 May 1828, p. 3.
64. *The Times*, 18 Nov. 1828, p. 2; 26 Nov. 1828, p. 3.
65. Ibid., 13 Nov. 1828, p. 3; 20 Nov. 1828, p. 3.
66. Ibid., 1 Dec. 1828, p. 2.

Chapter IX

1. John Bazant, 'Mexico from Independence to 1867', in Bethell, *Cambridge History of Latin America*, pp. 423, 433.
2. *The Morning Chronicle*, 24 June 1829, p. 2.
3. *The Times*, 30 Jan. 1829, p. 2.
4. *The Courier*, 4 June 1829, p. 4.
5. Ibid., 20 Mar. 1829, p. 4.
6. *The Times*, 21 Mar. 1829, p. 2.
7. Simon Bolívar, *Carta de Jamaica* (Caracas, 1965), p. 61.
8. Ibid., p. 63.
9. Ibid., pp. 66–7.
10. *The Morning Chronicle*, 26 June 1829, p. 3.
11. *The Times*, 28 May 1829, p. 2.
12. Public Record Office, Kew Gardens, (hereinafter PRO) London, FO 15/8, fol. 217.
13. PRO, FO 15/8, fol. 225, fols. 135–7.
14. White to Rodríguez, Valparaiso, 24 Feb. 1829, *Correspondence*, no. 309.
15. White to Rodríguez, Valparaiso, 4 May 1829, *Correspondence*, no. 313; Rodríguez to White, Santiago, 9 May 1829, *Correspondence*, no. 314.
16. Backhouse to Ewing, London, 8 April 1829, *Correspondence*, no. 83.
17. *The Morning Chronicle*, 11 Mar. 1828, p. 3.
18. *The Times*, 7 April 1829, p. 4.
19. *The Courier*, 22 April 1829, p. 2.
20. Ibid., 23 April 1829, p. 2.
21. *The Times*, 23 April 1829, p. 2.
22. Ibid., 20 Jan. 1829, p. 3.
23. *The Morning Chronicle*, 28 Mar. 1829, p. 2; 31 Mar. 1829, p. 4.
24. Ibid., 2 April 1829, p. 2.
25. Ibid., 30 April 1829, p. 2; 27 April 1829, p. 2.
26. *The Times*, 27 April 1829, p. 2.
27. *The Morning Chronicle*, 14 May 1829, p. 3; 19 May 1829, p. 4; *The Times*, 14 May 1829, p. 2; 19 May 1829, p. 2; 21 May 1829, p. 2.
28. *The Morning Chronicle*, 21 May 1829, p. 3; 23 May 1829, p. 2.
29. *The Times*, 22 May 1829, p. 4.
30. Ibid., 25 May 1829, p. 2.
31. *The Morning Chronicle*, 29 May 1829, p. 3; Sturz, *A Review* p. 14.
32. *The Morning Chronicle*, 29 May 1829, p. 3; 1 June 1829, p. 2; 4 June 1829, p. 2; *The Times*, 29 May 1829, p. 3; 12 June 1829, p. 2.
33. *The Times*, 30 May 1829, p. 2; 8 June 1829, p. 2; *The Morning Chronicle*, 30 Dec. 1829, p. 2.
34. Bolívar to Sucre, Lima, 20 Jan. 1825, quoted in Ron L. Seckinger, 'South American Power Politics During the 1820's', *Hispanic American Historical Review*, (May 1956), LVI, pp. 241–5.
35. Seckinger, 'South American Power Politics', p. 252.
36. *The Morning Chronicle*, 4 Jan. 1827, p. 4.
37. Ibid., 9 Jan. 1827, p. 7; 10 Jan. 1827, p. 3.
38. Ibid., 13 Jan. 1827, p. 3.
39. Ibid., 27 Jan. 1827, p. 3.
40. *The Times*, 21 May 1827, p. 2.
41. *The Morning Chronicle*, 27 Jan. 1827, p. 3.
42. *The Times*, 31 Mar. 1827, p. 1.
43. Ibid., 4 May 1827, p. 3.
44. *The Morning Chronicle*, 30 Nov. 1827, p. 3.
45. Ibid., 11 Dec. 1827, p. 3.
46. Walter Dupouy (ed.), *Sir Robert Ker Porter's Caracas Diary, 1825–1842* (Caracas, 1966), p. 45.
47. Ibid., pp. 213–14.
48. Ibid., pp. 235–6.
49. Ibid., p. 270.
50. *The Courier*, 27 Sept. 1827, p. 3.
51. Ibid., 11 Oct. 1827, p. 3.
52. *The Morning Chronicle*, 7 Feb. 1827, p. 2.
53. *The Times*, 28 Feb. 1828, p. 2.
54. Ibid., 22 April 1828, p. 3.
55. Ibid., 5 Sept. 1828, p. 3.
56. Ibid., 29 Sept. 1828, p. 2.
57. McCulloch, 'Mining Companies', p. 749.
58. *The Morning Herald*, 3 April 1828, p. 4.
59. A. C. Todd, *The Search for Silver: Cornish Miners in Mexico, 1824–1947* (Padstow, Cornwall, 1977).
60. *The Times*, 22 Oct. 1828, p. 1; 20 Oct. 1828, p. 1.
61. Ibid., 27 Oct. 1828, p. 2.
62. *The Times*, 16 Dec. 1828, p. 2; 18 Dec. 1828, p. 2.
63. Ibid., 26 Dec. 1828, p. 2.
64. *Prospectuses of Firms*, III, fol. 67.
65. *The Morning Chronicle*, 19 May 1828, p. 4.

66. Ibid., 30 Dec. 1828, p. 2.
67. Claudio Véliz, 'Egaña, Lambert, and the Chilean Mining Associations of 1825', *Hispanic American Historical Review*, LV, pp. 638, 639–41 (1975); Carlos Marichal, *A Century of Debt Crisis in Latin America* (Princeton, 1989) pp. 51–3.
68. McCulloch, *A Dictionary*, p. 746.
69. Ibid., pp. 747–8.

Chapter X

1. Hobson, *The Export of Capital*, pp. 110–11.
2. See discussion in D.C.M. Platt *Finance, Trade and Politics in British Foreign Policy, 1815–1914* (Oxford, 1968), pp. 35–53.
3. Webster, *Britain and the Independence of Latin America*, I, Appendix II.
4. Charles Fenn, *Compendium of the English and Foreign Funds* (London, 1837), pp. 59–61, 73, 74, 81. Fenn also reported that a loan of £600,000 had been made to the Mexican state of Guadalajara during the lending boom, but that it had gone into default and now was it 'almost unknown on the Stock Exchange'. An examination of the prospectus files at the British Museum, however, reveals that the borrower was a textile enterprise in Guadalajara, Spain, not the Mexican state of that name. Unfortunately, subsequent commentators have repeated Fenn's assertion, thus perpetuating the error.
5. Platt, *Latin America and British Trade*, pp. 36–8.
6. Dupouy, *Porter's Caracas Diary*, p. 934.
7. The circular is reprinted in full in Platt, *Finance, Trade and Politics*, Appendix II.
8. *Prospectuses*, vol. Fac-Gla.
9. Turlington, *Mexico*, pp. 59–62.
10. Backhouse to Warrington, London, 24 Feb. 1836, in *Correspondence*, no. 93.
11. Turlington, *Mexico*, pp. 91–8; Henry Ayres (ed.) *Fenn's Compendium of the English and Foreign Funds* (London, 1855, ed.), p. 195.
12. Turlington, *Mexico*, pp. 117–35; For further details of the intervention see Henry Wheaton, *Elements of International Law* (C. H. Dana ed., 1864), pp. 105–10.
13. Alfred Tischendorf, 'The British Foreign Office and the Renewal of Anglo-Mexican Diplomatic Relations, 1867–1884', *Inter-American Economic Affairs*, XI (1957) pp. 37, 39; 'The Anglo-Mexican Claims Commission, 1884–1895, *Hispanic*

American Historical Review, XXXVII, (1957) p. 470; Turlington, *Mexico*, pp. 5–6, 200–11.
14. *The Times*, 19 Feb. 1831, p. 3.
15. *The Morning Post*, 19 Feb. 1831, p. 2.
16. Malcolm Deas, 'Venezuela, Colombia and Ecuador: The First Half-Century of Independence', in Bethell, *The Cambridge History of Latin America*, pp. 507–13.
17. Dupouy, *Porter's Caracas Diary*, pp. 457–8.
18. Edward B. Eastwick, *Venezuela, or Sketches of Life in a South American Republic, with the History of the Loan of 1864*, (London, 1868), p. 323. The Venezuelan decree approving the arrangement is contained in *Cuerpo de Leyes de Venezuela* (Caracas, 1851), I, pp. 178–81.
19. Ayres, *Fenns Compendium* (1855 ed.) p. 282; *Sixtieth Annual Report of the Council of the Corporation of Foreign Bondholders for the Year 1933* (London, 1934) pp. 500–501 (hereinafter *1933 Report*).
20. Wilson to Palmerstone, Caracas, 10 Feb. 1847, PRO, FO 199/12, fols. 1537–9.
21. *1933 Report*, p. 501.
22. Eastwick, *Venezuela*, p. 324; *Prospectuses*, vol. Ott-Wel.
23. *Prospectuses*, Vol. Ott-Wel.
24. *Fenn's Compendium* (1876 ed.), p. 505; Eastwick, *Venezuela*, p. 328 (emphasis in original).
25. *1933 Report*, p. 502.
26. Addington to Powles, London, 28 Oct. 1842, *Correspondence*, no. 202.
27. *1933 Report*, p. 151.
28. *1933 Report*, pp. 151–2.
29. *Prospectuses*, vol. Cla-Cux.
30. *1933 Report*, pp. 152–3.
31. Hubert Herring, *A History of Latin America* (New York, 1956), pp. 478–81. Deas, 'Venezuela, Colombia and Ecuador', p. 524.
32. Ayres, *Fenn's Compendium* (1855 ed.) p. 155.
33. *1933 Report*, pp. 190–1.
34. *First Report of the Council of the Corporation of Foreign Bondholders*, p. 42.
35. *Sixth Annual General Report of the Council of the Corporation of Foreign Bondholders for the Year 1878* (London, 1879), p. 21; *1933 Report*, p. 191.
36. Palmerstone to Chatfield, London, 28 Feb. 1835, PRO, F.O. 15/18, fols. 7–9.
37. Committee of Central American Bondholders to the Supreme Government of Central America, London, 10 Mar. 1836,

PRO, F.O. 15/18, fol. 247.

38. Read to Palmerstone, London, 10 Mar. 1836, PRO, F.O. 15/18, fol. 248.

39. Chatfield to Palmerstone, Guatemala, 1 July 1836, PRO, F.O. 15/18, fol. 10.

40. Chatfield to Palmerstone, Guatemala, 18 Mar. 1837, 2 May 1837, PRO, F.O. 15/19, fol. 61.

41. Thomas Karnes, *The Failure of Union: Central America 1824–1960* (Chapel Hill, 1961), pp. 243–54.

42. Mario Rodríguez, *A Palmerstonian Diplomat in Central America: Frederick Chatfield, Esq* (Tuscon, 1964), pp. 114–20; *1933 Report*, pp. 167, 262, 274, 312, 407, Ernst H. Feilchenfeld, *Public Debts and State Succession* (New York, 1931) p. 297, n. 120.

43. Robert Dunlop, *Travels in Central America, being a journal of nearly Three Years Residence in the Country* (London, 1847), pp. 324–5.

44. Great Britain, House of Commons, 'Report of the Select Committee on Loans to Foreign States', in *Parliamentary Papers, Reports of Committees*, XI, pp. xxx–xxxvi (hereinafter *Committee Reports*).

45. Chatfield to Palmerstone, Guatemala, 5 Jan. 1849, PRO, F.O. 15/57, fol. 34.

46. Palmerstone to Chatfield, London, 2 May 1849, PRO F.O. 15/57; Palmerstone to Chatfield, London, 2 Feb. 1850, FO 15/64; Rodríguez, *Palmerstonian Diplomat*, pp. 306–7, 311–12.

47. *Prospectuses*, vol. Rhe-Sco; *1933 Report*, p. 392.

48. The fraud is described in detail in Alfredo Leon Gómez, *El Escándalo del Ferrocarril* (Tegucigalpa, 1978) and in 'La Deuda Exterior y el Ferroccarril', *Revista del Archivo y Biblioteca Nacionales* (Tegucigalpa, 1952), p. 31.

49. *Committee Reports*, pp. iii et seq.

50. *Committee Reports*, pp. xix–xxi.

51. See discussion in Craig Dozier, *Nicaragua's Mosquito Shore: The Years of British and American Presence* (Birmingham, Ala. 1985), pp. 52–106.

52. *Second Annual General Report of the Council of the Corporation of Foreign Bondholders for the Year 1874* (London, 1875), p. 48; *1933 Report*, p. 326.

53. *1933 Report*, p. 276; *Prospectuses*, vol. Gre-Hyd.

54. Wayne M. Clegern, 'New Light on the Belize Dispute', *American Journal of International Law*, LII (1958), pp. 280, 283–4.

55. Ibid., pp. 291–3.

56. *1933 Report*, pp. 276–7.

57. Simon Collier, 'Chile from Independence to the War of the Pacific', in Bethell, *Cambridge History of Latin America*, III, pp. 583, 585–95.

58. Six Chilean loan prospectuses from 1858 to 1875 are in *Prospectuses*, vol. Can-Cit.

59. *Prospectuses*, vol. Can-Cit and accompanying correspondence.

60. Wilson to De Pando, Lima, 1 July 1833, *Correspondence*, no. 255.

61. Ayres, *Fenn's Compendium* (1855 ed.), pp. 196–7.

62. Ibid., pp. 198–9. W. M. Mathew, 'The First Anglo-Peruvian Debt and its Settlement', *Journal of Inter-American Studies* II, (1) (1970), p. 81.

63. *Prospectuses*, vol. Ori-Phi.

64. Fourth Annual General Report of the Council of the Corporation of Foreign Bondholders for the Year 1876 (London, 1877), pp. 34–40.

65. *Prospectuses*, vol. Ori-Phi and accompanying correspondence.

66. Moreno to García, London, 18 Feb. 1831, and 25 Feb. 1832, in José Luis Muñoz Azpiri, *Historia Completa de las Malvinas* (3 vols. Buenos Aires, 1966), I, pp. 373–84.

67. Fitte, *Historia* p. 178.

68. Ibid., pp. 202–10.

69. Ibid., p. 211.

70. Ayres, *Fenn's Compendium*, (1855 ed) pp. 145–6.

71. Fitte, *Historia*, pp. 303–4; *Prospectuses*, vol. Ang-Bar.

72. Ayres, *Fenn's Compendium*, (1855 ed) pp. 141–2; Normano, *Brazil: A Study of Economic Types*, pp. 154–5. See *Prospectuses*, vol. Bra-Can.

73. Hyde Clarke, 'On the Debts of Sovereign and Quasi-Sovereign States, Owing by Foreign Countries', *Journal of the Statistical Society*, XLI (London, June 1878), pp. 299, 303.

74. Morgan and Thomas, *The Stock Exchange*, p. 88. Also see generally, Clarke, 'On the Debts of Sovereign and Quasi-Sovereign States', pp. 299, 309, 313–18.

75. McCulloch, 'Mining Companies', p. 748; House of Commons, Great Britain, *Report of Committee on Joint Stock Companies*, Parliamentary Papers, III (1844) Appendix 4 (2), pp. 340–5.

76. *British Foreign Investment in Latin America, 1822–1949*, p. 35, Table 4 at p. 32, Table 5 at p. 34.

Chapter XI

1. Fitte, *Historia*, p. 211.
2. Gunn, Matthews, Schurman, Weibe *Disraeli Letters*; no. 21.
3. *Disraeli Letters*, no. 351.
4. *The Morning Chronicle*, 2 Dec. 1826, p. 2.
5. Martineau, *History of England*, I, p. 352.
6. Harriet Martineau, *Autobiography* (3 vols., London, 1877), I, p. 129.
7. Ibid., p. 239.
8. Benjamin Disraeli, *Vivian Grey* (5 vols., London, 1826), II, p. 107.
9. Thomas Ingoldsby, 'The Merchant of Venice', *The Ingoldsby Legends* (London, no date), p. 254.
10. William Makepeace Thackeray, *The History of Samuel Titmarsh and the Great Hoggarty Diamond* (London, 1849). First published in 1841 in Frasers Magazine.
11. Charles Dickens, *Dombey and Son* (London, 1983), p. 158.
12. Humphries, *Liberation in South America*, p.161.
13. Christopher Richardson, *Mr John Diston Powles: or the Antecedents, as a Promoter and Director of Foreign Mining Companies, of an Administrative Reformer* (London, 1855).
14. Donoso, *José de Irisarri*. David Vela, 'Antonio José de Irisarri', Revista Conservadora, IX (Oct. 1964, Managua), pp. 33, 36.
15. Sergio Fernandez Larraín, *Luis López Méndez y Andrés Bello* (Santiago, 1969); Restrepo, *La Revolución en Colombia*, IV, p. 428, n. 3.
16. Backhouse to Zebadúa, London, 6 Nov. 1830, PRO, F.O. 15/10.
17. Marcial Zebadúa, *Manifestación Pública del Ciudadano Marcial Zebadúa sobre su Misión Diplomática cerca a su Majestad Británica* (Guatemala, 1832).
18. Foreign Office to Castellón, 17 Aug. 1844, PRO, F.O. 15/39.
19. Frank G. Dawson, 'People in Finance: Gregor MacGregor', *The Banker*, (London, Jan. 1982).
20. *Dictionary of National Biography* (London, 1896) XLVI, pp. 190–2.
21. Rafael Caldera, *Andrés Bello: Philosopher, Poet, Philogist, Educator, Legislator, Statesman* (London, 1977); Miguel Luis Amunátegui, *Vida de Don Andrés Bello* (Santiago, 1882).
22. Dawson, 'The Influence of Andrés Bello', pp. 253, 299–303.
23. Carlos Calvo, *Le Droit international*

théorique et practique (7 vols. 1896), I, p. 109.
24. John Ford, 'Rudolph Ackermann: Publisher to Latin America' in *Bello y Londres*, I, p. 197, John Ford, *Ackermann, 1783–1983* (London, 1983), pp. 84–8.
25. *Dictionary of National Biography* (London, 1891), XXV, pp. 324–5; L. Oppenheim, *International Law*, (2 vols. 7th ed. 1948, E. Lauterpacht ed.), I, pp. 268, 759, 761.
26. Bushnell, *The Santander Regime*, pp. 118–22.
27. J. M. Velasco Ibarra, *Experiencias Jurídicas Hispanoamericanas: Bolívar, Alvarez, Alberdi* (Buenos Aires, 1943), pp. 15–16.
28. Jenks, *Migration of British Capital*, pp. 58–60, Platt, *Latin America and British Trade*, pp. 28–9.
29. Marichal, *A Century of Debt Crisis*, pp. 53–5.
30. *The Courier*, 29 Sep. 1825, p. 2.
31. Robert Crassweller, *Peron and the Enigmas of Argentina* (New York, 1987), p. 63.
32. *The Times*, 19 Feb. 1831, p. 3.
33. *The Morning Post*, 19 Feb. 1831, p. 2.
34. *The New Times*, 13 Sept. 1822, p. 4.
35. Bennett to Ellíce, Guatemala, 16 Sept. 1828, PRO, F.O. 15/8, fols. 189–90.
36. Platt, *Finance, Trade and Politics* pp. 34–53.
37. Turlington, *Mexico*, pp. 7, 100–4; Alfred P. Tischendorf, 'The British Foreign Office' pp. 37, 39–41.
38. Henry Wheaton, *Elements of International Law*, pp. 105–10, n. 41 (Charles Dana ed. 1866).
39. Edwin M. Borchard, *The Diplomatic Protection of Citizens Abroad* (New York, 1915), p. 313 n. 1; Amos S. Hershey, 'The Venezuelan Affair in the Light of International Law', *American Law Register*, LI (1902), p. 249.
40. *Gaceta del Gobierno del Salvador en la América Central*, 18 Dec. 1856, p. 3, PRO, F.O. 39/1, fol. 69.
41. *Twycross v. Dreyfus*, 5 ch. D. 605, 616 (C.A. 1877).
42. Clarke, 'On the Debts of Sovereign and Quasi-Sovereign States', pp. 299, 335.
43. State Immunity Act 1978; Foreign Sovereign Immunities Act, 28 U.S.C., sections 1330, 1332 (a) (2)–(4), 1441 (d), 1602–1611 (1976).
44. Donald R. Shea, *The Calvo Clause* (Minneapolis, 1955), pp. 11–21.
45. See discussion in Borchard, *Diplomatic Protection*, pp. 792–4 and in Amos S.

Hershey, 'The Calvo and Drago Doctrines', *American Journal of International Law*, I (1907), p. 26.

46. Hershey, 'The Calvo Clause', p. 26; Borchard, *Diplomatic Protection*, pp. 308–10.

47. Borchard, *Diplomatic Protection*, pp. 318–22; J. G. Starke, *Introduction to International Law* (London, 9th ed. 1984), pp. 292–3.

Chapter XII

1. Max Winkler; *Foreign Bonds: An Autopsy* (Philadelphia, 1933), pp. 204–5.

2. Ibid., p. 179.

3. Clifford Dammers, 'A Brief History of Sovereign Defaults and Rescheduling', in David Suratgar (ed.), *Default and Rescheduling Corporate and Foreign Borrowers* (Euromoney Publications, London, 1984), pp. 77, 82–4; Michael Hoeflich, 'Historical Perspectives on Sovereign Lending', in Michael Gruson and Ralph Reisner (eds.), *Sovereign Lending: Managing Sovereign Risk* (Euromoney Publications, London, 1984), pp. 21, 25–7.

4. Dick Murray, 'Lambeth's Foreign Cash in Revealed', *The Evening Standard* (London), 3 Mar. 1988, p. 5.

5. Chapter IX, *supra*, at pp. 181–2.

6. Chapter X, *supra*, at pp. 196–7, 207–8.

7. *The Financial Times*, Euromarket letter and Report, no. 619, 8 Feb. 1988, p. 24.

8. Chapter VIII, *supra*, at p. 162.

9. Chapter X, *supra*, at pp. 196, 208, 210.

10. Chapter X, *supra*, at pp. 196, 200, 202, 207, 209.

11. Peter Montagnon, 'Midland swaps debt for goods with Peru', *The Financial Times* (London), 16 Sept. 1987, p. 6.

12. Chapter IX, *supra*, p. 178.

13. Chapter X, *supra*, p. 204.

14. *Prospectuses*, vol. Gre-Hyd.

15. *Prospectuses*, vol. Ori-Phi.

16. Chapter X, *supra*, p. 206.

17. *The Independent* (London) 10 Nov. 1989, pp. 20, 21; Susan George, *A Fate Worse Than Debt* (London, 1988); Christine A. Bogdanowicz-Bindert (ed.) *Strategies and Controversies by Key Stakeholders* (New York, 1989).

18. Sue Branford and Bernardo Kucinski, *The Debt Squads: The US, the Banks and Latin America* (London, 1988), p. 55.

19. Barbara Stallings, *Banker to the Third World: U.S. Portfolio Investment in Latin America, 1900–1986* (Berkeley, 1987), pp. 294–301.

BIBLIOGRAPHY

I. NEWSPAPERS AND JOURNALS

The Times (London) 1820–30
The Morning Chronicle (London) 1820–30
The Morning Herald (London) 1822–30
The Courier (London) 1822–30
John Bull (London) 1822–8
The Edinburgh Advertiser 1822–5
The Edinburgh Evening Courant 1822–5
The Sunday Times (London) 1822–8

Also, miscellaneous issues of other newspapers, including *The Star, The Post, The Manchester Guardian, The Aberdeen Chronicle, The Scotsman* during 1822–6. Also *The Edinburgh Review, The Quarterly Review* (1822–8) and various others. Only *The Times* is indexed for the years covered here, and poorly at that.

The Banker since 1982 has carried numerous articles on the current debt crisis, as have *Euromoney*, the *International Financial Law Review, The Financial Times,* and other journals and newspapers in Great Britain and in the United States.

II. GENERAL REFERENCE WORKS AND DIRECTORIES

The Annual Register, or a view of History, Politics and Literature (1822–6) (London)
Council of the Corporation of Foreign Bondholders, *Annual Reports* (1872–1933) (London).
Course of the Exchange (1822–30) (London).
Critchett & Woods, *The Post Office London Directory* (1822–5) (London).
Dictionary of National Biography.
Gaceta de Colombia (1821–31), Banco de la República de Colombia Facsimile Edition (4 vols., Bogotá, 1973).
Gaceta del Gobierno de Guatemala (1822–5).
Kent's *Original London Directory* (1822–5) (London).
Pigot and Co's *London & Provincial New Commercial Directory for 1823–24* (London).
Robson & Co., William, *Robson's London Commercial Directory, Street Guide and Carrier's List for 1822* (1st ed. London, 1824).
The Stock Exchange Yearbook (1874–1880) (London).
The Times, Tercentenary Handlist of English & Welsh Newspapers, Magazines and Reviews (London, 1920).

III. BOOKS AND MONOGRAPHS

Amunátegui, Miguel Luis, Vida de Don Andrés Bello (Santiago, 1882).

Andreades, A., The History of the Bank of England 1640–1903, (C. Meredith (trans.), 7th ed., London, 1924).

Andrews, Joseph, Journey from Buenos Ayres Through the Provinces of Córdoba, Tucuman and Salta to Potosi (London, 1827).

Anonymous, The Contractor Unmasked, being Letters to one of the Contractors of the Colombian Loan Occasioned by His Recent Pamphlet, by a Member of the Honourable Society of Lincolns Inn (London, 1823).

Ayerst, David, Guardian: Biography of a Newspaper (London, 1971).

Banco Central del Ecuador, La Deuda Exerna del Ecuador (Quito, 1981).

Barriga Villalba, Antonio Mariá, El Empréstito de Zea y el Préstamo de Erick Bollmann de 1822 (Bogotá, no date).

Beaumont, James, A., Travels in Buenos Ayres and in the Adjacent Provinces of Rio de la Plata (London, 1828).

Bello, Andrés, Principios de Derecho Internacional (Caracas, 1847).

Bello, Andrés, Obras Completas de Andrés Bello (Caracas, 1954).

Bethell, Leslie (ed.), The Cambridge History of Latin America, from Independence to c.1870, III (Cambridge, 1985).

Bierck, Howard, La Vida Pública de Pedro Gual (Caracas, 1947).

Blanch, Lesley, The Game of Hearts: Harriette Wilson and her Memoirs (London, 1957).

Blanco–Fombona, Rufino, Grandes Escritores de America (Siglo XIX) (Madrid, 1917).

Bolívar, Simón, Carta de Jamaica (Caracas, 1965).

Borchard, Edwin M., The Diplomalic Protection of Citizens Abroad (New York, 1915).

Borchard, Edwin M., and Wynne, William H., State Insolvency and Foreign Bondholders (2 vols., New Haven, 1951).

Branford, Sue, and Kucinski, Bernardo, The Debt Squads: The US, the Banks and Latin America (London, 1988).

Bull, Hedley and Watson, Adam (eds.), The Expansion of International Society (Oxford, 1984).

Bushnell, David, The Santander Regime in Gran Colombia (Newark, Del., 1954).

Butler, E. M. (ed.), A Regency Visitor: The English Tour of Prince Puckler-Muskau Described in his Letters 1826–1828 (London, 1957).

Caldera, Rafael, Andrés Bello: Philosopher, Poet, Philologist, Educator, Legislator, Statesman (London, 1977).

Carr, Raymond, Spain, 1808–1939 (Oxford, 1966).

Castillo, Bernal, Díaz del, The Discovery and Conquest of Mexico (A. P. Maudsley (trans.), New York, 1956).

Creevey, Thomas, The Creevey Papers: A Selection from the Correspondence & Diaries of the late Thomas Creevey MP (London, 1923).

Cecil, Algernon, British Foreign Secretaries, 1807–1916: Studies in Personality and Policy (London, 1927).

Clapham, John, The Bank of England: A History (2 vols., Cambridge, 1944).

Crassweller, Robert, Perón and the Enigmas of Argentina (New York, 1987).

Dickens, Charles, Dombey and Son (London, 1983).

Disraeli, Benjamin, *An Inquiry into the Plans, Progress, and Policy of American Mining Companies* (London, 1825).

Disraeli, Benjamin, *Vivian Grey* (5 vols., London, 1826).

Dixon, Peter, *Canning: Politician and Statesman* (London, 1976).

Donoso, Ricardo, *Antonio José de Irisarri, Escritor y Diplomático* (Santiago, 1966).

Duguid, Charles, *A History of the Stock Exchange* (London, 1902).

Dozier, Craig, *Nicaragua's Mosquito Shore: The Years of British and American Presence* (Birmingham, Ald, 1985).

Dunn, Frederick, *The Protection of Nationals: A Study in the Application of International Law* (Baltimore, 1932).

Dupouy, Walter (ed.), *Sir Robert Ker Porter's Caracas Diary, 1825–1842* (Caracas, 1966).

Eastwick, Edward, *Venezuela, or Sketches of Life in a South American Republic, with a History of the Loan of 1864* (London, 1865).

Emden, Paul H., *Regency Pageant* (London, 1936).

Emden, Paul, H., *The Money Powers of Europe in the Nineteenth Century* (London, 1937).

English, Henry, *General Guide to the Companies Working Foreign Mines* (London, 1825).

English, Henry, *A Complete View of the Joint Stock Companies formed During the Years 1824 and 1825* (London, 1827).

Fenn, Charles, *A Compendium of the English and Foreign Funds and the Principle Joint Stock Companies Forming an Epitome of the Various Objects of Investment Negotiable in London* (London, 1837). The *Compendium* was re-issued and updated throughout the century under different editors.

Feilchenfeld, E., *Public Debts and State Succession* (New York, 1931).

Ferns, H. S., *Britain and Argentina in the Nineteenth Century* (Oxford, 1980).

Fernandez Larraín, Sergio, *Luis López Méndez y Andrés Bello* (Santiago, 1969).

Fitte, Ernesto, F., *Historia de un Empréstito: La Emisión de Baring Brothers en 1824* Buenos Aires, 1962).

Ford, John, *Ackermann 1783–1983: The Business of Art* (London, 1983).

Fundación La Casa de Bello (ed.), *Bello y Londres* (2 vols., Caracas, 1980).

Gibson, Charles, *Standing Guard: Protecting Foreign Capital in the Nineteenth and Twentieth Centuries* (Berkeley, 1985).

Gómez, Alfredo Leon, *El Escándalo del Ferrocarril* (Tegucigalpa, 1985).

Gunn, J. A. W.; Matthews, John; Schurman, Donald, M.; and Wiebe, M. G., *Benjamin Disraeli Letters: 1815–1834* (Toronto, 1982).

Graham, Maria, *Journal of a Residence in Chili during the Year 1822, and a Voyage from Chili to Brasil in 1823* (London, 1824).

Graham-Yool, Andrew, *The Forgotton Colony: A History of the English-Speaking Communities in Argentina* (London, 1981).

Hackett, James, *Narrative of the Expedition which Sailed from England in 1817 to Join the South American Patriots* (London, 1818).

Hall, Capt. Basil, *Extracts from a Journal written on the Coasts of Chile, Peru and Mexico, in the Years 1820, 1821 and 1822* (2 vols., London, 1824).

Haring, Clarence, N., *Empire in Brazil: A New World Experiment with Monarchy* (Cambridge, Mass., 1958).

Head, Francis, B., *Reports Relating to the Failure of the Rio Plata Mining Association* (London, 1827).

Head, Francis, B., *Journeys Across the Pampas and Among the Andes* (Edwardsville, Ill., 1967).

Hendriks, Herman, *A Statement of Facts in Reference to the Formation of the Haytian Mining Company* (London, 1827).

Herd, Harold, *The March of Journalism* (London, 1952).

Herring, Hubert, *A History of Latin America* (New York, 1956).

Hibbert, Christopher, *The Making of Charles Dickens* (London, 1983).

Hippisley, Gustavus, *A Narrative of the Expedition to the Rivers Orinico and Apure, in South America, which Sailed from England in November, 1817* (London, 1819).

Hobson, Charles K., *The Export of Capital* (London, 1914).

Hobson, Harold; Knightly, Philip; Russell, Leonard, *The Pearl of Days: An Intimate Memoir of the Sunday Times (1822–1972)* (London, 1972).

Holdsworth, William, *A History of English Law*, (17 vols., London, 1922–72).

Humboldt, Alexander von, *Personal Narrative of Travels to the Equinoctal Regions of America during the Years 1799–1804* (Tomasina Ross, trans., London, 1851).

Humphreys, Robert, A., (ed.), *British Consular Reports on the Trade and Politics of Latin America, 1824–1826* (London, 1940).

Humphreys, Robert, A., *Liberation in South America, 1806–1827: The Career of James Paroissien* (London, 1952).

Inman, Samuel G., *Inter-American Conferences 1826–1854: History and Problems* (Washington, 1965).

Jefferson, J. C. *The Life of Robert Stephenson F. R. S.* (2 vols. London, 1864).

Jenks, Leland H., *The Migration of British Capital to 1875* (London, 1827).

Jerman, B. R., *The Young Disraeli* (Princeton, 1970).

Kaletsky, Analole, *The Costs of Default* (New York, 1985).

Karnes, Thomas, L., *The Failure of Union: Central America, 1824–1960* (Chapel Hill, 1961).

Kent, James, *Commentaries on American Law* (New York, 1836).

Key, Hans Reinheimer, *Topo: Historia de la Colonia Escocesa en las Cercanías de Caracas 1825–1827* (Caracas, 1986).

Kindleberger, Charles, *Manias, Panics and Crashes: A History of Financial Crises* (London, 1981).

Kingleberger, Charles, *A Financial History of Western Europe* (London, 1984).

Lambert, Eric T. D., *Carabobo 1821* (Caracas, 1974).

Lauterpacht, Hersch (ed.), *Oppenheim's International Law* (2 vols., 7th ed. 1948).

Levandis, John A., *The Greek Foreign Debt and the Great Powers 1821–1898* (New York, 1944).

Lynch, John, *The Spanish American Revolutions, 1800–1826* (London, 1973).

Maceroni, Francis, *Memoirs of the Life and Adventures of Colonel Maceroni* (2 vols., London, 1828).

MacKenzie, Mauricio, *Los Ideales de Bolívar en el Derecho Internacional Americano* (Bogotá, 1955).

Manchester, Alan K., *British Preeminence in Brazil: Its Rise and Decline* (Chapel Hill, 1933).

Mancini, J. *Bolívar* (Mexico, 1914).

Manning, William, R., (ed.), *Diplomatic Correspondence of the United States Concerning the Independence of the Latin American States* (3 vols., New York. 1925).

Marchand, Leslie, A., *Byron: A Portrait* (London, 1970).

Marchand, Leslie, (ed.), *Byron's Letters and Journals* (6 vols., New York, 1973).

Marichal, Carlos, *A Century of Debt Crises in Latin America* (Princeton, 1989).

Martineau, Harriet, *A History of England During the Thirty Years Peace, 1815–1845* (London, 1848).

Martineau, Harriet, *Autobiography* (3 vols., London, 1877).

McCulloch, John A., *A Dictionary, Practical, Theoretical and Historical, of Commerce and Commercial Navigation* (London, 1832).

Mendoza, C., *La Junta del Gobierno de Caracas y sus Misiones Diplomáticas en 1810* (Caracas, 1936).

Morgan, E. Victor, and Thomas, W. A., *The Stock Exchange: Its History and Functions* (London, 1962).

Morrison, Stanley, *The English Newspaper* (London, 1932).

Mulhall, Michael J., *The English in South America* (London, 1878).

Normano, José F., *Brazil: A Study of Economic Types* (Chapel Hill, 1935).

O'Connell, D. P., *State Succession in Municipal Law and International Law* (2 vols., Cambridge, 1967).

Ortíz, Sergio Elias, *Doctor José María del Real, Jurisconsulto y Diplomático* (Bogotá, 1969).

Palacios Moreyra, Carlos, *La Deuda Anglo Peruana, 1822–1890* (Lima, 1983).

Peters, Harold E., *The Foreign Debt of the Argentine Republic* (Baltimore, 1934).

Phillimore, Robert, *Commentaries upon International Law* (3rd ed., London, 1870).

Platt, D. C. M., *Finance, Trade and Politics in British Foreign Policy, 1815–1914* (Oxford, 1968).

Platt, D. C. M., *Latin America and British Trade 1806–1914* (London, 1972).

Powell, J. H., *Richard Rush, Republican Diplomat* (Philadelphia, 1942).

Reeve, Henry (ed.) *The Greville Memoirs: A Journal of the Reigns of King George IV and King William IV by the Late Charles C. F. Greville* (3 vols., London, 1877, 3rd ed.).

Restrepo, Jośe M., *Historia de la Revolución de la República de Colombia* (6 vols., Besançon, 1858).

Richardson, Christopher, *Mr John Diston Powles, or the Antecedents as a Promoter and Director of Foreign Mining Companies of an Administrative Reformer* (London, 1855).

Rippy, J. Fred, *British Foreign Investment in Latin America, 1822–1949* (Minneapolis, 1959).

Rodríguez, Mario, *A Palmerstonian Diplomat in Central America: Frederick Chatfield, Esq* (Tucson, 1964).

Rodríguez, Ramón Armando, *Diccionario Biográfico, Geográfico e Histórico de Venezuela* (Madrid, 1967).

Rafter, M., *Memoirs of Gregor MacGregor* (London, 1820).

Saldarriaga, R. Botero, *Francisco Antonio Zea* (Bogotá, 1955).

Sánchez, Alirio Duque, *Francisco Antonio Zea* (Merida, 1970).

Schatan, Jacobo, *World Debt: Who is to Pay?* (London, 1987).

Shea, Donald, *The Calvo Clause* (Minneapolis, 1955).

Shuttleworth, Nina, *A Life of Sir Woodbine Parish* (London, 1910).

Smart, William, *Economic Annals of the Nineteenth Century* (2 vols., London, 1917).

Soltera, María, *A Lady's Ride Across Honduras* (London, 1884).

Stallings, Barbara, *Banker to the Third World: US Portfolio Investment in Latin America, 1900–1986* (Berkeley, 1987).

Stapleton, George, *The Political Life of the Right Honourable George Canning* (3 vols., London, 1831).

Sturz, J. J., *A Review, Financial, Statistical and Commercial of the Empire of Brazil and its Resources* (London, 1837).

Summerson, John, *Georgian London* (London, 1986).

Temperley, Harold, *The Foreign Policy of Canning 1822–1827* (London, 1925).

The Times, The History of the Times: 'The Thunderer' in the Making, 1785–1841 (London, 1935).

Thomas, A., and Thomas, A. G., Jr., *Non-Intervention: The Law and its Import in the Americas* (Dallas, 1956).

Tirado Mejía, Alvarado, *Introducción a la Historia Económia de Colombia* (Bogotá, no date).

Todd, A. C., *The Search for Silver: Cornish Miners in Mexico, 1824–1947* (Padstow, Cornwall, 1977).

Trevelyan, George Macauley, *British History in the Nineteenth Century and After (1782–1919)* (London, 1948).

Turlington, Edgar, *Mexico and her Foreign Creditors* (New York, 1930).

Velaśquez, Ramon J. (ed.), *Los Libertadores de Venezuela* (Caracas, 1983).

Walker, Alexander, *Colombia, being a Geographical, Statistical, Agricultural, Commercial and Political Account of that Country* (2 vols., London, 1822).

Webster, Charles, K., *Britain and the Independence of Latin America 1812–1830* (2 vols., London, 1938).

Wheaton, Henry, *Elements of International Law* (Charles Henry Dana, ed., 1864).

White, R. J., *Life in Regency England* (London, 1969).

Williams, Keith, *The English Newspaper: An Illustrated History to 1900* (London, 1977).

Winkler, Max, *Foreign Bonds: An Autopsy* (New York, 1932).

Wrightman, Gavin and Humphries, Steve, *The Making of Modern London: 1815–1914* (London, 1983).

Ziegler, Philip, *The Sixth Great Power: Barings, 1762–1929* (London, 1988).

IV. ARTICLES

Alberich, José, 'English Attitudes Towards the Hispanic World in the Time of Bello as Reflected by the *Edinburgh* and *Quarterly Reviews*', in John Lynch (ed.), *Andrés Bello: The London Years* (London, 1982).

Allen, Victor, 'The Prince of Poyais', *History Today* (Jan., 1952), p. 53.

Bazant, John, 'Mexico from Independence to 1867', in Leslie Bethell (ed.) *The Cambridge History of Latin America, from Independence to c.1870*, III (Cambridge, 1985).

Bethell, Leslie, and de Carvalho, J. H. 'Brazil from Independence to the Middle of the Nineteenth Century', in Leslie Bethell (ed.), *The Cambridge History of Latin America, from Independence to c.1870*, III (Cambridge, 1985).

Bonilla, Heraclio, 'Peru and Bolivia from Independence to the War of the Pacific', in Leslie Bethell (ed.), *The Cambridge History of Latin America, from Independence to c.1870*, III (Cambridge, 1985).

Bull, Hedley, 'The Emergence of a Universal International Society', in Hedley Bull and Adam Watson (eds.), *The Expansion of International Society* (Oxford, 1984), p. 11.

Clark, Hyde 'On the Debts of Sovereign and Quasi-Sovereign States, Owing by Foreign Countries', *Journal of the Statistical Society*, XLI, p. 299 (London, June 1878).

Clegern, Wayne, M., 'New Light on the Belize Dispute', *American Journal of International Law* (1958) LII, p. 281.

Dammers, Clifford, 'A Brief History of Sovereign Defaults and Rescheduling', in David Suratgar (ed.), *Default and Rescheduling: Corporate and Foreign Borrowers* (Euromoney Publications, London, 1984).

Dawson, Frank Griffith, 'William Pitt's Settlement at Black River on the Mosquito Shore: A Challenge to Spain in Central America', *The Hispanic American Historical Review* (1983) LXIII, p. 677.

Dawson, Frank Griffith, 'People in Finance: Gregor MacGregor', *The Banker*, p. 27 (London, Jan., 1982).

Dawson, Frank Griffith, 'The Influence of Andrés Bello on Latin American Perceptions of Non-Intervention and State Responsibility', *The British Yearbook of International Law*, *1986* (Oxford, 1987), p. 257.

Eakin, Marshall, C., 'Business Imperialism and British Enterprise in Brazil: The St. John del Rey Mining Company, Limited, 1830–1960', *The Hispanic American Historical Review* (1966) LXVI.

Gilmour, Robert Louis, and Harrison, John Parker, 'Juan Bernardo Elbers and the Introduction of Steam Navigation on The Magdalena River', *The Hispanic American Historical Review* (1948), XXVIII, p. 335.

Hasbrouck, Alfred 'Gregor MacGregor and the Colonization of Poyais', *The Hispanic American Historical Review* (1927), VII, p. 438.

Hershey, Amos, 'The Calvo and Drago Doctrines', *American Journal of International Law* (1907), I, p. 26.

Hoeflich, Michael, 'Historical Perspectives on Sovereign Lending', in Michael Gruson and Ralph Reisner (eds.), *Sovereign Lending: Managing Sovereign Risk* (London, 1984).

Huck, Eugene, R., 'Economic Experimentation in a Newly-Independent Nation: Colomba under Francisco de Paula Santander, 1821–1840', *The Americas* (Washington DC, 1973), XXIV, p. 17.

Jones, Calvin, P., 'The Spanish-American Works of Alexander von Humboldt as Viewed by Leading British Periodicals, 1800–1830', *The Americas* (1973), XXVIX, p. 442.

Lynch, 'Gran Bretaña y la Independencia Latinoamericana, 1810/1829' in Fundación Casa de Bello (ed.), *Bello y Londres* (2 vols., Caracas, 1980).

Mathew, W. M. 'The First Anglo-Peruvian Debt and its Settlement, 1822–1849; *Journal of Latin American Studies* II, (1), (1970), p. 81.

Mendoza, C., 'La Misión de Bolivar y López Méndez a Londres', *Boletín de la Academia de Historia* (Caracas, 1935), XVIII, p. 643.

Nava, Julian, 'The Illustrious American: The Development of Nationalism in Venezuela under Antonio Guzmán Blanco', *The Hispanic-American Historical Review* (1965), xlv, p. 527.

Rippy, J. Fred, 'Early British Investments in the Latin American Republics', *Inter-American Economic Affairs*, (1952), vi, p. 1.

Sambrano Urdaneta, Oscar, 'Cronología Londinense de Andrés Bello', in Fundación La Casa de Bello (ed.), *Bello y Londres* (2 vols., Caracas, 1980).

Seckinger, Ron L., 'South American Power Politics During the 1820's', *The Hispanic American Historical Review* (May, 1956), lvi, p. 241.

Smith, Roberts, 'Financing the Central American Federation 1821–1838', *The Hispanic American Historical Review* (1963), xliii, p. 483.

Temperley, Harold, 'French Designs of Spanish America in 1820–25', *English Historical Review* (1925), xl, p. 34.

Temperley, Harold, 'Canning and the Conferences of the Four Allied Governments at Paris, 1823–1826', *American Historical Review* (1925), xxx, p. 16.

Tischendorf, Alfred, P., 'The British Foreign Office and the Renewal of Anglo-Mexican Diplomatic Relations, 1867–1884', *Inter-American Economic Affairs* (1957), xi, p. 37.

Tischendorf, Alfred, P., 'The Anglo-Medican Claims Commission, 1884–1885', *The Hispanic-American Historical Review* (1957), xxxvii, p. 471.

Vela, David 'José Antonio de Irisarri', *Revista Conservadora* (Managua, Oct. 1964), ix, No. 49, p. 33.

Véliz, Claudio, 'Egaña, Lambert and the Chilean Mining Associations of 1825', *The Hispanic American Historical Review* (1975), lv, p. 638.

Williford, Miriam, 'Utilitarian Design for the New World: Bentham's Plan for a Nicaraguan Canal', *The Americas* (1971), xxvii, p. 75.

INDEX